The Foe Within

The Foe Within

Fantasies of Treason and the End of Imperial Russia

WILLIAM C. FULLER, JR.

Cornell University Press

ITHACA AND LONDON

First published 2006 by Cornell University Press

Printed in the United States of America

Library of Congress Cataloging-in-Publication Data

Fuller, William C.
  The foe within : fantasies of treason and the end of Imperial Russia / William C. Fuller, Jr.
    p. cm.
  Includes bibliographical references and index.
  ISBN-13: 978-0-8014-4426-5 (cloth : alk. paper)
  ISBN-10: 0-8014-4426-8 (cloth : alk. paper)
  1. Russia—History—Nicholas II, 1894–1917. 2. World War, 1914–1918—Russia. 3. Treason—Russia—
History. 4. Espionage, German—Russia—History. 5. Miasoedov, Sergei Nikolaevich, 1866–1915.
6. Sukhomlinov, Vladimir Aleksandrovich, 1848–1926. I. Title.
  DK264.8.F88 2006
  940.3'47—dc22

                         2005032279

Cloth printing   10 9 8 7 6 5 4 3 2 1

To Richard and Irene Pipes

Contents

Maps

Acknowledgments

The research for this book was largely accomplished at the following archives in Moscow: the Russian State Military-Historical Archive (RGVIA), the State Archive of the Russian Federation (GARF), and the Archive of the Foreign Policy of the Russian Empire (AVPRI). A small amount of primary research was also done at Britain's Public Record Office. I thank the staff at each of these institutions for their kind assistance. I owe a debt of gratitude, as well, to the librarians of the Lenin Library in Moscow, the Widener Library at Harvard University, and the Naval War College Library for their help with this project. Andrei Ganin of Moscow State University, a talented historian in his own right, tracked down the photographs that illustrate this book. The maps were prepared by Darin T. Grauberger of the University of Kansas. I am deeply indebted to them both.

Several colleagues provided me with advice and support. Michael Stanislawsky at Columbia University gave me some useful bibliographical pointers about questions of Jewish history. Thomas Owen at Louisiana State University shared his vast knowledge about the history of Russian capitalism and generously supplied me with material from his comprehensive database of prerevolutionary Russian corporations. I benefited greatly from discussing many of the topics treated in this book with Bruce Menning of the U.S. Army Command and General Staff College. Daniel Orlovsky at Southern Methodist University and Gregory Freeze at Brandeis University read the book in manuscript and contributed extremely valuable suggestions. I must also express my thanks to Eric Lohr at American University, who kindly allowed me to read his unpublished manuscript "Enemy Alien Politics within the Russian Empire during World War I." And Aleksandr Georgievich Kavtaradze, the greatest living expert on the imperial army, gave me invaluable aid during my research trips to Moscow. All errors in this book are, of course, my responsibility.

A small amount of material on the Russian experience in the First World War in chapters 5 and 7 previously appeared in William C. Fuller, Jr., "The Eastern Front," in *The Great War and the Twentieth Century,* ed. Jay Winter, Geoffrey Parker, and Mary Habeck (New Haven: Yale University Press, 2000), pp. 30–68, and is reprinted with permission of Yale University Press.

Note on Dates and Names

The Julian calendar used in Imperial Russia lagged twelve days behind the Gregorian calendar used in western Europe in the nineteenth century and thirteen days in the twentieth. It is for this reason that Russia's February Revolution of 1917 actually took place in March, according to Western reckoning. I have provided dates according to the Julian calendar but have also supplied the Gregorian date for events that occurred outside Russia, and for correspondence between Russia and the West.

The stress in Russian Christian names is irregular, although it often falls on the penultimate syllable. This is the case with two of the names that we will frequently encounter in the book: Miasoedov, pronounced Myas-o-YED-ov, and Sukhomlinov, pronounced Sukh-om-LEEN-ov.

Abbreviations

The following abbreviations are used in the text and footnotes.

op.   catalog
f.   collection
d.   file
l.   sheet
CI   counterintelligence
N. A.   Nachrichten Abteilung (Intelligence Section, German General Staff)
BE   *Entsiklopedicheskii slovar'*. 84 vols. Izdateli Brokgauza i Efrona. St.
        Petersburg, 1881–1907.
AVPRI   Arkhiv Vneshnoi Politiki Rossiiskoi Imperii
        Archive of the Foreign Policy of the Russian Empire, Moscow
GARF   Gosudarstvennyi Arkhiv Rossiiskoi Federatsii
        State Archive of the Russian Federation, Moscow
RGVIA   Rossiiskii Gosudarstvennyi Voenno-Istoricheskii Arkhiv
        Russian State Archive of Military History, Moscow
PRO   Public Record Office, London

The Foe Within

Introduction

A Hanging in Warsaw

On March 18, 1915, at 10:35 in the morning a special field court-martial came to order within the Citadel of Warsaw. The room chosen for the proceedings was large, unheated, and unfurnished save for some chairs and a green felt-covered table, behind which sat the presiding judge, Colonel Lukirskii, and his four colleagues. In the dock was Lieutenant Colonel Sergei Nicholaevich Miasoedov, age forty-nine, an interpreter attached to the staff of the Russian Tenth Army. He stood accused of espionage on behalf of Germany and was on trial for his life.

Miasoedev was stunned by the suddenness of his arrest and arraignment. He had managed to send a message to his mother begging her to petition General N. V. Ruzskii, commander of the Northwest front, for his release. "I am unconditionally not guilty either in deed or intention," he wrote, "and I don't know what I am accused of."[1] As far as Miasoedov was concerned, he was the victim of some insane misunderstanding: the trial was a mistake, and he was certain that everything would quickly be cleared up and his innocence established. But as the hours went by, as witnesses marched forward to testify and as the depositions of the absent were read into the record, Miasoedov's confidence began to falter. When he was told that he would not be permitted any defense, he finally recognized that he was truly in mortal danger. At 6:15 p.m. the court adjourned to consider the evidence. Less than two hours later, the judges reconvened to deliver the verdict. Miasoedov was declared guilty of points 1a, 2, and 3 of the indictment. The punishment was to be death by hanging.

---

1. O. G. Freinat, *Pravda o dele Miasoedova i dr. Po offitsial'nym dokumentam i lichnym vospominaniiam* (Vilna, 1918), pp. 36–37.

1

2   The sentence having been pronounced, the chairman of the court then turned to the prisoner and asked him if he had anything to say.

At first Miasoedov was silent. Suddenly he shouted that he wanted to send a telegram to the emperor, that he wanted a chance to say farewell to his mother; overcome by emotion, he crumpled to the floor in a swoon.[2] Guards quickly revived him and led him away to a holding cell on the third floor of the Citadel's military prison.

For the next several hours Miasoedov was sustained by the hope of clemency. He scribbled telegrams to his daughter, Musa, and his mother urging them to entreat for clemency on his behalf. "I have been condemned by a field court," he wrote his daughter, "I swear that I am innocent. Implore the Sukhomlinovs [the minister of war and his wife] to save me. Beg the emperor to spare my life."[3] As more and more time passed, however, the colonel's febrile optimism gave way to blackest despair.

At midnight an Orthodox priest, Father V. V. Kristaner, visited Miasoedov in his cell. As Kristaner was leaving, Miasoedov called out for permission to visit the toilet. Captain D. M. Eremev unlocked the cell and escorted the condemned man to the water closet in the corridor. Miasoedov closed and latched the door behind him. After a few minutes, he was suddenly heard to cry out: "Now! Now!" Eremev screamed to the guards to break down the door. Miasoedov was discovered leaning against the wall with blood trickling down the front of his shirt; he had removed his pince-nez, smashed the lenses into fragments, and had slashed himself three times in the throat. Only Eremev's intervention had prevented him from severing the carotid artery.

Back in his cell, Miasoedov was given first aid by the army doctor M. D. Voitsekhovskii. When his wounds had been dressed, Miasoeodov appealed to see the priest one more time. Father Kristaner heard Miasoedov's final confession and administered communion. Almost as soon as this ritual had concluded, a party of guards seized Miasoedov, dragged him into the corridor and thence to the scaffold located on the glacis outside the inner citadel.[4] At 3:13 a.m. the noose was tightened around his neck.[5] As the gallows was merely a twelve-foot-high crossbar with no drop, it is said that Miasoedov strangled for fifteen minutes at the end of the rope before he died.[6] When the body stopped twitching, it was cut down, wrapped in a coarse tarpaulin, and loaded into a military truck. The corpse was driven outside the city and consigned to an unmarked grave.

In the aftermath of this barbaric execution, "spy mania" swept the Russian Empire. The tsarist police detained scores of people, searched hundreds of apartments,

---

2. B. B-ago [B. Buchinskii], "Sud nad Miasoedovym," *Arkhiv russkoi revoliutsii*, vol. 14 (Berlin, 1924), p. 145.

3. Rossiisski Gosudarstvennyi Voenno-Istoricheskii Arkhiv (hereafter RGVIA), f. 962, op. 2, d. 104, ll. 69–70.

4. Testimony of Eremev and Kristaner, Protocol of March 26, 1915, RGVIA, f. 962, op. 2, d. 104, ll. 89–93, 96–97; Stefan Król, *Cytadela Warszawska* (Warsaw, 1978), p. 217.

5. Miasoedov was executed at 3:50 Petrograd time. Warsaw time was twenty-seven minutes behind.

6. Lieutenant A. Bauermeister, *Spies Break Through: Memoirs of a German Secret Service Officer*, trans. Hector Bywater (New York, 1934), p. 6.

The Konstantine Gates, Warsaw Citadel.
The Citadel was the site of Miaosedov's trial
and execution.

and confiscated thousands of pages of documents. Among those picked up in the first
wave of arrests were Miasoedov's estranged wife, his brother-in-law, his mistress, his
business partners, even some casual acquaintances, including a liquor store owner, a
man who had once lent him a typewriter, and another who owned a railway buffet
where he had occasionally bought snacks.[7] By the third week in April, thirty people
had been indicted in the case; dozens of other arrests would ensue.[8]

Later in the spring of 1915 German and Austro-Hungarian forces broke through
the Russian lines between Gorlice and Tarnow and drove the Russian army back some
three hundred miles. By the time the front restabilized at the end of the year one hundred and fifty thousand Russian soldiers were dead, another seven hundred thousand
were wounded, and over three hundred thousand more had been taken prisoner.[9]
The Germans' advance, which took them to the gates of Riga in the north and the
outskirts of Tarnopol' in the south, produced an exodus of almost two million civilian refugees. All of Russian Poland and virtually all of Lithuania were now under German military occupation. The outcry to do something about the "traitors" responsible for the "Great Retreat" touched off the second wave of arrests in connection with
the Miasoedov affair in late 1915 and early 1916. And this time the reverberations of
the colonel's case reached the highest political levels of the Russian Empire. On April
20, 1916, General V. A. Sukhomlinov, who had served as minister of war from 1909 to
the spring of 1915, was summarily taken into custody and packed off to the fortress of
SS. Peter and Paul. He was charged with nonfeasance, malfeasance, and high treason.
Among his purported "crimes" was his personal relationship with Miasoedov. Released to house arrest by order of Nicholas II in October 1916, Sukhomlinov was
jailed again after the February Revolution of 1917. Tried by the Provisional Government, he was convicted in September 1917 and condemned to life imprisonment at
hard labor.

At the time, in certain military circles—and not just liberal ones—the Miasoedov
affair, with its purported revelations about elaborate networks of spies organized by
Germany long prior to 1914, was taken as the principal explanation for the reverses
and catastrophes that Russia had endured since the beginning of the world war. Many

7. Letter of P. K. Karpova, April 26, 1915, RGVIA, f. 801, op. 28, d. 170, l. 30.
8. List of persons arrested, April 24, 1915, RGVIA, f. 2003, op. 2, d. 1073, l. 87.
9. Cyril Falls, *The Great War, 1914–1918* (New York, 1959), p. 124.

4 years later, there were those who remained convinced that Miasoedov's treacherous communications with the enemy had been the root cause of every Russian military disaster from the annihilating defeat at Tannenberg in August 1914 to the destruction of the XX corps in February 1915.[10] In memoirs published in 1956, M. D. Bonch-Bruevich, a tsarist officer who subsequently became a Soviet general, was still loudly trumpeting Miasoedov's guilt and boasting of his personal role in cracking the case.[11] On the opposite side of the political fence, Anton Denikin, one of the most important White generals to fight against the Bolsheviks during the Civil War, never wavered in his belief that Miasoedov had been a spy.[12]

In contemporary civil society, it became an article of faith among both the liberal and moderate right opposition that Miasoedov had been guilty of treason and espionage as charged. There was considerable public demand that severe punishment be meted out to anyone even remotely implicated in his treachery. M. V. Rodzianko, the president of the Russian parliament, the Duma, was quoted as saying, "Even those who cleaned Miasoedov's boots ought to be hanged."[13] As for Sukhomlinov, although there were doubts about whether he was a "conscious" German agent, there was broad agreement that his "light-mindedness," negligence, and taste for shady company had gravely compromised Russia's national security.[14]

Under these circumstances, it is not surprising that many of the allied diplomats and journalists accredited to Russia came around to the view that German spies had sabotaged Russia's military performance. France's ambassador to Petrograd, Maurice Paleologue, wrote in his diary for March 1915 that "the precise and continuous information" that Miasoedov had transmitted to the Germans had been instrumental "in that series of defeats which had recently obliged the Russians to evacuate East Prussia."[15] Robert Wilton, who served as the correspondent of the *Times* of London in Petrograd during the war, later opined that the Germans' great military success of the

---

10. General-Lieutenant Khol'msen, *Mirovaia voina. Nashi operatsii na Vostochno-Prusskom fronte zimoiu 1915 g.* (Paris, 1935), pp. 278–279; M. V. Rodzianko, *Krushenie imperii. Gosudarstvennaia duma i fev. 1917 revoliutsiia* (Valley College, N.Y., 1986), p. 114.

11. M. D. Bonch-Bruevich, *Vsia vlast' sovetam* (Moscow, 195), pp. 65–66. Two other figures who were active in investigating the Miasoedov case also maintained to the end of their lives that the lieutenant colonel had indeed been a traitor. See General'nogo Shtaba Gen.-Maior Batiushin, *Tainaia voennia razvedka i bor'ba s nei* (Moscow, 2002), pp. 138–139; Vladimir Orloff, *The Secret Dossier: My Memoirs of Russia's Political Underworld,* trans. Mona Heath (London, 1932), pp. 62–73. Batiushin's defense of the "evidence" against Miasoedov is, however, unconvincing, while Orlov's narrative about the case is fraught with so many errors of fact that it impeaches itself.

12. Anton Denikin, *The Career of a Tsarist Officer: Memoirs, 1872–1916,* trans. Margaret Patoski (Minneapolis, 1975), pp. 201–202; A. I. Denikin, *Ocherki russkoi smuti. Krushenie vlasti i armii. Fevral'-sentiabr' 1917 g.* (Paris, n.d.; repr., Moscow, 1991), p. 11.

13. Freinat, *Pravda o dele,* p. 121.

14. V. I. Gurko, *Features and Figures of the Past: Government and Opinion in the Reign of Nicholas II,* trans. Laura Matveev (Palo Alto, 1939), pp. 551–554; Count V. N. Kokovtsov, *Iz moego proshlogo. Vospominaniia, 1903–1919,* vol. 2 (Paris, 1933), pp. 61–62; A. N. Naumov, *Iz utselevshikh vospominanii, 1868–1917* (New York, 1955), pp. 317–319.

15. Maurice Paléologue, *La Russie des Tsars pendant La Grande Guerre. 20 Juillet 1914–2 Juin 1915* (Paris, 1921), p. 319.

late winter of 1915, in which they had "nearly crumpled up the whole of the Nieman front" was due to the aid of "Colonel Miasojedov [*sic*], their secret agent on the Staff of General Siever's corps."[16]

Since many of the earliest histories of the Russian Revolution were written by liberal émigrés, or by English, French, and American writers with personal connections to the liberal or liberal-right milieu, certitude about Miasoedov's treason became a standard feature of the historiography of Russia. Frequently, accounts of the case were embellished with misinformation and rumors that were credulously served up as unalloyed truth. In *The Fall of the Russian Monarchy,* for example, the British authority on Russia Bernard Pares reported that Miasoedov had confessed to being a German agent on the eve of his execution, and had justified his treason by explaining that "only the triumph of Germany could save the autocracy in Russia."[17] In his three-volume French-language history of Russia (1932), the distinguished historian and Kadet politician Paul Miliukov insisted that the conviction of Miasoedov "corroborated the rumor, which had raged through the whole country, that treason had penetrated into the very heart of the army."[18] Richard Wilmer Rowan, a specialist on espionage, published a book in 1929 that depicted wartime Russia as honeycombed with traitors and enemy agents but nonetheless touted the exposure and conviction of Miasoedov and Sukhomlinov as brilliant triumphs of Russian counterintelligence work.[19] And Victor Kaledin, nephew of the famous Cossack general, in his two volumes of purported "memoirs" about the prerevolutionary secret service, also devoted considerable attention to the affair. Actually these were not memoirs at all but melodramatic fictions that owed a great deal to Saxe Romer's Fu Manchu series. According to Kaledin, Miasoedov and Sukhomlinov were both spies, as was their protectress, Alexandra, empress of Russia. In Kaledin's version, Miasoedov finally confessed his treason to Princess G., "a young, voluptuous, utterly depraved Lesbian of the extremist type," during a sexual encounter arranged by the Russian secret service in his death cell.[20]

Of course, Kaledin's racy trash took in only the hopelessly naive, but it is nonetheless possible to argue that the difference between his distortion of the record and that to be found between the covers of real works of history and authentic volumes of reminiscences was only a matter of degree. In addition to the works already cited, a host of memoirs devoted to the last days of the ancien régime by army officers, bureaucrats, and civilian politicians all pushed the view that Miasoedov had been guilty as charged. More often than not their narratives contained garbled facts,

---

16. Robert Wilton, *Russia's Agony* (London, 1918), p. 224.

17. Bernard Pares, *The Fall of the Russian Monarchy* (New York, 1939), p. 221.

18. Paul Miliukov et al., *History of Russia: Reforms, Reaction, Revolutions,* trans. Charles Lam Markmann, vol. 3 (New York, 1969), p. 325.

19. Richard Wilmer Rowan, *Spy and Counterspy: The Development of Modern Espionage* (New York, 1929), pp. 162–169.

20. Viktor K. Kaledin, *14–O.M. 66. K: Adventures of a Double Spy* (New York, 1932); *F.L.A.S.H. D 13* (New York, 1930), pp. 42, 263–268 (quote on p. 266).

6 outright mistakes, and glaring improbabilities.[21] Perhaps as a result of the "anti-Mia-soedov" strain in the literature, even more recent accounts have perpetuated some of the mythology about the affair.[22]

But the notion that Miasoedov (and Sukhomlinov too, for that matter) were trai-tors, although widespread, was not universal. As early as the fall of 1915, it was being whispered at general headquarters that Miasoedov had been framed.[23] Many reac-tionaries and ultra-monarchists soon arrived at the conclusion that the Miasoedov and Sukhomlinov cases had been cooked up, either to deflect public scrutiny from the incompetence of the high command or as part of a sinister left-wing plot to dis-credit the monarchy.[24] As General A. I. Spiridovich wrote, Miasoedov was "the expi-atory sacrifice for the military failure of Stavka [Russian General Headquarters] in East Prussia."[25] Such charges acquired still more credibility after the publication of O. G. Freinat's pamphlet about the case in 1918.[26] Freinat, a bureaucrat in the Ministry of the Interior who had personally been a defendant in one of the trials that followed Miasoedov's execution, used a battery of legal documents that had somehow fallen into his hands to argue forcefully that Miasoedov had not been guilty. In 1967 histo-rian George Katkov, relying heavily on Freinat, highlighted the case, which he con-strued as a politically motivated miscarriage of justice, as one of the most important events in the prehistory of the February Revolution.[27] In the same year the famous Soviet scholar K. F. Shatsillo published an article based on some (but by no means all) of the relevant archival materials in which he too exonerated Miasoedov.[28] Fi-nally, in 1969 there appeared émigré historian Aleksandr Tarsaidze's *Chetyre mifa* (*Four Myths*), a book that scrutinized the published evidence against Miasoedov and Sukhomlinov and proclaimed the innocence of both.[29]

21. For example, P. P. Isheev, *Oskolki proshlogo. Vospominaniia 1889–1959* (New York, n.d.), p. 100, represents Miasoedov as having married into the family of the German industrialists, the Til'mans; Vladimir Korostovets, *Seed and Harvest*, trans. Dorothy Lumby (London, 1931), p. 247, falsely claims to have studied the entire dossier.

22. Popular historian Ward Rutherford's 1972 book on the Russian army in the First World War (reprinted in 1992) contains a factual error in virtually every sentence it devotes to the case. Ward Ruther-ford, *The Tsar's War 1914–1917* (Cambridge, 1992), pp. 27–28, 155, 278. Rutherford tells us, inter alia, that Miasoedov was arrested, tried, and acquitted of treason in 1912, that he was the lover of Ekaterina Sukhom-linova, that Sukhomlinov emigrated to Switzerland after the Revolution, that he dedicated his memoirs to the kaiser, etc. Every one of these statements is false. Error has even crept into works of serious scholarship See W. Bruce Lincoln, *Passage Through Armageddon: The Russians in War and Revolution, 1914–1918* (New York, 1986), p. 112. There are mistakes even in this excellent book. Lincoln writes incorrectly that Miasoe-dov "had been dismissed from the army in 1907 and again in 1912 because his superiors had strongly sus-pected him of being in the pay of Germany."

23. Mikh. Lemke, *250 dnei v tsarskoi stavke (25 sent. 1915–2 iulia 1916)* (Peterburg, 1920), p. 190.

24. P. G. Kurlov, *Gibel' imperatorskoi Rossii* (repr., Moscow, 1992), p. 187.

25. General A. I. Spiridovich, *Velikaia voina i fevral'skaia revoliutsiia*, vol. 1 (New York, 1960), p. 110.

26. See Freinat, *Pravda o dele*.

27. George Katkov, *Russia 1917: The February Revolution* (London, 1967), pp. 121, 125, 127.

28. K. F. Shatsillo, "'Delo' Polkovnika Miasoedova," *Voprosy istorii* 42, no. 4 (1967): 103–116.

29. Aleksandr Tarsaidze, *Chetyre mifa* (New York, 1969).

Today, owing to the research of Katkov, Shatsillo, and, to a lesser extent Tarsaidze, the dominant interpretation holds that Miasoedov was never convincingly proved to be a German spy.[30] Still further, in recent years a series of monographs on the Russian army have presented V. A. Sukhomlinov's tenure as war minister in a neutral or even favorable light and have thus, either implicitly or explicitly, raised serious questions about the circumstances surrounding his arrest and trial.[31]

Although the broad outlines (if not all of the scabrous details) of the Miasoedov affair have long been known to specialists, the declassification of Russian archives in the 1990s provides an opportunity for reassessment. The complete story of these interlocking cases and the spy mania that gripped Imperial Russia during the World War has never before been fully revealed. It is an astonishing story, full of vivid incident, populated by a cast of characters from all levels of European society. Among those directly or indirectly involved in the affair were the emperors of both Russia and Germany, Baltic noblemen, high-ranking generals, courtesans, armament profiteers, simple peasants, the leaders of several political parties, Jewish businessmen, tsarist ministers, political police agents, German spymasters, and Grigorii Efimovich Rasputin. But the Miasoedov/Sukhomlinov affair commands attention for reasons other than its dramatis personae or the twists and turns of its "plot." In the first place, the affair is intrinsically important in the political and military history of Russia, but second, an investigation of the case[32] can contribute to social and cultural history as well, for it serves as a window into a Russian society already in the throes of decomposition.

From the standpoint of politics, the most obvious significance of the case is that it helped lay the groundwork for the February Revolution. It did so by cheapening and debasing the authority and prestige of the dynasty. If Miasoedov had been a spy, it was widely assumed that the protection of V. A. Sukhomlinov had been instrumental to the success of his felonious activities. But if that were so, perhaps Sukhom-

30. Hugh Seton-Watson, *The Russian Empire, 1801–1917* (London, 1967), pp. 710–711. A recent historiographical backlash against the theory of Miasoedov's innocence is worth noting. In the past few years, several Russian-language publications have appeared that endeavor to burnish the reputations of the intelligence and counterintelligence services of both Soviet and tsarist Russia. An example is Batiushin, *Tainaia voennaia razvedka.* Batiushin was an investigator closely involved in the case, and in this intelligence manual he makes occasional reference to it. The book also contains a sympathetic biography of Batiushin that largely adopts his version of events. See also I. I. Vasil'ev and A. A. Zdanovich, "General N. S. Batiushin. Portret v inter'ere russkoi razvedki i kontrrazvedki," pp. 190–257. This strand of interpretation has been echoed in at least one work of recent Western scholarship: Alex Marshall, "Russian Military Intelligence, 1905–1917: The Untold Story behind Tsarist Russia in the First World War," *War in History* 11, no. 4 (2004): 393–423. Marshall writes: "Given Miasoedov's dubious past . . . perhaps Russian intelligence in 1915 got the right man, albeit by dishonourable means" (p. 412).

31. See, for example, Norman Stone, *The Eastern Front, 1914–1917* (New York, 1975), pp. 24–34, 197–199; Allan K. Wildman, *The End of the Russian Imperial Army: The Old Army and the Soldiers' Revolt (March–April 1917)* (Princeton, 1980), pp. 65–68, 92–93; William C. Fuller, Jr. *Civil-Military Conflict in Imperial Russia 1881–1914* (Princeton, 1985), pp. 237–244; Bruce W. Menning, *Bayonets before Bullets. The Imperial Russian Army, 1861–1914* (Bloomington, 1992), pp. 221–234.

32. I shall henceforth refer to the Miasoedov and Sukhomlinov cases together as "the case."

8 linov was himself a traitor. And, since Nicholas II had personally chosen Sukhomlinov to head the Ministry of War, since he had trusted him and confided in him, what did this imply about the former's judgment and qualifications to rule? Still further, how many hundreds of thousands of lives had been unnecessarily sacrificed at the front because of treachery either obtusely ignored or guilefully abetted by some of the highest officials in the regime? Reasoning like this became quite common in 1915 and 1916 both in civil society and in the frontline trenches.[33] Indeed the Miasoedov/Sukhomlinov cases may have been even more damaging to the monarchy than the lurid scandals associated with Rasputin. The very names Miasoedov and Sukhomlinov became synonyms for "traitor," much as the name Quisling would forty years later. After the Bolsheviks seized power, the prominent historian Iu. V. Got'e confided to his diary: "The more you think about it the clearer it becomes that the society that gave birth to Nicholas II with his Rasputins, Miasoedovs and Sukhomlinovs should have ended as it has ended."[34] In other words, Got'e (who was far from being a radical) was arguing that wartime treason had proved that the tsarist system was rotten to the core and that the putrescence of that system to an extent justified its elimination by sanguinary revolution. As we shall see, the affair gave birth to a peculiar grammar of treason, in which the traditional monarchism that had held the empire together for generations was equated not with loyalty but with its exact opposite.

The case is no less revealing about party politics and political culture in Russia, both prior to 1914 and during the war itself. The origins of political parties in Russia, the rancorous relations between successive tsarist governments and Dumas, the rigidification of political attitudes during the war, the eventual emergence of the "Progressive Bloc"—all have served as subjects for monographs in many languages. But what the Miasoedov/Sukhomlinov case brings home is the unsavory realization that much of Russian politics in the era of the so-called constitutional experiment was actually an utterly ruthless and completely unprincipled struggle for power. Narrative histories of the last years of Russia's ancien régime often call attention to the unscrupulousness of the Bolsheviks ("tactical flexibility" to their admirers), to the venality of the ministers, to the decadence of high society, and to the ineptitude of Nicholas II. But the conduct of some of the liberal and conservative politicians (as well as that of some of the generals) who took part in the Miasoedov/Sukhomlinov affair was so morally depraved that it takes one's breath away.[35] It is a vile deed to sacrifice the life of an innocent man for political expediency. But it is viler still to compound the crime by destroying his family, besmirching his honor, and spattering his very name with excrement. Those involved may have salved their consciences by emphasizing their good intentions or the imperatives of national emergency, but in the

33. Tsuyoshi Haskegawa, *The February Revolution: Petrograd 1917* (Seattle, 1981), p. 574.

34. Iurii Vladirimovich Got'e, *Time of Troubles: The Diary of Iurii Vladimirovich Got'e*, trans. Terence Emmons (Princeton, 1988), p. 271.

35. Haskegawa, *February Revolution*, pp. 28–29, rightly denounces the liberals for their part in the M/S affair. As we shall see, however, it was not only the liberals whose deeds were censurable.

end what they did was not only evil but dangerous. The fetid atmosphere of hate and paranoia that they helped create and encourage could not be dispelled after tsarism collapsed. The malignant influence of that atmosphere continued to undermine the war effort while contributing to the erosion of the claim to rule made by tsarism's successor, the Provisional Government.

This brings us to the issue of popular attitudes and mentalities. One of the most interesting puzzles connected with the case is that extremely flimsy evidence was received with such mass credulity. Of course, the experience of World War I inspired popular hysteria on the home front in many belligerent countries.[36] The belief that traitorous conspirators were responsible for the bulk of Russia's misfortunes obviously satisfied some deep psychological needs. But the particular form that spy mania assumed in Russia during the war years was conditioned by a profound ambivalence about capitalism, by both overt and latent anti-Semitism, and by certain cultural stereotypes about women.

Finally, there are features of the Miasoedov/Sukhomlinov cases that eerily foreshadow and anticipate the legal practices that would become common in Stalin's Soviet Union. The comparison to be drawn obviously does not concern the severity of the repression. It would be obscene to equate the abuses perpetrated in the Miasoedov case, bad as they were, with the terror and mass murder unleashed by Stalin in the 1930s. But what is similar about the judicial and police procedures of 1915 and 1937 is the general concept of presumptive guilt. In the Miasoedov case, as later in the era of high Stalinism, everyone who fell under suspicion was considered a potential traitor. This meant that no effort had to be made to establish a motive, no resources had to be expended searching for eyewitnesses, and no time had to be wasted weighing the evidence. Opportunity (that is, the physical possibility that the defendant could have committed the crime) and association (that is, contacts with other allegedly suspicious persons) were considered sufficient to establish culpability.

36. Sir Samuel Hoare, who served in Russia at the time of the affair, and who was one of the few foreigners to have strong reservations about what was going on, made an explicit analogy between the case "and the spy mania that swept England in the first year of the war." See his book *The Fourth Seal: The End of a Russian Chapter* (London, 1930), p. 54.

1

Verzhbolovo

Miaso" is the Russian word for "meat," and in literal translation the name Miasoedov means "clan of the meat eaters" or "clan of the carnivores." Because meat was scarcely the regular fare of the common people in medieval eastern Europe, the name by itself implied a rather high status. The Miasoedovs were indeed an ancient gentry family and could trace their origins back to the Grand Duchy of Lithuania. In 1464 one Iakov Miasoed arrived in Muscovy from Lithuania and swore his allegiance to Grand Prince Ivan III Vasilievich. The descendants of the line he founded appear episodically in the records of the Muscovite period, occupying posts in the armed forces, the court, and the bureaucracy. On several occasions they were granted estates in usufruct (*pomest'ia*) as rewards for their services.[1] Although eventually the family split into different branches, the one with which we are concerned was concentrated in the northwestern borderlands of the Russian Empire.[2]

Sergei Nikolaevich Miasoedov was born in Vilna, the old capital of Lithuania, on July 5, 1865. His father, Nikolai, was a landholder who owned an estate in the White Russian province of Smolensk, to the east. Although not particularly affluent, Sergei Nikolaevich's parents were relatively well connected. Various relatives and friends of the Miasoedovs were prominent in St. Petersburg society and the government bureaucracy, and Nikolai himself was distinguished enough to become for a time the marshal of the Smolensk nobility. Nonetheless, the Miasoedovs' shortage of ready

1. Aleksandr Bobrinskii, *Dvorianskie rody. Vnesennye v obshchii gerbovnik Vserossiiskoi Imperii*, pt. 1 (St. Petersburg, 1890), p. 552.
2. On other branches of the family see "Miasoedovy," *Entsiklopedicheskii slovar'*, vol. 20, pub. F. A. Brokgauz and I. A. Efron (St. Petersburg, 1897), p. 386 (hereafter *BE*).

money destined Sergei from the earliest age for a military career, both because an education was virtually free for children of the gentry in the special military schools maintained by the tsarist state and because the salary he would draw upon graduation would enable him to support himself.

Sergei accordingly matriculated at the Fourth Moscow Kadet Corps (which provided a general secondary education) and then moved on to the prestigious Alexander Infantry College for two years of advanced instruction in military arts and sciences. In the spring of 1885, several months shy of his twentieth birthday, he was commissioned a second lieutenant and joined the 105th Orenburg Infantry Regiment. Except for the two years he completed as adjutant to the commander of the 17th Army Corps (1888 and 1891), Sergei Nikolaevich spent all of his active-duty service with the Orenburg Infantry, where he was apparently popular and well regarded.[3]

Even as a young adult, Miasoedov made a considerable impression on his contemporaries. He was urbane, witty, and possessed a gift for languages, particularly German, which he spoke, read, and wrote fluently. Moreover, he was tall, handsome, imposing, and physically powerful. An acquaintance later recalled that Miasoedov sometimes demonstrated his strength by snapping copper coins in two with his fingers.[4] He did, however, have a pair of bodily flaws: first, a tendency to corpulence (which became more pronounced as he aged), and second, extremely weak vision (for which military authorities authorized him to wear spectacles).

In the fall of 1892 Miasoedov changed careers. Retiring from the army, he enrolled in the Separate Corps of Gendarmes—a militarized police force under the direct control of the Russian Ministry of the Interior.[5] The gendarmes had been created during the reign of Nicholas I as the overt arm of Russia's political police. By the late nineteenth century, the corps of gendarmes, which mustered slightly less than a thousand officers and slightly more than one hundred thousand enlisted men, was the only truly national police organization Russia had. There were gendarme administrations located in every province, in many of the principal towns, and in the more important fortresses. Special gendarme divisions patrolled the streets of Petersburg, Moscow, and Warsaw, while separate gendarme commands were attached to each railroad line. In addition, gendarme officers staffed the urban *okhrannye otdeleniia*, the secret political police organs that were collectively and colloquially known as the Okhrana.[6] As this might suggest, although the gendarmes had many collateral duties, including the inspection of passports and the maintenance of public order during fairs, parades, and outdoor assemblies, the corps' main purpose was the detection and investigation of political crime.

---

3. General A. I. Spiridovich, *Velikaia voina i fevral'skaia revoliustiia*, vol. 1 (Paris, 1960), p. 108.

4. P. P. Isheev, *Oskolki proshlogo. Vospominaniia 1889–1959* (New York, n.d.), p. 106.

5. This move was by no means unusual: by the early 1890s steep reductions by the government in military spending had resulted in a situation in which bureaucrats and officials in other ministries and services of the tsarist state were better compensated than army officers of equivalent rank. See William C. Fuller, Jr., *Civil-Military Conflict in Imperial Russia, 1881–1914* (Princeton, 1985), pp. 14–15.

6. "Zhendarmy," *BE*, vol. 22 (St. Petersburg, 1894), pp. 718–719.

Lieutenant Colonel Sergei Miasoedov

Miasoedov's transition into the separate corps of gendarmes appears to have been a smooth one. Although there were important differences between the gendarmes and the tsarist armed forces in terms of institutional and organizational culture, all of the corps' officers were men who, like Miasoedov, were veterans of service in the regular army. By law, no one could become a gendarme officer who had not completed three years of duty as an army officer.[7] To be sure, the uniform of the gendarme officers was distinctive, but they bore military ranks identical to those used in the line cavalry. Indeed, in the event of war, the corps immediately came under the jurisdiction of military authorities. Even in peacetime, the gendarmes were officially listed on registers of army manpower.

Miasoedov's first assignment was with the gendarme administration in Olonets, a province northeast of Petersburg that abutted the Finnish border. In less than a year he was transferred to the Minsk gendarmes; four months later he was relocated again, this time to Verzhbolovo, a small town located in Suvalki province on the frontier of East Prussia. On January 17, 1894, Sergei Nikolaevich Miasoedov took up his post as deputy head of the Verzhbolovo gendarmes, or, to give its title in full, the Verzhbolovo section of the St. Petersburg-Warsaw police administration of railroads.[8] Verzhbolovo, also known by the German name of Wirballen and the Lithuanian one of Virbalis, would be Miasoedov's home base for the next sixteen years.

By all accounts, Verzhbolovo was a most unattractive spot, chiefly memorable, as one English traveler put it, for "its sordid surroundings and high wavy trees."[9] Here a small stream (spanned by a crude plank bridge) and some stands of barbed wire delimited the extent of Russia's sovereignty and separated the Russian from the German empire. There was no industry to speak of in the town, and such shops as it boasted catered to the needs of the agricultural villages in the hinterland. Perhaps its only claim to fame (before the Miasoedov treason trial made it notorious) was the fact that Russia's great landscape painter Isaac Levitan (1860–1900), the son of a railway employee, had been born in the nearby hamlet of Kibarty.

As assistant to Colonel Shpeier, head of the Verzhbolovo gendarmes, Miasoedov had responsibility for the security of a prescribed section of the Warsaw-Petersburg railway line. He was also supposed to assist the frontier guard and the customs department in the never-ending struggle against smuggling.[10] He was expected to be especially vigilant in preventing the import of subversive propaganda or weapons. The majority of his time was, however, filled with activities far more routine and pedestrian: the registration of people and the inspection of passports. It was his task to validate the documents of all travelers who sought to enter or exit Russia through the Verzhbolovo checkpoint. After he was promoted to head of the Verzhbolovo gen-

7. Mikhail Alekseev, *Voennaia razvedka Rossii ot Riurika do Nikolaia II*, vol. 1 (Moscow, 1998), p. 122.

8. See Miasoedov's service record, February 6, 1915, RGVIA, f. 801, op. 28, d. 163, l. 44.

9. Bernard Pares, *My Russian Memoirs* (London, 1931), p. 56.

10. See E. K. Sukhova, "Pogranichnaia strazha i kontrabanda v Rossii nachala XX veka," *Voprosy istorii*, no. 7–8 (1991): 234–237.

14 darmes in May 1901, he was empowered to issue passes to Russian subjects for temporary trips abroad on his own authority.

It might at first glance seem that this gloomy backwater was a less-than-ideal billet for a worldly and presumably ambitious man like Miasoedov. Yet far from expressing dissatisfaction with his assignment, the young lieutenant of gendarmes soon built a comfortable life for himself, developing a large network of friends in Verzhbolovo, across the border in the German town of Eydtkuhnen, in the Polish province of Suvalki, and in the Lithuanian provinces of Kovno, Kurland, and Vilna. Miasoedov clearly owed many of these social contacts to his skill with rifle and shotgun. An enthusiastic hunter, he became a valued guest at the numerous shooting parties organized by local landholders. It was a common passion for hunting that brought him together with the Til'mans, a wealthy Russo-German family of industrialists with interests in steel, copper, iron, zinc, and machine tools, who owned factories in both empires. It was hunting that also led to his acquaintance with the agriculturist Edward Fuchs and the importer Eduard Valentini, both German subjects long resident in Russia. Finally, it was this sport that led to Miasoedov's marriage.

Samuil Gol'dshtein had come to Russia as a nearly indigent German-Jewish émigré decades before. Through hard work and business acumen he was by the 1890s the proprietor of a substantial tannery in the city of Vilna, the empire's most important center for the hide trade. The value of the Gol'dshtein firm—approximately 400,000 rubles—made it a solid fixture in the economic life of the city and surrounding province. As was the case with many other successful entrepreneurs before and since, Samuil was determined to give his family those luxuries and advantages he had been denied in his youth. He accordingly bought the country estate Novyi Dvor (New Court) as a vacation residence. His sons Pavel and Albert frequently arranged hunting weekends on the grounds of the property, to which local army and gendarme officers were invited. It was apparently at one of these affairs that Miasoedov met Klara Samuilovna, one of the two Gol'dshtein daughters, whom he courted and married in 1895.[11]

Miasoedov's marriage brought him Klara's dowry of 115,000 gold rubles, a substantial sum of money in those days. At the same time, it not only linked him to the Gol'dshtein family but also connected him in complex ways with all their clients and kinfolk. The number of persons to whom he could apply for advice and aid increased, as did the number of people who had reciprocal claims on him. One such party was Frantz Rigert, the husband of Klara's sister Maria. In 1905 Rigert imposed on Miasoedov to serve as his partner and front man in a land-purchasing deal. Working together, Rigert and Miasoedov acquired a large estate of 932 *desiatiny* (2,500 acres) in Sventsiansk *uezd,* Vilna province. Although Rigert advanced the entire down payment and was the real owner of "Sorokpol," the only name on the deed was Miasoedov's. The reason was simple: as a nobleman Miasoedov was able to take

11. Three children were born to the couple: Maria (November 29, 1896), Sergei (March 2, 1898), and Nikolai (October 31, 1901). Order on retirement of Miasoedov, 1912, RGVIA, f. 801, op. 28, d. 164, l. 258.

out the low-interest loan of 25,000 rubles from the Nobles' Land Bank that financed the sale.[12] The pattern was a familiar one and would be repeated throughout Miasoedov's life, for there would be many other transactions in which Miasoedov would in effect sell his name, influence, or position to the less nobly born in exchange for hard cash.

But as we have seen, marriage had made Miasoedov a man of substance in his own right. He lost little time in taking advantage of the alteration in his circumstances. He bought a large building in Vilna that, when rented out to the army as a barracks, produced an annual income of 3,000 rubles.[13] He also built himself a new house with an unusual and expensive stone facade that provoked much comment in Verzhbolovo.

As a married man and house owner Miasoedov was now in a position to reciprocate the hospitality he had received over the years and quickly became known for giving exceptionally splendid and entertaining parties. He took great pains to cultivate the society of military officers, and both German and Russian military men were guests at his fetes. Prince P. P. Isheev of the Eighth "Alexander III" Dragoon Regiment later explained why an invitation to the Miasoedovs was so highly prized: "The attractive hostess, interesting visiting German ladies, the extensive hospitality—all of this, speaking frankly, appealed to us young bachelors who were utterly bored in this remote outpost."[14] But Miasoedov did more than simply relieve the officers' ennui. Cornet P. M. Shurinov recalled that Miasoedov was always doing small favors for him and his comrades, furnishing them free passes for border crossings and using his contacts with the railroad to upgrade their sleeping accommodations, to give but two examples.[15] Indeed, the widespread knowledge that Miasoedov was a "soft touch" for passes abroad, neither delaying their issue nor demanding bribes for them (as so many other tsarist officials did) won him the respect of the local civilian population.[16]

From the foregoing, one might conclude that Miasoedov was just another bureaucrat vegetating in provincial obscurity. But Miasoedov was no ordinary official, because despite its outward drabness Verzhbolovo was special for at least three reasons. In the first place, it lay athwart one of Russia's most important avenues of entrance and egress. Second, it was located in the northeast borderlands of the empire, territories whose ethnic, cultural, and economic profile was strikingly different from that of Great Russia proper. And finally (although this was unknown to most people) it possessed strategic significance as one of the principal staging areas for Russian intelligence operations against Germany. The unique characteristics of Verzhbolovo and the provinces around it helped define the three lives Miasoedov led during this

12. Bank document, November 26, 1913, RGVIA, f. 962, op. 2, d. 114, ll. 106–107.

13. *Vsia Vil'na* (Vilna, 1915), p. 197; letter of Klara Miasoedov to Frantz Rigert, October 23, 1914, RGVIA, f. 801, op. 28, d. 166, l. 99; legal document, November 30, 1904, RGVIA, f. 962, op. 2, d. 113, l. 324.

14. Isheev, *Oskolki proshlogo*, p. 106.

15. RGVIA, f. 2003, op. 2, d. 1063, l. 246.

16. Interrogation of V. O. Rodzevich, May 16, 1915, RGVIA, f. 801, op. 28, d. 165, l. 186.

16   period: as gendarme officer, businessman, and intelligence agent. Miasoedov recognized and exploited the opportunities his environment provided him. But his activities would sow the seeds of his later troubles.

Gateway to Russia

At the turn of the century there were but two convenient portals for international train travel into Russia from the rest of Europe. One of these was the border crossing station of Alexandrovo, which commanded the rail links to Warsaw, Ukraine, and Moscow. The other was the station at Verzhbolovo, which was used by passengers bound for St. Petersburg or points in the Baltic provinces. An express train could cover the 462 miles between Berlin and Eydtkuhnen in ten and a half hours. From Eydtkuhnen it was a verst (roughly two-thirds of a mile) to Verzhbolovo, where there would be a halt of at least an hour for passport and customs inspection. Once that had been concluded, another 555 miles (and fifteen hours) separated travelers from the capital of the Russian Empire.[17] Persons departing St. Petersburg for western Europe would travel this route in reverse, stopping at Verzhbolovo for border formalities. After 1901 these formalities were under Miasoedov's exclusive oversight.

Sergei Nikolaevich took advantage of his position to ingratiate himself with all the dignitaries, both Russian and foreign, whose railway journeys were interrupted in Verzhbolovo. He extended every courtesy to the wealthy, powerful, and highly placed, greeting them personally, attending to their comfort, even on occasion winking at their violation of the custom regulations.[18] He introduced himself to the tsar and most of the other prominent members of the house of Romanov as well as to representatives of every other ruling European dynasty. His motives were, of course, transparent, for he believed that intimacy with the great was a sort of power and that their good will might be translated into influence at some later date, much as money deposited in a bank can be subsequently withdrawn. What could be described as Miasoedov's "campaign of deference" produced tangible results: he rapidly accumulated twenty-six Russian and foreign decorations, although many of the medals and orders he collected (such as the Siamese Order of the White Elephant, Fourth Class) were scarcely prestigious.[19] In any event, Miasoedov certainly succeeded in calling attention to himself.

One of those whose attention he attracted was none other than the emperor of Germany, Wilhelm II. Now it happened that Wilhelm's favorite pastime was hunting, a recreation he engaged in with such frequency and gusto that he is said to have per-

---

17. Ruth Kenzie Wood, *The Tourist's Russia* (New York, 1912), p. 17; Karl Baedeker, *Russia with Teheran, Port Arthur and Peking: A Handbook for Travellers* (Leipzig, 1914; repr., New York, 1970), p. 34.

18. M. D. Bonch-Bruevich, *Vsia vlast' sovetam* (Moscow, 1957) p. 62.

19. Order on retirement of Miasoedov, 1912, RGVIA, f. 801, op. 28, d. 164, l. 256.

The train station at Verzhbolovo (courtesy of the V. Z. Zvetkov Collection)

sonally killed over fifty thousand game animals in the course of his life.[20] The hunting lodge he prized above all others was his East Prussian estate of Rominten, which was adjacent to Eydtkuhnen on the Russian frontier. Every fall, Wilhelm and his entourage removed to Rominten for several weeks of stag and elk shooting. Clothed in a ridiculous faux-medieval hunting uniform of Wilhelm's own design, the emperor's guests would awaken every morning at 5:00 a.m. to the backfiring of the convoy of automobiles which was to take them to pre-prepared shooting platforms deep within the forest.[21] There they would assume their positions and wait for the beaters to drive the game to the slaughter.

Hearing good reports of him from German diplomats and learning of his reputation as a keen outdoorsman, Wilhelm in 1904 invited Miasoedov to take part in the Rominten hunt. The emperor evidently must have found Miasoedov good company, for he issued a repeat invitation in 1905. On this occasion (September 18) Wilhelm insisted that the lieutenant colonel of gendarmes stay for lunch at the lodge, where he made a point of drinking to the health of his Russian guest. There would be several other encounters between the German monarch and the Russian gendarme in Rominten over the next two years. Of course, Miasoedov dutifully reported every detail of these innocuous meetings to his superiors, but in later years stories of his "friendship" with the emperor of Germany would arouse suspicion, as would the signed photograph with which Wilhelm had presented him to commemorate his visits.[22]

20. Thomas August Kohut, *Wilhelm II and the Germans* (New York, 1991), p. 10.
21. Anne Topham, *Memories of the Kaiser's Court* (London, 1914), p. 243.
22. Miasoedov note of September 21, 1905, RGVIA, f. 801, op. 28, d. 163, l. 43.

18   Miasoedov thus parlayed his visibility as supervisor of an important border crossing post into an extensive (if shallow) acquaintance with many in the highest echelons of Russian and European society. But there was another way in which Verzhbolovo would exert a profound influence on Miasoedov's life. The town was located in a region that had become a corridor for out-migration from Russia. Assisting émigrés was a lucrative business, one in which Miasoedov himself would become deeply involved.

The Northwest Borderlands and the Problem of Jewish Emigration

Russia's northwestern borderlands included the Polish province of Suvalki, the three Lithuanian provinces of Grodno, Vilna, and Kovno, and the Baltic provinces of Kurland, Estland and Livonia. Centuries before, these territories had belonged to the Grand Duchy of Lithuania. All had come under Russia's control in the 1700s: Estland and Livonia as the spoils of Peter the Great's successful war against Sweden, the rest as a consequence of the partitions of Poland. By the turn of the century the six provinces boasted a combined population of about 7.1 million people. Taken together, they also comprised a region distinct in terrain, economy, and ethnicity.

The northwest borderlands were a densely forested territory checkered with swamps, rivers, and lakes. The majority of the population was involved in agriculture. Rye, wheat, barley, oats, and flax were cultivated, as were fruit, potatoes, and tobacco. Saltwater fishing was an important occupation along the Baltic coast, while Suvalki was known for the quantity and quality of its freshwater catch. Such industry as existed was chiefly concentrated in the working of forest, animal, and agricultural products. As already noted, Vilna's tanneries were famous, as were the textile factories at Belostok in Grodno. There were also a number of distilleries, breweries, and tobacco-processing plants scattered throughout the region. Despite these enclaves of prosperity, the northern borderland provinces were overall abjectly poor.

The most distinctive feature of the region's economic life, however, was the degree to which it was "outward" oriented. Numerous economic links bound the six provinces to western Europe, and to Germany in particular. For example, Prussia absorbed virtually all of the wheat and potatoes that were the principal crops of Suvalki. A substantial proportion of the timber felled and cloth spun in Grodno, and of the apples and pears harvested in Vilna, were also destined for shipment to Germany. Labor power was another commodity that the northwest borderlands exported. By the early years of the twentieth century hundreds of thousands of Russian subjects, chiefly from Lithuania and the White Russian provinces further east, were crossing over into Germany to take up temporary agricultural jobs every spring and summer.[23] Nor was the movement of goods and people exclusively from east to west: Su-

23. On the eve of the First World War, Russia would be supplying Germany with four hundred thousand of these migrant workers each year. British Foreign Office, *Russian Poland, Lithuania and White Russia: Foreign Office Publication no. 44* (London, 1920), p. 68. During the First World War, when Britain imposed a naval blockade of Germany, one of the factors that exacerbated domestic food shortages within the Reich was the cutoff in the supply of Russian agricultural labor.

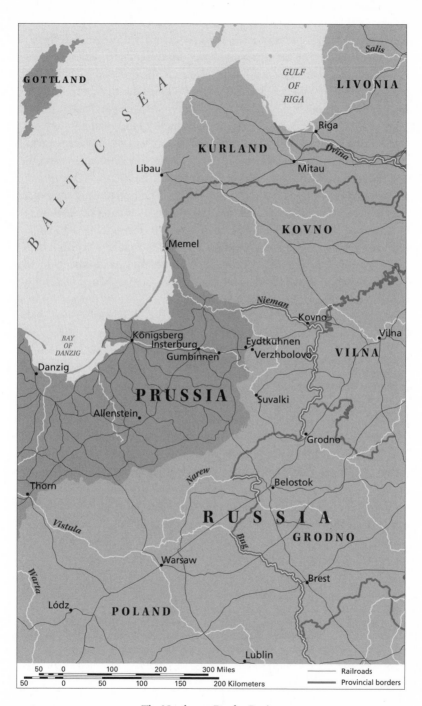

The Northwest Border Region

20 valki province was notorious for its smuggling rings, which specialized in running contraband liquor and tobacco from Germany into Russia.[24]

A remarkable religious, cultural, and ethnic diversity distinguished these northwestern borderlands. The territory was home to Lithuanians, Poles, Swedes, Germans, Finns, Jews, Latvians, Estonians, Russians, Belorussians, Ukrainians, and Tatars. The region's population was in fact so heterogeneous that although there were dominant ethnic groups in several of the six provinces (the Latvians in Livonia, the Lithuanians in Suvalki), in *none* of them was a single ethnicity an absolute majority. Almost as noteworthy as the region's population mix was the number of émigrés it produced. Among the groups who lived in the region, the Lithuanians and the Jews evinced the greatest propensity to leave Russia for good.

In the case of the Lithuanians, overpopulation, land hunger, and the general depression of the agricultural economy were the motors of emigration.[25] Jews had even stronger reasons than the Lithuanians to contemplate abandoning the Russian Empire, for they were oppressed by legislation designed to isolate them from the Christian population and to minimize their opportunities for advancement. By 1897 5.2 million Jews—half of world Jewry—were subjects of the tsar. Ninety percent of Russia's Jews lived in the so-called pale of settlement, the twenty-five provinces to which imperial law principally confined them.[26] Located on the western fringe of the empire, the pale consisted of the ten provinces of Poland in addition to thirteen others in Ukraine, Belorussia, and Lithuania plus the Crimea and Bessarabia. All the provinces of the northwest borderlands, save the two Baltic ones, were thus part of the pale, and consequently had populations with high concentrations of Jews. Over 25 percent of the inhabitants of Kovno were Jews, as were almost a fifth of the residents of Grodno.

In final twenty years of the nineteenth century the tsarist regime adopted a set of policies that exacerbated the plight of the Jews. The "temporary laws" of May 1882, which severely curtailed their right to buy or sell land, stimulated a mass migration of Jews from country to town, where they swelled the ranks of the urban poor. Other laws in 1886 and 1887 established strict quotas for Jewish enrollment in gymnasiums and universities, depriving thousands of educational opportunity.[27] When the state instituted an alcohol monopoly in 1894, another heavy blow fell upon the Jews. Since at that time 52 percent of all taverns and 55 percent of all distilleries in the pale were Jewish owned, the edict brought ruin to tens of thousands.[28]

24. Stanislaw Chankowski, "The Attitude of the Jewish Population of Augustow Province toward the January (1863) Insurrection," *Landsmen* 2, nos. 2 and 3 (1991–92): 35–36.

25. So powerful were these motivations that it has been estimated that approximately a quarter of the Lithuanian population emigrated from Russia in the fifty years prior to the outbreak of the First World War. Piotr S. Wandycz, *The Lands of Partitioned Poland, 1795–1918* (Seattle, 1974), p. 243.

26. Isaac M. Rubinow, *Economic Conditions of the Jews in Russia* (Washington, 1907; repr., New York, 1975), p. 488.

27. Samuel Joseph, *Jewish Immigration to the United States from 1881 to 1910* (New York, 1914), p. 62.

28. Charles Ruud and Sergei Stepanov, *Fontanka, 16. Politicheskii sysk pri tsariakh* (Moscow, 1993), pp. 280–281.

Making matters still worse for the Jews was an upsurge in anti-Semitism within the turn-of-the-century Russian Empire. Anti-Semitic organizations proliferated and demanded still greater restrictions on the Jews and even Jewish converts to Christianity, suggesting that at least some of this new Jew hatred was founded on inchoate ideas about Jewish "racial" characteristics, rather than traditional religious bias.[29] Eventually, the anti-Semitic movement in Russia erupted into violence: the Kishinev pogrom of April 1903 in which thirty-eight Jews were butchered was followed that summer by the still more bloody anti-Jewish rioting in Gomel. Large numbers of pogroms occurred throughout the empire in the fall of 1904 and in the revolutionary year 1905 there were over six hundred of them.[30] Poverty, legal discrimination, and the growing threat of physical violence were therefore all-important reasons behind the Jewish emigration. It is unsurprising, therefore, that of the 2,315,868 Russian subjects who emigrated to the United States between 1881 and 1910, over 48 percent were Jews.[31] Transporting emigrants to the United States was an extremely lucrative business. Packed into squalid dormitories in steerage, the travelers typically paid as much as five pounds a head, or 50 percent of the cabin-class fare. From 1860 to 1880 British steamship lines had dominated this business.[32] But as eastern and southern Europe became the source of more and more passengers, new competition—from the United States, but particularly from Germany—mounted effective challenges to British supremacy in oceanic transport.

The convenience of direct sailings from the continent was not the only tool the German shipping companies used to build their market share and their profits. Another was outright monopoly and price fixing. In 1891 Albert Ballin, the brilliant director of the Hamburg-American Line, organized the major European lines (except those of Britain and France) into the North Atlantic Steam-Ship Association, a cartel that established uniform minimum steerage-class ticket prices and tried to assign each of its members a specified percentage of the annual emigrant traffic.[33] Ballin's "pool," which had controlled 35 percent of the Atlantic passenger traffic, grew still larger in 1902, when Ballin struck a deal with J. P. Morgan to bring in additional shipping companies and to set prices and establish percentages not only for steerage but for first- and second-class passages as well.[34]

Finally, the German steamship lines were able to draw on the support of the German government itself in their struggle to dominate the emigration business. In the

29. Hans Rogger, *Jewish Policies and Right-Wing Politics in Imperial Russia* (Berkeley, 1986), pp. 33, 38.

30. Ruud and Stepanov, *Fontanka,16*, p. 295; S. N. Dubnow, *History of the Jews in Russia and Poland from the Earliest Times until the Present Day,* trans. I. Friedlander, vol. 3 (Philadelphia, 1920; repr., New York, 1975), pp. 80, 100, 116, 128.

31. Joseph, *Jewish Immigration,* p. 164.

32. Francis E. Hyde, *Cunard and the North Atlantic 1840–1973: A History of Shipping and Financial Management* (Atlantic Highlands, N.J., 1975), p. 81.

33. Bernhard Huldermann, *Albert Ballin,* trans. W. J. Eggers (London, 1922), pp. 23, 31, 33.

34. Lamarr Cecil, *Albert Ballin: Business and Politics in Imperial Germany 1888–1918* (Princeton, 1967), pp. 46–47.

22   summer of 1892, an outbreak of cholera in the port of Hamburg resulted two years
later in the promulgation of new regulations to control transit travel across Germany.
Henceforth eastern European emigrants en route to Prussian ports would be admitted to Germany only through special health inspection stations. At these stations, the
requirement for a transit visa was not just a clean bill of health; a passenger also had
to produce valid tickets for a transatlantic crossing on the Norddeutsche Lloyd or
Hamburg-American lines. Since the two firms participated in the management of the
inspection stations and maintained booking offices nearby, prospective emigrants
could buy their tickets on the spot and proceed on their way. But anyone without an
approved ticket or the money to purchase one was arrested and forcibly deported
from Germany. In short, if you wanted to go to America from Germany, you would
have to take passage on a German vessel. As the American consul general in Hamburg dryly remarked, this arrangement was "an extremely interesting combination
of hygienic and commercial management."[35] As a result of skillful business practices,
the operation of the pool, and the regulations of 1894, Norddeutsche Lloyd and
Hamburg-American were together carrying over a quarter of a million emigrants to
the United States every year by the turn of the century.[36]

Before prospective Russian Jewish émigrés dealt with foreign governments and
shipping companies, they had to get out of Russia in the first place, which was by no
means a simple task. The tsarist regime was ambivalent about the entire question of
emigration, even by Jews, an attitude that appears somewhat odd, given the general
anti-Semitism in the official circles of the day. Although St. Petersburg relaxed many
of the legal barriers to emigration in 1892, the procedures for acquiring formal permission to leave remained costly, onerous, and time-consuming. Any person desiring
to quit the empire permanently had to acquire a special passport, which often entailed a three-month wait. Moreover, the application process involved protracted
contact with Russian bureaucrats, who were known to make trouble for men of military age who could not produce army discharge papers. It was also no secret that
venal Russian officials often tried to squeeze payments out of émigrés over and above
those required by law. Although the statutory price for a passport was 15 rubles,
bribes could easily double or triple that cost.[37]

The inevitable upshot was that thousands of would-be emigrants did not even
bother to apply for exit permits and tried instead to cross the border illegally. The
great German steamship companies saw opportunity in all of this and soon got into
the business of organizing illegal border crossings as a service for their clients. Company agents were dispatched into Russia's western provinces to sell transatlantic
steamship tickets. For an additional fee (usually 50 percent of the face value of each
ticket), agents guaranteed the safe passage of émigrés from Russia into Germany. The

35. Zosa Szajkowski, "Sufferings of Jewish Emigrants to America in Transit Through Germany," *Jewish Social Studies* 39, nos. 1–2 (1977): 106.

36. René Fabre, *Les Grandes Lignes de Paquebots Nord-Atlantique* (Paris, 1928), p. 52; Cecil, *Albert
Ballin*, p. 25.

37. Rogger, *Jewish Policies*, pp. 183–184.

agents would take care of every detail from the hiring of peasant guides to the bribing of the border guards. Once across the frontier, emigrants would immediately be taken to an approved health inspection station, such as the one at Eydtkuhnen, where they would be registered and given medical examinations before proceeding to one of Germany's Baltic ports by rail.[38]

The Verzhbolovo region soon became a center for the smuggling of emigrants from Russia to Germany, a fact of which Miasoedov was well aware. In May of 1903, he wrote a comprehensive paper about the illegal emigration movement, which he forwarded to the governor of Suvalki province. In view of what would happen subsequently, it is worthwhile pausing for a look at the contents of Miasoedov's report.

Miasoedov began by noting that illegal emigration had reached epidemic levels in his segment of the frontier. In the spring and summer it was not uncommon for between one hundred and three hundred people to make illegal border crossings in the vicinity of Verzhbolovo every day. As this had been going on for years, the total number of people who had violated the frontier in this section of Suvalki province was very large. According to the incomplete information he had been able to obtain, from 1892 to 1902 at least 118,510 Russian illegals had been processed at Eydtkuhnen en route to Hamburg.[39] In Miasoedov's opinion, Suvalki province had become a mecca for illegal emigrants not only because of the health inspection station at Eydtkuhnen but also because of the boundless venality and wholesale corruption of the local Russian authorities. The culprits here were the Braunshtein brothers of Kibarty.

The Braunshteins were agents for the Grinman steamship booking company of Eydtkuhnen. Active everywhere in the northwest borderlands, they attracted customers with fairy tales about the glories of life in America, sold overpriced tickets to the gullible, and were heavily involved in the illegal border crossings. To facilitate their criminal operations, they "had bought up practically the entire local police of Volkovyshskii district"—the frontier district that included Verzhbolovo. According to Otto Grinberg, the proprietor of a currency exchange office in Verzhbolovo, even former district chief Link was on the Braunshteins' payroll. In sum, "since the local police and the lower ranks of the border guards do not have the willpower to resist constant temptation, they eventually give in, take bribes, and pander to the emigration movement." As a result, the Braunshteins conducted themselves as if the Russian border did not exist.[40]

This sorry state of affairs had two additional consequences, both of them dismal. First, because the Braunshteins were in collusion with the police, they virtually monopolized the steamship-ticket business in the region, which enabled them to fleece the poor. In Vilna the Braunshteins could get 115–20 rubles for the same ticket to New York that went for 80 rubles in Eydtkuhnen. Second, the Braunshteins' disregard for

---

38. Gerald Sorin, *A Time for Building: The Third Migration, 1880–1920*, vol. 3 of *The Jewish People in America*, ed. Henry L. Feingold (Baltimore, 1992), pp. 42–43.

39. Miasoedov report, May 20, 1903, RGVIA, f. 962, op. 2, d. 112, l. 413.

40. Ibid., ll. 383–384, 409, 415.

24 the law attracted emulators. Smuggling rings had become more numerous and more active. Dangerous felons were taking advantage of lax border controls in the district to escape from Russia into Germany or from Germany into Russia, while the same lack of oversight made revolutionaries increasingly prone to use this stretch of the frontier to import subversive political literature.[41]

In Miasoedov's view, a law enforcement crackdown was not the solution to illegal emigration through the district: although this might briefly stem the flow of emigrants, it would have no effect on the economic distress that was the underlying cause of emigration. Instead, he recommended that the imperial government alter policy and permit the emigration of any subjects who desired to leave. Stamp charges on passports should be reduced, and passports themselves should be priced on a sliding scale, with the neediest applicants charged no more than 3 to 5 rubles. Finally, to combat the abuses and swindles perpetrated by such men as the Braunshteins, the sale of transatlantic steamship tickets *within* Russia should be legalized, so as to encourage competition. Both the state and the people would benefit if reputable businessmen like Samuel Freidberg of Libava dominated the emigration business, rather than scoundrels like the Braunshteins. Freidberg, Miasoedov added, owned a legal emigration bureau that was officially licensed and beyond reproach.[42]

On one level, Miasoedov's 1903 paper could be taken as the work of a courageous and public-spirited civil servant, who sought only what was best for his country. Certainly, the report impressed the governor of Suvalki province, who forwarded it to the central Ministry of the Interior, which in 1906 appointed Miasoedov to a special interdepartmental commission on emigration and Russia's domestic transportation industry.[43] There was, however, more to Miasoedov's report than this. Although its views on emigration and its compassion for the less fortunate may well have been genuine, Miasoedov also had personal reasons for writing as he did: he had his own financial stake in the emigration movement. A concealed purpose of the report, then, was to advance the pecuniary interests of Miasoedov's friends and business partners by undermining their competitors.

Take, for example, the Otto Grinberg whom he had named as his source for the dishonesty of District Chief Link. Grinberg ran an office that changed money and made small loans; Miasoedov had invested in this office, despite the fact that as a gendarme officer he was forbidden by law to do so. But Grinberg was also a principal in Gerts, Grinberg and Levinson, a steamship-booking agency in Eydtkuhnen, which was a rival of the Braunshteins' employer, the Grinman firm. Since Miasoedov had also made investments sub rosa in Gerts, Grinberg and Levinson, he stood to profit by blowing the whistle on the Braunshteins' underhanded doings.[44] Miasoedov's ties to Samuel Freidberg, whose emigration bureau he held up as a model of probity, were even more interesting.

41. Ibid., ll. 409, 415.

42. Ibid., ll. 415–417.

43. P. E. Shchegolev, ed., *Padenie tsarskago rezhima*, vol. 4 (Leningrad, 1925), p. 517.

44. For Miasoedov's connection to Grinberg see note of February 6, 1915, RGVIA, f. 962, op. 2, d. 160, l. 26.

The Freidberg family had a long record of involvement in the emigration busi- 25
ness and, as a result, had an equally long record of run-ins with the police. In 1887,
Samuel and his father, Iankel, had been ordered out of the frontier zone for assisting
illegal emigrants to leave the empire. In 1891, two of Samuel's brothers were sentenced
to terms of administrative exile in Mogilev province for the same offense. In the late
eighties Samuel had moved to Hamburg, where he became (at least nominally) a convert to Christianity. Upon his return to Russia in 1897 he settled in the port city of
Libava and established himself as a merchant of the first guild. At the turn of the century, he and his third brother, Boris, founded Karlsberg, Spiro and Company, which,
as Miasoedov accurately observed in his report, was a licensed firm specializing in
legal emigration. Not surprisingly, Samuel now incurred the wrath of everyone in the
region who made money from legal or illegal emigration. If the Freidbergs succeeded,
they would imperil the livelihood of hundreds of people. The Freidbergs' enemies retaliated by harassing them with newspaper libels, attempted blackmail, anonymous
denunciations, and police raids. At some point, Samuel Freidberg turned to Miasoedov, whom he knew from Verzhbolovo, and retained him to provide political protection.[45] It is clear that one objective of Miasoedov's 1903 report was to launch a bureaucratic counterattack on the Freidbergs' business adversaries. Moreover, if the
Braunshteins were guilty of corrupting the police to put pressure on their competitors, were the Freidbergs behaving any differently in hiring Miasoedov to do the
same thing? Eventually, Sergei Nikolaevich would enter into still more intimate business dealings with the Freidbergs, dealings whose consequences would literally prove
fatal for him.

Russian capitalism had many faces, of course, but the face of capitalism as represented by the emigration business in Russia's northwest borderlands was a particularly ugly one. The objective of the emigration firm was to expand the customer base
not by offering more attractive prices or better services but by suborning venal and
greedy tsarist officials to turn the power of the state against the competition. In sur-
reptitiously working on behalf of Grinberg and the Freidbergs, Miasoedov was not
merely taking sides in a petty dispute between antagonistic groups of Jewish businessmen. The commercial conflict over emigration in the Russian northwest had international as well as local dimensions, for it both echoed and was partially driven by
the bitter struggle among German, British, and American steamship companies for
control over the entire transatlantic passenger traffic. There were powerful interests
standing behind the Freidbergs, and still more powerful interests lurking behind their
rivals.

Miasoedov and Military Intelligence

It is one of the ironies of the Miasoedov affair that there exists unequivocal evidence of Miasoedov's spying in the service of but one country: his own. There was

45. RGVIA, f. 962, op. 2, d. 112, l. 423; letter of assistant chief of Kurland gendarmes, February 20, 1915,
RGVIA, f. 801, op. 28, d. 168, l. 35.

26 nothing unusual about this. Rather the reverse. Given his position as head of an important frontier station, he would have been guilty of inexcusable misconduct had he not engaged in espionage.

In the early twentieth century, Russia's military intelligence system was rudimentary, decentralized, and underfunded. Although the main staff and after 1906 the newly created general staff were supposed to collect and analyze all intelligence, these organizations did not actively control the majority of intelligence operations, which more often than not were managed by Russia's military attachés and the staffs of the military districts into which the empire was divided.[46] Since the paltry sum of 35,000 rubles was typically a district's entire annual budget for intelligence work, district staffs had no choice but to rely on other agencies to help in the collection of intelligence. One of the agencies most active in this effort was the Separate Corps of Gendarmes, whose frontier officers had been required by law to perform intelligence functions since 1880.[47] Typically, a gendarme was asked to develop a network of informants in the border region who (it was hoped) could provide the local district staff with some sense of military dispositions on the other side of the frontier.

As a part-time intelligence officer, Miasoedov did precisely this. He debriefed teamsters, peddlers, and other people who made frequent trips back and forth to Germany. He also recruited his own agents—among them German workers, Russian expatriates, and religious sectarians. He even enlisted members of his own extended family as sources. He persuaded his brother-in-law Albert Gol'dshtein to move to Königsberg in Prussia to continually monitor military activities at the fortress there. But Miasoedov's labors for Russian military intelligence extended far beyond the mundane and ordinary, for he personally conducted reconnaissance missions in the field. In the spring of 1906 he went to the German city of Mannheim, where he purchased a top-of-the-line Benz automobile for 6,500 rubles. He employed this vehicle (to which he had added a secret compartment) on numerous occasions to drive into Germany. In the guise of an innocent tourist, he thoroughly reconnoitered the territory south and southeast of the Mazurian lakes.[48]

How important were the contributions to Russian military intelligence of the gendarmes in general and of Miasoedov in particular? A. A. Samoilo, who ran the intelligence bureau in Kiev district and who later served in the intelligence section of the central general staff, was on the whole dismissive of the efforts of frontier gendarme officers. The information they supplied, he maintained, was often fragmentary, incoherent, and consequently worthless.[49] But Samoilo's negative evaluation is flatly contradicted by that of one of his predecessors in the Kiev intelligence office, who wrote that gendarme officers who "lived permanently in the frontier zone, who

46. William C. Fuller, Jr., "The Russian Empire," in *Knowing One's Enemies: Intelligence Assessment Before the Two World Wars*, ed. Ernest R. May, pp. 103–108 (Princeton, 1984).

47. Alekseev, *Voennaia razvedka*, vol. 1, p. 122.

48. Deposition of I. P. Vasil'ev, assistant chief of counterintelligence, general staff, RGVIA, f. 962, op. 2, d. 160, ll. 58–60, 100.

49. A.S. Samoilo, *Dve zhizni* (Leningrad, 1963), pp. 102–103.

were completely familiar with the local population, and who possessed their own networks of spies" could perform services of "enormous value in the area of secret espionage."[50] Indeed, the failure of the Russian military to build up its own substantial rings of spies inside Germany can only have enhanced the value of the information provided by the gendarmes' agents. As late as April 1907, Vilna Military District had on its payroll but one agent who was resident in Germany. Warsaw Military District had none at all.[51]

As for the intelligence activities of Miasoedov himself, we have the testimony of Walter Nicolai, a career German intelligence professional who rose to become the German Empire's supreme intelligence chief during World War I. According to Nicolai, during his years in Verzhbolovo, Miasoedov "was one of the most successful" intelligence operatives that Russia ever had. One reason for this, as Nicolai ruefully noted, was the high prestige Miasoedov acquired as a participant in Wilhelm II's imperial hunts. Miasoedov's personal relationship with the German emperor intimidated the Prussian police, who refrained from interfering with him or even tailing him when he came to Germany, although they had ample reason to believe that he was there not to see the sights but to spy.[52]

No *direct* evidence to substantiate Nicolai's claim for the importance of Miasoedov's intelligence work has yet come to light. To my knowledge, no documents are extant that prove, for example, that the information supplied by Miasoedov had any impact on Russia's war plans. But if such evidence ever existed, it may well have been expunged from the archives, owing to the obloquy that subsequently attached itself to his name. Once Miasoedov had been executed for treason, how likely was it that the Russian General Staff would want the documentary record to show that it had entrusted the selfsame traitor with sensitive missions? Yet it can be stated with certainty that Miasoedov's intelligence operations were not low level and routine. For one thing, half of the money he used to buy his expensive Benz car came from a secret general staff subvention that had been approved by Nicholas II himself.[53] For another, even a cursory review of the kind of information he collected indicates that he was tackling one of issues that most troubled the leadership of the Russian army as it contemplated a future war.

By 1900 it was apparent that the most likely scenario for a general European war involved the powers of the Triple Alliance—Germany, Austria-Hungary, and Italy—squaring off against Russia and France. As Germany bordered both Russia and France, hostilities would oblige Berlin to choose one of them for the primary military blow while defending against the other. Since the war was expected to be short, its outcome might well be determined by the mistakes a nation's army either made or avoided in its opening stages, which in turn meant that knowledge of Germany's precise intentions was of the highest significance for Russia's national security. For Rus-

50. Alekseev, *Voennaia razvedka*, vol. 1, p. 123.

51. Ibid., vol. 2, pp. 181, 183.

52. W. Nicolai, *The German Secret Service*, trans. George Renwick (London, 1924), p. 27.

53. Report on activities of Miasoedov, February 12, 1915, RGVIA, f. 801, op. 28, d. 163, l. 54.

28 sian strategy to prevail in a European war, it had to be founded on an accurate prediction of what the Germans were going to do. Because of her superior mobilization speed, if Germany decided to deploy the bulk of her forces in the east, Russia's best course would be to array her own armies not along the frontier but deep inside Poland and Lithuania, to prevent their piecemeal destruction before the reserves could reinforce them. Alternately, if Germany threw most of her troops against France in the opening phase of the war, Russia should mass her forces closer to the border, so as to invade Germany and relieve the pressure on her beleaguered ally. As it happened, at the very end of 1905 General Alfred von Schlieffen finalized the plan that Germany would attempt to implement when World War I broke out in August 1914; as is well known, the Schlieffen plan made France, not Russia, the target of Germany's initial offensive. Although Russia soon got wind of the existence of the plan, she could not be entirely confident that it was the last word in German strategic thinking and that the Germans did not have an alternative scheme for a major attack in the east.[54]

The significance of Miasoedov's intelligence activities now becomes clear. By gathering information from his agents in Prussia and through his own personal reconnaissance, Miasoedov was searching for clues about the mystery at the heart of German strategy. If Germany truly intended to march against France in force in the event of war, it would be logical for her to make large investments in fortresses, blockhouses, and other defensive works on the Russian frontier, which is why Miasoedov and his agents spent so much time trying to determine whether Germany was actually doing this. When Miasoedov studied the number of railway stations east of the Vistula that were furnished with military platforms, he was looking for evidence that would either support or rebut the hypothesis that Germany would make her biggest initial thrust against Russia.[55] Since the Russian General Staff did not rule out the possibility that Germany was capable of altering her strategic focus at the very last minute, Miasoedov took precautions to deal with that eventuality as well.[56] During a crisis, his agent, Rubin, an employee in an East Prussian bicycle factory, was instructed to send coded telegrams to Russian intelligence officers working under cover

54. Russia was correct to entertain these doubts at this time. The Schlieffen plan, which was drafted in response to the European situation as it stood in 1905, was never intended to be Germany's unalterable design for future war. See Arden Bucholz, *Moltke, Schlieffen and Prussian War Planning* (New York, 1991), pp. 195–196; see also William C. Fuller, Jr., *Strategy and Power in Russia, 1600–1914* (New York, 1992), p. 442. In 1912, however, Russian planners became convinced that Great Britain would enter into a general European war as a French ally, and that therefore the Germans would most probably level their hardest initial blow against France.Personal communication from Prof. Bruce Menning, U.S. Army Command and Staff College, May 26, 2000.

55. Deposition of I. P. Vasil'ev, assistant head of counterintelligence, general staff, RGVIA, f. 962, op. 2, d. 160, ll. 58–60.

56. An April 1914 report by Lieutenant General Iu. N. Danilov, Russia's deputy chief of staff, while correctly predicting that the Germans would attack France with the bulk of their forces at the very beginning of a general European war, nonetheless refused to exclude the possibility that the Germans might have a variant plan that struck Russia the heaviest initial blow. See V. M. Gilensen, "Germanskaia voennaia razvedka protiv Rossii (1871–1917 gg.)," *Novaia i noveishaia istoriia*, no. 2 (1991): 159–162.

in Copenhagen. If Rubin observed large troop concentrations in the vicinity, he was to wire "I am sending the typewriter to Malmö"; if he noticed only light concentrations, the message was to read "I am sending the typewriter to Bern."[57]

It bears stressing that there were no watertight bulkheads separating Miasoedov's three lives as official, businessman, and spy; indeed, each of these lives interpenetrated the others. He took advantage of his official status to further his business interests, used his commercial contacts as sources of intelligence, did business deals with certain of his agents, and so forth. But Miasoedov also made enemies in each of his spheres of activity: within the Russian bureaucracy, within the emigration and steamship industries, and within the intelligence service of Germany. In a real sense, the misfortunes that subsequently befell him could all be traced back to his years in Verzhbolovo.

The Troubles Begin: The Mission of Cornet Ponomarev

For his first twelve years in Verzhbolovo, Miasoedov appears to have enjoyed extremely cordial relations both with his immediate superiors in the borderlands and with the high functionaries of the Ministry of the Interior back in Petersburg. To be sure, his service record was not spotless: three times he was issued mild citations (*zamechaniia*) for "inappropriate language" and "tactless" conduct toward railway passengers, and on one other occasion he received a sterner reprimand (*vygovor*) for insulting a postal clerk.[58] These instances of official displeasure were, however, comparatively few and relatively trivial.

But everything changed in 1906. Toward the end of that year, someone in or near Verzhbolovo authored an anonymous denunciation of Miasoedov that worked its way up the chain of command to the desk of the director of the department of police. This letter accused Miasoedov of shameful dereliction of duty: not only was the gendarme colonel failing to suppress smuggling in his district, but he was even trafficking in contraband himself by sneaking untaxed wine and liquor into Russia from Germany. Rather than dismiss this unsubstantiated complaint out of hand (as it most likely would have done earlier), the department of police decided to launch an investigation.

There were two reasons for this. The first had to do with the empire's internal crisis. Russia's string of defeats in her war against Japan, the rising hostility to the government on the part of land-hungry peasants, mistreated factory workers, and alienated intellectuals, as well as that same government's obdurate refusal to even consider a program of meaningful reforms, all combined in 1905 to touch off a full-blown revolution. Although the worst was over by the end of that year, strikes, demonstrations, street warfare, and rural unrest smoldered on into early 1907 before burning out completely. It was the fact of revolution, then, that lent the charges made against Mi-

---

57. RGVIA, f. 801, op. 28, d. 166, ll. 22–23.
58. Note of February 6, 1915, RGVIA, f. 962, op. 2, d. 160, ll. 26–27; RGVIA, f. 962, op. 2, d. 121, ll. 1–2.

30 asoedov in 1906 particular gravity. If Miasoedov was insufficiently vigilant in the struggle against smuggling, he was not just depriving the treasury of customs revenues but potentially imperiling public order, even the survival of the regime. Revolutionary terrorism of unprecedented intensity then gripped the empire: between October 1905 and December 1907 over nine thousand people were slaughtered or maimed by terrorists, who in many cases used weapons manufactured abroad to perpetrate their outrages. All around Russia's land perimeter, revolutionaries were infiltrating the border with shipments of firearms, cartridges, and high explosives. If illegal arms were coming into Russia through the Verzhbolovo region, this had to be stopped immediately, and Miasoedov deserved exemplary punishment.

Yet there was another reason why the department of police now elected to scrutinize Miasoedov. In 1906, Maksimilian Ivanovich Trusevich, a former prosecutor, had been appointed the director of the department. Trusevich, whose talent as an investigator was later described by an admiring subordinate as "almost Dostoevskiian," is probably best remembered for his efforts to break Russia's revolutionary parties from the inside by launching waves of double agents against them.[59] Nervous and high-strung, he was the sort of man who was quick to take offense and never forgot or forgave any slight. One of the people against whom he nursed a grudge was Miasoedov. The precise origin and nature of Trusevich's hostility to the gendarme officer are still obscure. Apparently, Trusevich felt that he had been badly treated by Miasoedov or his assistant during a trip he had made to Verzhbolovo in his capacity as assistant St. Petersburg prosecutor. Then, too, there may have been friction as a result of Trusevich's 1904 inquiry into the unintentional detonation of a homemade terrorist bomb in Petersburg's Northern Hotel, for which Miasoeodov obtained some physical evidence.[60]

To head up the investigation of Miasoedov, Trusevich turned to a certain Cornet Ponomarev, a gendarme officer then attached to the St. Petersburg Okhrana. A thoroughly unpleasant and unscrupulous individual, Ponomarev had acquired a nasty reputation while still a student at the St. Petersburg Mining Institute, in part for his efforts to denounce his own professors to the authorities for political unreliability.[61] After completing his studies, he gave up on engineering and instead sought admission to the secret political police. The ambitious Ponomarev was jubilant about his special mission to Suvalki province, for he realized that its success could be the making of his career. In accordance with his instructions, he avoided any contact with the railway gendarmes after arriving in Verzhbolovo in late 1906, and told only the local office of border guards about the nature of his assignment. He also persuaded the Vilna Okhrana to lend him some of its operatives as assistants.

These men were *filery*, or professional surveillance agents. Although at least one post-Revolutionary memoirist went to great lengths to defend the sterling moral

---

59. A. P. Martynov, *Moia sluzhba v otdel'nom korpuse zhandarmov*, ed. Richard Wraga (Palo Alto, 1972), p. 325; Ruud and Stepanov, *Fontanka, 16*, p. 334.

60. RGVIA, f. 962, op. 2, d. 101, l. 3.

61. O. O. Gruzenberg, *Yesterday: Memoirs of a Russian Jewish Lawyer*, trans. Don C. Rawson and Tatiana Tipton (Berkeley, 1981), p. 129.

character of the roughly one thousand *filery* employed throughout the empire, the Okhrana often recruited them from the ranks of criminal lowlifes and derelicts.[62] In any event, this was certainly the background of the team seconded to Ponomarev. As soon as he met with his flunkies from Vilna, Ponomarev explained that their collective purpose was quite simply the destruction of Miasoedov. They would accomplish this in two stages: by organizing a series of additional anonymous denunciations to further blacken the colonel's name in St. Petersburg and silence his supporters; and by collecting the evidence to arrest and convict him on smuggling charges.

But Ponomarev was soon disappointed. Although he did manage to persuade several people—including petty bureaucrats, barflies, and at least one disgruntled gendarme corporal—to put their names to letters calumniating Miasoeodov (letters that would dog Miasoedov for years to come), it proved difficult to nab his target in the act of transporting contraband.[63] Even after several weeks of clandestine observation, his team was still unable to collect solid proof of any wrongdoing by Miasoedov. Given the absence of evidence, Ponomarev decided to cook some up. One evening, when Miasoedov was visiting friends in Eydtkunen, Ponomarev arranged to have his agent Dontsov sneak across the border and plant dynamite and revolvers in the false compartment of the colonel's Benz automobile. This scheme disastrously misfired: Miasoedov caught Dontsov in the act of breaking into the car, thrashed him savagely with a walking stick, and forced him to sign a full confession.[64]

Ponomarev's second attempt at organizing a provocation against Miasoedov was an even greater fiasco. Miasoedov had the habit of shopping at a general store in Eydtkunen run by a merchant named Schuler. When Ponomarev tried to bribe Schuler to "accidentally" wrap up some handguns along with Miasoedov's next purchases, the store owner punched the hapless cornet in the face and ejected him into the street with the sole of his boot. Still worse, Schuler immediately sent Miasoedov a letter with a full account of the affair.[65]

By this point Ponomarev was at his wits' end. Since Miasoedov was now on his guard and moreover possessed written proof of the cornet's plot against him in the form of Dontsov's confession, it was highly unlikely that a third attempt at entrapment would succeed where the previous two had failed. In a last bid to salvage something from his mission, in March 1907 he made contact with a band of smugglers led by Lev and Petr Kudriavtsev, oddly enough both former clerks in the Verzhbolovo customs office. Through intermediaries, Ponomarev hired the Kudriavtsevs to transport a shipment of goods from Germany into Russia. Unbeknownst to them, Ponomarev had previously secreted small arms, ammunition, and revolutionary literature in the packages. Since he had already alerted the customs service, the Kudriavtsevs

62. P. P. Zavarzin, *Rabota tainoi politsii. Vospominaniia* (Paris, 1924), p. 35.

63. Letter of Miasoedov to Sukhomlinov, September 1909, RGVIA, f. 962, op. 2, d. 101, l. 4; letter of Miasoedov to N. A. Maklakov, June 1912, RGVIA, f. 962, op. 2, d. 112, l. 503.

64. Memorandum, Main Administration of Military Justice, April 18, 1915, RGVIA, f. 962, op. 2, d. 66, l. 60.

65. RGVIA, f. 962, op. 2, d. 101, l. 4; also K. F. Shatsillo, "'Delo' Polkovnika Miasoedova," *Voprosy istorii* 42, no. 4 (1967): 106.

32 were arrested as soon as they presented themselves at the frontier. Ponomarev evidently hoped that this incident would simultaneously elevate his own stock as a crime fighter and discredit Miasoedov, who of course had done nothing to apprehend the "dangerous" gang of contrabandists who had been operating under his very nose.

Since Suvalki province was juridically in a state of emergency, the case fell under the jurisdiction of military law, which prescribed the death penalty for arms smuggling. On April 2, 1907, the eleven defendants were arraigned before the temporary military court in Vilna.[66] Although all of them proclaimed their innocence, guilty verdicts and executions seemed a foregone conclusion: after all, illegal weapons were in their possession when they were arrested. Yet events took a different and surprising turn when Miasoedov was sworn in as a character witness for the accused. One of the defense attorneys, O. O. Gruzenberg, famed as one of the most brilliant lawyers in Russia, immediately saw an opening. As part of his examination of Miasoedov, Gruzenberg asked whether the former had any information about the affiliation of any of the accused with the revolutionary movement. Sergei Nikolaevich at first refused to answer this question on the grounds of state security. But Gruzenberg invoked a precedent (which, inter alia, was usually honored only in tsarist military courts) that held that the interests of justice trumped those of state secrecy. The presiding judge, Major General Baron Osten-Saken, then instructed Miasoedov to respond.

Miasoedov began by admitting that, as far as he knew, none of the defendants had ever been suspected of revolutionary activity. But he did not stop there. Gruzenberg remembered that it was "though a dam had burst inside of him. . . . [D]isclosures, each more surprising than the last, flowed forth in a raging torrent."[67] He recounted the whole story of Ponomarev's conspiracy to frame him and strongly implied that Ponomarev's methods by no means deviated from the customary practices of the Okhrana. Since Miasoedov's testimony established beyond question that Ponomarev had a history of evidence tampering and perjury, all eleven defendants were acquitted forthwith.

The oppositionist press immediately realized that this case offered a delicious opportunity to bludgeon the government. Criticism of the interior ministry, and of the Okhrana in particular, became still more strident when someone made the stupid blunder of assigning Ponomarev, now a lieutenant, to the security detail at the Tauride Palace, where the newly created State Duma (or Parliament) held its meetings. *Rech'*, the daily organ of the Constitutional-Democrats (Kadets), the important liberal political party, hooted that "if Mister Ponomarev does not consider the promotion he has received satisfactory, if he wishes to distinguish himself one more time, will he plant dynamite and weapons within the Tauride Palace?"[68] Public ridicule soon induced the government to remove Ponomarev from his post and to reassign him quietly to Riga.

66. "Sudebnye vesti," *Novoe vremia,* April 7 (20), 1907, p. 3.

67. Gruzenberg, *Yesterday,* pp. 127–128.

68. "Duma i Kornet Ponomarev," *Rech',* April 8(21), 1907, p. 2.

M. I. Trusevich was furious, as was his boss, Minister of the Interior P. A. [33] Stolypin. It was Stolypin's obligation to pacify a country awash in revolutionary violence and terrorism. For Stolypin, terrorism was no mere abstraction, for it had already nearly claimed the lives of members of his family. On August 12, 1906, Socialist Revolutionary Maximalists had exploded bombs in Stolypin's summer home on Apektarskii island in Petersburg, killing twenty-seven and wounding sixty-two, including Stolypin's four-year-old son and fourteen-year-old daughter.[69] Although Stolypin believed that a program of substantive reforms was a necessary tool in combating the revolution, he was not squeamish about applying the instruments of repression.[70] It was not accidental that "Stolypin necktie" had already become popular slang for a hangman's noose. In his view, the Okhrana and police were the frontline troops in a war for the survival and future of Russia, and he could not overlook the fact that Miasoedov, even if unintentionally, had brought these organs of state security into disrepute. Noting that he found "the statements given by Lt. Colonel Miasoedov in court incompatible with the performance of his duty," he ordered the head of the gendarmes corps to transfer Miasoedov "to somewhere in the interior provinces, but in any event no nearer than the longitude of Samara."[71]

Miasoedov understood well that a transfer like this would be tantamount to a sentence of banishment; after all, Samara was located on the extreme eastern fringe of European Russia. He therefore tried to mobilize his friends and family connections in an effort to have his reassignment rescinded or countermanded. By some accounts, he went so far as to enlist the chief of the general staff, F. F. Palitsyn, as well as dowager empress Maria Fedorovna, to intercede on his behalf.[72] All these efforts came to naught. Knowing that as long as Trusevich ran the police department, he could anticipate an unrelieved diet of Okhrana harassment even if he accepted relocation to eastern Russia, on September 27, 1907, Sergei Nikolaevich Miasoedov resigned his commission as a lieutenant colonel in the Separate Corps of Gendarmes. He was forty-one years old and a civilian for the first time in his adult life.

The Northwest Russian Steamship Company

Sergei Nikolaevich's resignation from the gendarmes decisively altered his circumstances for the worse. Not only had he been forced to accept degradation in status by leaving the corps of gendarmes, but he was now also deprived of a steady income. As Klara's dowry was mostly exhausted and he had been judged ineligible for a pension, Miasoedov confronted the very real specter of imminent poverty. At the

69. Anna Geifman, *Thou Shalt Kill: Revolutionary Terrorism in Russia, 1894–1917* (Princeton, 1993), pp. 21, 74–75.

70. On Stolypin's views about how to suppress the revolution see: V. S. Diakin, *Samoderzhaviae, burzhuaziia i dvorianstvo v 1917–1911 gg.* (Leningrad, 1978), pp. 19–20.

71. Note on Miasoedov's service record, February 6, 1915, RGVIA, f. 962, op. 2, d. 160, l. 27; Shatsillo, "'Delo,'" p. 107.

72. *Padenie tsarskago rezhima*, vol. 3 (Leningrad, 1925), p. 371. (testimony of S. P. Beletskii); on Palitsyn, see Miasoedov to Stolypin, September 1, 1909, RGVIA, f. 962, op. 2, d. 101, l. 2.

34 very end of 1907 he paid a call on O. O. Gruzenberg in his Vilna law office. He appeared so haggard and frightened that Gruzenberg initially did not even recognize him. Miasoedov explained to Gruzenberg that he was in dire need of a job in the private sector, for the enmity of the secret police would prevent him from ever working for the state again. Gruzenberg recalls him as having said, "You don't know what the Okhrana is like. It's a hornet's nest. I've stepped on it and I shall never be forgiven. If I had gone over to the revolutionaries or committed a major crime, they would have forgiven me more easily than for the testimony I gave in court." Since Miasoedov held Gruzenberg responsible for eliciting that testimony, he appealed for his help in finding a position in banking or industry. Gruzenberg expressed his sympathy and promised to do what he could, which, as it transpired, was not much.[73]

Compounding Miasoedov's distress was an acute marital crisis. Miasoedov's penchant for recreational adultery had long irritated and humiliated his wife. Shortly after he left the gendarmes, Klara learned of yet another of his serial infidelities (in this case with the wife of a local doctor) and threatened to leave him. Miasoedov promised to break off the relationship and composed a lengthy note begging his wife to relent. "I will do everything that I ought to do as an honorable man, husband and father and I believe that it would be the greatest vileness if I do not justify your confidence on the occasion of this, my last chance."[74]

In the end, it was the contacts Miasoedov had made among the entrepreneurs of the northwest borderlands that came to the rescue. In 1908 the brothers Samuel and Boris Freidberg decided to expand their horizons by opening a modest steamship company of their own. For the past several years the transatlantic passenger trade had been highly volatile: fare wars among British and continental firms as well as the American depression of 1907 had chilled revenues for all of them. Albert Ballin responded to this crisis by negotiating yet another expansion in the transatlantic pool. In 1908 he engineered the establishment of a truly inclusive steamship cartel comprising all the principal companies both on the continent and in Britain, including Cunard, which had adamantly opposed Ballin's pool arrangement since its inception in 1891.[75] The Freidbergs saw a niche for themselves on the fringes of the newly enlarged pool and planned a service that would carry emigrants from Libava across the Baltic and North Sea to Hull, where they could connect to Liverpool and make the transoceanic passage with the Cunard line. Boris Freidberg had been Cunard's agent in Libava for some time and was confident of the English firm's good will. Since the pool's elaborate price-fixing mechanisms guaranteed Cunard 13 percent of the annual Atlantic passenger revenues, the Freidbergs believed that their venture could not fail.

In November 1908 the Freidbergs approached Miasoedov and offered him the chairmanship of the new concern, which they named the Northwest Russian

73. Gruzenberg, *Yesterday,* pp. 129–130.
74. Letter of Miasoedov to Klara, February 4, 1907, RGVIA, f. 801, op. 28, d. 167, l. 29.
75. Fabre, *Les Grandes Lignes,* pp. 51–52; Huldermann, *Albert Ballin,* p. 65–66, 111–112.

Steamship Company. Sergei Nikolaevich readily agreed. In the same month, they 35
submitted the proposed charter of their company to the inspection of the Russian
government, as was required by law.[76] With the approval of the Russian Council of
Ministers, the company was formally incorporated.

The Northwest Russian Steamship Company was capitalized at 600,000 rubles.
Samuel Freidberg held 1,000 and Boris another 240 of its 2,400 shares, giving the
brothers majority control. According to the incorporation papers, the other shareholders were Sergei Miasoedov; his wife, Klara; Baron Otton Grotgus; and Robert
Falk.[77] The company was based in Libava, with branch offices in Odessa and Minsk,
headed respectively by David Freidberg (the youngest of the brothers) and Israel Frid.
Sergei Nikolaevich Miasoedov was listed as chairman of the board of directors at an
annual salary of 6,000 rubles.[78] At the first meeting of stockholders and directors,
held in Petersburg on February 4, 1908, the company announced that it would soon
inaugurate sailings on the steamers *Georgios I* and *Leopold II,* each of 1,679 gross tons,
which it had recently leased in Denmark from the United Steamship Company (*Det
forenede Dampskibs-Selskab*).[79]

But the Northwest Russian Steamship Company did not prove to be the financial
bonanza for Miasoedov that it seemed. The aftershocks of the 1907 economic down-
turn in America persisted much longer than most people had expected, accounting
for a reduced demand for transatlantic tickets that dragged on almost to 1910. Moreover, despite its indirect affiliation with the pool, Northwest faced formidable competitive challenges from the moment it opened its offices. In 1906 the Russian Volunteer Fleet, a quasi-private company subsidized by the Russian government, declared
it would begin direct sailings between Libava and New York. Ballin's Hamburg American line immediately retaliated on behalf of the pool by buying up 51 percent of the
shares of the Russian East Asiatic Steamship Company, a putatively Russian firm that
was actually controlled by Danish interests.[80] Russian East Asiatic then declared that
it would acquire and outfit vessels to make its own voyages between the empire's
Baltic ports and the United States. The purpose of this initiative was to provide the
Volunteer Fleet with such stiff competition that it would be ground into powder.

Although Ballin acquired Russian East Asiatic as a weapon against the Volunteer
Fleet, in the final analysis it was a weapon that he did not have to use. The Volunteer

76. Any new joint stock company in Russia had to win the approval first of the ministry most nearly
concerned with its business, and then of the Council of Ministers as a whole. See Howard P. Kennard, ed.,
The Russian Year-Book for 1912 (London, 1912), p. 29.

77. RGVIA, f. 2003, op. 2, d. 1063, ll. 109–110; Freinat report on Northwest Russian Steamship Company, 1909, RGVIA, f. 962, op. 2, d. 112, l. 423.

78. O. G. Freinat, *Pravda o dele Miasoedova i dr. Po offitsial'nym dokumentam i lichnym vospominaniiam* (Vilna, 1918), p. 11.

79. Both vessels had been built in 1888 by Burmeister and Wain, Denmark's oldest manufacturer of
iron- and steel-hulled ships. See F. Holm-Petersen and A. Rosendahl, *Fra Sejl til Diesel. Dansk Skibsfart,
Søhandel og Skibsbygning, vol. 3* (n.p., n.d.), pp. 231, 244. Also see *Lloyd's Register of Shipping: From 1 July
1914 to 30 July 1915,* vol. 1 (London, 1914), "Register of Steamers," O number 93 and S number 595.

80. Ole Lange, *Den Hvide Elefant. H. N. Andersens Eventyr og ØK 1852–1914* (Viborg, 1986), pp. 57–59.

36 Fleet ran into financial difficulties, and its Libava-New York steamship route never really got off the ground. At this point, however, something extremely odd took place. In 1907 Russian East Asiatic's original Danish shareholders bought their stock back from Ballin.[81] They then announced that under its new management Russian East Asiatic would be going into the American passenger business after all. Russian East Asiatic declined to join the international steamship pool, and by 1908 its biweekly direct sailings from Libava to New York were serious breaches in the pool's monopoly. Russian East Asiatic's success was bad news for Cunard and devastating news for the Freidbergs' Northwest Russian Steamship Company. Since Russian East Asiatic could get emigrants to America more quickly than could Cunard in combination with such feeder lines as Northwest, the latter were at a real competitive disadvantage. By 1913 sixty thousand people a year were traveling from Libava to New York on the ships of the Russian East Asiatic Company. This was over 20 percent of the total number of Russian subjects who emigrated to America that year.[82]

Russian East Asiatic rapidly became an economic powerhouse in Libava. It built its own docks, warehouses, and hotels and organized transportation to Libava for prospective emigrants from other Russian Baltic ports. Russian East Asiatic also became thoroughly ruthless in defense of its customer base and took steps against Cunard's most important feeder line in Libava, the Freidbergs' Northwest Russian Steamship Company. For this purpose it bribed important provincial officials, just as many other businesses did.

The most valuable such man in Russian East Asiatic's pay was Libava's chief of police, Colonel Podushkin. Podushkin was ideally placed to make life miserable for the Freidberg brothers and did so at every possible opportunity. He also had a personal bias against Miasoedov: as coincidence would have it, he had struck up a close friendship with Lieutenant Ponomarev while the two had served together in Riga. Podushkin had scabrous articles about the Northwest Russian Steamship Company placed in the *Voice of Libava,* a prominent local newspaper that just happened to be owned by one of Russian East Asiatic's directors. He closed down the Kni emigration bureau of Robert Falk, another of Northwest's principals, on suspicion of passport forgery. He tried to instigate criminal proceedings against Karlsberg and Spiro for encouraging illegal emigration. And he regularly denounced Northwest to the authorities in Petersburg for real or imagined contraventions of the commercial code. He was particularly scathing about Miasoedov's role at Northwest; the former gendarme, he complained, "is giving these yids the cover of his name."[83]

Miasoedov, Northwest, and the Ministry of the Interior

Miasoedov was therefore the chairman of a seriously troubled firm. Podushkin was on the warpath against the company, and the business climate for steamship en-

---

81. N. R. P. Bonsor, *North Atlantic Seaway,* vol. 3 (Jersey, Channel Islands, 1979), pp. 1350–1351.
82. Lange, *Den Hvide Elefant,* p. 170.
83. Report to governor of Kurland, September 12, 1911, RGVIA, f. 962, op. 2, d. 101, ll. 5, 8–9, 11.

terprises was bad in general. Yet if Miasoedov realized that his involvement with Northwest would not make him rich, perhaps he could at least console himself with the thought that he was drawing a handsome salary, fully 60 percent more than he had earned in the gendarmes.[84] Or could he? It is evident that Miasoedov's entire annual compensation of 6,000 rubles was never paid to him in full. Basically, the "management" and "proprietorship" of the company were purely notional: Northwest's charter was merely a facade that permitted Samuel Freidberg simultaneously to lay claim to the legal protections of incorporation and to conceal the true extent of his family's control of the enterprise. The distribution of Northwest shares did not accurately reflect the distribution of power within the firm at all. Robert Falk, for example, received shares with a face value of 100,000 rubles for an investment of only 40,000.[85] The Freidbergs compelled Baron Grotgus, who had paid nothing for his stock, to sign it back over to them in the immediate aftermath of Northwest's formal incorporation.[86] And although Miasoedov later insisted that he had bought his own 220 shares for 55,000 rubles, we have already observed that in 1907 and 1908 he did not have that kind of money.[87]

Why, then, did the Freidbergs need Grotgus and Miasoedov? What was the purpose of the charade? The answer is that Podushkin, despite his coarse anti-Semitic slurs, had been fundamentally correct about what was going on: they were front men, people who could get the attention of the influential and powerful, potential insurance policies against disaster. Grotgus subsequently confessed that his chief contribution to the firm, for which he received an emolument of 50 rubles a month, had been "to smooth over misunderstandings with the authorities."[88] It is clear that although Miasoedov was both better paid and much more closely involved in Northwest's affairs than the impecunious Baltic nobleman, his real position in the company was not substantially different.

While Miasoedov's chairmanship of Northwest thus brought him a small income, it was no substitute for a full-time job, let alone a new career. In mid 1909, however, Trusevich's dismissal from the Department of Police suddenly opened the possibility of his resuming his old one. To accomplish this Miasoedov would have to move to St. Petersburg, the better to deploy his network of family connections. The Freidbergs generously offered to underwrite the costs of his move and insisted on paying his rent in the capital, since his apartment would double as an office for the Northwest Steamship Company. Sergei and Klara first lodged on Bol'shaia Moskovskia Street before taking even more commodious quarters on Kolokol'naia.

In September 1909, Miasoedov petitioned Interior Minister Stolypin for reinstatement in the Separate Corps of Gendarmes. Depicting himself as the pitiable vic-

84. On military and police salaries see A. M. Anfimov and A. P. Korelin, eds., *Rossiia. 1913 god. Statistiko-dokumental'nyi spravochnik* (St. Petersburg, 1995), pp. 289–290.

85. Zhizhin Report, May 30, 1915, RGVIA, f. 2003, op. 2, d. 1073, l. 111.

86. RGVIA, f. 2003, op. 2, d. 1073, l. 109.

87. Letter of Miasoedov to A. A. Makarov, 1912, RGVIA, f. 962, op. 2, d. 66, l. 14.

88. RGVIA, f. 2003, op. 2, d. 1073, ll. 109–110.

38 tim of a sinister conspiracy, he gave Stolypin his own exculpatory version of what had happened at Verzhbolovo and Vilna in 1907. He insisted that he had intended no disrespect to the police by his words in the Vilna trial, that he had testified only under compulsion, and that left-wing lawyers, not he, had been responsible for leaking his deposition to the press. He also detailed the services he had performed in the cause of law and order during his fourteen years in Verzhbolovo, massaging the facts considerably: "I conducted a merciless struggle against illegal emigration. . . . I nipped in the bud all attempts at strikes, owing to the authority that I enjoyed in Verzhbolovo among the railway workers and the local population. I detained masses of revolutionaries, and seized thousands of copies of revolutionary publications. I always gave complete cooperation to the Okhrana and its agents."[89] Yet none of Miasoedov's arguments and appeals had any weight with Stolypin. He instructed his deputy, P. G. Kurlov, to inform Miasoedov that his case would not be reopened, and that he would *never* be readmitted to governmental service under any circumstances whatsoever.

On top of this bureaucratic defeat, something then occurred that for sheer horror dwarfed every calamity that Miasoedov had previously suffered taken together: Nikolai, the Miasoedovs' beloved eight-year-old son, was crushed to death in a freak elevator accident in Petersburg.[90] This was a shattering blow, and both Sergei and Klara were inconsolable. Some marriages cannot survive a catastrophe as dire as the loss of a child, whereas others seem mysteriously to grow stronger on a diet of shared grief. Although the Miasoedovs' marriage had not been particularly healthy for years, the latter seems to have happened in their case. Klara stopped threatening to leave her husband, and Miasoedov ceased his philandering and spent more time at home. His restraint may have had more to do with his mental condition than with any moral scruple, however, for he plunged into a deep and paralyzing depression that temporarily deprived him of his taste for food, sport, and companionship, as well as his desire for women.

Now it is time for us to start unraveling a different skein in our story. For the moment we will leave Sergei Nikolaevich in the darkened study of his Petersburg apartment, mourning his dead boy, brooding over his personal and professional failure, and contemplating the shambles of his life through the bottom of a vodka glass.

---

89. Letter of Miasoedov to Sukhomlinov, September 1, 1909, RGVIA, f. 962, op. 2, d. 101, l. 3.
90. Klara Miasoedova interrogation, May 12, 1915, RGVIA, f. 962, op. 2, d. 160, l. 107.

2

Kiev

S prawling across hills and ravines on bluffs overlooking the middle reaches of
the Dniepr River, Kiev was the most ancient and famous Slavic settlement in
the Russian Empire. Regarded as the "mother of Russian cities," Kiev had
been the capital of old Rus', the trading state that had risen to prominence in
the ninth century and flourished until sacked by the Mongols in 1240. In the ensuing
centuries, the city had known Tatar suzerainty, Lithuanian occupation, and Polish
rule before passing into the control of Muscovite Russia in 1667.

By the beginning of the twentieth century Kiev was one of the most dynamic and
fast-growing cities in the Russian Empire. The population, 127,000 in 1874, had almost doubled by 1897, and would double again by 1910. When the war broke out in
1914, Kiev boasted a population of 626,000.[1] Tempos of growth like these put tremendous strain on the city authorities, as demand for municipal services far outstripped
supply. For example, at the point where the Dniepr flowed through Kiev, its water
was so notoriously contaminated that in 1907 a public health commission declared it
unpotable. But given the expense and limited capacity of the artesian wells that were
the only alternative, thousands of Kievans continued to drink it anyway, despite the
industrial effluvia and raw sewage that dyed the Dniepr an unmistakable shade of
sickly yellow.[2]

Like many other cities outside the Great Russian heartland of the empire, Kiev
was ethnically and culturally diverse. Although the city was officially "Russian" and
Russian was the language of bureaucracy, education, and commerce, the plurality of

---

1. Michael F. Hamm, *Kiev: A Portrait, 1800–1917*, rev. ed. (Princeton, 1995), pp. 103, 128, 230.
2. Hamm, *Kiev*, pp. 44, 48.

40 Kiev's residents were ethnic Ukrainians. In addition to the Russians and Ukrainians, long-established communities of Poles, Jews, and Belorussians coexisted in the city.

The foundation of Kiev's economy was the distillation and sale of beet sugar. As a result of the stiff tariffs imposed on imported cane sugar in the first half of the nineteenth century, a large vertically integrated industry had arisen in Ukraine devoted to the cultivation and processing of sugar beets.[3] In Kiev province alone over 184,000 acres were planted in sugar beets in 1892, producing a harvest of 900,000 tons.[4] Kiev had 117 plants where sugar was refined from this crop; many of the city's other factories were directly dependent on the sugar industry since they manufactured the pipes, valves, boilers, and other machinery with which the refineries were equipped.

But Kiev was also an important administrative center. In addition to its governor, Kiev also had a governor-general, a high official with extensive powers over the 13 million people who inhabited the 64,000 square miles that comprised the three provinces of Kiev, Podolia, and Volynia.[5] Kiev was notable from the military point of view as well. It was the headquarters of both the IX and XXI Army Corps and was the seat of its own military district, which included the Kiev, Podolia, Volynia governor-generalship, as well as the provinces of Chernigov, Kursk, Kharkov, and Poltava. Because of its common frontier with Austria-Hungary, Kiev District occupied a particularly sensitive position in Russia's national security calculations. In the event of a crisis, troops would be massed in the district against the Dual Monarchy; in the event of war, the district's chief would assume field command and lead those troops into battle. In early 1905 the commander of Kiev District was Lieutenant General V. A. Sukhomlinov, a man whose name would be inextricably linked to the Miasoedov affair.

Vladimir Aleksandrovich Sukhomlinov

Like Miasoedov, V. A. Sukhomlinov was the scion of a gentry family that had once seen better days. Born in Kovno in 1848, he was educated in Vilna's Alexander Cadet Corps and the Nicholas Cavalry School. Four years after he was commissioned in 1867, he matriculated at Imperial Russia's highest institution of military learning, the Nicholas Academy of the General Staff, where he acquired a reputation as an outstanding scholar. After graduating near the top of his class in 1874, he resumed an active-duty military career that was little short of brilliant, characterized by prestigious tours and rapid promotion. When war broke out between Russia and Turkey in 1877, Sukhomlinov wrangled an assignment with Russia's Danubian army and was awarded a gold-handled saber for bravery in action.

After the conclusion of peace and a brief stint of regimental command, he was appointed head of the Officers' Cavalry School in Petersburg, where he personally instructed the future Nicholas II in tactics. By the age of forty-two he was a major gen-

3. Walter McKenzie Pintner, *Russian Economic Policy under Nicholas I* (Ithaca, 1967), pp. 224–225.

4. Calculated on the basis of "Kievskaia gubernia," *BE*, vol. 15 (St. Petersburg, 1895), p. 258.

5. Calculated on the basis of material in A. M. Anfimov and A. P. Korelin, eds. and comps., *Rossiia 1913 god. Statistiko-dokumental'nyi spravochnik* (St. Petersburg, 1995), pp. 11–13.

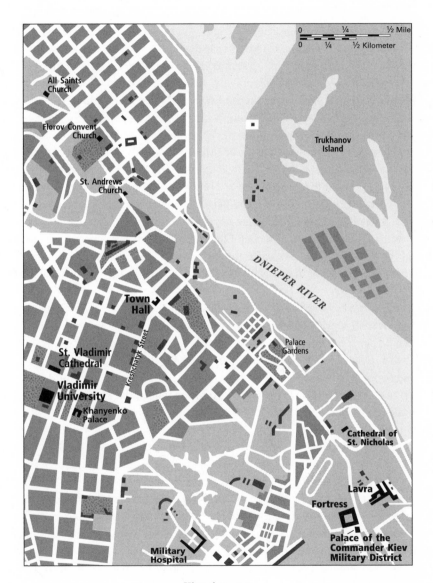

All Saints
Church

Florov Convent
Church

St. Andrews
Church

Trukhanov
Island

DNIEPER RIVER

Town
Hall

Kreshchatyk Street

St. Vladimir
Cathedral

Vladimir
University

Khanyenko
Palace

Palace
Gardens

Cathedral of
St. Nicholas

Lavra

Fortress

Military
Hospital

Palace of the
Commander Kiev
Military District

0   ¼   ½ Mile
0   ¼   ½ Kilometer

Kiev circa 1905

42 eral. Seven years later he took charge of the Tenth Cavalry Division. Two years after this posting, with his promotion to lieutenant general virtually foreordained, he was transferred to the Ukraine as chief of staff to the legendary M. I. Dragomirov, the commander of Kiev District.[6]

One of the most revered figures in the Russian army, Dragomirov was famous for his open panslavist sympathies, his francophilism, his wild eccentricity, and his thirst for alcohol. On one occasion during his early days in Kiev when he realized with horror that he had forgotten to wire Alexander III the customary congratulations on his name day, he sought to avert the imperial displeasure by cabling the belated, but plausible, excuse that "We have been drinking Your Majesty's health for the last three days straight!" only to receive the laconic "Time to stop" in reply.

But for all his quirks, Dragomirov was a serious and complex man. An authentic hero, he had become immensely popular throughout the empire for his martial feats during the Russo-Turkish War of 1877–78, particularly his timely relief of Stoletov's outnumbered force at the second Battle of Shipka Pass. At the same time, Dragomirov was a military theoretician of no mean gifts. An acknowledged expert in the field of military psychology (the subject of motivating the individual soldier in battle particularly fascinated him), he was also one of the empire's foremost tacticians. He had authored the principal textbooks on tactics in common use in late-nineteenth-century Russia and had made the training exercises he conducted in Kiev District the laboratory for his theories.

Dragomirov's charisma and power naturally attracted ambitious officers to him. After arriving in Kiev, Sukhomlinov slipped naturally into the role of the older man's protégé. In 1902, Sukhomlinov became deputy commander of Kiev District, and in 1904, when Dragomirov retired at the age of seventy-four, Vladimir Aleksandrovich was the logical candidate to succeed him. In early November of that year Sukhomlinov moved into the official residence of the commander, a large two-story structure surrounded by almost nineteen acres of fruit trees.

By this point Russia was again at war. This time her adversary was the empire of Japan, whose night torpedo attack on the Russian Pacific fleet in the Port Arthur roadstead in February 1904 had inaugurated hostilities. From any standpoint, the war was an unmitigated disaster for Russia. Since the Japanese perceived the objective of the war—the expulsion of Russia from both Korea and Manchuria—to be as much a matter of national survival as one of national prestige, the war elicited mass enthusiasm throughout the home islands. But in the eyes of most Russians, the war was being fought over remote and outlandishly named territories for purposes that few understood or cared about. It was more than apathy, however, that undermined Russia's military effort. Because the single-tracked Trans-Siberian railroad was Russia's only lifeline to the theater of war, Russia faced nearly insuperable difficulties in victualing, arming, and reinforcing her Far Eastern armies. Then, too, anxious lest Austria-Hungary and Germany take advantage of Russia's distraction in Asia to attack in Eu-

---

6. These details come from his service record. See RGVIA, f. 409, op. 1, d. p/sp 362–573, ll. 1–3.

rope, the Russian high command chose to prosecute the conflict while maintaining the empire's western defenses as intact as possible. This resulted in a series of selective unit transfers and partial mobilizations that neither provided Russia's eastern commanders with military superiority over the Japanese nor prevented the steep degradation of defense readiness in the west. Combined with Russia's misuse of her maritime power and the mediocre leadership of her Far Eastern generals, all of this produced an unending succession of battlefield defeats: at the Yalu, Liaoyang, the Sha-Ho, San-de-pu, and Mukden. After Russia's Baltic fleet steamed halfway around the world into Asiatic waters only to be sunk by the Japanese navy in the Tsushima straits (March 1905), Nicholas II decided to sue for peace.

Contributing to that decision was the Russian Empire's internal disarray. The unsuccessful war in Manchuria had had dangerous repercussions at home, for it amplified popular discontent with the autocratic government throughout every stratum of society. When on January 9 (22) 1905 ("Bloody Sunday") police and soldiers gunned down scores of peaceful demonstrators in St. Petersburg, protest gave way to violent revolution: waves of strikes engulfed the empire's factories, plants, and mines; peasant rebellion convulsed the country from Kursk to the Volga; terrorists launched thousands of attacks; and nationalist groups plotted armed insurrection all throughout the borderlands. In October, Nicholas II issued a proclamation promising substantive reforms, including the establishment of an elected legislature, or Duma, in the evident hope that this concession would pacify his dominions. Nicholas and his advisors had miscalculated, however, for the immediate effect of the October Manifesto was to inflame, rather than narcotize, revolutionary passion. Far from abating, antigovernmental violence actually intensified.

Kiev and its surrounding province saw its share of revolutionary upheaval during 1905. In January workers in some of the city's most important factories struck in sympathy with the victims of the Bloody Sunday massacre. Industrial strikes continued into February, when there were also strikes by a congeries of disparate nonproletarian groups, including bakers, hairdressers, and high school students. In the spring, there was an explosion of unrest throughout the rural districts of Kiev province that lasted through the summer.[7]

By October the center of gravity of the revolution had shifted from the countryside back to the city. Kiev's Vladimir University became a hotbed of revolutionary activity; antigovernmental meetings involving thousands of people took place every night. On October 18 (31), the day the promulgation of the October Manifesto became known, an enormous number of students and workers converged on Kiev's town hall, where they were harangued by the Bolshevik agitator A. G. Shlikhter.[8] An exchange of shots between demonstrators and police resulted in the use of troops to disperse the crowd, at a cost of at least 7 dead and 110 wounded.

7. Robert Edelman, *Proletarian Peasants: The Revolution of 1905 in Russia's Southwest* (Ithaca, 1987), pp. 94–97.
8. V. G. Sarbei et al., eds., *Istoriia Ukrainskoi SSR*, vol. 5 (Kiev, 1983), pp. 122–123.

44   One anomaly of 1905 in urban Russia was that the revolution gave rise to both left- and right-wing mass politics. The abrupt collapse of the town hall meeting of October 18 was the spark that brought a different sort of mob into the streets, one composed of monarchists, reactionaries, anti-Semites, and common criminals. Believing (or pretending to believe) that all Russia's troubles stemmed from the machinations of the Jews and socialists, such people needed no urging to mete out their own punishment to the "guilty." There ensued the horrific Kiev pogrom of October 18–20 (October 31–November 2), an orgy of looting, rapine, and murder chiefly directed against the factories, shops, homes, and persons of the Jews. This riot claimed the lives of between forty-seven and one hundred people and resulted in serious injury to at least three hundred more as well as the destruction of between 10 and 40 million rubles of property.[9] This pogrom and the others that swept southern Russia at approximately the same time were so annihilative that, in the words of Simon Dubnow, taken together they amounted to "Russia's St. Bartholomew's night."[10]

One reason for the monstrous scale of the Kiev pogrom of 1905 had been the paralysis of the local administration. The Kiev, Podolia, Volynia governor-general, N. V. Kliegels, a man more notable for his judgment of horseflesh than for his firmness of character, had become completely deranged by fear during the course of the year. Cravenly hoping to avoid responsibility, in the fall of 1905 he had attempted to surrender all his civil powers to the military. As Sukhomlinov was by then enjoying his customary annual vacation on the Riviera, Kliegels had approached the deputy military district commander, General Ivan Karas, with his request. Karas accepted but soon had second thoughts about the legality of this irregular transfer of authority. Confusion about who was the legitimate governor-general or acting governor-general thus contributed to the fatal hesitation to take decisive measures to stamp out the pogrom. It was only after Karas had telegraphed to Petersburg for instructions and received a direct order to restore order by force that he commanded his troops out of their barracks to suppress the mob.

The disastrous mismanagement of events in Kiev quickly resulted in a personnel shake-up. In view of the volatility of the situation, the central government decided that all civil and military powers in the region ought to be united in the hands of one man: V. A. Sukhomlinov. On October 19 (November 1), the Ministry of the Interior sent a wire to Biarritz directing Sukhomlinov to return immediately and assume the position of governor-general of Kiev, Podolia, and Volynia. Henceforth Sukhomlinov would have plenary authority over all the bureaucrats and all the soldiers within one of the most sensitive borderlands of the Russian Empire. He would also be one of the empire's most highly paid officials, for the combined salaries of his two posts totaled 51,000 rubles.[11]

9. Hamm, *Kiev,* p. 191.

10. S. N. Dubnow, *History of the Jews in Russia and Poland from the Earliest Times Until the Present Day,* trans. I. Friedlander, vol. 2 (Philadelphia, 1920; repr., New York, 1975), p. 128.

11. N. A. Epanchin, *Na sluzhbe trekh imperatorov. Vospominaniia* (Moscow, 1996), p. 372.

V. A. Sukhomlinov

Upon his arrival in Kiev in November 1905, Sukhomlinov acted vigorously to restore public confidence in the probity and competence of the government. He immediately had broadsheets pasted up throughout the city reading: "I have taken over the administration and I will tolerate no disorder."[12] He also fired several of the most unpopular local officials, including the corrupt city police chief V. Tsikhotskii. He also took steps to rein in the city's reactionary and anti-Semitic press, recognizing as he did the role that gutter journalism had played in fueling the hatred that led to the pogrom.[13]

Actions like these did not endear him to the political right in either the city or province of Kiev. It was whispered that Sukhomlinov was far too solicitous of the welfare of the Jews and was, moreover, too often to be found in their company, for he openly socialized with people whose names were Margolin, Furman, Fishman, and Faltser.[14] These whispers became still louder in the summer of 1906, when General A. P. Veretennikov became governor of Kiev province. Sukhomlinov detested Veretennikov, not least because of his overt participation in right-wing politics. A rabid anti-Semite, Veretennikov was a member of the Union of the Russian People, a mass organization with a protofascist agenda, whose insignia he proudly wore and whose activities he supported financially. In attempting to use his office to launch a new campaign of persecution against the Jews, Veretennikov found himself stymied by Sukhomlinov at every turn: Sukhomlinov countermanded his orders, forbade him to search Jews for false residency papers, and so forth. Relations between the two men deteriorated completely, and each of them schemed to discredit the other.

In the end it was Veretennikov who fell from office. One of his bad habits was his practice of signing any paper placed before him without reading it. In December 1905, someone in his office inserted a confession of incompetence in a portfolio of documents for his signature. When the text of Veretennikov's "statement" ("I affirm that I was never suitable and that I am completely incapable of governing the

12. V. A. Sukhomlinov, *Vospominaniia Sukhomlinova* (Moscow/Leningrad, 1926), p. 109.
13. A. A. Sidorov, "V Kieve," *Golos minuvshago*, nos. 1–3 (1918): 224.
14. Petrov Commission report, 1916, RGVIA, f. 962, op. 2, d. 164, l. 118.

46   province entrusted to me") was published first by the national Russian press and then by the *London Times,* a badly embarrassed government had little choice but to remove him.[15] On December 15, 1906, Interior Minister Stolypin abruptly transferred Veretennikov to Kostroma. P. G. Kurlov, his replacement in Kiev, was an officer much more to Sukhomlinov's liking, having been a pupil of his at the Nicholas Cavalry School.[16]

By late 1906 Sukhomlinov had consolidated a reputation as a philo-Semite and something of a liberal, making him an object of loathing on the extreme nationalist right.[17] Most of his enemies in Kiev suspected that he had been behind the deception that had cost Veretennikov his job. Subsequently he would acquire enemies across the entire political spectrum. Few postrevolutionary memoirs offer a positive evaluation of Sukhomlinov. To be sure, Father Georgii Shavelskii, who served as chief chaplain of the Russian army in the world war, described Vladimir Aleksandrovich as "intelligent, simple, warm of heart and sympathetic," but this was an atypical characterization.[18] In general he was depicted either as an archvillain of boundless malevolence or as a shallow, bureaucratic mediocrity. The diplomat Andrei Kalmykov, for instance, denounced Sukhomlinov as "the evil genius of Russia."[19] V. N. Kokovtsov, who later sat with him in the Council of Ministers, dismissed him as "an extremely flippant and superficial man, not without gifts, but utterly incapable of any assiduous labor, analysis, or work in accordance with a well-considered plan."[20]

Kokovtsov's account of his personality, albeit one-dimensional, did contain an element of truth. There is abundant evidence that, at least after Dragomirov's retirement, he was inclined to cut corners in the performance of his official duties. Contemporaries who served under him in Kiev observed that he delegated most of the quotidian business of the military district to General A. A. Mavrin, his chief of staff, and much of the day-to-day administration of the governor-generalship to his chief of chancellery, A. N. Neverov.[21] One of his subordinates, divisional commander N. A. Epanchin, recalled how dumbfounded he was when Sukhomlinov "inspected" the 167th Ostrozhskii Infantry Regiment in the summer of 1907 without leaving his Dniepr steamboat; on this occasion it was a passion for fishing, rather than a concern for military excellence, that had actually motivated his trip upriver.[22]

15. Veretennikov to V. D. Frederiks, May 25, 1910; clipping from *Russkoe slovo,* January 1910, RGVIA, f. 970, op. 3, d. 1505, ll. 5,8.

16. P. G. Kurlov, *Gibel' imperatorskoi Rossii* (Moscow, 1992), p. 74.

17. Kurlov, *Gibel',* pp. 74,79. [A. I. Guchkov and N. A. Bazili], *Aleksandr Ivanovich Guchkov rasskazyvaet* (Moscow, 1994), p. 60.

18. Georgii Shavel'skii, *Vospominaniia poslednego protopresvitera russkoi armii i flota,* vol.1 (New York, 1954; repr., Moscow, 1996), p. 263.

19. Andrew W. Kalmykow, *Memoirs of a Russian Diplomat: Outposts of the Empire, 1893–1917,* ed. Alexandra Kalmykow (New Haven, 1971), p. 257.

20. V. N. Kokovtsov testimony, December 19, 1916, RGVIA, f. 962, op. 1, d. 52, l. 296.

21. Epanchin, *Na sluzhbe,* p. 369.

22. Ibid., p. 370.

But there was more to Sukhomlinov than these assessments might suggest. In the first place, his high intelligence was beyond dispute and was conceded even by his most implacable opponents. It is this, of course, to which Kokovtsov's remark about his being "not without gifts" referred. Even if he preferred to leave the details to others, he had an extremely agile mind that enabled him "to grasp quickly the essence of any subject," as one member of his staff expressed it.[23] Second, he had a natural aptitude for foreign languages and read, spoke, and wrote German flawlessly. Moreover, throughout his many years of active duty he pursued a subsidiary career as a writer and published several volumes of short stories and essays, many under the pseudonym "Ostap Bondarenko." By inhabiting the persona of Bondarenko—purportedly a retired Cossack officer who respected tradition, prized common sense over sterile theory, and was dubious about innovation for innovation's sake—Sukhomlinov could contribute to the debate over the future of the Russian army, even criticize the higher echelons of military leadership, without risking punishment for insubordination. Whether composed with an audience of officers or of private soldiers in mind, the didactic and moralistic Bondarenko tales bespoke the belief in enlightenment and self-improvement he carried with him throughout his life. Almost all of Sukhomlinov's literary work appeared under the imprint of V.A. Berezovskii, a personal friend who was the owner of a famous military publishing company and the editor of Russia's most important privately issued military magazine, *Razvedchik* (*The Scout*).

Yet it was as a politician that Sukhomlinov truly excelled. Within the context of the autocratic system, he was an expert manipulator of people and events for the purpose of personal advancement. He was a master at tapping into the numerous patronage networks dispersed throughout the army, whether based on family connections, schoolhouse ties, or common regimental service. He knew how to both use and subvert bureaucratic organizations, he was very clever at the forging and dissolving of tactical alliances, and he adroitly employed his charm both to beguile his superiors and to cover his tracks. Despite the fact that he was short, bald, and unprepossessing (or rather, perhaps *because* of this fact), he cultivated exquisite manners and projected an image of affability and warmth. These were precisely the skills needed to survive and flourish in the world of autocratic politics. As we shall see, however, it was because he possessed these skills in abundance that his enemies would never forgive him.

A final singularity rounds out our sketch of Sukhomlinov. He was an uxorious man with an extremely high libido. Count Witte, one of the empire's greatest statesmen, gave voice to common knowledge when he referred to him as "a greater lover of the female sex."[24] Sukhomlinov's first marriage occurred shortly after the end of the Russo-Turkish war. His bride, Baroness Korf, came from a solid Russo-German family with excellent connections. (Her oldest sister, Mariia Ferdinandovna, was married

23. A. S. Somoilo, *Dve zhizni* (Leningrad, 1963), p. 91.
24. S. Iu. Vitte, *Vospominaniia*, vol. 3 (Moscow, 1960), p. 496.

48 to former minister of justice D. N. Nabokov, father of the distinguished jurist and politician V. D. Nabokov, whose own son would acquire international fame with such novels as *Pale Fire* and *Lolita.*) This union did not, however, last long; Vladimir Aleksandrovich was a widower within a year.

After a decent interval for mourning, Sukhomlinov married again. His new spouse, Elizaveta Nikolaevna Koreish, the ex-wife of a civil engineer, was an extroverted woman of bohemian temperament who relished the company of actors and artists. A native of Kiev, she was delighted at her husband's 1899 assignment to Dragomirov's staff. Because she still had numerous relatives and friends in the city, the couple was soon leading a busy social life.[25] The Sukhomlinovs hosted numerous receptions, dinner parties, and balls in their official residence, and Elizaveta Nikolaevna also became active in charitable work. Yet in the spring of 1904 all this marital happiness came to an abrupt end. Rumors began to circulate throughout the city that large sums of money—up to 40,000 rubles by some accounts—had been embezzled from the local branch of the Red Cross, of which Elizaveta Nikolaevna was trustee. Although an audit later turned up no irregularities in the Red Cross's books (either there had never been a deficit or someone had quietly made good the loss), Elizaveta fell into a deep depression. Shortly after this, she suddenly and unexpectedly died, by her own hand, according to some. Sukhomlinov oscillated between fits of melancholy and bursts of rage. He tried unsuccessfully to persuade the civil authorities to shut down the *Kiev Gazette,* the newspaper whose gossip and innuendo about the Red Cross and his wife he held responsible for her death.[26]

Nonetheless, it did not take Sukhomlinov long to recover from his domestic tragedy. He soon found consolation in the arms of a music hall singer by the name of Kaplan, with whom he formed a liaison in late 1904 or early 1905. This affair was short-lived, and it was during his annual vacation in the south of France in the fall of 1905 that he met the woman who would become his third wife: Ekaterina Viktorovna Butovich. At that point he was fifty-seven years of age, and she was barely twenty-three.

Ekaterina Viktorovna Butovich

Ekaterina was the daughter of Viktor Ivanovich Goshkevich, who worked as a printer and part-time journalist for the *Kievan,* the city's most important nationalist newspaper. The Goshkeviches were ethnic Ukrainians originally of the clerical estate, who numbered many parish priests on their family tree. Viktor lived with his wife, Klavdiia Nikolaevna, and their daughter in a cramped two-room apartment within the building that also housed the *Kievan*'s editorial offices. Ekaterina thus grew up in exceedingly modest circumstances, which deteriorated still further at the turn of the

25. On Sukhomlinov's second marriage see also V. I. Gourko, *Features and Figures of the Past: Government and Opinion in the Reign of Nicholas II,* ed. J. E. Wallace Sterling, Xenia Joukoff Eudin, and H. H. Fisher; trans. Laura Matveev (Palo Alto, 1939), pp. 551–552.

26. On this episode see Sidorov, "V Kieve," p. 225; Petrov Commission report, 1916, RGVIA, f. 962, op. 2, d. 164, l. 118; Mikh. Lemke, *250 dnei v tsarskoi stavke (25 sent. 1915–2 iuliia 1916)* (Petersburg, 1920), p. 260.

century when her father abandoned the family and ran off to Kherson. Desperate for income, Ekaterina's mother subdivided the tiny apartment, letting out half of it to lodgers. She was also able to bring in a little money by practicing as a midwife. Notwithstanding her near destitution, Klavdiia somehow managed to set aside enough to give her daughter a reasonable education. Ekaterina attended classes at the Kiev Gymnasium, qualified as a typist, and, by the age of nineteen, was employed as a secretary in the office of a notary/justice of the peace named Ruzskii at the meager salary of 25 rubles ($12.50) a month.[27] By that point Ekaterina was sick to death of the monotony, squalor, and humiliation of poverty. She was determined to escape into a better life at any cost, and in planning to do so she had one invaluable asset: her exceptional physical beauty.

It is said that even as a baby, Ekaterina Viktorovna had impressed everyone with her ethereal good looks. According to a story widely circulated in Kiev, when the famous artist V. M. Vasnetsov was commissioned to paint the icons and murals in Kiev's Vladimir Cathedral, he chose Ekaterina as his model for the figure of the infant Christ.[28] As an adult, she was popularly reputed be one of the most beautiful women in Russia. None other than Rasputin would later say that she was one of only two women in the world who had ever stolen his heart.[29] Another acquaintance would describe her as "a platinum blonde with wonderful blue eyes, a fascinating, intelligent, dangerous woman."[30] In his memoirs, Sukhomlinov wrote that her extraordinary beauty and grace were actually defects because they aroused envy and enmity against her, but he added (with more than a little self-satisfaction) that when he subsequently took her to the theater in Petersburg, all the binoculars in the house would be trained on their box rather than the stage.[31] Certainly, the surviving photographs of her would not seem to justify the extravagant claims made for her loveliness (although to be fair, most of these were taken after the onset of her serious medical troubles). There were in fact those who believed that her true sexual power inhered in her personality rather than any perfection of form. As an anonymous society lady expressed it, Ekaterina Viktorovna was "one of those small, slight, well-proportioned women who have more womanly grace than actual beauty. At first glance she seems insignificant, not even pretty, but her attractions seem to grow upon one; she does not dazzle but she fascinates and knows how to keep a strong hand over men."[32]

In 1902 a young nobleman, Vladimir Nikolaevich Butovich, paid a business call at the office of Ekaterina's employer. Butovich, twenty-eight, was an extremely affluent man, being the owner of a 6,750-acre estate known as Krupol' (Buckwheat Field)

27. V. Shulgin, *Gody-Dni-1920* (Moscow, 1991), p. 249. Coincidentally, Ruzskii was the uncle of N. V. Ruzskii, a soldier who held prominent command in World War I.

28. Ibid., p. 248.

29. The other woman was Anna Vyrubova, lady-in-waiting to the Empress Alexandra, and Rasputin's conduit to court. See Aleksandr Tarsaidze, *Chetyre mifa* (New York, 1969), p. 261.

30. Kalmykow, *Memoirs*, p. 257.

31. Sukhomlinov, *Vospominaniia*, p. 254.

32. "A Russian," *Russian Court Memoirs 1914–1916* (London, 1917), p. 142.

50

Opening of the Tsesarevich Military Hospital, September 10, 1915. Figure 1 is Vladimir Sukhomlinov. Figure 2 is E. V. Sukhomlinova. Figures 29 and 31 are Sukhomlinov's friends the Berezovskiis.

in Poltava province. Whether by using her looks alone or by a combination of looks and guile, Ekaterina Viktorovna soon had made a conquest of Butovich. He proposed and the pair married in early 1903.

On the face of it, this advantageous match would seem to have been the answer to Ekaterina's prayers, for it rescued her from the banality of underpaid menial toil and translated her into a world of leisure and riches. But although her husband worshipped her and denied her nothing, even settling an annual income of 20,000 rubles in rents upon her, Ekaterina was oddly restless.[33] The birth of her son, Iurii, was only a temporary relief from her mood of dissatisfaction. Wealth was all very well, but it was hard for Ekaterina to enjoy it in the rustic seclusion of Butovich's estate. Concluding that she was starved for excitement and society, in 1905 she persuaded her husband, who was detained in Russia by his business affairs, to let her travel alone to the resorts in the south of France. As we have seen, it was at Biarritz in the fall of that year that she had first been introduced to Sukhomlinov.

When she went to western Europe the following year, it was not, however, merely a pleasure jaunt. Sometime during the course of 1906 she had manifested symptoms of serious and chronic kidney disease, possibly some variety of pyelonephritis. When doctors insisted that she consult foreign specialists, in November 1906 Butovich escorted her to Berlin, where she underwent kidney surgery. Several months of convalescence in an exclusive German nursing home followed.

From the time of their very first meeting, Sukhomlinov had been smitten by the young woman. Upon her return to Russia in 1907, he traveled to Poltava to renew the acquaintance. He became a frequent guest in the Butovich household and paid suit to Ekaterina whenever her husband's back was turned. In between visits, there were fre-

33. Petrov Commission report, 1916, RGVIA, f. 962, op. 2, d. 164, l. 85.

quent presents and telegrams expressing passionate love (some of which Sukhomlinov signed "Azure," the name of Ekaterina's lapdog.)[34] It was either in the late spring or early summer of 1907, while Butovich was away on an extended trip to Kishinev, that Ekaterina finally succumbed to Sukhomlinov's importuning, and the two became lovers.[35]

When Butovich arrived home that July, he was greeted with the electrifying news that his wife wanted a divorce. Nor was that all. Ekaterina insisted that he accept all the legal blame for the divorce himself, that he renounce all claims to Iurii's custody, and that he make her a payment of 200,000 rubles. Butovich was thunderstruck. As he had detected no signs of strain in his marriage, he was flabbergasted not only by Ekaterina's insistence that they part but also by the outrageous selfishness of her additional demands. He angrily refused.

Blaming Sukhomlinov for the ruination of his private life, he immediately issued a challenge to a duel, which was, however, contemptuously ignored. In the hope of goading the general to fight, he began to pepper him with insulting letters, each more offensive than the last. Although Butovich's epistolary campaign did not have the effect he had desired, it did make Sukhomlinov stop and think. Aware that Butovich could cause much more trouble if he wanted to, Vladimir Aleksandrovich started to wonder whether pressing for the divorce was really his wisest move. At the end of July an inquisitive governess overheard Sukhomlinov telling Ekaterina Viktorovna that, all in all, it might be preferable if she remained Butovich's wife.

Ekaterina would have none of this. Although she had never really cared for Butovich, she truly was in love with Sukhomlinov, or at least believed herself to be. To be sure, the prospect of becoming the consort of the most powerful man in the southwest of the empire considerably exceeded any destiny she could have imagined for herself, and this doubtless predisposed her in the general's favor. But the letters she wrote him, the passion she evinced for him, and the loyalty she subsequently showed him all strongly suggest that her feelings were sincere. Over the next three months she spent as much time in Kiev with her lover as she could and when she was at home, she constantly entreated Butovich to consent to the divorce. In November she tried to penetrate the wall of Butovich's obstinacy with a sham suicide attempt. She ingested a large (although not fatal) quantity of opium and demonstratively refused to take the emetics the doctors offered her. This episode appears to have triggered a flare-up of her kidney disease. In December she went abroad for six months of treatment at an exclusive sanitarium near Nice. In the same month, seeking a change of scene to dull his personal pain, Butovich accepted a position with the Ministry of Education as a traveling school inspector.

Sukhomlinov's ardor for Ekaterina and his enthusiasm for the divorce had been rekindled. In May 1908, after her discharge from the sanitarium, he joined her at the

---

34. Shulgin, *Gody,* p. 253.

35. Virtually all of the following details come from letters to Butovich dated July 10 and 28, 1908. Their author was Fanny Rochat, Iurii's former governess. See RGVIA, f. 962, op. 2, d. 90, ll. 73–74.

52 Czech spa of Carlsbad. From there he wrote to his Kiev attorney, V. E. Nemetti, instructing him to present an ultimatum to Butovich: either he could amicably agree to the divorce or he could expect the general would use all means necessary to settle the matter in another way.[36] Butovich construed this message as the threat it so obviously was. According to one (admittedly scurrilous) account, Sukhomlinov followed this up by explicitly menacing Butovich with administrative exile if he remained non-compliant.[37] Whether intimidated or not, Butovich was now prepared to yield.

In June the young landowner sent word through intermediaries that he was finally willing to accede to the divorce but only on his own terms. Ekaterina would have to surrender all custodial rights to their child. Moreover, she should put any thought of a financial settlement out of her head; she would never receive a single kopeck from the husband she had betrayed. Perhaps owing to her infatuation with her elderly suitor or to the stunted development of her maternal instincts (or perhaps both), Ekaterina immediately accepted Butovich's first condition. It was the second stipulation—the one concerning money—that she refused.[38]

And it was this refusal that enraged Butovich beyond measure. Retracting his pledge to cooperate, he vowed to contest the divorce with every resource at his disposal: he leaked the story to the newspapers and fired off a series of petitions to the Ministry of the Interior in which he accused Sukhomlinov of moral turpitude and abuse of power. The deputy minister of war, A. A. Polivanov, even made a personal report about Butovich's complaints to the emperor; it was fortunate for Sukhomlinov that Nicholas II decided against opening an inquiry, noting merely that it was "inconvenient" that embarrassing stories should circulate about so eminent a person.[39]

Although Butovich failed to poison the highest echelons of the tsarist government against Sukhomlinov, this did not mean that the general was without problems. He was well aware that if Butovich really did contest it, the chances of obtaining a lawful divorce might be very slim. For Orthodox Christians, as Sukhomlinov, Ekaterina, and Butovich all were, questions involving marriage fell within the purview of the Holy Synod, a sort of ecclesiastical ministry that regulated both the temporal and spiritual affairs of Russia's state church. For theological reasons, Orthodoxy was committed to upholding the sacrament of matrimony and took a dim view of the very concept of divorce. Although the Church did recognize four legitimate grounds for dissolving a marriage—sexual incapacity, insanity, adultery, and abandonment— it was not inclined to grant many divorces.[40] In August Sukhomlinov drafted a letter to the Synod, inquiring whether there was not some sort of special dispensation that

36. Sukhomlinov letter to Nemetti, May 16, 1908, RGVIA, f. 962, op. 2, d. 52, l. 324.

37. V. A. Apushkin, *General ot porazhenii V.A. Sukhomlinova* (Leningrad, 1925), p. 26.

38. Butovich to N. M. Goshkevich, June 16, 1908, RGVIA, f. 962, op. 2, d. 90, ll. 20–21.

39. A. A. Polivanov, *Iz dnevnikov i vospominanii po dolzhnosti voennogo ministra i ego pomoshchika 1907–1916 gg.*, vol. 1 (Moscow, 1924), p. 50.

40. On divorce in Russia generally see Gregory L. Freeze, "Krylov vs. Krylova: 'Sexual Incapacity' and Divorce in Tsarist Russia," in *The Human Tradition in Modern Russia,* ed. William B. Husband, pp. 5–17 (Wilmington, Del., 2000). See also "Razvod," *BE,* vol. 26 (St. Petersburg, 1899), p. 135.

could be granted in his case. As Emperor Nicholas II was head of the Church, was it 53
not within his power to dissolve the Butoviches' union by simple decree?[41] The response that Sukhomlinov received from the Procurator of the Holy Synod was not encouraging: there could be no such thing as divorce by imperial edict in the Orthodox Church. The Procurator added that given Butovich's opposition, "the only possible basis for a divorce would be for Mrs. Butovich to accuse her husband of infidelity."[42] Still further, such an accusation would have to be backed up by tangible proof. In divorce cases, the Church demanded that adultery be substantiated by eyewitness testimony even if one of the parties to the marriage confessed to the offense.[43] As Butovich obviously had no intention of confessing to adultery, the matter of witnesses was all the more important. For help in finding credible witnesses, Sukhomlinov turned to his old friend Alexander Altschüller. Altschüller was already Sukhomlinov's closest confidant in the Butovich affair; indeed, the general had drafted the first version of his original letter to the Holy Synod on the stationery of one of Altschüller's companies.

Alexander Altschüller

Born an Austrian Jew, Alexander Altschüller was a convert to Lutheranism who had immigrated from the Hapsburg Empire to Kiev in 1870. Starting out as a factor for various German and Austrian concerns, he eventually amassed enough capital to open his own brokerage and shipping office. This office, which maintained branches in Tambov and Kozlov as well as Kiev, specialized in supplying the needs of the Ukrainian sugar beet industry and, as a sideline, imported agricultural machinery, one of the few categories of goods that Russia's notoriously high tariff schedules admitted duty free.[44] By the 1890s Altschüller's office had prospered to such an extent that it regularly paid out 90,000 rubles in profit every year.[45] Nor was this only source of his income. Owing to his friendship with the Brodskys, a family of Jewish industrialists who collectively controlled 25 percent of the Russian Empire's sugar production, he sat on the board of directors of Kiev's largest sugar refinery.[46]

At the turn of the century the South Russian Machine Works, a Kiev company that built cast-iron boilers and railway boxcars, was placed in receivership; the firm's creditors undertook its reorganization. The largest creditor was none other than

41. Sukhomlinov to the Holy Synod, October 3, 1908, RGVIA, f. 962, op. 2, d. 70, l. 2.
42. RGVIA, f. 962, op. 2, d. 52, l. 231.
43. Gregory L. Freeze, "The Orthodox Church and Emperor Nicholas II: A Confrontation over Divorce in Late Tsarist Russia," in *Stranitsy rossiiskoi istorii. Problemy, sobytiia, liudi. Sbornik statei v chest' Borisa Vasil'evicha Anan'icha,* ed. V. Paneiakh et al., p. 198 (St. Petersburg, 2003). I want to thank Professor Freeze for supplying me with a copy of this essay, a remarkable analysis of the Butovich divorce case based on Church sources.
44. RGVIA, f. 962, op. 2, d. 136, l. 36.
45. Testimony of Oscar Altschüller (Alexander's son and partner in this business), August 26, 1917, RGVIA, f. 962, op. 2, d. 146, l. 6.
46. Hamm, *Kiev,* p. 129.

54 Altschüller, whose office had been the factory's principal supplier of metal plate. In recompense for his losses, Altschüller was given the position of majority shareholder in the reconstituted enterprise. He also became its chief executive officer.[47]

It is fair to say that neither the company's other stockholders nor the Russian economy benefited at all from this transaction, for Altschüller proceeded to run the firm into the ground. He was a dealmaker rather than a manufacturer and was determined to squeeze the South Russian Machine Works for every drop of profit that he could. He made himself both the sole purveyor of raw materials to the factory and the sole agent for its sales, taking percentages at either end. He kept the company undercapitalized and committed it to fulfill orders at barely sustainable prices. It was doubtless for these reasons that in 1905 the South Russian Machine Works became one of the most radical and militant factories in the entire Ukraine. Throughout the year South Russian's 759 laborers struck earlier and more frequently than any other group of workers in the region. What the South Russian's factory hands wanted, of course, was a reduction in hours and a boost in pay, but because of the company's financial weakness, no negotiated compromise was possible; there simply was not enough money to satisfy the workers' demands.[48] The South Russian Machine Works therefore resorted to heavy-handed tactics in dealing with its labor problems. During the strike of February/March 1905, it fired the entire workforce, closed down, and reopened a few days later offering employment only to those who would agree to accept prestrike wages.[49]

None of this apparently bothered Altschüller in the slightest; because of his arrangements with South Russian Machine Works he was now making more money than ever before. In addition to the 35,000 rubles he annually took out of his shipping office, and the 10,000 he received as director of the Brodskii refinery, he collected another 15,000 in salary from South Russian, and 60,000 more in commissions from its business.[50]

Despite his modest beginnings, Altschüller had risen to become a prominent and influential businessman. Franz Josef's government in Vienna had appointed him an honorary consul of Austria-Hungary. He was at home in every European capital and visited all the fashionable spas. Back in Russia, he moved smoothly through the upper levels of Kiev society, where his facility with foreign languages, his dandyish dress, and his ready wit were much remarked upon.[51] An employee later recalled that although he was tightfisted when it came to small outlays, Altschüller never hesitated "to lay out large sums on dinners, flowers and the like, whenever it was necessary for him to make a good impression."[52] His guest list included not only his personal

47. RGVIA, f. 962, op. 2, d. 48, l. 123.

48. F. E. Los', ed., *Revoliutsiia 1905–1907 gg. na Ukraine. Sbornik dokumentov i materialov v dvukh tomakh*, vol. 2, pt. 1 (Kiev, 1955), pp. 118–119.

49. The militancy of the South Russian Machine Works in 1905 receives considerable attention in Hamm, *Kiev*. See particularly pp. 33, 178, 180, 187, 231.

50. Goshkevich interrogation, July 25, 1915, RGVIA, f. 962, op. 2, d. 134, l. 33; testimony of O. Altschüller, August 26, 1917, RGVIA, f. 962, op. 2, d. 146, ll. 5–6.

51. Goshkevich interrogation, July 25, 1915, RGVIA, f. 962, op. 2, d. 134, l. 31.

52. Ibid.

friends but also "people who were useful to his business because of the high social position they occupied."[53] More often than not, these functions were wildly successful.
"Nobody anywhere ever feeds you as well as Altschüller," observed one Kiev resident.[54]

It was Sukhomlinov's second wife, Elizaveta Nikolaevna, who had introduced
Altschüller to her husband shortly after his transfer to Kiev in 1899. The urbane Austrian had long been a friend of her family's.[55] Despite the disparity in their back-
grounds, the two men soon became intimate. Perhaps it was the fact of Altschüller's
status as a foreigner and outsider that made him one of the few people whom
Sukhomlinov felt he could trust with his confidences. Altschüller was a frequent
guest in the district commander's mansion and reciprocated this hospitality with the
still more lavish hospitality of his own. When Elizaveta Nikolaevna died in 1904, it
was Altschüller who helped Sukhomlinov to mourn. And when in 1908 Sukhomlinov
announced that he intended to wed Ekaterina Viktorovna, Altschüller was one of the
few people to stand by him at a time when most of his other friends, like Berezovskii,
sourly disapproved.[56]

Altschüller's sympathy for Sukhomlinov's new romance, taken together with his
willingness to help facilitate Ekaterina Viktorovna's divorce, cemented his ties with
the governor-general. In the fall of 1908 Butovich, Iurii, and the boy's new governess,
Mlle. Laurens, traveled to France for a lengthy vacation. Altschüller followed them
there and hired a team of private detectives to put them under surveillance.[57] He soon
accumulated a thick stack of notarized depositions from numerous employees of
Nice's Hôtel Château Des Baumettes testifying to the adulterous relationship between Butovich and Vera Laurens. Adolphe Ghibando, the headwaiter of the establishment, swore that he "had noticed that Monsieur Boutowicht [*sic*] had many times
gone into the room of Mlle. Vera Laurens at night, and had only emerged after several
hours and that his extreme familiarity towards her did not permit of any doubt that
there were intimate relations between the two of them, and that the entire staff of the
hotel was aware of this state of affairs."[58]

In the meantime there had been momentous changes in Sukhomlinov's career.
Russia's defeat in the Russo-Japanese War had made the necessity of thoroughgoing
military reform incontestable. A first effort in that direction had been the establishment in the summer of 1905 of a new organ, the Council of State of Defense. Under
the chairmanship of Nicholas II's second cousin, the Grand Duke Nikolai Nikolaevich, the council was supposed to unify all national security decision making for
both the army and the navy. At the same time, the general staff had been split off
from the Ministry of War and made an independent entity (as in Germany). This entailed downgrading the Ministry of War to a mere executive agency, responsible for

53. RGVIA, f. 962, op. 2, d. 136, l. 36.
54. Ekaterina Sukhomlinova interrogation, November 16, 1916, RGVIA, f. 962, op. 2, d. 52, l. 68.
55. Sukhomlinov interrogation, November 9, 1916, RGVIA, f. 962, op. 2, d. 52, l. 24.
56. Testimony of V. A. Berezovskii, February 3, 1917, RGVIA, f. 962, op. 2, d. 55, l. 70.
57. RGVIA, f. 962, op. 2, d. 52, ll. 26, 66.
58. Notarized statement of Ghibando, May 13, 1909, RGVIA, f. 962, op. 2, d. 88, l. 67.

56 equipping, feeding, and training the army, but not for war plans. It soon became evident, however, that to detach strategy and logistics so completely made little sense.
Conceding that the experiment had been a failure, in June 1908 Nicholas II disman-
tled the State Defense Council and resubordinated the general staff to the war ministry. In November 1908, Sukhomlinov learned that he had been nominated to take
over from F. F. Palitsyn, Nikolai's handpicked chief of staff. Both the emperor and the
minister of war, A. F. Rediger, agreed that Vladimir Aleksandrovich was the right
man for this sensitive job. To accept this promotion would entail a move to the capital. It would also entail a monetary sacrifice, for although the chief of the general staff
was responsible for matters of the utmost seriousness—including the collection of
intelligence and the preparation of Russia's war plans—his annual salary was only
16,000 rubles, a sum less than a third of what Sukhomlinov had been earning as
governor-general and military district chief in Kiev. Vladimir Aleksandrovich
nonetheless felt that he had no choice but to accede to his emperor's wishes. In early
December 1908 he entrained for St. Petersburg. Ekaterina Viktorovna soon joined
him there and took possession of a separate apartment attached to the official residence of the chief of staff.

Sukhomlinov did not, however, occupy this post for long. Within a few months
an even more dazzling promotion came his way. In March 1909 the Octobrists, the
center-right party that was dominant in the Third Duma, began a campaign of criticism against the government for the weakness and superficiality of its military reforms. Octobrist orators, particularly A. I. Guchkov, placed heavy emphasis on the
unwholesome meddling of the imperial family in military affairs. But War Minister
Rediger replied with a speech so tepid and unpersuasive that an infuriated Nicholas
summarily fired him and appointed Sukhomlinov in his stead. Vladimir Aleksandrovich immediately moved into the quarters of the minister of war—a forty-room
palace on the Moika Canal.

By June 1909 the Butovich divorce was in the hands of the spiritual consistory of
the St. Petersburg diocese. The consistory (an ecclesiastical court composed of bish-
ops) appeared willing to bend over backwards to accommodate the new minister of
war. When Ekaterina Viktorovna submitted the affidavits that Altschüller had
brought back from Nice, the consistory found the proofs of infidelity compelling and
applied to the Holy Synod for confirmation of the divorce decree. Butovich had,
however, been alerted to this development by his own sources in the Church hierarchy, and he contested the consistory's decision in a direct appeal to the Synod. Butovich argued that all of Ekaterina's "evidence" came from foreigners of dubious probity and was, moreover, merely hearsay, not the testimony of two *eyewitnesses*, as
canon law required.[59]

Despite the intervention of Nicholas II, who made it known that he wanted the
case resolved in Sukhomlinov's favor, the Synod declined to endorse the diocesan

---

59. Butovich also called attention to numerous other irregularities and illegalities in the proceedings.
See Freeze, "Orthodox Church and Emperor," p. 198.

consistory's recommendation. As far as the Synod was concerned, the standard of proof for adultery had not been met. Even when in September Nicholas II all but ordered the Synod to grant the divorce anyway, lest he use his "supreme power" to divorce the couple himself, the Synod would not budge.[60] The most it would do was charge the St. Petersburg consistory to conduct an additional verification of Ekaterina's evidence. This, of course, would produce still further delays. Moreover, what might the result of such an "additional verification" be? Butovich had dispatched his own agents to the French Riviera, where they either cajoled or bribed all of Altschüller's informants save one into retracting their statements. The exception was Ghibando, the headwaiter at the Hôtel Des Baumettes, who had in the interim committed suicide in a bout of alcoholic despondency. Although Ghibando's deposition had been the most damaging of all the materials Ekaterina Viktorovna had filed with the consistory, the circumstances of his death undermined its credibility.

Ekaterina Viktorovna and Vladimir Aleksandrovich now realized that the Synod's obstinacy had markedly improved Butovich's chances of blocking or at least postponing the divorce. Believing that he had the initiative, Butovich did everything he could to keep the scandal in the public eye. The longer the divorce case dragged on, the greater the probability that Sukhomlinov's other enemies would take a hand in it. In particular, Sukhomlinov suspected that A. L. Myshlaevskii, who had replaced him at the general staff, was employing family connections to influence key members of the Synod to vote against the divorce, in the hopes that this defeat would drive him from office.[61] Ekaterina Viktorovna and Vladimir Aleksandrovich were uncomfortably aware that they needed something else to buttress their collapsing suit. It was at this juncture that Anna Goshkevich came forward.

Anna Goshkevich (née Grek) was the twenty-seven-year-old daughter of a provincial judge. In 1906 she had married engineering student Nikolai Mikhailovich Goshkevich, Ekaterina Viktorovna's first cousin.[62] In the summer of 1906 the newly-weds spent part of their honeymoon at Butovich's Poltava estate. By 1908 the couple had settled in Petersburg, where Nikolai had found a low-level position with the Ministry of Trade. When they learned of Ekaterina Viktorovna's liaison with Sukhomlinov, they were at first overwhelmingly sympathetic to Butovich, whom they regarded as the aggrieved party. After some meetings with Ekaterina and Sukhomlinov, however, the Goshkeviches changed their minds and began to take the part of the general and his young mistress against Butovich. In the fall of 1909 Anna revealed to her husband that she was in a position to give explosive evidence that would ensure that the divorce suit was resolved in Ekaterina's favor: she insisted that during their stay at Krupol' in 1906 Butovich had attempted to rape her. When Nikolai asked her why she had not told him about this attack at the time, she answered that she was afraid that if she had, he would have killed Butovich.[63]

60. Ibid., pp. 199–200.
61. Polivanov, *Iz dnevnikov*, pp. 76, 78–79.
62. Anna Goshkevich statement, July 26, 1915, RGVIA, f. 962, op. 2, d. 51, l. 242.
63. N. M. Goshkevich statement, July 23, 1916, RGVIA, f. 962, op. 2, d. 134, l. 19.

58 Anna Goshkevich's testimony to the ecclesiastical authorities had just the effect she had predicted. Although some in her audience were bothered by discrepancies in her story, the consistory found for Ekaterina Viktorovna on the basis of Anna's statement and the Ghibando affidavit. Whether it was truly convinced that Anna's evidence supported the charge Ghibando had made, or whether it merely pretended to be convinced in order to defuse a dangerous confrontation with the emperor, the Synod reversed itself. On November 11 a plenary session of the Synod granted Ekaterina Viktorovna a divorce on the grounds of her husband's adultery.[64] Two days later Ekaterina and Sukhomlinov were married in accordance with the Orthodox rite. Among those present at the private ceremony were the Goshkeviches; the Berezovskiis; V. E. Nemetti, Sukhomlinov's attorney from Kiev; and Alexander Altschüller.[65]

Ekaterina Viktorovna's struggle to dissolve her union with Butovich had lasted twenty-eight months. It had been a messy and distasteful business that tarnished the reputation of the Sukhomlinovs for good. Despite the fact that the divorce had been technically lawful, as had Ekaterina's remarriage, the stink of scandal had attached itself to the war minister and his bride. It was a stink that could not readily be scrubbed away. In society there was a general sense that Sukhomlinov and Ekaterina had resorted to underhanded, perhaps even nefarious, methods in their dispute with Butovich. Even if these rumors were without foundation, Sukhomlinov's conduct in the affair had scarcely been exemplary. Antonii, Metropolitan of Petersburg, was overheard saying at a reception "the war minister had married in order to work in peace. What, however, would be the position of the Synod if every minister, in order to work in peace, wished to take another man's wife?"[66] As for Butovich, he refused to give up. He commissioned a pamphlet telling his side of the story, which he distributed free, in hundreds of copies.[67] In 1912 he would instigate legal proceedings against both Ekaterina Viktorovna and Anna Goshkevich, accusing them of slander and perjury.

How a person stood on the question of the Butovich divorce now became the litmus test of trustworthiness and reliability for the Sukhomlinovs. Anyone who had expressed doubts was perforce to be numbered among their personal enemies. Sukhomlinov's relations with some of his oldest friends, including the Berezovskiis, perceptibly cooled after 1909 because of their lack of enthusiasm for his spouse. By contrast, those who had expressed sympathy and support for the embattled couple in the two years before the divorce were deemed fully worthy of admission to the couple's inner circle, irrespective of any flaws in their character.

One person who fell into this category was Nataliia Iliarionovna Chervinskaia, who, although a cousin of Vladimir Butovich, conspicuously sided with Ekaterina, claiming that her own husband's abuse gave her a special empathy for Ekaterina's

64. Petrov Commission report, 1916, RGVIA, f. 962, op. 2, d. 164, ll. 261–262; Polivanov, *Iz dnevnikov*, p. 85.

65. RGVIA, f. 962, op. 2, d. 35, ll. 70–71.

66. Polivanov, *Iz dnevnikov*, p. 85.

67. Rediger memoir, RGVIA, f. 280, op. 1, d. 8, p. 54.

plight. Ekaterina was so affected by this unanticipated support that she impulsively invited Chervinskaia to move into the war minister's mansion, where she remained as a houseguest for several years. The Sukhomlinovs also felt themselves indebted to Nikolai and Anna Goshkevich. Ekaterina was able to arrange a suitable guerdon for them even before the divorce was finalized. In the summer of 1909 she had introduced Nikolai to Alexander Altschüller. At her urging, the Kiev businessman offered Nikolai a job as the Petersburg representative of the South Russian Machine Works. Nikolai gratefully accepted and set up an office in his apartment on Bolshaia Zeleninaia Street. As we shall see, Miasoedov also found a way to use the Butovich divorce to ingratiate himself with Sukhomlinov. This in turn would bring him back into uniform under circumstances and with consequences that were among the most dramatic in the entire "espionage" affair.

3

St. Petersburg

Given her incontinent ambition, Ekaterina Viktorovna must surely have been gratified by the extraordinary upward mobility she had experienced over the previous decade. In 1902 she had been a nameless secretary slaving away in a notary's dreary office; a year later she was the mistress of an enormous and lucrative provincial estate; but now, a mere five years after that, she had become the wife of the incumbent war minister, one of the most important and prominent officials in St. Petersburg. Nonetheless, Ekaterina's delight in her status and her expectation of social triumph proved evanescent when she discovered that there were some formidable barriers to her acceptance in Petersburg society. For example, an unwritten rule held that no divorced woman could ever be presented at court. Making matters still worse was the fact that Ekaterina Viktorovna's divorce had been particularly nasty, involving the public exchange of sordid charges between the parties and evoking a torrent of salacious gossip. As one contemporary noted, Sukhomlinov still bore "the filth of this unpleasant affair on his shoulders."[1] The most prominent salons in St. Petersburg would not receive the newly married pair. Even some of Sukhomlinov's oldest friends in the capital now barred their doors to him. Despite her husband's lofty official position, the *belle monde* had closed ranks to frustrate Ekaterina Viktorovna's social hopes.[2]

Although she may have been nonplussed by these social slights, she was not defeated by them. With characteristic energy and drive, Ekaterina Viktorovna did everything she could to maintain and enhance her husband's status. For example, she

1. V. Shulgin, *Gody-dni-1920* (Moscow, 1991), p. 235.
2 Anna Goshkevich testimony, October 18, 1916, RGVIA, f. 962, op. 2, d. 135, l. 55.

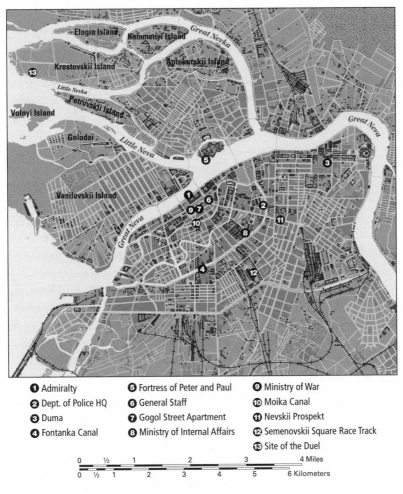

❶ Admiralty **❺** Fortress of Peter and Paul **❾** Ministry of War

❷ Dept. of Police HQ **❻** General Staff **❿** Moika Canal

❸ Duma **❼** Gogol Street Apartment **⓫** Nevskii Prospekt

❹ Fontanka Canal **❽** Ministry of Internal Affairs **⓬** Semenovskii Square Race Track

⓭ Site of the Duel

0	½	1		2		3		4 Miles
0	½	1	2	3	4	5		6 Kilometers

St. Petersburg circa 1910

62 prevailed upon Sukhomlinov to develop his ties to General E. V. Bogdanovich, whose impeccable connections to the court would be valuable in a campaign to have her spouse made a general of the suite, one of that select company of officers who were honorifically attached to the person of the emperor.[3] At the same time, being young and vivacious, she had no intention of living as a recluse. She gradually built up her own extensive network of friends. One of her detractors later wrote that "she created her circle of people, who, although not admitted in high society, nonetheless occupied one sort of visible position or another thanks to their business contacts or great wealth."[4] Industrialists, financiers, and members of the consular corps populated her receptions.

One of the few even quasi-respectable drawing rooms in which Ekaterina Viktorovna was still welcome belonged to Madame Lidiia Nikolaevna Viktorova, the wife of D. A. Viktorov, a senator in the department of cassation of the governing senate. Viktorova was quite tolerant of marital irregularities; she had been living apart from her husband for some time, and her discreet amour with a retired military prosecutor, General P. P. Maslov, was common knowledge in Petersburg society.

Now it happened that Madame Viktorova was one of Sergei Miasoedov's most important connections in the capital. Although not a blood relation, Lidiia had known the former gendarme since childhood and was so fond of him that she addressed him by the diminutive endearment "Seriozha." In a sense, Viktorova's salon became Miasoedov's general headquarters in his battle for reinstatement in government service. During their frequent visits to Viktorova's home both Miasoedovs buttonholed the other guests and steered the conversation around to Sergei's plight. In the summer of 1909, Viktorova introduced Klara Miasoedova to Ekaterina Viktorovna Sukhomlinova. Klara listened with concern to Ekaterina's story of the horrors Butovich was subjecting her to in his struggle to prevent the divorce. Later that summer, after Klara had read a particularly lurid newspaper article attacking Ekaterina Viktorovna's conduct in the case, she wrote her a letter of sympathy.[5] Ekaterina responded with a thank-you note, and in November, two weeks after her marriage to Vladimir Aleksandrovich, she paid her first call at the Miasoedovs' home. It was the beginning of a friendship between the two women that would lead to a striking improvement in Miasoedov's circumstances.

During 1910 the Miasoedovs and Sukhomlinovs became very intimate. The Sukhomlinovs attended parties organized by Sergei and Klara and reciprocated with invitations to functions at the Minister of War's residence. At these soirees the Miasoedovs rubbed shoulders with the other members of the Sukhomlinovs' circle, including Nikolai Goshkevich, Anna Goshkevich, and, with increasing frequency, Alexander Altschüller.

3. A. N. Berezovskii testimony, February 3, 1917, RGVIA, f. 962, op. 2, d. 55, l. 74.
4. M. D. Bonch-Bruevich, *Vsia vlast' sovetam* (Moscow, 1957), p. 66.
5. Klara Miasoedova interrogation, n.d., RGVIA, f. 962, op. 2, d. 160, l. 102.

The Miasoedovs and the Sukhomlinovs

The friendship between the Miasoedovs and the Sukhomlinovs ripened into an intense relationship that occasioned much comment. Other friends of the Sukhomlinovs were surprised at the intimacy between the two couples as well as the familiarity that Sukhomlinov permitted Miasoedov. After all, unsavory rumors—of smuggling, dishonest business practices, and questionable associations with Jews—clung to the former railway gendarme. Berezovskii later deposed that one day he was ushered into Sukhomlinov's drawing room only to find Miasoedov "sprawled" on the sofa. When he asked Vladimir Aleksandrovich why he put up with this, he replied it was for his wife's sake.[6] Anna Goshkevich also later claimed that when she once asked Ekaterina Viktorovna what she saw in Miasoedov, the former replied that he "is an excellent fellow. No one can set up a dinner or buy something as cheaply as he can."[7] Clearly Ekaterina found Sergei Nikolaevich clever, amusing, and useful. Sergei was only too happy to accommodate the war minister's spouse by indulging her whims and by performing such small services for her as acting as her agent at auctions and making reservations for her at foreign hotels. However, if Ekaterina found Sergei to be a resourceful and obliging general factotum, in Klara she found a confidante. There were many lively exchanges of letters between the two young women, particularly when Ekaterina traveled abroad, as she often did, for medical consultations and recuperation at fashionable spas.[8]

In the summer of 1910 Sergei left on a trip to Carlsbad to take the cure for a flare-up of his gout. The Sukhomlinovs, who also planned a journey to Carlsbad that year, prevailed on Klara to accompany them.[9] In August the two couples engaged nearby rooms in Carlsbad's sumptuous Grand Hotel Pupp.[10] Miasoedov, whose gout treatment had concluded successfully, energetically threw himself into the task of ensuring that his highly placed friends had the time of their lives. Ekaterina was later quoted as saying that the dinners Miaoseodov treated her to during this vacation were better than any she had ever eaten before.[11]

At some point during the time they all spent together in Carlsbad, Miasoedov was emboldened to ask Sukhomlinov to intervene to have him recalled to active duty in the army and offered a suitable billet. Might it be possible for him to be appointed the war minister's adjutant? Sukhomlinov, obviously in an expansive mood, readily agreed that this was an excellent idea. But Ekaterina Viktorovna objected, observing that many well-connected officers, particularly in the guards, coveted an adjutant's

6. Berezovskii testimony, February 3, 1917, RGVIA, f. 962, op.2, d. 55, l. 73.

7. Anna Goshkevich testimony, October 18, 1916, RGVIA, f. 962, op. 2, d. 135, l. 56.

8. See, for example, the sequence of letters from Ekaterina to Klara in the spring of 1910, RGVIA, f. 962, op. 2, d. 51, ll. 89–93.

9. Klara Miasoedova statement, May 1915, RGVIA, f. 962, op. 2, d. 160, l. 104.

10. Ibid., l. 96.

11. Nikolai Goshkevich statement, July 25, 1915, RGVIA, f. 962, op. 2, d. 134, ll. 35–36.

64 post; it would not do, she continued, to offend them needlessly by tapping the relatively obscure ex-gendarme for such an assignment. Sukhomlinov understood her logic but was still determined to do something for his new friend. He told Miasoedov he would have him reinstated in the Separate Corps of Gendarmes and then indefinitely assigned to the central Ministry of War.

Upon his return to Petersburg, Sukhomlinov was as good as his word, for he immediately telephoned his former student P. G. Kurlov, now deputy minister of the interior, to sound him out about Miasoedov's resuming a service career.[12] However, Interior Minister Petr Stolypin had still neither forgotten nor forgiven Miasoedov for his 1907 Vilna testimony and refused to do anything to help him even as a courtesy to his ministerial colleague. Sukhomlinov then went over Stolypin's head to Nicholas II, whom he tried to persuade to reinstate Miasoedov in the gendarmes by decree. When Stolypin got wind of Sukhomlinov's attempt to engineer a fait accompli, he was predictably incensed. Stolypin's fury reached new heights when V. N. Kokovtsov, minister of finance and consequently chief of the customs bureau, informed him that during the Verzhbolovo years his agents had once caught Miasoedov red-handed with smuggled goods and weapons hidden in his car.[13] That this episode had not, in fact, ever taken place made no difference; Stolypin was now convinced that Sukhomlinov's protégé was nothing more than a common criminal. Whether by pressuring Sukhomlinov or by direct appeal to the tsar, Stolypin was able to block Miasoedov's appointment in early fall of 1910.

For the moment there was nothing even Sukhomlinov could do to help Sergei Nikolaevich, who continued working in his nominal job with the Northwest Russian Steamship Company. The ensuing year was a troubled one for Miasoedov, for money was again extremely tight. In September 1910 he was able to raise 4,000 rubles from his friend Valentini by arranging the fictitious sale to him of all the furniture, clothing, and property in the Kolokolnaia apartment. The inventory prepared for this transaction listed tables, chairs, mirrors, three marble busts, twelve shotguns, a silver flatware service for twenty-four, twenty-three tablecloths, four suits, three overcoats, twenty-four shirts, thirty pairs of socks, seven hundred books, six hundred bottles of wine, and a smoking jacket—in short, all of the accoutrements of a well-born gentleman with a partiality for outdoor sport.[14] However, if Miasoedov had a gentleman's possessions, he was running low on the resources necessary to support a gentleman's standard of living. The sources offer fragmentary glimpses of him in these months, desperately pursuing one get-rich-quick scheme after another. None of these, including the Caucasian lumber deal about which he had been so hopeful, ever even turned a profit.[15]

12. P. G. Kurlov statement, August 8, 1916, ibid., l. 108.

13. V. N. Kokovtsov, *Iz moego proshlogo. Vospominaniia 1903–1919*, vol. 2 (Paris, 1933), p. 62; V. N. Kokovtsov statement, December 1916; RGVIA, f. 962, op. 1, d. 52, l. 295.

14. Bill of sale, September 30, 1910, RGVIA, f. 962, op. 2, d. 112, l. 429.

15. N. Goshkevich statement, July 26, 1916, RGVIA, f. 962, op. 2, d. 134, l. 65.

Perhaps it was to escape from the tension of his precarious economic situation that Miasoeodov now began yet another extramarital affair. His new lover, Evgeniia Stolbina, was the daughter of a Colonel Speier, who had once been Miasoedov's superior in the Verzhbolovo gendarme detachment. When Evgeniia grew up, she had married a gendarme officer named Stolbin and had moved with him to the capital. This marriage was not a success, and Stolbina soon tired of her spouse. Sometime in 1911 she ran into Miasoedov on a Petersburg street. As Stolbina had in fact been infatuated with him since adolescence, the pair soon drifted into a passionate physical relationship. Since Klara almost immediately came to suspect that Sergei Nikolaevich was once again betraying her, violent scenes and icy silences alternated in the Miasoedov household.[16]

Sukhomlinov, although still in principle committed to helping Miasoedov, was in 1911 distracted by a domestic crisis of his own. Ekaterina Viktorovna's health had deteriorated, and the doctors agreed that only radical surgery could save her life. As Sukhomlinov did not have the money to pay for Ekaterina's operation, Nicholas II authorized the outlay of 10,000 rubles for this purpose from a special emergency fund.[17] In July Ekaterina took the train for Berlin, where on July 28 the internationally celebrated nephrologist Professor Oskar Israel excised her entire left kidney.[18] Though she eventually recovered from this procedure, her convalescence was a long and painful one. Moreover, the operation did not produce any dramatic improvement in her medical condition, leaving Sukhomlinov to worry about how much time Ekaterina had before she succumbed to a potentially fatal attack.

On September 1, 1911, Dmitrii Bogrov, a sociopath with ties to both the tsarist secret police and the terrorist wing of the Socialist Revolutionary Party, shot and mortally wounded Interior Minister Stolypin in the Kiev opera house.[19] Because of uncertainty about Bogrov's authentic allegiance, some doubt remains to this day about the motivation for this savage crime.[20] As minister of the interior and chairman of the Council of Ministers, Stolypin had restored order after the Russian Revolution of 1905 and had inaugurated a series of imaginative reforms designed to confer political and social stability on the empire. Although his death was not the unmitigated catastrophe it is sometimes represented to be—by 1911 he was mentally exhausted, politically isolated, and increasingly ineffective—it is nonetheless clear that Russia scarcely benefited from the loss of her most talented statesman. But if Russia did not benefit,

---

16. Klara Miasoedova statement, May 1915, RGVIA, f. 962, op. 2, d. 160, l. 107; Assistant Procurator, Warsaw, to Stavka, February 5, 1916, RGVIA, f. 2003, op. 2, d. 1073, l. 219.

17. Kokovtsov's statement, December 1916, RGVIA, f. 962, op. 2, d. 52, l. 288.

18. Ibid., l. 93; Ekaterina Sukhomlinova testimony, November 21, 1916, RGVIA, f. 962, op. 2, d. 136, l. 45.

19. For an excellent description of this in English see Anna Geifman, *Thou Shalt Kill: Revolutionary Terrorism in Russia, 1894–1917* (Princeton, 1993), pp. 238–240.

20. The best explanation to date holds that Bogrov hoped that this spectacular act of terrorism would allay the growing suspicion in SR circles that he was betraying the party's secrets to the local Okhrana. See Richard Pipes, *The Russian Revolution* (New York, 1990), pp. 188–190.

66 S. N. Miasoedov did. With Stolypin out of the picture, Sukhomlinov could again revive his suit for Miasoedov's reinstatement in the gendarmes, and on September 28, Sergei was back in a lieutenant colonel's uniform. On the very same day he was seconded by the interior ministry to the Ministry of War as "officer for special assignments" (*ofitser osobykh poruchenii*). On October 27 (November 9) Ekaterina Viktorovna wrote Miasoedov a brief note from Cap d'Ail congratulating him on his new position, wishing him success, and thanking him for the sable muff he had sent her.[21]

Borrowing money to send his benefactress a valuable gift was not the only way in which Sergei jubilantly celebrated his good fortune. On November 24, Miasoedov rendezvoused with Stolbina in Belostok, then whisked her off for a weekend of sex at Warsaw's exclusive Bristol Hotel.[22] Upon his return to Petersburg, Miasoedov resumed his practice of entertaining lavishly. On December 31, 1911, the Miasoedovs gave a New Year's Eve party at their apartment on Kolokolnaia Street. Among the guests were Sukhomlinov and Ekaterina Viktorovna, the Goshkeviches, General N. M. Kamenev and his wife, and Miasoedov's German friend, the pharmaceutical importer Valentini.[23] Miasoedov evidently laid out a great deal of money for this evening, and by all accounts it was an enormous success. If anything cast a shadow over the festivities, it was the fact that several people whom the Miasoedovs had invited were conspicuously absent. Sukhomlinov's most senior adjutant Staff-Captain Lev Bulatsel' refused to attend, as did his colleague Colonel V. S. Botkin. So, too, did the Berezovskiis. Madame Berezovskaia is supposed to have said, half-jokingly, that she "wouldn't go to Miasoedov's since she did not want [one day] to sit with him in the prisoners' dock."[24]

Miasoedov at the Ministry of War

The precise nature of Miasoedov's duties at the Ministry of War was to become one of the most controversial issues in his entire case. Some of Sukhomlinov's adversaries would accuse the war minister of having used Miasoedov to build up an enormous secret organization to probe the political loyalty of the Russian officer corps. Others asserted that Miasoedov had been given a high post in Russian counterintelligence. For his part, Sukhomlinov vigorously denied that Miasoedov had ever had any sensitive assignment whatsoever. None of these three characterizations of Miasoedov's war ministry job were remotely accurate.

To be sure, Sukhomlinov did initially have Miasoedov work on the question of revolutionary propaganda in the Russian army, but this was primarily a matter of compiling syntheses of reports prepared by others. Miasoedov was also instructed to keep a register of incoming information about political unrest in the ranks of the

---

21. Letter of Ekaterina Sukhomlinova to Miasoedov, November 15, 1911, RGVIA, f. 962, op. 2, d. 135, l. 23.

22. RGVIA, f. 962, op. 2, d. 169, l. 122.

23. N. Goshkevich statement, July 25, 1915, RGVIA, f. 962, op. 2, d. 134, l. 36.

24. V. A. Berezovskii testimony, February 3–8, 1914, RGVIA, f. 962, op. 2, d. 55, l. 75.

army, which entailed business trips to Kovno, Vilna, and Minsk in November 1911 and February 1912.[25] Yet Miasoedov had nothing to do with the network of political informers within the Russian officer corps. Such a network in fact existed, but it was the creation of N. P. Zuev, who directed the Department of Police between 1909 and 1913.[26] Far from tolerating this sort of police espionage within the officer corps, Sukhomlinov was its ferocious and implacable opponent. In his opinion, allowing the police to recruit officers to report on the political opinions of their comrades-in-arms was a grievous insult to the collective honor of Russian officers. Moreover, such practices could only result in the complete destruction of the army's morale. For these considerations he gave his full backing to the military district commanders, who were unanimous in their struggle against this pernicious police meddling in the military's internal affairs.[27] Nonetheless, Sukhomlinov did toy with the idea of making Miasoedov his informal liaison to the Department of Police. Because of Sergei Nikolaevich's years of service in the gendarmes, Sukhomlinov reasoned that he would be the ideal person to represent the war ministry's position in consultations with the political section of the police department. Officials at the latter institution, however, had a long memory and would have none of this.[28]

It is equally clear that Miasoedov would very much have liked a formal position in military intelligence or counterintelligence. Indeed, on the eve of his reinstatement in the gendarmes he wrote Sukhomlinov requesting a position in the intelligence field.[29] He had of course acquired considerable experience in and a taste for intelligence operations during his years in Verzhbolovo. Perhaps he was also aware that Russia's military intelligence services had recently undergone reorganization and modest expansion. This was particularly true of counterintelligence. Only a few months before Miasoedov's reentry into state service, counterintelligence, whose functions were previously shared by both army and police, became an exclusively military undertaking, and CI offices were set up in all the military districts as well as in the general staff in Petersburg.[30] Soon after reporting for duty at the war ministry, Miasoedov evidently decided to explore the possibility of a posting to the intelligence department. He went to see Colonel N. A. Monkevits, the head of the special office of the first section of the general staff, which oversaw military intelligence and counterintelligence, and asked to be taken on. Monkevits curtly refused, claiming later (and that "later" deserves special emphasis) that his reasons had been his low estimation of Miasoedov's moral character and his hunch that the gendarme was a person capable of "filthy deeds."[31]

25. Letter of Miasoedov to Sukhomlinov, June 16, 1912, RGVIA, f. 962, op. 2, d. 66, l. 23; Miasoedov service record, 1912, RGVIA, f. 801, op. 28, d. 164, l. 258.

26. Charles Ruud and Sergei Stepanov, *Fontanka, 16. Politicheskii sysk pri tsariakh* (Moscow, 1993), p. 234.

27. See the testimony of S. P. Beletskii, himself subsequently director of the police department. *Padenie tsarskago rezhima*, vol. 4 (Leningrad, 1925), p. 516.

28. RGVIA, f. 962, op. 1, d. 43, l. 140.

29. Letter of Miasoedov to Sukhomlinov, n.d., RGVIA, f. 962, op. 2, d. 51, l. 73.

30. Alekseev, *Voennaia razvedka*, vol. 2, pp. 49–51.

31. Petrov Commission report, RGVIA, f. 962, op. 2, d. 164, ll. 208–209.

68   Soon after this rebuff, Miasoedov turned up at the general staff building again, this time asking for Lieutenant Colonel V. A. Erandakov. Erandakov, another gendarme officer on loan to the Ministry of War, was Monkevits's chief of counterintelligence. Miasoedov explained that Sukhomlinov found it desirable to have direct and unfiltered access to the counterintelligence information collected by Erandakov's office. It was Sukhomlinov's desire that Erandakov furnish these raw data to Miasoedov, who would make a digest for regular oral reports to the minister of war. Erandakov indignantly refused: without a written order from Sukhomlinov, he said, he would do nothing of the kind. A day or so later, Miasoedov returned with a *precis verbale* of a conversation between himself and Sukhomlinov, which laid out the procedure exactly as Miasoedov had originally described it. However, this document, which was dated February 8, 1912, bore Miasoedov's signature alone.[32] Erandakov showed Miasoedov's paper to Zhilinskii, the chief of the general staff, who told him to disregard it.

The third time Miasoedov visited Erandakov it was to summon him to a confidential face-to-face meeting with the minister of war. According to Miasoedov, it was Sukhomlinov's express order that Erandakov's superiors were to be kept in the dark about this. Between 8:00 and 9:00 p.m. on the appointed day, Miasoedov and Erandakov took an official car over to Sukhomlinov's palace. Once they had arrived and had been ushered in to war minister's private study, Sukhomlinov commanded Erandakov to do what Miasoedov had originally told him to. Further, there would never be any formal or official acknowledgment of Miasoedov's mission. There would be no paper trail of any kind; Erandakov would receive his orders exclusively by telephone or in person. Finally, Erandakov was forbidden to divulge any details of the operation to higher-ups in the chain of command at the general staff.[33]

Miasoedov thus did get into the counterintelligence business, but through the back door and in a highly irregular way. The materials supplied by Erandakov served as the basis for briefings that Miasoedov delivered to Sukhomlinov several times a week. In general, the information on which Miasoedov reported concerned the activities of persons suspected of espionage on behalf of foreign powers. It consisted of denunciations, sometimes signed, but more often anonymous. Surveillance reports were also included, as were photographs and copies of perlustrated letters prepared in the bureau of foreign censorship. In time, Erandakov himself took part, preparing counterespionage summaries of his own for the war minister's use.

What did Sukhomlinov possibly hope to gain by organizing this weird project? Although ironclad evidence is lacking, a number of explanations suggest themselves. First, there is the possibility that Sukhomlinov was seriously concerned about the security and reliability of the counterintelligence office. By employing Miasoedov as his informal agent, the war minister might be able to draw his own independent conclu-

32. Ibid., l. 213.

33. V. A. Erandakov testimony, May 5, 1916, RGVIA, f. 962, op. 2, d. 47, ll. 249–251; RGVIA, f. 962, op. 2, d. 145, ll. 58–59.

sions about the gravity and extent of foreign espionage within Russia as well as the accuracy of the general staff's assessment of it. Because of the trauma of the Manchurian war (in which Japanese agents had repeatedly compromised Russian security) and also because of the ongoing international instability, there was indeed a great deal of inchoate anxiety within the Russian army about foreign espionage. Sometimes this assumed extreme forms. At about the same time that Miasoedov was settling into his new war ministry post, General Staff Chief Ia. G. Zhilinskii called Erandakov in to inform him that he had received an anonymous tip that Colonel Monkevits was himself a traitor. But regardless of Monkevits's official position, Zhilinskii insisted that he be placed under observation. Erandakov, who was embarrassed by the idea of spying on his boss, nevertheless obeyed Zhilinskii by handing the task over to the St. Petersburg Okhrana.[34] It is worth noting that Sukhomlinov himself had doubts about Monkevits's loyalty and discussed his apprehensions with none other than Miasoedov.[35]

As this example illustrates, any accusation, regardless of its source or credibility, was sufficient to put the machinery of military counterespionage into motion. This meant that Erandakov's office possessed vast quantities of data about hundreds, if not thousands, of totally innocent people, some of whom were doubtless Sukhomlinov's personal enemies. Even if surveillance reports turned up no proof of treason, there was certain to be information about their sexual habits, vices, and financial status. Still further, since *all* personal letters written by *every* tsarist minister, governor-general, governor, Duma member, senator, and army general were subject to perlustration; since thousands of such letters were read, and in many cases copied by the police; and since these copies usually fell into the hands of counterintelligence, CI possessed a treasure trove of data about the attitudes, opinions and innermost thoughts of the highest echelon of the Russian elite.[36] This, then, is another reason Sukhomlinov may have wanted Miasoedov to be his eyes and ears in counterespionage: he understood that knowledge of this kind could be a source of power, particularly valuable in the conduct of the intrigues that were the very fabric of political life in the Russian autocracy. That this was indeed one of Sukhomlinov's motivations is substantiated by Erandakov's recollection that Sukhomlinov was particularly interested in getting the lowdown about high war ministry officials and about persons whom he believed to be personally ill disposed to him.[37]

A third motive, however, might have been purely defensive. Clearly, Erandakov's files included information about people close to Sukhomlinov and even about Sukhomlinov himself. If Sukhomlinov wanted to avert unpleasant surprises, if he wanted to prevent his enemies from using such information against him, he had to be apprised of it in advance. In that event he might either suppress it or, if a leak occurred, take steps in advance to minimize the damage.

34. Erandakov testimony, May 5, 1916, RGVIA, f. 962, op. 2, d. 47, l. 249.

35. Miasoedov letter to Sukhomlinov, June 16, 1912, RGVIA, f. 962, op. 2, d. 66, l. 24.

36. Mikhail Alekseev, *Voennaia razvedka Rossii ot Riurika do Nikolaia II*, vol. 1 (Moscow, 1998), p. 126.

37. *Padenie tsarskago rezhima*, vol. 4 (Leningrad, 1925), p. 519.

70   If Sukhomlinov therefore discerned numerous advantages in opening a secret channel to the counterintelligence service, why did he trust Miasoedov to be the middleman? The answer is a simple one. Like his contemporaries, Sukhomlinov instinctively understood something about late imperial politics that many historians have overlooked: kinship and personal relationships were often much more important than official or professional ones. One reason for this was the structure of the imperial government itself, which was guaranteed to produce enmity both laterally (among the ministries), and vertically (within the ministries). The conflicting institutional interests of the ministers meant that groups of them would always be at odds, regardless of who was in office. Thus the minister of finance, whose duty was to hold down government expenditures, was the inevitable antagonist of the minister of war, who was obliged to demand high outlays from the treasury to stockpile large quantities of modern arms.[38] Likewise, the Ministry of Trade and Industry, which was committed to the country's economic development, generally supported the interests of factory owners, while the Ministry of the Interior, concerned as it was with public tranquillity, often tilted in favor of factory workers for whom, on one occasion, it actually organized its own union.

It was the permanent hostility among the ministries that accounted for the bizarre status within the upper echelons of the Russian bureaucracy enjoyed by Prince M. M. Andronnikov, who later played a sinister role in the Miasoedov affair. Described by a contemporary as a "scented person of servile behavior and dyed facial hair," Andronnikov was a journalist, swindler, and pederast whose only official position was a minor sinecure at the Holy Synod.[39] Yet the prince was received everywhere and by everybody. The explanation for the unsavory prince's astonishing access to Russian men of state was really quite straightforward: the web of contacts he had spun throughout Petersburg was so extensive that he was uniquely positioned to tell a minister what his rivals were actually up to. The fact that Andronnikov was also a purveyor of gossip and unreliable slander did not detract from the value of the solid news he also had to impart.[40]

If the rifts among the ministries not only made possible but also even necessitated the activities of someone like an Andronnikov, divisions within the ministries were equally significant and pregnant with consequences. Just as was true in the Russian army, within every ministry there existed numerous patronage networks. Whether based on common school attendance, provincial service, kinship ties, or

38. David MacLaren McDonald, *United Government and Foreign Policy in Russia 1900–1914* (Cambridge, 1992), p. 177.

39. Anna Vyrubova, quoted in Edward Radzinsky, *The Rasputin File,* trans. Judson Rosengrant (New York, 2000), p. 335. According to police informants, Andronnikov led an "open life" and was noted for receiving guests from all levels of society at all times of the day and night. Among his guests were tsarist officials, junkers, cadets, enlisted soldiers, and high school boys. See Petrov Commission report, 1916, RGVIA, f. 280, op. 2, d. 164, l. 112.

40. See A. F. Rediger memoir, RGVIA, f. 280, op. 1, d. 8, p. 918; Ekaterina Sukhomlinova interrogation, November 21, 1916, RGVIA, f. 962, op. 2, d. 136, l. 51; A. Polivanov, *Iz dnevnikov i vospominanii po dolzhnosti voennago ministra i ego pomoshchika 1907–1916 gg.,* vol. 1 (Moscow, 1924), p. 77.

M. M. Andronnikov

simple election, these networks shared identical objectives: the maintenance and expansion of their own power. This was accomplished by advancing the interests of all its members collectively. If the leader of a particular group was promoted, its members could anticipate rising with him. But equally, were he to fall in rank or lose his post, his adherents would suffer demotions and firings as well, when his successor replaced them with men from his own network. Thus, in addition to the official place he occupied in the ministerial hierarchy, the typical bureaucrat also filled a specific position in the subterranean hierarchy of his patronage group. This system meant that there was a perpetual war among the factions within every ministry, for the satisfaction of any official's personal ambition depended completely on the discomfiture and disgrace of networks antagonistic to his own. Every tsarist minister consequently appreciated that the organization he headed was filled with people whose fondest wish was to see him removed and who were all too eager to realize their dream by engaging in intrigue. The apparent paranoia detectable in the behavior of many high officials in the late imperial period was really a comprehensible adaptive response to the environment in which they worked. Sukhomlinov had been wise, then, in the first months of his ministry to distrust Chief of Staff Myshlaevskii; as we will see shortly, he was on even firmer ground when he began to question the fidelity of the deputy he had inherited from Rediger, General A. A. Polivanov.

This is where Miasoedov came in. Because Sergei Nikolaevich occupied an unusual position, being simultaneously of the war ministry and exterior to its hierarchies, both official and unofficial, he had nothing to gain by betraying his patron Sukhomlinov. For his maneuver against counterintelligence to succeed, the war minister needed a man of unswerving loyalty and unshakable discretion. As Sukhomlinov's protégé, as an officer who owed the resumption of his government career *solely* to Sukhomlinov's intercession, Miasoedov exactly matched this profile. Indeed, it is possible that Miasoedov's responsibilities may have extended beyond the field of counterintelligence into intelligence collection itself. One tantalizing bit of evidence on this score dates from 1912. In late February of that year German police in Eydtkuhnen arrested the head of the Verzhbolovo railway postal office, Robert Falk, a man who perhaps not coincidentally was also one of Miasoedov's closest associates in

72 the Northwest Russian Steamship Company. The charge was espionage. Although the Russian government was able to secure Falk's release after only twenty-one days in custody, it is by no means unlikely that he had actually been guilty. Given what we know of Miasoedov's predilection in Verzhbolovo for employing his business acquaintances on spying missions, it is tempting to infer that Sergei Nikolaevich was still planning and occasionally directing occasional operations for the Russian General Staff.[41]

In any event, it is now obvious why Sukhomlinov never would (or could) admit what the colonel of gendarmes really did during his tenure at the war ministry. To confess that he had initiated an executed "traitor" into most restricted secrets of military counterintelligence would have been a revelation so damning that it could not possibly have been explained away. Writing in emigration, Sukhomlinov observed that the chief of the general staff had refuted the charge that Miasoedov had ever been associated with counterespionage; what conveniently went unmentioned, of course, was the fact that Zhilinskii's ignorance about this subject was the result of Sukhomlinov's own machinations.[42]

Sukhomlinov at the Ministry of War

If there was much going on behind the scenes during Sukhomlinov's first years at the Ministry of War, there was also a large amount of important business that was conducted in the limelight of stage center. Sukhomlinov's elevation to ministerial rank in March 1909 had been greeted with considerable approbation in the army, particularly in the upper tiers of military leadership. According to A. F. Rediger, Sukhomlinov owed his initial popularity to his association with Dragomirov, to the St. George's Cross that he had won for valor against the Turks, and to his reputation as a combat general more comfortable in the field than in the chancellery. In conservative military circles it was hoped that he would check or even reverse some of Rediger's more unpalatable innovations.[43] Sukhomlinov met these expectations to some extent; he did in fact water down the new system of regimental purchasing that Rediger had believed would promote honesty and efficiency but against which many of the most senior colonels in the army bridled, perhaps for this very reason. Yet although willing to make some concessions to army traditionalists (he was the author of the "Ostap Bondarenko" essays, after all), Sukhomlinov was no reactionary. He was, on the contrary, firmly committed to the cause of military reform. His accession to power had coincided with the sorry denouement of the 1908–9 Eastern crisis, in which Germany and Austria-Hungary had banded together to humiliate a militarily weak Russia by forcing her to swallow Vienna's annexation of Bosnia and Herzegovina. This episode illustrated how far the Russian army still had to go to recover from its Manchurian disaster. It also demonstrated to a Russian military elite still

41. See A. S. Rezanov, *Nemetskoe shpionstvo* (Petrograd, 1915), pp. 279–280.
42. V. A. Sukhomlinov, *Vospominaniia Sukhomlinova* (Moscow/Leningrad, 1926), pp. 317–318.
43. A. F. Rediger memoir, RGVIA, f. 280, op. 1, d. 8, p. 931.

worried about the potential renewal of hostilities with Japan that the danger of a general European war was becoming ever more real.[44] Sukhomlinov was determined to prepare the army for either of these eventualities to the best of his ability. As minister, he consequently presided over the introduction of a large program of reforms.[45] Broadly speaking, these reforms fell into three categories: manpower, strategy, and technology.

With regard to manpower, Sukhomlinov's most significant accomplishment was his thorough overhaul of the reserve system. Formerly, in the event of war, reservists called to the colors were either fed into preexisting units to swell their numbers or placed in special support or auxiliary formations in the rear. In Sukhomlinov's entirely justified opinion, this approach was counterproductive, for it ensured that reservists would be vastly inferior in training to army regulars, even as it deprived field generals of the additional troops that might tilt the scales of victory in the opening phase of any war. Sukhomlinov consequently disbanded the old territorial and fortress garrison reserve units and substituted a system of "hidden cadres." In the event of war, the officers and men of the hidden cadres would be detached from their units to form the nuclei of an additional 560 infantry battalions, which would be fleshed out by drafts of reserves.[46] Along with the reduction in the terms of active duty for draftees enacted in 1906 (which eventually produced a 25 percent increase in the pool of trained men available in a crisis), Sukhomlinov's reform resulted in the optimal exploitation of reserve manpower. When European war broke out in August 1914, almost a third of the infantry formations that Russia initially mobilized were the product of his hidden cadre system. If this system did not lead Russia to win the war in its first six months, it arguably at least prevented Russian defeat in the same period.

A second set of reforms concerned strategy. Ever since the Franco-Prussian War of 1870–71 had made the newly created German Empire Russia's most formidable potential enemy, the Russian Ministry of War had fretted about the problem of countering Germany's superior mobilization speed. Owing to the density of the German railway net, Berlin could call up its reserves and transport them to the frontier much more rapidly than could Petersburg. The Russian military leadership's solution was to compensate by deploying an ever-greater proportion of Russia's peacetime forces in the westernmost territories of the country. By 1893, 610,000 soldiers—almost 45 percent of the army—were stationed in Kiev, Vilna, and Warsaw Military Districts.[47] The idea here was that this dense concentration of troops, as well as the heavily defended fortresses of Osovets, Kovno, Grodno, Warsaw, Ivangorod, and Novoge-

---

44. William C. Fuller, Jr., *Strategy and Power in Russia 1600–1914* (New York, 1992), pp. 418–423.

45. The intellectual foundation for this reform program was the massive report on the empire's defense needs of August 1908 that had been prepared by his predecessor as chief of staff, F. F. Palitsyn, and the latter's talented assistant M. V. Alekseev. See K. F. Shatsillo, *Ot portsmutskogo mira k pervoi mirovoi voine. Generaly i politika* (Moscow, 2000), pp. 131–134.

46. Bruce Menning, *Bayonets before Bullets: The Imperial Russian Army 1861–1914* (Bloomington, 1992), pp. 226–227; L. G. Beskrovnyi, *Russkaia armiia i flot v nachale xix veka. Ocherki voenno-ekomonicheskogo potentsiala* (Moscow, 1986), pp. 13–14.

47. Fuller, *Strategy and Power*, pp. 341–343.

74 orgievsk, would make it impossible for Germany to crush Russia decisively with early attacks before Russia's own mobilization could be completed. In 1910 Sukhomlinov's defense reorganization plan revised this time-honored approach to the empire's defense by transferring 128 battalions of infantry from Kiev and Vilna districts into the interior of the country. There were several advantages to this redeployment. Since the units affected were moved into the densely populated regions that supplied them with the reserves they needed to reach wartime strength, Russia could mobilize faster than ever before. At the same time, by shifting the center of gravity of the army to the east, Sukhomlinov enhanced the empire's strategic flexibility, its ability to respond to military emergencies in either Asia or Europe. Sukhomlinov's proposal to demolish the western fortresses complemented his reorganization plan. Because the army would now mobilize farther east, the fortresses' protective role in the initial phase of a European war would be redundant. Moreover, Sukhomlinov argued that improved long-range artillery had made the fortresses obsolete in any case; the cost of maintaining them, let alone upgrading them to withstand the firepower of modern ordnance, would run to hundreds of millions of rubles—sums that would be better expended on the needs of the field army.[48]

This plan was enormously controversial at the time. As we shall see shortly, it stirred up considerable domestic opposition. But it also caused a public outcry in France, where it did not go unnoticed that the reorganization reduced the speed with which Russia could mount the offensive against Germany on which Paris counted in the event of general war in Europe. France's former minister of foreign affairs, Theophile Delcassé, spoke openly of the "imbecilities that are being committed by the [Russian] Minister of War."[49] Sukhomlinov was alarmed enough by the firestorm of criticism to send Prince Andronnikov on a confidential mission to France to reassure opinion makers. Eventually the French were mollified, but only after they realized that the Germans and Austrians were seriously worried about the extent to which the 1910 reforms would augment Russian offensive power.[50]

The third target of Sukhomlinov's reform program was military technology. The Russo-Japanese War had drawn down the Russian army's stockpiles of weapons and munitions, and these had to be replenished as soon as possible. Indeed, the war had demonstrated that the peacetime targets of cartridges per rifle and shells per artillery tube had to be substantially increased. The land war in Manchuria had also proved the value of other armaments, such as machine guns and mountain artillery, which had previously been underestimated. During Sukhomlinov's first twelve months in office, his ministry adopted two new heavy howitzers for standard use and made its first large orders for the 1909 mountain gun, which was significantly lighter, and consequently superior, to earlier models. The number of machine guns in the army's arsenal, approximately one thousand on the eve of the Russo-Japanese war, had

48. On this subject see ibid., pp. 427–432; Menning, *Bayonets before Bullets*, pp. 223–227.

49. *Padenie tsarskago rezhima*, vol. 2 (Leningrad, 1924), p. 23.

50. David G. Herrmann, *The Arming of Europe and the Making of the First World War* (Princeton, 1996), pp. 132–136.

climbed to over four thousand by 1914, although this figure still fell almost 17 percent short of the statutory norm. Sukhomlinov was also sufficiently imaginative to foresee the military utility of motorized vehicles and aircraft. It was under him that the Russian army acquired its first airplanes. He also fought, albeit without much success, to enlarge the army's park of trucks and automobiles.[51] In the years before the outbreak of the world war, Sukhomlinov developed and pushed through four discrete rearmament programs—one in 1910, two in 1913, and yet another in 1914.[52]

As might have been expected, these initiatives were very costly. Taken together, the four rearmament plans projected spending an additional billion rubles above ordinary expenditures to meet the needs of Russia's land forces alone over a ten-year period. Russia's budget consequently rose steeply. By 1914 Russia was devoting 965 million rubles to the army and the navy, a sum almost 33 percent higher than 643 million she had disbursed in 1909 when Sukhomlinov took office.[53] The extraordinary growth in military spending was decisive in pulling Russian industry out of recession in 1910, and was one of the engines that drove Russia's economic boom in the last prewar years.[54] Throughout the empire, industrialists, financiers, and engineers schemed to secure their share of the defense-spending bonanza. Among those who had definite ideas on this score was Sukhomlinov's old friend from Kiev, Alexander Altschüller.

Altschüller and His Circle

In 1910, Altschüller's wife had died in Kiev after a lengthy illness. Claiming that he needed a change of scene, in the spring of that year he moved from Kiev to Petersburg. Although he continued to make several extensive trips abroad, and although he spent at least two months a year in Ukraine, the Russian capital was now his permanent base of operations; his son Oscar looked after his affairs in Kiev. Altschüller took a suite at number 12, Gogol Street, and furnished one of its six rooms as the new office of the South Russian Machine Works. He soon established himself comfortably in his new surroundings and assuaged his bereavement through an amour with a French cabaret singer called "Lucette," whom he eventually married.

Altschüller's social life in Petersburg increasingly came to revolve around the Sukhomlinovs, with whom he typically dined once a week. Sukhomlinov apparently looked on Altschüller as a virtual member of the family and addressed him either as "Papa" or by the affectionate diminutive "Sashechka."[55] Altschüller cemented his bonds to Ekaterina Viktorovna with numerous gifts, and he enjoyed the complete

51. On Sukhomlinov's particular interest in the automobile see *Padenie tsarskago rezhima*, vol. 6 (Moscow/Leningrad, 1926), pp. 192–193.

52. Beskrovnyi, *Russkaia armiia i flot*, pp. 80–82, 87–91; Peter Gatrell, *Government, Industry and Rearmament in Russia, 1900–1914: The Last Argument of Tsarism* (Cambridge, 1994), pp. 132–134.

53. William C. Fuller, Jr., *Civil-Military Conflict in Imperial Russia 1881–1914* (Princeton, 1985), p. 227.

54. Gatrell, *Government, Industry and Rearmament*, pp. 155–156.

55. M. I. Kolomnina testimony, January 1917, RGVIA, f. 962, op. 2, d. 137, l. 26.

76 run of the Sukhomlinovs' home.[56] Berezovskii later testified that on one peculiar occasion he telephoned Sukhomlinov's private office number only to have the phone answered by Altschüller, who obstinately pretended to be the minister of war, and who abandoned the crude hoax only when Berezovskii exploded in rage. Sukhomlinov was somewhat defensive but all the same unrepentant about his relationship with Altschüller, whom he defended to Berezovskii as a "dear and very fine person."[57] In 1911, General N. N. Ianushkevich, head of the war ministry chancellery, encountered Altschüller for the first time coming out of Sukhomlinov's home office. Ianushkevich was stunned into silence at hearing Altschüller address the war minister in the second personal singular (*ty*), which in Russian, as in other continental languages, connotes extreme closeness and familiarity. When the chief of staff asked Sukhomlinov who this extraordinary, Jewish-looking individual was, the later explained that Altschüller was an old and close friend from his Kiev days and added that "some very decent people are found among the Jews"—an opinion that flabbergasted Ianushkevich, one of Russia's most fanatic anti-Semites.[58]

What were Altschüller's true reasons for settling in Petersburg? One of these may have been a concern for his personal safety. In 1909 a self-styled "patriot"—most likely a business competitor—had denounced Altschüller to the Kiev Okhrana as an Austrian spy. Although intensive surveillance turned up nothing incriminating, Altschüller, who eventually learned what had happened, may have realized that it could eventually prove dangerous for him to remain in Kiev now that his old friend and protector had moved on to higher office in the capital.[59]

But there can be little doubt that avarice, as much as if not more than fear, lay behind Altschüller's move, for he was bent on twisting his relationship with the Sukhomlinovs to his own pecuniary advantage. The Kiev attorney V.-N. Z. Finn, who at one time occupied a seat on the board of the South Russian Machine Works, commented that Altschüller saw his friendship with the war minister as an easy road to greater wealth, since he "could, for example, receive enormous commissions from the purchase of lands for war ministry proving grounds, and from the sale to the war ministry of unnecessary materials, and could also earn large honoraria for petitioning [the minister] on behalf of various persons."[60] Evidence substantiates Altschüller's involvement in swindles of exactly the kind identified by Finn. Altschüller sold his goodwill to people seeking pensions and compensation from the Ministry of War, while at the same time using his inside knowledge to "mediate" between the ministry and potential contractors and vendors, sometimes working in partnership with Prince M. M. Andronnikov.[61]

56. Ekaterina Sukhomlinova testimony, November 16, 1916, RGVIA, f. 962, op. 2, d. 52, l. 69; Ekaterina Sukhomlinova statement, November 21, 1916, RGVIA, f. 962, op. 2, d. 48, l. 124; RGVIA, f. 962, op. 2, d. 136, l. 45.

57. RGVIA, f. 962, op. 2, d. 55, l. 2.

58. N. N. Ianushkevich deposition, September 14, 1916, RGVIA, f. 962, op. 2, d. 134, ll. 156–157.

59. RGVIA, f. 801, op. 28., d. 164, l. 108.

60. V.-N. Z. Finn statement, n.d., RGVIA, f. 962, op. 2, d. 136, ll. 37–38.

61. See, for example, *Padenie tsarskago rezhima*, vol. 6, p. 64; RGVIA, f. 962, op. 2, d. 134, l. 23; A. I. Guchkov and N. A. Bazili, *Aleksandr Ivanovich Guchkov rasskazyvaet* (Moscow, 1994), p. 96.

The Gogol Street apartment was Altschüller's headquarters for all his business dealings, both legitimate and illegitimate. Even after he took over South Russia's Petersburg ventures himself, he kept Nikolai Goshkevich on the company payroll. Goshkevich was a person who had had serious difficulty finding his niche in life. Altschüller's offer to hire Goshkevich in 1909 had therefore been a very attractive one. His base salary from the South Russian Machine Works was 400 rubles a month, a considerable improvement over the pathetic stipend he had received as a petty clerk at the Ministry of Trade. In addition, Goshkevich had the possibility of earning commissions from the firm, which obligingly agreed to defray the cost of his flat. In order to throw still more income Goshkevich's way, Altschüller introduced him to Maksim Il'ich Veller in the fall of 1909.

Although a Russian subject, Veller had attended the University of Berlin to evade the tsarist government's anti-Jewish higher education quotas. In the mid 1880s he had briefly been an employee of the Russian Foreign Ministry, a career that ended abruptly in 1888, when as secretary to Russia's naval attaché in Germany he was arrested and held for six weeks by German authorities on suspicion of espionage. This melancholy experience appears to have purged him of any desire to continue in state service; henceforth he devoted himself to business. In 1907 he relocated to Petersburg, where he opened an import/export office.

Initially, Veller's interest in Goshkevich was explained by his closeness to the people around Sukhomlinov and to Sukhomlinov himself. He candidly explained to Goshkevich that he wanted to be introduced into this milieu both because he hoped to steer lucrative military orders to some of the domestic and foreign factories he represented and because he dreamed of one day becoming the contractor-in-chief for the entire Ministry of War.[62] He promised Goshkevich large cash payments if he could help him in either of these matters, in addition to 50 percent of the profits on any orders he was instrumental in arranging. As a token of good faith, he also put the engineer on retainer as a consultant to his firm.[63]

Goshkevich lost no time in exerting himself on Veller's behalf. He introduced Veller to A. I. Zotimov, Sukhomlinov's private secretary, at a dinner he arranged at the "Contant," a deluxe Petersburg restaurant. He also acquainted Veller with Staff-Captain V. G. Ivanov, a ballistics expert who had been given a desk job in the procurement office of the Main Administration of Artillery after having been severely maimed by an explosion while testing fuses. Ivanov, who occupied an apartment in the same building as Goshkevich, was as eager to be corrupted by Veller as Goshkevich had been, and was completely willing to assist Veller in negotiations with the Ministry of War—for an appropriate price, of course.

But Veller's interest in the Goshkeviches soon transcended the realm of mere rubles and kopecks. In September 1909 Nikolai brought Veller home to meet his wife. Veller found Anna Andreevna so seductive and desirable that he immediately vowed

---

62. Petrov Commission report, 1916, RGVIA, f. 962, op. 2, d. 164, l. 152.

63. Anna Goshkevich testimony, July 9, 1915, RGVIA, f. 962, op. 2, d. 51, l. 236; Nikolai Goshkevich testimony, July 23–25, 1916, RGVIA, f. 962, op. 2, d. 134, l. 46.

78 to win her for himself. Apparently Anna soon came to reciprocate his illicit passion: within two months she had become Veller's mistress.

Nikolai Goshkevich clearly knew what was going on, and whether or not he condoned his wife's affair, he certainly did not object to it. Veller, whose annual income exceeded 100,000 rubles, began to make frequent "loans" to Anna Andreevna. These payments, which amounted to at least 12,000 rubles a year, went directly into the Goshkevich budget, producing a dramatic improvement in the Goshkeviches' standard of living.[64] In June 1910 Veller not only rented a dacha for the Goshkeviches on Petersburg's fashionable Kamennyi Ostrov but actually moved in with the couple for the entire summer. That December he advanced Anna 1,500 rubles to cover the first six months' lease on an opulent apartment in Nikolaevsk Street, which she furnished lavishly, also at Veller's expense. When Anna came into a small inheritance at about this time, it was again Veller who advised her on investing it and who bought her a portfolio of interest-bearing bonds. Anna and Veller became so brazen about their relationship that they openly traveled abroad on vacation together.[65]

The fact that Veller was sleeping with his wife did not temper the zeal with which Nikolai Goshkevich continued to promote his patron's interests. On one of Petersburg's pleasant "white nights" in 1910, the Sukhomlinovs attended a crayfish supper at the Goshkeviches' dacha. It was at this feast that Veller finally attained his goal of a face-to-face meeting with Sukhomlinov. Owing to the intercession of Staff-Captain Ivanov (and perhaps that of Sukhomlinov as well), the firms Veller represented began to do better in the competition for war ministry contracts. When the ministry awarded orders for two-wheeled carts and saddles to one of these companies in 1910, Veller immediately pressed 4,000 rubles on Goshkevich.[66] The Goshkeviches' sudden prosperity raised some eyebrows at the Ministry of War, where the rumor circulated that the formerly insolvent engineer was now spending on the order of 50,000 rubles a year. Sukhomlinov's adjutants, in particular, suspected Goshkevich of abusing his family ties to Ekaterina Viktorovna to enrich himself.[67]

Miasoedov, Sukhomlinov, and Their Enemies

Thus it was that Altschüller, Goshkevich, and Veller, no less than Miasoeodov, all profited from their relationship with Sukhomlinov. As it transpired, however Sergei Nikolaevich was not to have much of a future in the war ministry, despite Sukhomlinov's favor and protection. To comprehend the train of events in the winter and spring of 1912 that led to his downfall, we must pause and take the measure of his enemies and those of his benefactor, the minister.

---

64. M. I. Veller testimony, August 9, 1916, RGVIA, f. 962, op. 2, d. 134, l. 113; Anna Goshkevich testimony, July 26, 1915, RGVIA, f. 962, op. 2, d. 51, l. 242.

65. RGVIA, f. 962, op. 2, d. 164, l. 133; Veller testimony, August 9, 1916, RGVIA, f. 962, op. 2, d. 134, ll. 113–114.

66. Goshkevich testimony, July 23–25, 1916, RGVIA, f. 962, op. 2, d. 134, ll. 47–48.

67. Petrov Commission report, 1916, RGVIA, f. 962, op. 2, d. 164, l. 133.

To begin with, there were those whose hostility to Miasoedov stemmed from his support of the Freidbergs' emigration and steamship business—most notably, the Russian East Asiatic Steamship Company. On the eve of Miasoedov's appointment to the war ministry, Russian East Asiatic orchestrated another round of harassment against the Freidbergs. Highly negative articles about them appeared in the local press. Although Boris Freidberg was able to put a halt to this negative publicity by paying off a venal journalist, he was less lucky in countering Russian East Asiatic's manipulation of government officials.[68]

Libau police chief Podushkin, who, as already noted, had been heavily bribed by Russian East Asiatic, authored reports accusing the Northwest Steamship Company of unsound practices and fraud. The most serious charge he lodged against Northwest was that it was a fictitious company; he asserted that the real operators of the steamship service were Danes, who were using Northwest as a cover to gain privileges not extended to foreign concerns by Russian law. Miasoedov had to refute these slurs in a letter to the governor of Kurland province. Although he did not succeed in having Podushkin reprimanded, he did manage to relieve the pressure on his business associates, albeit temporarily.[69]

Miasoedov also remained in the black books of the Ministry of the Interior, and especially its Department of Police. The latter organization had still not forgiven Miasoedov for the Vilna debacle of 1907. Sergei Nikolaevich had particular reason to dread Colonel A. M. Eremin, a former Cossack officer who in 1910 had been promoted to head of the Department's Special (or Political) Section. Regarded even by his admirers as a cold and saturnine personality, Eremin numbered among his few good friends none other than Colonel Podushkin. As if that were not bad enough, Miasoedov had reason to believe that Eremin coveted his billet as officer for special assignments at the war ministry.[70] In fact, when Eremin had first learned of Miasoedov's appointment in October 1911, he had immediately penned a memorandum for file about the latter's unfitness for sensitive duties.[71]

But Sergei Nikolaevich's appointment to the war ministry made him new enemies at the same time as it roused his old foes. Sukhomlinov's senior adjutant, Staff-Captain Lev Bulatsel', disliked Miasoedov personally and resented the way in which the gendarme colonel had supplanted him in the minister's affections. Arguing that Sukhomlinov "easily fell under the influence of suspicious persons, for whom he had some sort of weakness," Bulatsel' took it upon himself to preserve his boss from the consequences of his misjudgments by driving Miasoeodov out of the war ministry at the earliest opportunity.[72] Another of Sukhomlinov's officer adjutants, Lieutenant

---

68. RGVIA, f. 962, op. 2, d. 167, l. 24.

69. Report to governor of Kurland, September 12, 1911, RGVIA, f. 962, op. 2, d. 101, ll. 7–12.

70. On Eremin see A. P. Martynov, *Moia sluzhba v Otdel'nom Korpuse Zhandarmov. Vospominaniia*, ed. Richard Wraga (Stanford, 1972), pp. 160, 334; Miasoedov to Kokovtsov, June 5, 1912, RGVIA, f. 962, op. 2, d. 66, l. 20; note by Miasoedov, September 1911, RGVIA, f. 962, op. 2, d. 101, l. 15.

71. General staff memorandum, RGVIA, f. 2000, op. 1, d. 8230, ll. 8–9.

72. Ministry of Justice letter to Petrov Commission, August 1915, RGVIA, f.962, op. 2, d. 43, l. 158.

80   Colonel V. S. Botkin, also soon came to hate and envy Miasoedov. That Botkin, a habitual drunkard, had any job at all was due to the position occupied by his brother, the celebrated E. S. Botkin, personal physician to the imperial family.[73] As already noted, Bulatsel' and Botkin had telegraphed their feelings about Miasoedov when they rudely avoided his New Year's Eve party at the very end of 1911.[74] Lieutenant Kolomnin, a former war ministry adjutant who had had to retire when his syphilis reached its tertiary stage, also joined Bulatsel' and Botkin in the alliance against Miasoedov. Although one might think that an alcoholic like Botkin and a venereal patient like Kolomnin were hardly in a position to do Miasoedov much harm, the reverse was actually the case. The two men were dangerous because of their connections: N. I. Guchkov, mayor of Moscow and brother of Russia's leading Octobrist politician, was married to a Botkin; Kolomnin was the grandson of A. S. Suvorin, founder of Russia's most widely read daily newspaper, *Novoe Vremia* (*New Times*).

    As for Sukhomlinov's enemies, they were legion. First there were the other ministers, who were virtually unanimous in their jealousy of Vladimir Aleksandrovich's special rapport with the tsar. In Russia's autocratic political system, power depended on controlling, even if only temporarily, the way in which the emperor saw the world. Sukhomlinov's great skill at doing this derived from his understanding of the essential solipsism at the heart of autocracy: what the emperor believed to be true, or could be induced to believe was true, was by definition true. But Sukhomlinov's influence with Nicholas II also derived from an astute insight into the tsar's character. Recognizing that Nicholas took small pleasure in ruling the empire and saw his crown as a burden to be born out of resignation to duty, Sukhomlinov divined that the best way to win over his sovereign was to make sure he was constantly amused. By keeping the imperial ennui at bay, Sukhomlinov earned Nicholas's gratitude and conspicuously distinguished himself from the other ministers of state. He consequently festooned his reports with anecdotes, witticisms, and surprise twists. As a result, according to the head of the court chancellery, Sukhomlinov held the tsar "in suspense right up to the last minute, even if his audience lasted a couple of hours."[75] Vladimir Aleksandrovich's colleagues were naturally offended by his aptitude for getting the emperor to do as he wished, for they knew that the more resources Nicholas was persuaded to assign to the Ministry of War, the less would remain for all of them. Although all the ministers therefore resented Sukhomlinov to some degree, two of them—Kokovtsov and Makarov—bore the war minister particular ill will.

    After the assassination of Stolypin, Minister of Finance V. N. Kokovtsov assumed the chairmanship of the Council of Ministers, thus becoming de facto head of the Russian government. As previously noted, the very structure of the Russian ministerial system would have made Kokovtsov antagonistic to any minister of war. But the

---

73. Guchkov and Bazili, *Guchkov rasskazyvaet*, p. 93.

74. Petrov Commission report, 1916, RGVIA, f. 962, op. 2, d. 164, l. 190.

75. A. A. Mossolov, *At the Court of the Last Tsar*, ed. A. A. Pilenco; trans. E. W. Dickes (London, 1935), p. 234.

relationship of Kokovtsov and Sukhomlinov was complicated by deep personal antipathy. Certainly the two men could not have been more unlike in personality, for
they had nothing in common but egotism. Whereas Sukhomlinov was flamboyant,
openhanded, and perennially disorganized, Kokovtsov was inhibited, thin-skinned,
and a meticulous stickler for detail.[76] Kokovtsov was decidedly of the view that Russia's interests would best be served by evicting Sukhomlinov from his post, for he
feared that the war minister was reinforcing the emperor's authoritarian impulses. At
the same time, he believed that Sukhomlinov was careless, lazy, and superficial.
"Complete chaos," Kokovtsov sourly opined, held sway in Sukhomlinov's department.[77] A. A. Makarov shared Kokovtsov's convictions on this score. Educated as a
lawyer, Makarov had been tapped as minister of the interior at Kokovtsov's urging.
Although ambitious, he was a somewhat dull and unimaginative bureaucrat, possess-
ing all the charm of a "notary public," in Nicholas's memorable phrase.[78]

Within the military some opposed Sukhomlinov because of policy differences:
the war minister's extensive reform program had its share of detractors, who rallied
to block its implementation and were on occasion successful in doing so. Owing to
their obstruction, for instance, Sukhomlinov had to disavow his plan to raze all the
western fortresses. But personal animus and ravening careerism were also at work.
Take the case of the deputy minister of war, General A.A. Polivanov.

Restricted in his ability to move his shoulder and neck as a result of the Turkish
bullet wound he had suffered back in 1877, Polivanov had graduated from the Academy of the General Staff as first in his class. Despite his physical disability, he had
steadily risen in the military hierarchy and had served successively in Kiev Military
District and the main staff, where he had edited the army's official journal and newspaper. Selected by Rediger as deputy minister, he had remained in this position after
Rediger fell. A cultivated soldier with a well-deserved reputation as a theater lover,
Polivanov possessed administrative talents of the first order.[79] He had secretly opposed Sukhomlinov virtually from the very moment he took office. Now it is true
that Polivanov was considerably to the left of his chief in terms of national politics
and cultivated good relationships with the leaders of the Duma, but the real key to his
animosity was his unsatisfied hunger for advancement: Sukhomlinov was the obsta-
cle to his accession to ministerial rank.

The Grand Duke Nikolai Nikolaevich, the emperor's first cousin once removed,
was another potent figure who stood against Sukhomlinov within the army. Appointed chairman of the Council of State Defense in the summer of 1905, Nikolai became the virtual dictator of Russia's national security. In 1908, however, the short-

76. Paul Miliukov, *Political Memoirs, 1905–1917*, ed. Arthur P. Mendel; trans. Carl Goldberg (Ann
Arbor, 1967), pp. 236–237.

77. Kokovtsov testimony, December 19–24, 1916, RGVIA, f. 962, op. 2, d. 52, ll. 288, 296.

78. V. I. Gurko, *Features and Figures of the Past*, ed. J. E. Wallace Sterling, Xenia Joukofff Eudin, and
H. H. Fisher, trans. Laura Matveev (Stanford, 1939) p. 519.

79. A. M. Zaionchkovskii, "Vvedenie," in Polivanov, *Iz dnevnikov*, pp. 12–14; V. A. Teliakovskii,
Vospominaniia (Moscow/Leningrad, 1965), pp. 176–177.

82 comings of this arrangement led to the disbanding of the council and Nikolai's relegation to the command of St. Petersburg Military District. The word "hatred" is
probably too insipid a term to describe Nikolai's feelings toward Sukhomlinov,
whom he blamed for advising the emperor to abolish the Council.[80] Nikolai, who
manifested the classic symptoms of manic depression, thus begrudged Sukhomlinov
the power that had so recently been his. He had his own ideas about how to reform
the Russian army, ideas to which Sukhomlinov showed no deference at all. The two
were barely on speaking terms; when Sukhomlinov wanted to communicate something to the grand duke, he typically used Andronnikov as an intermediary.[81] What
made Nikolai a particular menace was not only his membership in the imperial family but also his extensive network of contacts and disciples within the officer corps.
When World War I broke out and Nikolai Nikolaevich went to the front as supreme
commander of all Russia's forces, he became more redoubtable still.

It would, of course, be a daunting task to prepare an exhaustive catalog of
Sukhomlinov's enemies in the army, but there is one more person who deserves attention, if only because of his subsequent prominence in the case: General N. I.
Ivanov. Ivanov, a hardworking although boorish officer, was widely (although erroneously) rumored to be the son of a common soldier. Morbidly sensitive about his
personal appearance, Ivanov tried to conceal his ugliness behind an enormous set of
bushy whiskers. When he came to Kiev as Sukhomlinov's replacement, he brought
with him an entirely new leadership team, including General M. V. Alekseev, later
famed as the chief of staff at Russian General Headquarters in World War I. Although
Ivanov was quite open about his negative attitude toward the war minister, the origin
of his antipathy remains obscure. Ivanov's own explanation—that he had found Kiev
Military District in shambles owing to Sukhomlinov's incompetence—does not ring
true.[82] More likely than not, frustrated ambition was the source of his antipathy. For
his part, Sukhomlinov did not trust Ivanov, whom he privately referred to as "that
blockhead." His low opinion was only confirmed by Ivanov's inaugural address to the
Kiev garrison in January 1909. On that occasion, either by accident or design, Ivanov
omitted Sukhomlinov's name from the list of previous district chiefs.[83] Sukhomlinov
was sufficiently offended to make a point of never subsequently doing Ivanov any favors. And this, of course, meant that Ivanov was frozen in place. As long as Sukhom-

---

80. S. Iu. Vitte, *Vospominaniia,* vol. 3 (Moscow, 1960), p. 509. It should be noted that K. F. Shatsillo has
argued that what really convinced the emperor to abolish the council was its conspicuous lack of enthusiasm for rebuilding Russia's blue-water navy, a cause to which Nicholas II was personally committed. Shatsillo, *Ot portsmutskogo mira,* pp. 146–47.

81. *Padenie tsarskago rezhima,* vol. 1 (Leningrad, 1924), p. 372.

82. Testimony of December 21, 1916, RGVIA, f. 962, op. 2, d. 52, l. 301, for Ivanov's characterization of
his relationship with Sukhomlinov. It should be noted that Norman Stone's depiction of the Russian army
as split between the aristocratic followers of the Grand Duke Nikolai Nikolaevich and plebeian Sukhomli-
novites is a vast oversimplification of a much more complex reality. Still further, some of the evidence that
Stone adduces to support his hypothesis is flatly wrong. For instance, he describes Ivanov as a member of
Sukhomlinov's clique. See Norman Stone, *The Eastern Front, 1914–1917* (New York, 1975), p. 27.

83. N. A. Epanchin, *Na sluzhbe trekh imperatorov. Vospominaniia* (Moscow, 1996), pp. 372, 375.

linov held power in Petersburg, Ivanov knew that a promotion either for him or for anyone else in his patronage network was highly unlikely.

The third group of Sukhomlinov's enemies was composed of Duma politicians. Sukhomlinov was, of course, anathema to the left, which regarded him (as indeed it would have regarded any other minister of war) as the personification of tsarist military despotism. But Sukhomlinov's most dangerous foes actually occupied the center-right. The Union of October 17, or Octobrist Party, had been founded early 1906 on a platform of support for moderate reform and opposition to revolution. Known for its superpatriotism and xenophobia, the union had many members with affiliations to industry and trade, although it would be misleading to identify it, as have some, as Russia's "capitalist" party. The single largest faction in the Third Duma, it had cooperated to an extent with P. A. Stolypin, supporting his agrarian reforms and his policies of Russification in the borderlands. The relationship between the chairman of the Council of Ministers and the Octobrists was not, however, a placid one and had in fact become severely frayed as a result of the "western zemstvo crisis" in the spring of 1911, when large numbers of Octobrists had attacked Stolypin for bypassing the parliament and introducing a system of local government in the western quarters of the empire by emergency degree.[84] Nonetheless, collaboration with Stolypin had ensured the party access to the highest circles of the government, and when Stolypin was killed in September, the party saw its influence dwindle. The new ministers, as well as the court, seemed inclined to reassert tsarist absolutism at the Duma's expense. The most visible leader of the Octobrist Party, Aleksandr Ivanovich Guchkov, was determined to turn this situation around.

A. I. Guchkov was born in 1863 into a wealthy family of Moscow merchants, which had originally made its fortune in textile manufacturing. Highly educated, he had taken a degree in history from Moscow University in 1885 and had followed this up with five years of postgraduate study in classical philology in Berlin and Heidelberg. Despite his scholarly achievements, his was no serene temperament, for he was mercurial, quarrelsome, and high-strung. He was also a braggart, a bully, and a serial adulterer, whose daughter later ruefully reminisced that the Guchkov family "never returned to the same sea-side resort two summers running, because the second summer all the babies in prams looked embarrassingly like me."[85] While in his thirties he had made a habit of rushing off to scenes of global crisis. Thus he had traveled to Turkey at the time of the Armenian massacres in 1895. In 1899 he had fought for the Boers against the British in South Africa, where he picked up a leg wound that left him lame for the rest of his life. In 1900 he turned up in Manchuria for the Boxer uprising, and in 1905 in Macedonia for the nationalist revolt there. During the Russo-

84. Ben Cion-Pinchuk, *The Octobrists in the Third Duma 1907–1912* (Seattle, 1974), pp. 148–150; Geoffrey Hosking, *The Russian Constitutional Experiment: Government and Duma, 1907–1914* (Cambridge, 1973), pp. 137–147; Terence Emmons, *The Formation of Political Parties and the First National Elections in Russia* (Cambridge, 1983), pp. 104–105.

85. Quoted in William Gleason, "Alexander Guchkov and the End of the Russian Empire," in *Transactions of the American Philosophical Society*, vol. 73, pt. 2 (Philadelphia, 1983), p. 79.

84 Japanese War he had worked for the Red Cross in the Far East until captured by the Japanese, and, upon his release, had been instrumental in organizing the Union of 17 October.

Perhaps because of his amateur soldiering in the South African veldt, Guchkov fancied himself a defense expert; as a member of the Duma Committee on State Defense, he always sought the limelight when military issues or appropriations were raised in the popular assembly. Guchkov's own military expertise was, however, overrated, and subsequent generations of historians have tended to take his claims about it at face value. It is high time to dispense with the notion that Guchkov was some sort of Cassandra, whose prescient warnings and brilliant insights about military reform—had they only been heeded by a hidebound military establishment—might have saved Russia from defeat in the world war. No one would deny that Guchkov was authentically popular among the officers and men of Russia's armed forces; his sincere devotion to improving the conditions of service and raising pay and benefits deservedly won him many admirers. Nor is it in dispute that Guchkov espoused opinions (many reasonably technical) on a variety of military issues. But these were not the result of his own learning and ratiocination; rather, he parroted what a large web of informants told him. Among these men were General V. I. Gurko, the editor in chief of the official history of the Russo-Japanese war, who, along with his staff, regularly prepped Guchkov to speak on questions of defense legislation.[86] Other sources included several of Russia's foreign military attachés; certain military district chiefs of staff; N. I. Ivanov, commandant of Kiev district; and Deputy War Minister A. A. Polivanov.[87]

These men, and others besides, supplied Guchkov with all kinds of information about procurement, weapons systems, even the intelligence assessments of the Russian army, much of which was acutely sensitive or even highly classified. Their reasons for breaching security and violating the chain of command were varied. Principled opposition to the current direction of Russia's military policy undoubtedly played a great role. However, one is left with the distinct impression that baser motivations were also at work: several of Guchkov's *mouchards* stood to benefit professionally if only Sukhomlinov could be driven from office.

Guchkov subsequently claimed that when Sukhomlinov took over the war ministry he had extended the hand of friendship to the general, only to have his knuckles rapped. Sukhomlinov evinced little interest in cooperating with Russia's elected legislature. Nicholas II had, in fact, forbidden the war minister to attend Duma sessions. When the presence of a representative from the war ministry was required at the Duma, Sukhomlinov sent Polivanov in his stead. Sukhomlinov would not even receive the members of the Duma defense committee, although he did permit them to be briefed in informal meetings by Polivanov, Ianushkevich, Lukomskii, and Mysh-

---

86. Guchkov and Bazili, *Guchkov rasskazyvaet*, p. 7.

87. Ibid., pp. 56, 59–60. See also Gosudarstvennyi arkhiv Rossiiskoi Federatsii (hereafter GARF), f. DP OO, d. 144 1913, l. 119.

A. I. Guchkov

86 laevskii, among other ministry officials.[88] In large measure because Sukhomlinov would not accord Guchkov the respect and influence that he believed were rightfully his, the Octobrist politician concluded that the war minister was a man "indifferent to the needs of the army."[89] With the smug self-righteousness that was one of his most odious personality traits, Guchkov decided that Sukhomlinov had to be removed from his ministry for the good of Russia's national security. He, Guchkov, would be the instrument of Sukhomlinov's destruction. After all, how difficult could this be? Had not Guchkov ousted Rediger, the previous minister of war, with his March 1909 speech about the Romanov family and the military? To the consternation of the Octobrist, however, parliamentary oratory and interpellation did not shake the emperor's confidence in Sukhomlinov but rather strengthened it.

Guchkov became obsessed with expelling Vladimir Aleksandrovich from the government, and he was not squeamish about the means to be used to encompass that end. As he later confessed in his Riviera exile: "I thought that if we could not polish off the war minister by criticizing his activities, we might be able to wring his neck with a scandal."[90] The materials to concoct such a scandal were soon at hand.

The Intrigues of Winter and Spring 1912

The spring of 1912 brought the synergistic conjunction of several intrigues: plots by the Russian East Asian Steamship Company, the Ministry of the Interior, and Sukhomlinov's adjutants against Miasoedov; a right-wing conspiracy against Polivanov and Guchkov; and a cabal hatched by Polivanov and Guchkov against Sukhomlinov.

It was the adjutants who made the first move. In January, Bulatsel' went to see Colonel Eremin at the Office of the Special Section of the Department of Police. Explaining that he and his comrades were determined to free Sukhomlinov from the baleful influence of such a "scoundrel" as Miasoedov, Bulatsel' begged Eremin to rummage through the files of his department for ammunition that could be used to discredit the newly reinstated gendarme. Since Eremin nurtured his own grudges against Miasoedov, he not only immediately agreed to do as Bulatsel' requested but also volunteered to write the report and provide Sukhomlinov with a verbal synopsis himself. As it happened, he did not have to look very hard for his material.[91]

A. S. Gubonin, an interior ministry official, had compiled the most extensive list of charges against Miasoedov in the possession of the Department of Police at the very end of 1906. All the old complaints against Sergei Nikolaevich were laid out here: that he had engaged in improper commercial transactions, that he was involved in illegal emigration, that he consorted with Jews, and so forth. It was simplicity itself for Eremin to dust off Gubonin's paper and take it with him to Sukhomlinov's office.

---

88. V. Kobylin, *Imperator Nikolai II i General-Ad"iutant M.V. Alekseev* (New York, 1970), pp. 80–82.
89. Guchkov and Bazili, *Guchkov rasskazyvaet*, p. 58.
90. Ibid., p. 95.
91. Petrov Commission report, 1916, RGVIA, f. 962, op. 2, d. 164, ll. 191–192.

The war minister was, however, underwhelmed by the Gubonin memorandum, which, as he calmly observed, was nothing more than a grab bag of unsubstantiated allegations. Eremin reluctantly had to concur but rejoined that the fact that the allegations were unproven did not mean that they were not true.[92] He returned to the police department and busied himself with digging up further dirt on Miasoedov.

When Sergei Nikolaevich learned about what had happened, he immediately took sensible measures to defend himself. Tracking down Gubonin in Petersburg, Miasoedov persuaded him to admit in the presence of two witnesses that he had never believed in the credibility of his own 1906 report since all the information in it had come from the lips of the criminal scum who worked for the notorious Cornet Ponomarev, the Okhrana agent whose attempt to frame innocent men for capital crimes had been exposed in the Vilna military court.[93]

About this time a new series of anonymous accusations began to dribble into the war ministry. The target this time was A. A. Polivanov, who, the letters declared, was actually the highest-ranking Austro-Hungarian spy in Russia.[94] Sukhomlinov's response to these missives was to send Miasoedov to see Polivanov and ask him who he suspected was behind the attempt to smear him.[95]

The accusations were most likely composed by someone close to retired Staff-Captain P. M. Mikhailov. Mikhailov, a graduate of the General Staff Academy, part-time journalist and full-time agent provocateur, was a man of such questionable ethics that he makes everyone we have encountered to this point seem a model of rectitude and self-restraint. In 1909 Guchkov had hired Mikhailov as the secretary of the Duma Committee on State Defense. This was a most peculiar appointment, to say the least, and is explicable only by presuming that Guchkov was ignorant of Mikhailov's ultrareactionary political beliefs. Mikhailov at once set himself to spy on Guchkov and soon forwarded Sukhomlinov an extensive list of the military officers with whom the former was secretly in correspondence, which resulted in abrupt transfers out of the capital for many of them. When Guchkov caught wind of his secretary's treachery and fired him, Mikhailov retaliated both publicly and privately: publicly, by publishing an article ("Ex-Subaltern Guchkov") denigrating the Octobrist's competence in military affairs; and privately, by authoring or instigating anonymous denunciations of both Guchkov and his closest allies in the army establishment. Perhaps because they feared being victimized themselves, Polivanov and Guchkov abandoned all scruples as they launched their intrigue against Sukhomlinov. It is conceivable that they may have believed that the war minister himself was pulling Mikhailov's strings, although there is no evidence to substantiate that this was true. In any event, both Polivanov and Guchkov were aware that they were under attack, and this awareness, along with their knowledge of Miasoedov's putative involve-

92. Eremin testimony, August 23, 1917, RGVIA, f. 962, op. 2, d. 145, l. 38.
93. Miasoedov to N. A. Maklakov, February 24, 1913, RGVIA, f. 962, op. 2, d. 66, l. 33; Miasoedov to Maklakov, June 1912, RGVIA, f. 962, op. 2, d. 112, l. 503.
94. Anonymous letter to Sukhomlinov, April 27, n.y., RGVIA, f. 962, op. 2, d. 51, l. 71.
95. Sukhomlinov, *Vospominaniia Sukhomlinova*, p. 189.

88 ment in investigating the "espionage" charges concocted by Mikhailov's associates, may account for the form that their intrigue took.

Their objective was to persuade or force Nicholas II to dismiss Sukhomlinov and replace him with Polivanov. Pressure would be applied upon the tsar from two different directions at once: the other ministers would be induced to coalesce in opposition to Sukhomlinov while educated public opinion would be mobilized to demand the war minister's ouster. There was a natural division of labor. Polivanov undertook to organize the ministerial common front, and Guchkov, the public opinion side of the affair. Precise timing, as well as excellent coordination with the Ministry of the Interior and the press, was essential if this two-pronged intrigue was to succeed. The attacks on Sukhomlinov both within the government and within the pages of the newspapers would hinge on the war minister's relations with Lieutenant Colonel Sergei Miasoedov.

It was Sukhomlinov's practice to break the routine of office work in Petersburg with periods of travel throughout the provinces and outlying territories of the empire. In fact, so numerous and extensive were these personal inspection tours that his critics charged him with undertaking the majority with no other purpose than to inflate his salary by collecting expenses.[96] Polivanov and Guchkov, however, realized that they could turn the minister's frequent absences from the capital to their advantage. In March 1912 Sukhomlinov boarded his private railway carriage for an inspection trip to Turkestan, leaving Polivanov behind as acting minister. On March 18 an official communication from Minister of the Interior A. A. Makarov arrived at the office of the war minister. As Sukhomlinov was not present, his deputy opened and read the memorandum in his place.

Dated March 16, Makarov's letter was a full-bore assault on the honesty and reliability of Sergei Miasoedov. It noted that after his retirement from the gendarmes, Miasoedov had founded an emigration company "with a certain Jew, Freidberg," adding that "this company, like other emigration offices causes significant financial losses to the state by its misdeeds." Not only had Miasoedov thus taken part in the dubious Northwest Russian Steamship Company, but he had scandalously continued to work on its behalf even after resuming governmental service, in direct contravention of the law. Most shocking of all, there was reason to believe that something even darker was lurking at the heart of the matter: Freidberg was a man with extremely suspicious acquaintances. For example, one person with whom he occasionally did business was Joseph Katsenlenbogen, who had been convicted in 1907 of attempting to obtain foreign passports under false pretenses. In turn, Katsenlenbogen was in business relations with one Franz Lentser, the representative of the central German bureau that hired seasonal agricultural workers in Russia. And Lentser, Makarov concluded, was also a secret agent of the German General Staff.[97]

96. See, for example, Bonch-Bruevich, *Vsia vlast' sovetam*, p. 67. For the views of Finance Minister Kokovtsov see RGVIA, f. 962, op. 2, d. 52, l. 297
97. RGVIA, f. 962, op. 2, d. 66, l. 11, for the text of this letter.

Polivanov states in his diary that he was "shocked" by Makarov's sinister revelations.[98] Whether he was being disingenuous or not, he moved immediately to ensure that they would be widely circulated. He showed the letter to V. N. Kokovtsov, chairman of the Council of Ministers, and Ia. G. Zhilinskii, chief of the general staff. Then, and only then, did he forward it to its original addressee, General Sukhomlinov.[99]

Sukhomlinov returned to Petersburg in early April furious with Polivanov for having divulged the contents of Makarov's memorandum to people other than himself. He called Miasoedov into his office, informed him of Makarov's charges, and ordered him to prepare an explanation and rebuttal. The gendarme colonel was absolutely dumbfounded by what he was told: over the years he had been accused of all sorts of abuses and crimes but never treason. Worse, however, was still to come, for the real storm cloud over the hapless colonel's head had yet to break.

The April 13 issue of the *Evening Times* (*Vechernee vremia*), a popular St. Petersburg paper, ran an unsigned article under the headline "To Whom Is Military Counterintelligence in Russia Entrusted?" This exposé declared that there was evidence that lately Austria-Hungary's access to Russian military secrets had improved dramatically. Was it merely a coincidence, the article asked, that at about the same time a certain gendarme colonel had been attached to the central ministry of war and given a job with intelligence responsibilities? Although Miasoedov was nowhere identified by name, more than enough details were supplied to leave no doubt about whom the "certain gendarme colonel" was.[100] On April 14 the *Evening Times*'s sister paper, *New Times* (*Novoe vremia*), published an interview with Guchkov, who vouched for the accuracy of all the information that had appeared in the *Evening Times* and confirmed that Sergei Nikolaevich Miasoedov was indeed the officer in question.

When B. A. Suvorin, editor in chief of the *Evening Times,* came to work on the morning of the fourteenth, Miasoedov was waiting for him at the office door. The two men already knew each other; Suvorin had in fact been an occasional guest in Miasoedov's home. The gendarme colonel demanded that the journalist reveal who was responsible for the terrible libels against him. He was completely innocent, he asserted, and could prove it. Suvorin, who had really authored the April 13 article himself, declined to respond to Miasoedov's angry query but told the gendarme that he would consider publishing a refutation if Miasoedov would care to write one. He then hurried into his editorial office without a further word.

This vague promise that the *Evening Times* might eventually permit him to defend himself was not, however, satisfactory to Miasoedov. He needed vindication and he wanted it immediately. Throughout the day Miasoedov sent several messages to Suvorin begging for an opportunity to meet with him. If Suvorin would but hear him out, he would surely be convinced of Miasoedov's blamelessness and would print the retraction that Miasoedov desperately craved. Suvorin brushed off every one of Mia-

98. Polivanov, *Iz dnevnikov*, p. 111.
99. *Padenie tsarskago rezhima*, vol. 6, p. 63.
100. See the press clipping, RGVIA, f. 962, op. 2, d. 66, l. 66.

90 soedov's approaches. Toward the end of the day, he received a final note from the gendarme, this time containing a challenge to a duel. Suvorin ignored this, too. It was evidently this final rebuff that goaded Miasoedov into a paroxysm of rage.

On Sunday, April 15, Suvorin attended the horse races at the trotting track in Semenovskii Square. Miasoedov, who had followed him there, shoved his way through the crowd toward the journalist. Suddenly materializing in front of Suvorin, Sergei Nikolaevich struck him a tremendous blow across the top of the head with a riding crop. The stunned Suvorin crumpled to his knees, then staggered to his feet and grappled with his antagonist. Here accounts differ. Suvorin later claimed (and this claim, inter alia, was never corroborated by any other eyewitnesses) that at this point Miasoedov pulled a revolver from the pocket of his tunic and menaced him with it. In any event, the two men were separated and physically restrained; Miasoedov turned on his heel and walked away, the whole time shouting curses and imprecations at Suvorin, who, he said, was too craven to fight.[101]

Miasoedov's friends appreciated his frustration. On April 17 Sukhomlinov sent a letter to Ekaterina Viktorovna in France. "Miasoedov," he wrote, "has caned Boris Suvorin for libeling him in the *Evening Times*. There was no other possible outcome." Vladimir Aleksandrovich only regretted that the "scoundrel" Suvorin had not been more thoroughly humiliated.[102] Two days later Boris Freidberg wrote Miasoedov from Libava that he "was stung to his very soul by the unspeakable impudence and gall of those who would stoop to such a vile calumny" and added that "your friends and acquaintances, who know you well, have never for a moment doubted your complete honesty and devotion to your duty."[103]

Guchkov in the meantime had used the appearance of the articles to make Miasoedov's function at the war ministry the subject of parliamentary inquiry. A special, closed session of the Duma Committee on State Defense was scheduled for April 19. There was no way Sukhomlinov could avoid an appearance at this meeting: to refuse to attend would have been taken as an admission that the newspaper stories were true. At 2:30 in the afternoon on the appointed day Sukhomlinov strode into the committee room, flanked by Chief of Staff Zhilinksii and Ianushkevich, the acting chief of the war ministry chancellery.

Sukhomlinov began by emphasizing that the newspaper accounts had misrepresented war ministry policy and falsely characterized both Miasoedov and his job. Since there did not exist, nor had there ever existed, a secret counterintelligence organ within the ministry, Miasoedov could not possibly have been in charge of one. Both intelligence and counterintelligence were centralized in the general staff. Moreover, Miasoedov had never carried out "any responsible assignments" at all on behalf of the ministry or the minister. Sukhomlinov concluded his statement with the ob-

101. For Suvorin's version of these events see testimony of August 24, 1917, RGVIA, f. 962, op. 2, d. 145, ll. 93–95. See also Guchkov and Bazili, *Guchkov rasskazyvaet*, p. 96; Kokovtsov, *Iz moego proshlogo*, vol. 2, p. 61.

102. RGVIA, f. 962, op. 2, d. 66, l. 55.

103. Freidberg to Miasoedov, Aptil 19, 1912, RGVIA, f. 962, op. 2, d. 113, ll. 6–7.

servation that certain bits of information contained in the articles were highly classified, and that he had already instructed the military-judicial administration to investigate the leak.

Guchkov responded that he knew that "on several occasions Miasoedov had been
entrusted with secret inquiries outside the boundary of normal duties." Contrary to
what Sukhomlinov had said, there was indeed an office within the ministry that kept
tabs on the political views of Russian officers. When Sukhomlinov denied that this
was so, Guchkov produced a secret war ministry circular dated March 14, 1910 and
asked him to account for it. This document required military district staffs to collect
and retain material supplied by the gendarmes on the political reliability of officers,
which of course suggested that these data would eventually be dispatched to some
sort of central ministerial bureau. Sukhomlinov responded truthfully that the ministry's personnel office—the main (*glavnyi*) staff—rather than a clandestine bureau,
was what the circular referred to, and that the circular had in any case been countermanded at the end of 1910. But Guchkov merely waved the paper in the air, as if to say
that this was the tangible substantiation that the war minister was lying.[104]

The Duel

Miasoedov was meanwhile in a state of desperation. The original stories in the
Evening Times and *New Times* had by now been picked up and reprinted by provincial
newspapers throughout the empire. Although Sukhomlinov obviously had sympathy
for his plight, Vladimir Aleksandrovich was also too skillful at autocratic politics not
to take prudent steps to distance himself from his one-time protégé. On the very day
the first article appeared, Sukhomlinov suspended Miasoedov from duty and wrote
Makarov that he had done so "in view of your letter of March 16th."[105] What was
going on here was obvious: Sukhomlinov was keeping his options open by preparing
a paper trail that could prove useful if he finally decided to get rid of Miasoedov.

In a letter of April 14, Miasoedov pleaded with Vladimir Aleksandrovich for a
chance to exonerate himself. "The only result of my abrupt dismissal will be to make
it possible for our enemies to say that in selecting me you made a mistake which you
have now hastened to correct to please the press. But I will be completely shamed by
this."[106] The next day he wrote again, insisting that the war ministry immediately
conduct a full-scale investigation of the charges against him. He had nothing to fear
from such an inquiry and was even willing to submit to arrest if that was thought
necessary.[107]

Yet if Sukhomlinov initiated a military judicial investigation (and in fact he did),
Miasoedov feared that it would be weeks, perhaps months, before he was cleared officially. He felt that he had to do something dramatic to impress the fact of his inno-

104. RGVIA, f. 962, op. 2, d. 51, ll. 148–149, for the secret journal of the committee meeting.
105. Sukhomlinov to Makarov, April 13, 1912, RGVIA, f. 962, op. 2, d. 66, l. 12.
106. Makarov to Sukhomlinov, April 14, 1912, RGVIA, f. 962, op. 2, d. 66, l. 13.
107. Miasoedov to Sukhomlinov, April 15, 1912, RGVIA, f. 962, op. 2, d. 66, l. 16.

92 cence on the public. The coward Suvorin had, of course, declined his challenge. There remained his other tormentor, Aleksandr Guchkov.

Whatever can be said of his other personal qualities, Guchkov was a man of indisputable physical bravery. He was also a pistol expert whose favorite garden-party trick was shooting cigarettes out of people's mouths. Nor was he a stranger to dueling. In May 1908 he had forced the Kadet politician and historian Paul Miliukov to apologize for a critical remark on the floor of the Duma by threatening him with a duel.[108] In a duel fought in November of the following year Guchkov put a bullet through the shoulder of Count A. A. Uvorov, a member of his own political party—an escapade that earned him a week's confinement in a fortress.[109] When on April 18 Miasoedov challenged Guchkov to meet him on the field of honor, the latter immediately accepted.

On April 19 a meeting was held at the apartment of P. N. Krupenskii, a Duma deputy who had agreed to serve as one of Guchkov's seconds. In addition to Krupenskii, A. I. Zvegintsev, Guchkov's other second, attended, as did the two officers—Captain V. D. Abelov and Captain D. N. Miasodoev (Sergei's brother)—who represented the challenger. The conditions and rules governing the duel were soon agreed upon. The participants would fight with pistols on Sunday, April 22. They would be placed forty-five paces from each other. At the signal, each of them would advance ten paces and fire. There was a division of opinion over only one issue. Miasoedov's seconds (in accord with his instructions) urged that in the event no one was injured in the first exchange of shots, the duel be repeated up to two more times, so that blood might be spilled and honor satisfied. As Guchkov's seconds spurned this proposal, the matter was resolved by drawing lots, which resulted in a victory for Guchkov's side: the two men would fire at each other only once.[110]

Although dueling was tolerated within the Russian officer corps (there were in fact circumstances under which it was virtually mandatory), duels between civilians or officers and civilians were forbidden by Russian law. Since the impending gun battle was openly discussed in the capital, and even written about in the newspapers, the police took extraordinary steps to prevent it. They placed Guchkov and his seconds under twenty-four-hour surveillance and instructed special police detachments in the city's outlying suburbs to be on the alert for the dueling party. On the morning of April 22, however, Guchkov managed to elude his police tail by alighting from his taxi on Morskaia Street, running through a building that opened onto the Moika, and engaging another taxi there.

At eleven o'clock the principals, their seconds, and the obligatory doctor rendezvoused on Krestovskii Island in the estuary of the Neva River. Preparations for the combat were, however, quickly interrupted by the arrival of a sizable contingent of police, who had been tipped off by a sharp-eyed bridge watchman. Yet neither

108. GARF, f. 555, op. 1, d. 4, ll. 2–3.
109. Polivanov, *Iz dnevnikov*, p. 86.
110. See the protocol of the seconds' meeting in RGVIA, f. 962, op. 2, d. 112, l. 439.

Guchkov nor Miasoedov was willing to postpone their confrontation; they and their companions only pretended to comply with the order to disperse. Within an hour the dueling party had reassembled on the western coast of the island, not far from a military rifle range. There, on the shore of the Gulf of Finland, the two men were given revolvers and led to their places. Miasoedov was the first to squeeze off a shot. Perhaps owing to trouble with his pince-nez, the near-sighted gendarme missed his adversary completely. After a moment of hesitation Guchkov then raised his pistol and "demonstratively fired into the air." With that the duel concluded, and Miasoedov indignantly turned his back on Guchkov instead of shaking his hand, as was the customary practice.[111]

Aftermath

The duel had unfortunate consequences for both participants. It was Miasoedov who suffered the most direct damage. Unwilling to back Sergei Nikolaevich in the teeth of all of the negative publicity, Sukhomlinov arranged for his discharge from the Separate Corps of Gendarmes. In accord with an imperial decree (backdated to April 17), Miasoedov was retired into the reserve militia of Petersburg province "for family reasons" and awarded an annual pension of 484 rubles.[112]

But Guchkov did not emerge from the duel unscathed either. Although his self-dramatizing entrance into the Duma the following Monday with his uninjured arm in a sling won him a round of applause, his conduct throughout the mysterious affair stimulated critical comment in newspapers and magazines of a variety of political orientations.[113] There was one set of questions in particular that many found perplexing: If Guchkov knew beyond the shadow of a doubt that Miasoedov was really an Austrian spy, then why on earth had he accepted the latter's challenge? Was it not the case that a traitor was by definition incapable of giving satisfaction? And if that was so, was not Guchkov's agreement to exchange shots with Miasoedov (not to mention his bullet in the air) tantamount to a confession that his accusations against the officer were false? As the prominent attorney O. O. Gruzenberg put it: "One must assume that spies are not the sort of men with whom one would care to fight a duel."[114] Guchkov was hard-pressed to devise credible answers to these questions, for he had none.

Polivanov was another casualty of the scandal. Although he had hoped to replace Sukhomlinov before the month was over, he was instead hoisted by his own petard. Nicholas II was at this time vacationing in his palace at Livadia on the Crimean coast.

111. "Duel' mezhdu A. I. Guchkovym i S. N. Miasoedovym," *Rech'*, no. 110 (1912).

112. Order on retirement of Miasoedov, 1912, RGVIA, f. 801, op. 28, d. 164, l. 257.

113. V. Shulgin, *Gody-Dni-1920* (Moscow, 1991), p. 271. S. S. Oldenburg, *Last Tsar: Nicholas II, His Reign and His Russia*, vol. 3 of *The Duma Monarchy, 1907–1914*, trans. Leonid I. Mihalap and Patrick J. Rollins; ed. Patrick J. Rollins (Gulf Breeze, Fla., 1977), p. 113.

114. O. O. Gruzenberg, *Yesterday: Memories of a Russian Jewish Lawyer*, trans. Don C. Rawson and Tatiana Tipton (Berkeley, 1981), p. 131.

94 The adjacent resort of Yalta was abuzz with rumors about the clash between Guchkov and Sukhomlinov in the Duma and about the obscure and apparently disreputable gendarme colonel Miasoedov. Much of this talk was disseminated by V. N. Kokovtsov, who had arrived at the spa on April 21.[115] But Sukhomlinov was already en route to the Crimea himself. On April 23 Nicholas II received him in an audience at Livadia. The war minister must have deployed his characteristic charm to good effect, for he walked out of the interview with exactly what he wanted: his reconfirmation in office and a warrant in his pocket removing Polivanov from his post and assigning him to the Council of State. Once the tsar was apprised of Polivanov's close association with Guchkov, he probably required little convincing in any case. Nicholas had taken a strong dislike to Guchkov ever since his attack on the military aptitude of the Romanov dynasty three years before, and this dislike had congealed into loathing just one month previously, when Guchkov had denounced Rasputin from the rostrum of the Duma—an act the emperor had construed as a disgusting attempt to meddle in his private, family life.[116]

Reconstructing the Machinery of the Plot

It remains to clear up the mysteries surrounding the scandal in the spring of 1912. In retrospect it is clear that the "damaging revelations" in the Makarov letter of March—all of the material about Katsenelenbogen, Lentser, etc.—were supplied by Colonel Eremin, who fished them out of the vast sewer of perlustrated mail to which he had access. It is not unlikely that he did so with the connivance of his friend Podushkin, who, as we have seen, was in cahoots with the Russian Eastern Asiatic Steamship Company, a commercial rival of Northwest. The probability is also high that, in collusion with Polivanov, Makarov timed the release of his letter to the war ministry to coincide with Sukhomlinov's absence in Turkestan. Had Sukhomlinov been the first to read the letter, he would certainly have looked into the allegations it contained, but he would never have allowed it to leave the filing cabinets of the ministry of war, let alone reach the desk of Prime Minister Kokovtsov. But that is precisely where Polivanov bore it, clearly aware that he was thereby impugning the competence and judgment of his chief.

As for the newspaper campaign against Miasoedov, it was Guchkov's project from beginning to end. Guchkov had good personal relations with the Suvorin family (as well as the help of Kolomnin) which enabled him to plant stories in both the *Evening Times* and *New Times*. As Boris Suvorin later admitted at Sukhomlinov's trial, he wrote the article of April 13 not only at Guchkov's urging but also virtually at

115. Kokovtsov, *Iz moego proshlogo*, vol. 2, pp. 62–64.

116. G. E. Rasputin, a Siberian peasant and self-styled *starets*, or holy man, had been introduced to the imperial couple in 1905. He owed his influence with the emperor and empress largely to his mysterious ability to control the bleeding attacks of their son, Aleksei, who suffered from hemophilia. But both Nicholas and Alexandra also came to view Rasputin as an authentic spokesman for Russia's peasant masses. See Dominic Lieven, *Nicholas II: Twilight of the Empire* (New York, 1993), pp. 164–167.

his dictation.[117] The "interview" of April 14 was similarly contrived: Guchkov composed both the questions and the answers.[118]   95

Did Guchkov have evidence of any kind linking Miasoeodov to espionage? He claimed he did, and he further claimed that the evidence was ironclad. But on any occasion when he was asked to produce this evidence, even when he was tendered an official request by judicial authorities, he steadfastly declined to do so, declaring sententiously that had to protect his sources.

Now as it happened, one of the charges made in the newspaper campaign—that Austrian intelligence had been increasingly successful of late in breaching Russian military secrecy—was incontrovertibly true. Russian counterintelligence was painfully aware that a variety of classified data, including defense estimates, technical specifications of weapons, information about the political affiliations of high-ranking officers, and so forth, was coming into Vienna's possession.[119] As General Danilov of the general staff noted: "Insofar as it is possible to judge . . . the Austrians dispose of a large and well-informed network of agents in St. Petersburg."[120]

That the Russians had such a good picture of what the Austrian intelligence knew about them was the result both of their interception of the messages that passed between Austria's military attachés and Vienna and of their extraordinary achievements in penetrating the Austro-Hungarian army itself. Russia's greatest intelligence asset in the Dual Monarchy was Colonel Alfred Redl, who for several years served as the head of the Austro-Hungarian military intelligence bureau. A homosexual who may have been blackmailed into treason but who was also paid at least half a million Austrian crowns for his services, Redl had been recruited by the Russians around about 1902. He furnished his Russian handlers with copies of Austrian mobilization documents, identified Austrian agents in Russia, and supplied microphotographs of the most important Austro-Hungarian General Staff reports, which, in Sukhomlinov's words, he "constantly and systematically" forwarded to Kiev, Warsaw, and Petersburg.[121] Although Redl had been exposed and forced to commit suicide in 1913, his death did not stanch the flow of high-level politico-military intelligence about Franz Josef's empire, for St. Petersburg benefited from the efforts of other well-situated traitors, including servants in the home of the mistress of Baron Moritz Auffenberg von Komarow, Austria's minister of war.[122]

---

117. Suvorin testimony, August 24, 1917, RGVIA, f. 962, op. 2, d. 145, l. 93.

118. Guchkov and Bazili, *Guchkov rasskazyvaet*, p. 97.

119. See, for example, RGVIA, f. 400, op. 323, d. 38, ll. 48–50, for a secret Russian document retrieved by Russian intelligence from the Austro-Hungarian army.

120. Petrov Commission report, 1916, RGVIA, f. 962, op. 2, d. 164, l. 129.

121. Sukhomlinov interrogation, August 4, 1916, RGVIA, f. 962, op. 2, d. 134, l. 97.

122. On Redl, see also Holger H. Herwig, *The First World War: Germany and Austria-Hungary 1914–1918* (London, 1997), pp. 65, 74. The best recent study of Redl, based upon Austrian sources, employs his bank records to argue for a later recruitment date. See John Schindler, "Redl—Spy of the Century?" *International Journal of Intelligence and Counterintelligence* (forthcoming). I would like to thank Dr. Schindler for supplying me with a copy of this manuscript and permitting me to cite it. On Auffenberg see the testimony of General Ivanov, December 21, 1916, RGVIA, f. 962, op. 2, d. 52, l. 301.

96   Of course, Guchkov had no knowledge of any of these triumphs of Russian intelligence collection. But he did know that Russian counterintelligence was nervous about the outflow of Russian secrets to Vienna because N. I. Ivanov, Sukhomlinov's successor in Kiev, had so informed him. However, Ivanov never identified Miasoedov as the source of the leak and probably never even mentioned him to Guchkov by name.[123] This was no surprise. Neither in Kiev nor St. Petersburg nor anywhere else was there solid evidence proving or even suggesting that Miasoedov had spied on behalf of Austria. It would, in fact, have been much more plausible if Guchkov had accused Altschüller, although, as we shall see in the next chapter, there was no evidence against him either.

To be sure, Guchkov was aware of the contents of the Makarov letter, which Polivanov had divulged to him. But that document hinted at a connection between Miasoedov and Berlin, not Miasoedov and Vienna. Further, Guchkov had had dealings with the police before and was alive to the ease with which they could cook up completely spurious allegations. Moreover, the statement that an acquaintance of an acquaintance of a friend of "x" worked for enemy intelligence was so vague as to be functionally meaningless.

It is difficult not to conclude that Guchkov's press attack on Miasoedov was at best unprincipled and at worst truly vicious. In feeding his vanity, advancing his political agenda, and helping his friend Polivanov, he did not care if he irrevocably besmirched the reputation of an innocent man. Sacrificing Miasoedov was simply too convenient to waste time worrying about.

Miasoedov was understandably bitter, for he comprehended more quickly than many other people what had happened and why. On April 20 he wrote Guchkov that he was convinced that the latter had trumpeted his vile accusations in the newspapers even though he knew them to be false. In Miasoedov's opinion, Guchkov "had been consciously playing a dirty political game the entire time, a game whose goal had been the elevation of Polivanov to the post of war minister."[124] As he later pointed out in a note to Sukhomlinov, "I was only the scapegoat. The blow was aimed at you, but fell with all its weight on me."[125]

123. RGVIA, f. 962, op. 2, d. 52, l. 301. See also Guchkov and Bazili, *Guchkov rasskazyvaet*, p. 95.
124. Miasoedov to Guchkov, April 30, 1912, RGVIA, f. 962, op. 2, d. 112, l. 446.
125. Miasoedov to Sukhomlinov, June 16, 1912, RGVIA, f. 962, op. 2, d. 66, l. 25.

4

Realignments and Betrayals

Would there be no end to Miasoedov's misfortunes? It was as if the past were repeating itself. In Sergei's opinion, in 1907 he had been unjustly removed from the service and in 1912 it had happened to him again. This time, of course, there was an additional overlay of rancor, since the person he held responsible for his involuntary retirement was not some sworn enemy but Sukhomlinov, whom he had trusted and regarded as a friend. And just as in 1907, Miasoedov responded to his degradation by appealing to higher authorities for a reconsideration of his case.

In a letter of June 1912, he furnished Prime Minister V. N. Kokovtsov with his version of the scandals that had occurred earlier that winter and spring. Here he provided an extensive and rather accurate account of the manner in which the defamatory stories about him had been cooked up and spread. Miasoedov was particularly caustic about the role he believed (correctly) that police colonel Eremin had played in circulating the slander that had found its way into Makarov's memorandum to the Ministry of War in March 1912. He complained that Eremin had abused and was continuing to abuse his job as custodian of all of the perlustrated mail in Russia. "It is always possible for Eremin to come up with any 'information' or 'data' that suits him. Taking advantage of his extraordinary position in the service, Eremin can accuse anyone he wants of anything he likes, being confident of his immunity to punishment, since the information provided by the Special Section of the Department of Police is never verified."[1] But it was such a "verification" that Miasoedov now demanded; even a cursory inquiry would reveal that the "information" that Eremin had

1. Miasoedov to Kokovtsov, June 5, 1912, RGVIA, f. 962, op. 2, d. 66, l. 19.

97

98 collected against him was fraudulent and falsified. For this reason, Miasoedov called on Kokovtsov to order the charges against him investigated.

Rather than doing this, Kokovtsov merely passed Miasoedov's letter on to the Ministry of the Interior (MVD), with a request for its comments, which predictably were that Miasoedov's plea was without merit. At the same time, the ministry was remarkably candid about the reasons why it held such a low opinion of the retired colonel. It was no secret, wrote Beletskii of the MVD's police department, that Minister Makarov had a negative attitude toward Miasoedov. But that low opinion had nothing at all to do with the recent accusations; rather, it had everything to do with "the conduct of Miasoedov in court on 2 April 1907 in the Cornet Ponomarev affair. The minister has not changed his view of Miasoedov from that time to this."[2] When Miasoedov had predicted to the attorney Gruzenberg that his court testimony in Vilna would bring him the implacable enmity of the organs of internal security, he had been right. When Makarov fell from power in December 1912 as a result of another Rasputin scandal, his replacement, the notorious reactionary N. A. Maklakov, was no more inclined than his predecessor to hear Miasoedov out, even though he was a close friend of Miasoedov's aunt, Countess Sol'skaia.[3]

The last court of appeal was the emperor. It was Klara who signed her name to her husband's carefully drafted petition. Requesting that Sergei Nikolaevich be restored to duty by imperial order, this document averred that the Ministry of the Interior itself had connived with Guchkov and the Octobrist Party in a sordid plot to eliminate "a loyal officer" and "compromise General Sukhomlinov." The proof of the MVD's complicity was the fact that it could easily have refuted Guchkov's malicious calumny about Miasoedov's supposed "treason" had it really cared to do so. Despite (or perhaps because of) these potentially explosive allegations, Klara's appeal to the throne was also rejected.[4]

Given what had happened, it is not difficult to understand Miasoedov's frame of mind. He believed himself to be surrounded by false friends and persecuted by cabals of relentless enemies. Sukhomlinov was the particular object of Miasoedov's wrath. A whole series of notes climaxed in Miasoedov's letter to his former patron of June 16, 1912, which Miasoedov described as "probably the last I shall ever write you." The fact that the minister of war had abandoned him at the first sign of trouble was only one of Miasoedov's grievances. It was almost worse that the defense Sukhomlinov had mounted of his one-time protégé had been both flaccid and inaccurate. Sukhomlinov had, for example, asserted in the Duma that Miasoedov had fulfilled only low-level and unimportant assignments during his months at the war ministry, a statement that both men knew to be utterly untrue. Miasoedov concluded by observing that "my position is such that I am almost ready to put a bullet through my head. It is only

2. Beletskii to minister of interior, November 23, 1912, RGVIA, f. 962, op. 2, d. 134, l. 56.

3. Letter of Miasoedov to Maklakov, November 1912, RGVIA, f. 962, op. 2, d. 112, l. 506; letter of Miasoedov to Maklakov, February 1913, RGVIA, f. 962, op. 2, d. 66, ll. 31–33.

4. Klara Miasoedova to Nicholas II, RGVIA, f. 962, op. 2, d. 101, l. 20.

the shame of pusillanimity and my obligation to my children that dissuade me from such a deed."[5] Sukhomlinov's rejoinder—that he considered all of his actions toward Miasoedov to have been both tactful and correct—stung the ex-gendarme to the quick.[6] Sukhomlinov, Miasoedov wrote to his wife, was nothing other than "a big pig." Miasoedov reminded Klara that Madame Viktorova had originally warned them that Sukhomlinov was "an egotist and heartless" and that "he associated with people as long as he needed them, but thereafter discarded them like squeezed lemons without any regret."[7]

Although it was the case that the war minister saw only harm in any continued association with Miasoedov, this did not mean that he did nothing to counter the charges of treason with which Sergei Nikolaevich had been besmirched. After all, Sukhomlinov realized that accusations of espionage within the highest levels of the war ministry reflected badly on him as well. In the aftermath of the newspaper scandal, Vladimir Aleksandrovich had put into motion three inquiries designed to allay public concern about security in his department and to corroborate the testimony he had delivered at the Duma Commission on State Defense. The crucial point was to establish officially that Miasoedov had never held a formal position in either Russia's intelligence or counterintelligence service. If Miasoedov had not had access to secrets, ipso facto he could not have betrayed any.

At Sukhomlinov's request, the general staff, the Main Administration of Military Justice, and the staff of the Separate Corps of Gendarmes all detailed officers to look into this question. Of course, Sukhomlinov knew in advance what the outcome would be. None of the investigations would come up with any documentary material linking Miasoedov to Russian military intelligence because there was no such material to be found. Sukhomlinov had been very careful to keep the true nature of Miasoedov's duties secret from virtually everyone in his ministry. Not the chief of the general staff, not the heads of the ministry's main administrations, and not even Sukhomlinov's private secretary, Zotimov, could say with any confidence that they knew how Miasoedov had spent his time. There was no hard evidence; all instructions to Erandakov had been issued either face-to-face or over the telephone. As the minister had foreseen, all three investigatory bodies dutifully found that Miasoedov was innocent of any affiliation with the Russian secret service. In addition to establishing this "fact," functionaries of the Main Administration of Military Justice had also interviewed Guchkov and Suvorin. As neither of them would produce any evidence or name any source for the charge that Miasoedov was guilty of treason (thus shielding themselves from prosecution for perjury), military juridical authorities quickly concluded that the newspaper allegations had been baseless. On May 16 the Main Administration of Military Justice released a report exonerating Miasoedov,

5. Miasoedov to Sukhomlinov, June 16, 1912, RGVIA, f. 962, op. 2, d. 66, ll. 23–26, quote on l. 26.

6. Miasoedov to Klara, June 18, 1912, RGVIA, f. 962, op. 2, d. 51, l. 95.

7. Letters of Sergei to Klara, June 18 and July 20, 1912, RGVIA, f. 962, op. 2, d. 135, ll. 26, 28.

100 which was published as an official bulletin the next day in the army newspaper *Russkii invalid*.[8] By this point Miasoedov, who had retained an attorney, had already instigated civil proceedings against Boris Suvorin for libel.[9]

So much for the official inquiries. But Sukhomlinov did not stop here, for toward the end of April he tasked Colonel Erandakov personally to keep an eye on Miasoedov for a while. Sukhomlinov particularly desired Erandakov to collect all the information he could about Miasoedov's friends and acquaintances. Had the war minister come to suspect that Sergei Nikolaevich might really be in the hire of a foreign power? It is possible that Sukhomlinov wanted to be absolutely certain of Miasoedov's innocence; when asked about this episode subsequently, he testified that in view of the public furor, he did not think that having Miasoedov watched was "superfluous."[10] But it is much more likely that what actually bothered Sukhomlinov was the thought that there might be unsavory incidents in Miasoedov's past and present life, even unconnected to espionage, which the minister's enemies might eventually unearth and seek to exploit.

Erandakov dogged Miasoedov's footsteps for approximately a month. During that time he noted that Sergei Nikolaevich was on good terms with numerous members of the German colony in St. Petersburg and knew many Russians who also had German friends. These were scarcely earth-shattering revelations, given the size of the German community in the capital, Miasoedov's admiration for German culture, and his aptitude for the German language. To be sure, not all of Miasoedov's contacts boasted spotless reputations. At least some tsarist officials thought that his friend Eduard Valentini's business involved more than the importing of foreign medicine. Then there was Anna Aurikh, the German-born widow of a Russian captain, who supported herself by freelancing for Berlin newspapers and was thought to be a sympathizer with, if not a member of, the Menshevik Party. Another acquaintance, General Greifan of the Russian Quartermaster Corps, had been an intimate of Count Lelio Spannocchi, the Austrian military attaché in Petersburg who had been expelled from Russia in 1911 for his involvement in the sensational Untern-Shternberg espionage case.[11] Of course, all these details appeared much more sinister in retrospect than they did at the time. The point was that whatever Miasoedov's acquaintances

<hr />

8. Petrov Commission report, 1916, RGVIA, f. 962, op. 2, d. 164, ll. 195–200, 202; Main Staff memorandum, May 1912, RGVIA, f. 962, op. 2, d. 171, l. 1.

9. Miasoedov to A. N. Konstantinov, RGVIA, f. 962, op. 2, d. 112, l. 453.

10. Sukhomlinov testimony, August 3, 1916, RGVIA, f. 962, op. 2, d. 134, l. 92.

11. Petrov Commission report, 1916, RGVIA, f. 962, op. 2, d. 164, ll. 222–224. Baron Eduard Rudolfovich Untern-Shternberg was a retired officer and self-styled freelance journalist living in Petersburg in straitened circumstances. In 1910 Count Spannocchi approached him and requested that he use his contacts in the Duma to obtain reports on the demolition of the western fortresses then proposed by the Russian Ministry of War. Alfred Redl tipped off the Russians, who arrested, tried, and convicted Untern-Shternberg for espionage. Interestingly, one of the star witnesses against him at his trial was P. M. Mikhailov, whom Guchkov had appointed to be secretary of the Duma defense committee. See Georg Markus, *Der Fall Redl* (Vienna, 1984), pp. 137–139.

were doing or were suspected of doing, Erandakov's surveillance turned up no evidence that Miasoedov was involved in treason or spying. "My observation of Miasoedov," he wrote, "produced no serious data."[12]

During the investigation of Sukhomlinov four years later, however, Erandakov conveniently "remembered" that notwithstanding the absence of conclusive proof, he had already been positive in the spring of 1912 that Miasoedov was a foreign agent.[13] This self-aggrandizing statement was clearly supposed to impress his interrogators with his intelligence, acumen, and vigilance, but by making it Erandakov opened himself to charges of criminal misconduct. If, as a loyal counterintelligence officer, he had known "beyond doubt" of Miasoedov's treason in 1912, why had he not done more to unmask the blackguard? At the very least he should have prolonged the surveillance of Miasoedov, but Erandakov had not even bothered to keep the ex-gendarme's dossier active. Perhaps his own loyalty was not beyond question. When Erandakov realized how close he had come to incriminating himself, he made haste to retract his original testimony. In 1912 he had not yet developed a "firm conviction" of Miasoedov's guilt. All he had been persuaded of at the time was that Miasoeodov was a "scoundrel" owing to his "Germanophilism" and his dealings with an emigration office "that exploited its clients."[14]

The Woes of Sukhomlinov

Sukhomlinov had his hands full in the spring of 1912. Thwarting the Guchkov-Polivanov plot involved manipulating the emperor's perceptions. To counteract bad publicity he had to settle matters so that war ministry investigations would clear Miasoedov of any wrongdoing. Partly as an act of self-defense and as a future insurance policy, he also found it expedient to fire Miasoedov and arrange that he be spied on. But at the very moment when the minister was busily managing the fallout from the Miasoedov newspaper, racetrack, and dueling scandals, his old antagonist, Ekaterina's former husband, Butovich, was preparing to renew his attacks.

Butovich once again had recourse to the press. He published articles, particularly in *Zemshchina,* a right-wing gazette, which reopened the old wound of the divorce. He insisted that all the evidence used against him in the Holy Synod had been fraudulently obtained or manufactured. He charged that Sukhomlinov's helpmates in this chicanery included not only Altschüller and Lieutenant Colonel N. N. Kuliabko (former head of the Kiev Okhrana) but also even Dmitrii Bogrov, Stolypin's assassin! In tandem with this latter absurdity, Butovich also reiterated all his previous accusations: that Ekaterina had been an unfit mother more interested in money than the welfare of her son; that Sukhomlinov had threatened him with commitment to a

12. Erandakov testimony, May 5, 1916, RGVIA, f. 962, op. 2, d. 47, ll. 252–253.
13. Minister of Justice to the Petrov Commission, August 11, 1915, RGVIA, f. 962, op. 2, d. 43, l. 143.
14. RGVIA, f. 962, op. 2, d. 47, l. 253.

102 mental institution or administrative exile to Siberia; and so forth.[15] Ekaterina Viktorovna was in Italy when Butovich's articles began to appear and entrained for Petersburg at once. Upon her return she was able to prevail upon several papers to print her letter of rebuttal, which angrily denounced Butovich's allegations as lies and described her married life with him as "a living hell."[16]

However, Butovich's new bid to play for public sympathy was but one part of his strategy for hurting his ex-wife and her new husband. Simultaneously he sued Anna Goshkevich and Ekaterina Viktorovna in civil court for slander. His suit maintained that Anna had perjured herself by stating that he had sexually attacked her, and that Ekaterina had done the same by swearing that he had had an adulterous relationship with Vera Laurens, their son's governess. This was a shrewd maneuver on Butovich's part, for by calling both of these bits of evidence into question, he was casting grave doubt on the legality of the Sukhomlinovs' marriage; after all, the synod had granted the divorce on the exclusive bases of the attempted rape of Anna Goshekevich and Butovich's supposed extramarital philandering.

Butovich's attorneys now filed papers with the court that included an affidavit from a French doctor who had examined Vera Laurens and pronounced her a virgin. It is of course quite possible that this testimonial to Laurens's chastity was accurate in every respect, but it is not impossible that Butovich had obtained it by bribing an accommodating doctor. There exists a letter to Butovich from one of his anonymous informants at the Holy Synod that can be read as enhancing the plausibility of the latter interpretation. Offering his covert help in the suit, this clerk advised Butovich to "rely on me and be confident of success. Then you will have the unobstructed power to screw whomever you want in the cunt or the ass. You will even be able to use people involved in the case like Laurens and Goshkevich as if they were whores."[17] There is no record that Butovich was offended at all by these sentiments or by this characterization of his appetites.

Whether authentic or not, however, the mere existence of the Laurens medical report was the worse news possible for the Sukhomlinovs. If only the document would disappear! To the consternation of Butovich, it proceeded to do just that, mysteriously vanishing from the files of the tsarist Ministry of Justice, along with other materials submitted by Butovich's lawyers. As neither Butovich nor his legal team had taken the salutary precaution of keeping copies, the St. Petersburg circuit court dismissed Butovich's slander case on June 23, 1912, for lack of evidence.[18] Although people muttered that there was probable cause to arrest Sukhomlinov on suspicion of theft, the tsarist Ministry of Justice, which ascribed the loss of the documents to an

15. Great Britain, Public Record Office (hereafter PRO), Foreign Office (hereafter FO) 371/1469. See page 301 for the report of Lieutenant Colonel Knox, Britain's military attaché, concerning this dispute, as well as the dismissal of Polivanov.

16. RGVIA, f. 962, op. 2, d. 136, l. 55; clipping from New Times, May 8, 1912, RGVIA, f. 962, op. 2, d. 88, l. 74.

17. Anonymous note from consistory, Holy Synod, to Butovich, RGVIA, f. 962, op. 2, d. 88, l. 41.

18. Petrov Commission report, 1916, RGVIA, f. 962, op. 2, d. 164, l. 132.

innocent clerical error, declined to act. There was uproar in the Duma not only among the Octobrists and Kadets but even among deputies further to the right, who believed that the affair of the "lost" documents had debased Russia's prestige and exposed her to international ridicule.[19]

Though the collapse of Butovich's legal action was obviously a relief to Vladimir Aleksandrovich, this welcome event did not mean that henceforth the minister was free of care, for he had one problem that grew more neuralgic with every passing week: lack of money. It is true that when Sukhomlinov moved from Kiev to Petersburg to become chief of the general staff, he had accepted an enormous pay cut: his base salary had fallen from almost 60,000 to 16,000 rubles a year. When he received his ministerial portfolio, that sum had increased by a mere 2,000 rubles. However, the minister's base pay of 18,000 rubles was only a fraction of his compensation, for he also received a variety of allowances—for travel, entertaining, and stabling (just to mention a few)—that elevated his total cash emolument from the treasury to 62,695 rubles per annum.[20] As this total slightly exceeded what Sukhomlinov had earned in Kiev, one might suppose that he was handsomely if not munificently provided for.

Yet money went a lot further in the capital of Ukraine than it did in the capital of the entire empire. Moreover, Sukhomlinov's position as minister entailed financial burdens considerably heavier than any he had known as a provincial governor-general. For example, he was personally responsible for the wages of the sixteen servants who staffed his two official residences.[21] Whereas in Kiev Sukhomlinov had managed to get away with giving one and only one large-scale party a year, in Petersburg his rank obliged him to host numerous social events each month. There were also Ekaterina's large medical expenses to contend with, as well as the bills she ran up while traveling abroad. Ekaterina appears to have used her doctors' recommendation that warm climates were good for her health to justify these annual high-priced foreign trips. She was absent from St. Petersburg several months every year, residing in such locations as the south of France, Italy, Greece, Smyrna, Egypt, and Morocco. In the letters and telegrams she sent her husband while away there were frequent requests to cable more money.[22]

Indeed, it is fair to say that Ekaterina had a highly developed sense of personal entitlement where money was concerned—perhaps the psychological residuum of her penurious childhood and youth. She is said to have spent freely, even extravagantly, on such items as sable furs, Parisian gowns, and objets d'art from Fabergé. Certain of her critics subsequently averred that it was not unusual for her to run through 100,000 rubles a year.[23] Such charges must, of course, be taken with a very

19. See report of Knox, May 27, 1912, PRO. FO 371/1469, 301, and V. Shulgin, *Godi-dni-1920* (Moscow, 1991), pp. 259–262.

20. Petrov Commission report, RGVIA, f. 962, op. 2, d. 164, l. 88.

21. N. Goshkevich testimony, July 25, 1915, RGVIA, f. 962, op. 2, d. 134, l. 34.

22. See, for example, Sukhomlinov to Ekaterina, October 13, 1910, RGVIA, f. 962, op. 2, d. 60, l. 10.

23. See, for example, Petrov Commission report, 1916, RGVIA, f. 962, op. 2, d. 164, ll. 88–86; Anna Goshkevich testimony, October 18, 1916, RGVIA, f. 962, op. 2, d. 135, l. 54.

104 large grain of salt, in view of the questionable motives of those who advanced them. Tales of Ekaterina's excessive spending also fit all too conveniently into one of the most enduring narratives spun about the Sukhomlinov affair: that, at bottom, it was the story of an officer, once honorable and upright, who was ruined in the very twilight of his life by the insane whims of his young bride. It is a story in which Sukhomlinov plays the role of the dupe and Ekaterina Viktorovna that of the "Dostoevskian" woman and seductress.[24] One official report drafted after Sukhomlinov's arrest put it this way: "Falling under the influence of a depraved and cynical woman, he [Sukhomlinov] lived exclusively for her and for her caprices."[25]

What is not in dispute, however, is that the Sukhomlinovs' budget was seriously out of balance. To meet his bills Sukhomlinov had to turn to other sources of income, which, in his case, were quite limited. Vladimir Aleksandrovich collected no rents, since, like the majority of Russian noblemen, he owned neither lands nor estates. His book royalties, which usually totaled a mere 300–400 rubles a year, did not help very much either. He therefore had to draw on his savings, which by late 1908 amounted to almost 57,000 rubles in cash and securities. He tried speculating on the stock market. One of his friends, an engineer by the name of Urbanskii, had a reputation for financial wizardry. At his direction, Sukhomlinov made some extremely fortunate investments, which may have netted him a profit of as much as 55,000 rubles. However, the stock market was by nature volatile, and it was unwise for a man to bank too much on it, as Sukhomlinov learned to his pain in the fall of the 1912 when the outbreak of the First Balkan War triggered a steep decline in the value of shares on the St. Petersburg bourse.[26] Matters grew so bad that Sukhomlinov's devoted housekeeper, Mariia Frantsevna Kiun'e, grew reluctant to ask him for small sums for domestic expenses, owing to the long face he assumed whenever she did.[27] It was apparently about this time—late in 1912—that Sukhomlinov's inhibitions weakened and he began to accept bribes.

The Corruption of Sukhomlinov

It was inevitable that the vast sums Russia appropriated for military modernization in the years leading up to the world war would command the attention of international arms manufacturers. A great deal of the money Russia was proposing to spend would go for the purchase of advanced technology. The loss of the Baltic fleet in the Russo-Japanese war and the threat of Turkish naval predominance in the Black Sea meant that millions of rubles would be lavished on the construction of capital ships and coastal defenses. There would also be large investments on behalf of the army, particularly to increase its stocks of artillery, machine guns, and ammunition.

24. See, for example, M. D. Bonch-Bruevich, *Vsia vlast'sovetam* (Moscow, 1957), p. 66.
25. Note on Sukhomlinov, 1916, RGVIA, f. 962, op. 2, d. 133, l. 1.
26. RGVIA, f. 962, op. 2, d. 164, l. 6; material on military unpreparedness, August 11, 1915, RGVIA, f. 962, op. 2, d. 43, l. 125.
27. N. Goshkevich testimony, July 25, 1915, RGVIA, f. 962, op. 2, d. 134, l. 34.

As Russia's domestic arms industry, although robust, lacked the capacity to carry out the entire program in as timely a fashion as was desired, there were considerable opportunities for foreign concerns to share in the windfall. Such titans of the industry as France's Schneider-Creusot, Germany's Krupps, Austria's Skoda, and Britain's Vickers all vied with each other for lucrative Russian military contracts; this competition had as much to do with greasing the appropriate palms as it did with offering quality goods at attractive prices.

The biggest winner was the firm of Vickers Limited. By 1900 Vickers was a huge Anglo-American conglomerate with interests in shipbuilding, munitions, railroads, and steel. Even in an era of predatory capitalism, Vickers stood out for its total lack of scruples in pursuing foreign orders. Vickers's success in winning contracts from the governments of such countries as Turkey, Spain, Italy, Brazil, and Japan was more often than not due to its assiduous courtship and generous remuneration of key military and political figures.[28]

The firm's business in Russia was in the hands of one of its directors and top salesmen, the notorious Greek-born polyglot Basil Zaharoff, who had been cultivating the empire's grand dukes, admirals, and generals since the late nineteenth century. Zaharoff is said to have made particularly effective use of his association with the ballerina Kshinskaia, who, after losing her place as mistress to the emperor, took up with Grand Duke Sergei Mikhailovich, inspector general of the Russian artillery.[29]

The post-1906 Russian military buildup offered full scope to Zaharoff's talents. Vickers was soon given a contract to erect a naval shipyard in Nikolaev, which upon completion was to be managed by the Nikolaev Shipbuilding Company, a Russian concern. In order to steer business its way, this latter firm, which was partially owned by Vickers, spent 100,000 rubles on buying the goodwill of officials at the Russian Ministry of Marine. This sum (and its purpose) was actually entered into the company's books, and was so reported to London in October 1912 by the incredulous British naval attaché.[30]

Nineteen twelve was a banner year for Vickers's sales to Russia's land forces as well. It won the right to produce light machine guns for the army, despite the fact that its bid of 1,750 rubles per gun was almost 43 percent higher than the 1,000 rubles tendered by Russia's own Tula Armament Works.[31] Vickers was also engaged to build an enormous armament plant at Tsaritsyn for the Russian Artillery Works Company, 20 percent of the stock of which it conveniently also owned. This enterprise in turn became the recipient of many of the war ministry's largest and most valuable con-

28. See, for example, Philip Noel-Baker, *The Private Manufacture of Armaments*, vol. 1 (London, 1936), pp. 72, 142, 152–153.

29. Richard Lewinsohn, *The Mystery Man of Europe: Sir Basil Zaharoff* (Philadelphia, 1929), pp. 95–98; 114–119; Anthony Allfrey, *Man of Arms: The Life and Legend of Sir Basil Zaharoff* (London, 1989), pp. 57–58, 74–76, 82–83.

30. PRO.FO.371/1469.77. The Corrupt Practices Act of 1906 made it a crime for any British company to resort to bribery to gain foreign orders; this was one parliamentary act that Vickers consistently ignored.

31. RGVIA, f. 962, op. 2, d. 48, l. 120.

106 tracts; the ministry placed 40 million rubles' worth of orders with the Russian Artillery Works in the first half of 1914 alone.[32]

Sukhomlinov's support for all these ventures was bought and paid for. Vickers made at least one payment of 50,000 rubles to the minister in 1913, and there were probably several others.[33] The go-between was doubtless P. I. Balinskii, the chief executive of the Russian Artillery Works Company, who in previous years had worked for Zaharoff as one of Vickers's agents in Russia. Sukhomlinov had been acquainted with Balinskii for more than a quarter of a century.[34]

Nor was Vickers the minister's exclusive benefactor. Having given in to temptation once, Vladimir Aleksandrovich apparently found it easier and easier to compromise his principles on every subsequent occasion. It is highly likely that he also took money from Nikolai Svirskii, another old acquaintance, to whose son he had stood godfather. Svirskii, a furniture manufacturer who had long resided in France, returned to Petersburg a few years before 1914 as the representative of several French armament concerns. In 1913 he brokered a deal between the Russian War Ministry and France's Gyro Company for the production of twelve-inch shells. When he subsequently set up Promet, an armament firm of his own, military contracts rained down upon him like confetti, including one for the production of artillery fuses worth over 7 million rubles.[35] It is also highly probable that Alexander Altschüller's son Oskar won a contract for gun carriages for the St. Petersburg Metallurgical Works by making a bribe to the minister the centerpiece of his lobbying effort.[36]

The Sukhomlinov Circle after 1912

Thus it was that Sukhomlinov finally joined his friends and acquaintances in feeding at the trough of military procurement. However, all was far from well within the retinue of profiteers and swindlers who surrounded the minister. Although much money was being made, bickering and disagreement came to replace amity and cooperation in the last few years before the outbreak of the world war. Several of the members of what we might describe as the "Sukhomlinov circle" broke their ties with one another; some broke off with Sukhomlinov himself; virtually all experienced dramatic changes in their personal fortunes. A few years later tsarist investigators would be baffled by the shifting patterns of these relationships, but that was because they saw them as the outward signs of widespread plots rather than taking these manifestations of human weakness, jealousy, and greed for what they were.

Consider the case of Alexander Altschüller. Although he continued to earn impressive sums by selling access to the war minister, Altschüller's core business went

32. Ibid., l. 119.

33. Petrov Commission material, 1916, RGVIA, f. 962, op. 2, d. 133, l. 2; Petrov Commission report, RGVIA, f. 962, op. 2, d. 164, l. 6.

34. Petrov Commission report, 1916, RGVIA, f. 962, op. 2, d. 164, l. 14.

35. RGVIA, f. 962, op. 2, d. 164, l. 40; RGVIA, f. 962, op. 2, d. 48, ll. 122–123.

36. N. Goshkevich testimony, July 23–26, 1916, RGVIA, f. 962, op. 2, d. 48, l. 124.

into steep decline. Years of mismanagement had taken their toll on the South Russian Machine Works, which by 1912 was almost one million rubles in debt to the Russian State Bank. Altschüller's fellow shareholders were extremely unhappy with the performance of the company, and in order to prevent the bank from placing the firm into receivership and to protect his investment, Durilin, another of the company's directors, plotted a takeover. When Altschüller put some of his own stock up for sale, Durilin quietly bought it up through intermediaries. In fact, Durilin acquired so many shares that he easily arranged for Altschüller's removal from the chairmanship and board of the company at a general shareholders meeting in 1913. Altschüller was compelled to sell off his remaining stake in South Russian and completely sever his connection to the firm.[37]

The shock of this business debacle caused Altschüller to reassess his mode of life. He regularized his domestic circumstances by finally marrying his French mistress, Lucette, even as he began to worry about his advancing age and his deteriorating health. In view of his worsening angina pectoris, his physician, Dr. Sventsitskii, warned him that continued exposure to the rigors of the Russian winter could prove fatal. Altschüller consequently decided to liquidate his affairs in Russia, and retire to the Austria he had abandoned over forty years previously. In 1913 he purchased an estate north of Vienna and signed over all his remaining interests in brokerage, shipping, and agricultural machinery to his son Oskar. In March 1914 he sold his Petersburg apartment and left the Russian Empire for good. Ekaterina Viktorovna gamely promised to visit him in Austria that summer, a promise that she would have kept had not the July crisis and world war intervened.[38]

Nikolai Goshkevich had sided with Durilin in his coup against Altschüller. Indeed, the relationship between Goshkevich and Altschüller had begun to fray even before the affairs of the South Russian Machine Works turned critical. One of the employees whom Goshkevich had hired for the Petersburg office had proved to be a thief, and Altschüller had blamed Goshkevich personally for the sums the miscreant had embezzled from the office accounts. For his part Goshkevich had come to resent Altschüller's insouciance in money matters, particularly those that affected Goshkevich himself. When Altschüller left South Russian, the new management raised Nikolai's salary and appointed him to take the Austrian's place as the firm's Petersburg representative. The company office was transferred to a room in Goshkevich's apartment. Goshkevich did not, however, devote himself exclusively to South Russian's affairs any more than his predecessor had done. He also worked for the Russo-American Chamber of Commerce and the Commercial Society of Mutual Credit and simultaneously collected commissions and kickbacks from such organizations as Prodamet, the Russian metallurgical syndicate, and from various consortia of foreign

37. RGVIA, f. 962, op. 2, d. 134, l. 63; V.-N. Z. Finn testimony, n.d., RGVIA, f. 962, op. 2, d. 136, l. 38; Stavka report, RGVIA, f. 2003, op. 2, d. 1063, l. 66.

38. RGVIA, f. 962, op. 2, d. 146, l. 20; RGVIA, f. 962, op. 2, d. 164, l. 124; N. Goshkevich testimony, July 25, 1915, RGVIA, f. 962, op. 2, d. 134, l. 30.

108   investors. It was during this same period that his marriage came to an end. In 1913 he formally separated from Anna, and they were finally granted a divorce in June 1914.[39]

It is not impossible that Anna's rupture with her lover, Maxim Veller, was the proximate cause of the dissolution of the Goshkevichs' marriage. Nikolai's indifference to his wife's shameless dalliance with the rich businessman provides the basis to presume that it was Veller's money rather than any mutual attraction or respect that had kept the couple together. But at last Veller tired of Anna and, moreover, came to suspect that she was entertaining other men behind his back. Around Easter 1913, Veller told Anna that the affair was over; he also informed her that he was cutting her off without a kopeck. It was only a few months later that Anna and Nikolai parted.[40]

Curiously, Veller and Nikolai remained on good terms. Yet perhaps this was not as odd as it appears, for both men still had a mutual interest in negotiating contracts with the war ministry's Main Artillery Administration, and both looked to Colonel V. G. Ivanov for back-channel help. Although Ivanov would insist at his own trial that he had had nothing to do with either man after 1912, the evidence indicates that this was a bold-faced lie.[41] What had actually happened was that Ivanov, who was morbidly afraid of having his dishonesty exposed, insisted in 1912 that henceforth all contact between him and his business partners be put on a conspiratorial footing. Neither Veller nor Goshkevich was to visit his office or telephone him from their homes. Instead of his real name, the pseudonym "Arthur" was to be used in both speaking and writing of him. Whether as a result of his dealings with Goshkevich and Veller or his association with others, by 1913, the year of Vickers's bonanza, there had been large and gratifying improvements in Ivanov's financial circumstances. Whereas in 1910 he had been so poor that he had humbly begged state charities for relief, by 1913 he was affluent enough to move into a luxurious seven-room apartment, to indulge in foreign travel, and to plan the purchase of a 100,000–ruble estate.[42]

Then there was the Georgian Vasilii Dumbadze, a relative latecomer. Like Veller, Dumbadze had gone to Germany for his postsecondary education and was a graduate of Leipzig University. An adventurer and confidence man, he managed to finagle his way into Petersburg society by falsely claiming kinship to General I. Dumbadze, Governor of Yalta, and by adopting the pose of a soigné man-about-town. He built relationships with General E. V. Bogdanov, a prominent member of the imperial suite, as well as with Altschüller, Veller, and Goshkevich in order to become close to War Minister Sukhomlinov. Hoping to influence Sukhomlinov to route a military railroad through some land he owned, Dumbadze hit on the idea of flattering the minister's vanity by proposing to write his biography. His instincts were correct. Not only was Sukhomlinov enthusiastic about this book project, but he also obligingly of-

39. RGVIA, f. 962, op. 2, d. 146, ll. 19, 27; N. Goshkevich testimony, 1916, RGVIA, f. 962, op. 2, d. 134, ll. 28–29, 40, 44, 48, 64.

40. M. I. Veller testimony, August 9, 1916, RGVIA, f. 962, op. 2, d. 134, ll. 114–116.

41. V. G. Ivanov testimony, July 31, 1916, RGVIA, f. 962, op. 2, d. 134, l. 78.

42. N. Goshkevich testimony, July 24, 1916, RGVIA, f. 962, op. 2, d. 134, ll. 26–27; note on surveillance, n.d., RGVIA, f. 2003, op. 2, d. 1063, l. 67.

fered to supply Dumbadze with materials. Shortly after the beginning of the war, the minister gave Goshkevich some documents to pass on to the enterprising Georgian. Included in the package was "A List of the Most Important Measures Carried Out by the War Ministry from 1909 to March 1914," a classified report that the general staff had compiled at Sukhomlinov's direction. Sukhomlinov apparently felt no qualms about allowing Dumbadze access to this document: although it contained the most comprehensive description of the ministry's military reforms, he believed that the secrets it contained had been rendered valueless by the coming of the war.

Because Dumbadze had no literary talent to speak of, he farmed the chapters of his book out to a team of ghostwriters. The manuscript was completed in December 1914 and the work appeared in print one month later. Dumbadze made sure that Sukhomlinov received a large shipment of complimentary copies. George V's government arranged for its translation and publication in Britain in order to inspire confidence in the military skill and prowess of the nation's Russian allies.[43]

If Sukhomlinov acquired a new friend in Vasilii Dumbadze, he was simultaneously discarding others. As time went by, the Sukhomlinovs came to see less and less of the Goshkeviches; Ekaterina Viktorovna (somewhat hypocritically) ascribed the chilling of her former warmth toward her cousin and his wife to her moral outrage at Anna's sexual wantonness.[44] Of greater consequence still was the Sukhomlinovs' rupture with Prince Andronnikov.

It became an idée fixe among the intelligentsia during that most paranoid of years, 1917, that the last stage of the tsarist autocracy had resembled a puppet theater. Although the naive might be taken in by the magnificence of the sets and the costumes, the wise were aware that there were "dark forces" behind the scenes making all the decisions and pulling the strings. Depending upon where one's political sympathies lay, these dark forces could be variously identified as Jews, Masons, the court camarilla, the Rasputin clique, Germans, or others. One name often mentioned in connection with dark forces was that of Prince M. M. Andronnikov. When Andronnikov was called to the witness stand after the February Revolution of 1917 to testify about his relationship with the Sukhomlinovs, he began his statement with the unconsciously hilarious assertion "I am not a dark force."[45]

Ekaterina Viktorovna later swore that she and her husband renounced any further contact with the prince in the spring of 1914, when they realized he was behaving as if he really were some sort of a clandestine power broker. It was only then, said Ekaterina, that she had grasped the full truth about Andronnikov's dishonest attempts to batten off the military budget by, for example, buying up lands in Turkestan through which a military railroad would have to pass. When she learned

43. V. M. Voblyi testimony, July 19, 1916, RGVIA, f. 962, op. 2, d. 134, ll. 1–3; Petrov Commission report, 1916, RGVIA, f. 962, op. 2, d. 164, ll. 241–242; RGVIA, f. 962, op. 2, d. 48, ll. 144–145; V. D. Doumbadze, *Russia's War Minister: The Life and Work of Adjutant-General Vladimir Alexandrovitsh Soukhomlinov* (London, 1915).

44. Ekaterina Sukhomlinova testimony, December 1916, RGVIA, f. 962, op. 2, d. 52, l. 71.

45. Andronnikov testimony, August 23, 1917, RGVIA, f. 962, op. 2, d. 145, l. 18.

110   that Andronnikov was openly boasting that anyone who wished to do business with her husband would have to approach him, Andronnikov, first, she regarded this piece of effrontery as unforgivable. It was at her insistence that Sukhomlinov repudiated Andronnikov; the prince was henceforth never again to be received in the minister's office or home.[46]

However, Ekaterina's story of the origin of the discord between Andronnikov and Sukhomlinov did not lack for competition; there were, in fact, several alternate versions of these events. According to Vladimir Aleksandrovich, it was he, rather than his wife, who had been the prime mover in severing relations with the prince; he also implied that he had made an enemy of Andronnikov by refusing to countenance his shady dealings in real estate and military contracts.[47] As for Andronnikov, he claimed that Sukhomlinov's hostility toward him stemmed from his manly attempt to open the minister's eyes to the vileness and untrustworthiness of such persons as Miasoedov and Altschüller, about whom he had warned the minister repeatedly.[48] A final explanation, offered by a prominent figure in the police department, took a completely different tack: in this telling the quarrel arose when Andronnikov went to Sukhomlinov and told him that his wife had begun an affair with A. I. Mantashev, the fabulously wealthy Baku oil tycoon in whose company she had recently completed an extensive tour of Egypt. When Sukhomlinov told Ekaterina what the prince had said, she heatedly denied everything and extracted a promise from her husband never to associate with the dirty-minded intriguer again.[49]

There is probably more to this latter version than to any of the others. Ekaterina obviously had had a fair sense of how Andronnikov made his living all along, which meant that she experienced no sudden revelation about his knavery in the spring of 1914. Sukhomlinov may have actually frustrated some of the prince's business deals with the war ministry around this time, but even if he did, he had previously smiled on them. It is equally obvious that Andronnikov did not harbor dark suspicions about Miasoedov and Altschüller, having actually collaborated with the latter on several occasions. It was much more in character for Andronnikov to have spread stories of adultery and illicit sex; gossip, after all, was his stock in trade. It was therefore likely that Andronnikov's accusation against Ekaterina Viktorovna (whether grounded or not), along with his evident attempt to supplant Altschüller (who was on the verge of leaving Russia) as gatekeeper to the person of the war minister, was the grounds for the row. We know that Andronnikov made an effort to patch things up by sending Sukhomlinov a pair of expensive cuff links as a peace offering. When Sukhomlinov accepted them while still instructing his servants to bar the door to Andronnikov, the prince knew that there would be no reconciliation.[50]

Parting company with Andronnikov had repercussions for Ekaterina's relations with Nataliia Chervinskaia. Chervinskaia, that relative of Butovich's who had sided

46. Ekaterina Sukhomlinova testimony, November 21, 1916, RGVIA, f. 962, op. 2, d. 136, l. 52.
47. V. A. Sukhomlinov, *Vospominaniia Sukhomlinova* (Moscow/Leningrad, 1926), pp. 256–257.
48. *Padenie tsarskago rezhima*, vol. 1 (Leningrad, 1924), pp. 373–374.
49. Ibid., vol. 2, p. 56.
50. A. F. Rediger memoir, RGVIA, f. 280, op. 1, d. 8, p. 918.

with Ekaterina during the divorce proceedings and who had lived with the Sukhomlinovs ever since, over the years had become a friend, confidante, and partisan of Andronnikov's. (Andronnikov had helped Chervinskaia invest her small capital, and she
had equally come to rely on money he "lent" her.) When Chervinskaia sought to intercede for the prince with her benefactress, Ekaterina told her that she would have to
choose between Ekaterina and Andronnikov. Chervinskia opted for the prince and
moved out of the Sukhomlinovs' palace in June 1914.[51]

Working in tandem, Andronnikov and Chervinskaia were a formidable pair of
enemies. Taking advantage of his unique entrée into Petersburg society and the Russian bureaucracy, Andronnikov scurried from drawing room to drawing room and
office to office, tattling about Sukhomlinov's venal acceptance of bribes and kickbacks. For her part, Chervinskaia established a salon in her new apartment that func-
tioned as a virtual anti-Sukhomlinov general headquarters. Among those who fre-
quented her home were Colonel Lev Bulatsel', Sukhomlinov's disgruntled former
aide; Colonel I. V. Gorlenko, another bilious ex-adjutant; and S. T. Varun-Sekret, the
deputy chairman of the Duma, who would play such a prominent and malicious role
during the official investigation of the war minister two years later.[52] Chervinskaia
and Andronnikov became still more dangerous after the outbreak of the war when
they enlisted the help of an ally much more powerful than either of them: the uncouth, self-anointed "holy man" from Siberia, Grigorii Efimovich Rasputin. Andronnikov, who had an extraordinary sensitivity to the subterranean politics of the court,
had attached himself to Rasputin in late 1914. Chervinskaia would be the hostess at
the notorious dinner parties with which Andronnikov regaled Rasputin at his
Fontanka apartment throughout the war, soirées at which the *starets* gorged himself
on boiled fish and sweet wine while engaging in informal conversation with the imperial ministers whom Andronnikov had so considerately invited. Since Rasputin
would begin to acquire real political influence in 1915, Andronnikov and Chervinskaia would eventually use their connection to Rasputin as the trump card in the
campaign they conducted against V. A. Sukhomlinov.

The Fortunes of Miasoedov

While all these realignments had been occurring within the minister's rarefied
circle, Miasoedov's affairs had not been proceeding at all well. Once again without
steady employment, he had returned to the Northwest Russian Steamship Company.
Among the lies, half-truths, and innuendo in Makarov's letter of March 1912 there
had been at least one accurate statement: as Makarov had charged, Sergei Nikolae-

---

51. RGVIA, f. 962, op. 2, d. 136, l. 53. Among the many items of misinformation contained in Edward
Radzinsky's book on Rasputin is the fallacious assertion that "Chervinskaia hated the sixty-two year old
minister for deserting her sister and marrying a younger woman." As we have seen, Chervinskaia was related to Butovich, not Elizaveta Nikolaevna Koreish; moreover, Elizaveta Nikolaevna had not been "deserted" by Sukhomlinov as the two were married at the time of her death. See *The Rasputin File*, trans. Judson Rosengrant (New York, 2000), p. 284.

52. Sukhomlinov, *Vospominaniia Sukhomlinova*, p. 258.

112 vich had not suspended all his dealings with Northwest after he reassumed the uniform but had instead merely scaled them back. He continued to "own" stock in the firm, for which he also occasionally did small favors. Evidence suggests that Miasoedov anticipated rejoining Northwest in a full-time capacity someday. In September 1911, on the eve of his appointment to the war ministry, Miasoedov had concluded an agreement concerning the company with the Freidberg family. The Freidbergs promised Miasoedov that after the expiration of ten years (that is, in 1921) they would accept him as chairman of the firm not only in name but also in fact.[53] What this document makes clear is that Miasoedov anticipated serving an additional decade in the gendarmes, retiring in his mid-fifties, and then pursuing a second career in business.

But things had not gone according to plan. Miasoedov had been forced to resume his job with Northwest under the old terms; it would be nine long years before he could count on a promotion to real executive responsibility. And although he was apparently paid more than he had been prior to his brief stint with the war ministry, his duties were still much more clerical than managerial. Virtually all the work of the firm was done in the Libava office. Letters prepared there to a variety of British and American shipping companies and banks were forwarded to Petersburg for Miasoedov to sign and post to their destinations.[54] Sergei was also expected to serve as liaison to tsarist government authorities, as he did, for example, in the spring of 1914 by defending the company's use of Jewish field agents in correspondence with the governor of Minsk.[55]

Despite the volatility of the emigration business, the Northwest Russian Steamship Company appears to have prospered moderately. Increasing revenues made it possible in 1911 for the firm to buy outright the two ships *Leopold II* and *Georgios I* that it had previously leased in Denmark. *Det forenede Dampskibs-Selskab* (the United Steamship Company), the vessels' original owner, transferred title to *Leopold* and *Georgios* in June and August, respectively; Danish sources reveal that the purchase price for the *Leopold*, which Northwest rechristened *Saratov*, was 100,000 rubles. The amount that Northwest paid for the *Georgios*, renamed *Odessa*, was not recorded.[56]

But Northwest Russian's modest success did not satisfy Miasoedov; the only way for him to earn more money through the company would be if it experienced explosive, rather than steady, growth. Accordingly, he importuned the Freidbergs to expand the scale and scope of the business at every opportunity. Might it not be possible for Northwest to inaugurate its own direct service from Russia to America, for instance? Samuel Freidberg found this idea preposterous. He wrote Miasoedov that the firm would continue to be a "feeder" line for Cunard, just as it always had been in

53. RGVIA, f. 962, op. 2, d. 167, l. 20.

54. Packet of letters, RGVIA, f. 962, op. 2, d. 112, ll. 458–501 passim.

55. Miasoedov to governor of Minsk, May 4, 1914, RGVIA, f. 962, op. 2, d. 112, ll. 467–468.

56. F. Holm-Petersen and A. Rosendahl, *Fra Sejl til Diesel. Dansk Skibsfart, Søhandel og Skibsbygning*, vol. 3 (n.p., n.d.), pp. 442, 467. Russian sources appear to be in error in dating this sale to 1913. See Petrograd Okhrana to Department of Police, February 21, 1915, RGVIA, f. 801, op. 28, d. 168, l. 63.

the past. The Freidbergs had neither the necessary capital nor the stomach to compete head to head with the giants of transatlantic shipping. As far as he was concerned, the subject was closed.[57]

Miasoedov also made an effort to persuade the Freidbergs to sell Northwest and give him part of the proceeds and even opened negotiations with the Danish shipping factor Katsenlenbogen on this subject. The Freidberg family was not interested in this suggestion either.[58] Thwarted in his efforts to squeeze more income out of Northwest, Miasoedov pursued other business opportunities. He was involved, for a time, in a venture to develop hydroelectric power in Transcaucasia, and in early 1914 visited Tiflis in the company of some German investors to discuss the matter. But once again, nothing came of it.[59]

There was more to Miasoedov's quest for income in the last prewar years than garden-variety avarice. His expenses had risen sharply. His children were older, and there were tuition payments and music lessons to think of. The principal drain on Miasoedov's bank account, however, was his mistress Evgeniia Stolbina, for by this point Sergei Nikolaevich was paying her an allowance of 210 rubles a month. As a result of this generosity, Miasoedov fell deeply into debt, for it was only by signing promissory notes that he was able to keep his head above water. Even so, an inspection of his banking records reveals that at the end of a typical year Miasoedov usually had no more than one or two hundred rubles in cash to his name.[60]

In January 1914 Stolbina's husband was transferred out of the capital to the gendarme detachment in Radzivillov. She declined to go with him, remained in Petersburg, and rented out a room in her apartment, first to a piano teacher named Izabella Kan and then to Nina Petrovna Magerovskaia, who had been her friend since their school days together at the Kiev Gymnasium. Stolbina and Magerovskaia now apparently set themselves up as courtesans and developed a small but select clientele among the military officers of the Petersburg garrison.[61]

Despite what investigators would later describe as her "dissipated" mode of life, Stolbina's feelings for Miasoedov had deepened over the years, as had his for her. The love letters they sent each other during this time were replete with evidently sincere, if syrupy, endearments.[62] More and more frequently, Sergei and Evgeniia spoke of marrying and starting a new life together. There were, however, two big obstacles to the realization of their dream. One was Miasoedov's wife, Klara, who would have to be convinced to agree to a divorce. This was so because she, not Sergei, was the aggrieved party who would have to appeal to the synod for a divorce decree on the

---

57. Freidberg to Miasoedov, July 14, 1914, RGVIA, f. 962, op. 2, d. 113, l. 27.

58. Matveev report, April 30, 1915, RGVIA, f. 801, op. 28, d. 167, ll. 23–24.

59. Chief of counterintelligence, general staff, to Matveev, June 24, 1915, RGVIA, f. 801, op. 28, d. 172, ll. 23–24.

60. Ibid., ll. 33ff. On January 1, 1915, for example, Miasoedov's bank account contained a mere 120 rubles and 87 kopecks.

61. Assistant procurator, Warsaw, to Stavka, 5 February 1916, RGVIA, f. 2003, op. 2, d. 1073, ll. 219–220.

62. See, for example, Miasoedov to Stolbina, RGVIA, f. 962, op. 2, d. 112, ll. 225, 266.

114 grounds of her husband's unfaithfulness. But money was also an issue, for as Sergei wrote Evgeniia, "to immediately break with the past and go off with you on 430 rubles a month is hardly sensible."[63]

Klara, who, as we have seen, had known about her husband's extramarital liaison almost from the beginning, grew ever more angry and hurt. It is likely that the combination of the affair and all the shocks the couple had experienced in the winter and spring of 1912 served to extinguish what was left of her love and respect for Sergei. In November 1912 she painted a bleak picture of the state of her marriage in a letter to her sister's husband, Frantz Rigert: "We only see each other at dinner. We feel nothing for each other but hostility."[64] A week later, at her urging, Sergei's brother Nikolai sent him a note of reproof. Nikolai observed that Sergei could not shirk the duty of apprising Klara of his future intentions concerning her, and concluded, "Do not hinder me from reminding you that your wife does not deserve such cruelty and shame."[65]

In 1913 Miasoedov eventually broached the subject of a divorce. Klara later claimed that she was fully prepared to accept the formal termination of the marriage, assuming, of course, that Miasoedov made adequate provision for her support and that of the children. But Sergei's offer to pay 3,000 rubles per year—i.e., the annual rent he received from his Vilna building—Klara dismissed as inadequate and insulting. As she observed in another letter to Rigert, Sergei's salary and pension came to over 7,000 rubles, while she and the two children were expected to subsist on a sum less than half as much. It simply wasn't fair.[66] If we are to believe what she later told military investigators, it was, moreover, not only her husband's meanness that led her to reconsider the wisdom of a divorce. The older of the children, Mariia (Musa) adored her father and tearfully implored Klara not to acquiesce in the breakup of their family. Klara gave in to Musa's importunings and told her husband that she did not want to discuss divorce again, even though she privately knew that ending rather than continuing the marriage would be much the better option for her. "I sacrificed myself because of my love for my children," was the way she subsequently characterized the decision she made at this time.[67]

But Stolbina began to grow impatient. When she pressed Miasoedov to explain why no progress was being made on the divorce question, he eventually had to admit that his wife's stubborn opposition was the problem. Stolbina was outraged. On the night of July 4, 1914, a truly witless (and possibly drunken) idea occurred to Miasoedov: he would take Stolbina over to his apartment for a final showdown with Klara. Sergei and Evgeniia arrived at the apartment on Kolokolnaia Street at 1:30 in the morning. There ensued an ugly and violent scene, with Evgeniia and Klara shouting curses and imprecations against each other, and eventually against Miasoedov, too.

63. Assistant procurator, Warsaw, to Stavka, February 5, 1916, RGVIA, f. 2003, op. 2, d. 1073, l. 222.
64. Matveev findings, April 30, 1915, RGVIA, f. 801, op. 28, d. 167, l. 29.
65. Nikolai Miasoedov to Sergei Miasoedov, November 30, 1912, RGVIA, f. 962, op. 2, d. 112, ll. 19–20.
66. Klara to Rigert, October 23, 1914, RGVIA, f. 801, op. 28, d. 166, ll. 99–100.
67. Klara Miasoedova interrogation, RGVIA, f. 962, op. 2, d. 160, ll. 107–108.

Furious with them both, Sergei turned on his heel and strode out of the apartment, slamming the door behind him on the two quarreling women. In a note she jotted down about this incident Klara stated that if she were suddenly to die "accidentally," it would behoove the police to investigate Stolbina on a charge of murder, as she was a person "capable of anything."[68]

Miasoedov departed Petersburg on the first available train to Libava. Stopping briefly to confer with Samuel and Boris Freidberg, he proceeded on to Germany. Needing to be alone, he spent several days in a Berlin hotel trying to think through the mess of his private life. The only person he informed of his whereabouts was Evgeniia Stolbina, who received a postcard telling her not to worry, that all was well and that he would return shortly. It is the last glimpse we have of Miasoedov prior to outbreak of the war just a few weeks later.

Sergei Nikolaevich, like many other Europeans of his time, greeted the coming of the war with a combination of enthusiasm and relief. Always patriotic, he realized that military emergency would force his recall to the army, where he hoped he would be able to find a job in which he could perform real services for his country. At the same time, the war would rescue him from his nasty and unpleasant domestic complications. His failures—in the service, in business, even in his marriage—would all be washed away and he need not dwell on them anymore. As if reborn, he would now have the opportunity simultaneously to bury the memories of the past and cover himself with glory. What he could not know, of course, was that the war had obloquy rather than glory in store for him. The war would be the last act in the play of Miasoedov's life, and owing both to human malevolence and simple bad luck, that last act would be brief.

68. Matveev findings, April 30, 1915, RGVIA, f. 801, op. 28, d. 167, ll. 29.

5

The First Phase of the War

On June 28, 1914, a nineteen-year-old consumptive named Gavrilo Princip fired a revolver into an open touring car on the streets of the Bosnian city of Sarajevo, killing the heir to the Austrian throne, the Archduke Franz Ferdinand, as well as his wife. There ensued six weeks of diplomatic crisis that eventually culminated in the outbreak of the First World War.

Contrary to what has often been written about it, the coming of the Great War was neither an accident nor a mistake. It was not the inevitable product of an arms race, nor the consequence of the septic polarization of the Great Powers into two antagonistic alliance systems. It was, in short, most definitely not the "war no one wanted." Rather, the statesmen of 1914 took actions that they knew entailed courting war, and the reason they did so was that the political objectives they pursued seemed important enough to justify accepting the risk of full-blown hostilities. In the case of every important power involved, Germany excepted, these objectives concerned either national survival or national security interests of the highest importance.

In Vienna it was correctly believed that the Sarajevo conspirators had been organized and armed by elements in the Serbian government. Were this outrage not punished, Vienna would in effect be giving a powerful boost to the forces of nationalism and of south Slav nationalism in particular—forces whose waxing strength represented the single greatest challenge to the continued existence of the Hapsburg Empire. For this reason, the ultimatum that Vienna tendered Belgrade on July 23 offered the Serbs the stark choice between renouncing their national sovereignty and going to war.

Equally compelling reasons induced the Russians to support their Serbian allies. Germany and Austria had humiliated Russia back in 1908, when Petersburg had been incapable of either preventing or receiving compensation for Vienna's annexation of Bosnia-Herzegovina. The Russian Council of Ministers did not believe that Belgrade was complicit in the Sarajevo *attentat* and noted that Vienna had produced no iron-clad evidence proving that this was the case.[1] The council was also strongly of the view that if Russia permitted Serbia to be crushed militarily, it would again be acquiescing in its own humiliation, this time with potentially fatal consequences. If Russia declined to help the Serbs, it would be relegated to the ranks of the second- or even the third-rate powers, and its influence and prestige would suffer throughout the world. Still worse, the regime's numerous domestic opponents would doubtless construe its inaction as weakness, a perception that could give birth to riot, disorder, and perhaps even revolution at home. The council conducted its deliberations, after all, against the backdrop of recent serious industrial strikes, which had been attended by violence and by the erection of barricades in many of the working-class districts of the capital. It was nonetheless only after significant hesitation as well as impassioned pleading by Sukhomlinov and Foreign Minister Sazonov that Nicholas II was induced to sign the order authorizing a general mobilization—against both Austria and Germany.

In Paris the government of the Third Republic held that French security could be preserved only through the maintenance of the balance of power, a balance that depended utterly on the cohesion and robustness of the Franco-Russian alliance. To stand by and look on while Germany and Austria squared off against Russia was therefore out of the question, for this would virtually guarantee a Russian defeat. A Europe without a strong Russia would be a Europe unsafe for France, for the entire continent would ultimately succumb to German domination. As this nightmarish outcome was completely unacceptable, France would stand with Russia, regardless of whether or not the evolving crisis produced a clear-cut *casus foederis*. Of course, given the immediate implementation of the Schlieffen plan at the beginning of the war, which involved Germany's delivering its heaviest initial military blow against the French in the west, there was no realistic chance of limiting the conflict to eastern or southern Europe.

It was the Schlieffen plan that also eventually brought the British into the fight. Although aligned with France and Russia, Britain was not formally allied with either and was therefore not legally obligated to send an expeditionary force across the English Channel. The Schlieffen plan, however, famously entailed Germany's violation of the neutrality of Belgium. It had been a cardinal principle of British foreign policy since the time of Henry VIII that British security required London's participation in any coalition designed to thwart the emergence of a European hegemon, particularly one who sought to control the low countries, the natural staging area for any invasion of England. This principle now inspired Britain to oppose Wilhelm II, just as in previous centuries it had inspired the nation's opposition to Phillip II, Louis XIV, and Napoleon.

---

1. See Iu. A. Pisarev, *Tainy pervoi mirovoi voiny. Rossiia i Serbiia v 1914–1915 gg.* (Moscow, 1990), p. 40.

118   It is difficult to resist the conclusion that the bulk of the responsibility for the war must therefore rest with Germany. Although all the belligerents eventually developed wish lists of territories they hoped to acquire at the expense of their defeated enemies, Germany was motivated by a lust for aggrandizement from the very beginning. The decision for war was, in the phrase of Fritz Fischer, "ein Griff nach der Weltmacht," or a grab for world power, for it was Germany's desire to overthrow the status quo, to redraw the boundaries of Europe, and to seize overseas colonies. Indeed, it was Berlin's notorious "blank check," its pledge of unstinting support, that encouraged the Austrians to tender their ultimatum to Belgrade in the first place. Vienna would never have acted as it did without the connivance and approval of Berlin. It was thus the choices that Germany made during the July crisis of 1914 that, more than anything else, caused the dispute between Serbia and Austria to balloon into a pan-European conflict.[2]

The Start of the War

On July 19 (August 1), 1914, Germany declared war on the Russian Empire. The news of the outbreak of the war elicited mass enthusiasm and patriotic demonstrations in St. Petersburg, as it did in many other European capitals.[3] Despite the indus-

2. From the foregoing it should be clear that I completely disagree with the view of the war's origins presented by Niall Ferguson in his recent *The Pity of War* (New York, 1999). Ferguson is a historian of great gifts who has written an extraordinary book. But in his eagerness to invert the conventional wisdom about the war he has advanced some interpretations that I find to be, in a word, perverse. Consider, for example, his argument against the Fischer thesis that Germany was in the end responsible for the war and that it really did seek European hegemony, if not world power. Ferguson maintains that it was only after the war started that Germany arrived at a set of extreme annexationist aims (the Bethmann "September Program"). It did not draft plans, for instance, to seize and hold French and Belgian territory until two months after the war had begun, which meant that it could not possibly have launched the war to gain these particular objectives. Moreover, if Britain had stayed neutral (as Ferguson passionately believes it should have done), the Germans would never have developed such territorial ambitions in the first place. See pp. 169–173.

This argument disregards the inconvenient fact that however much or however little land the Germans proposed to annex after they had won, they started the war with the intention of altering the European balance of power in their favor permanently. Germany proposed to dominate the continent of Europe. Perhaps the British Empire could have lived with this arrangement, although I heartily doubt it. A Germany much stronger in economic, military, and naval resources than it had been prior to 1914 would have been a constant threat to the security of the British Isles. Still further, Germany's decision to use the Schlieffen plan at the beginning of the war unavoidably entailed Germany's violation of Belgian neutrality. But Ferguson cannot explain why anyone in Britain should have believed Berlin's promise that it would evacuate Belgium as soon as victory had been achieved.

Finally, even if Britain should have viewed Germany's intentions on the continent as benign, neither Russia nor France had any reason to adopt the same perspective. Russia had no territorial designs on Germany, and the German secret service knew it. To be sure, France was a revisionist power in the sense that it wanted to recover Alsace and Lorraine. But France was incapable of action against Germany without Russian aid, and Russia would never have taken up arms in exclusive support for a French bid at revanche. It therefore follows that in 1914 Russia fought in defense of the status quo and Germany fought against it.

3. There were, however, serious draft riots in seventeen of European Russia's fifty provinces. These are discussed in Josh Sanborn, "The Mobilization of 1914 and the Question of the Russian Nation: A Reexamination," *Slavic Review* 59, no. 2 (2000): 267–289. This provocative article unfortunately does not adduce

trial violence that had gripped Petersburg a mere few weeks earlier, tens of thousands of Russians of all social classes streamed into the great square before the Winter Palace on July 20 to hear the tsar read his war proclamation from its balcony. Waving placards, icons, and pictures of the emperor, his subjects listened in silence as Nicholas II appealed to them to defend the motherland in exactly the same words Alexander I had used in 1812. Nicholas concluded his peroration by quoting his imperial predecessor's pledge never to make peace as long as a single foreign soldier remained on Russian soil.[4] The crowd saluted the emperor's speech with tumultuous cheers and then, in an act of eerie spontaneity, with the mass singing of the Russian national anthem. Of course, Nicholas conveniently overlooked the fact that there were currently no foreign soldiers on Russian soil as well as the fact that Russia's war plans mandated the rapid *Russian* invasion of neighboring territory. Nonetheless, the tsar, so often tone-deaf in public settings, had hit exactly the right rhetorical pitch. This war, he was telling his subjects, was a defensive war that had been forced on Russia. But more than this, the war was not just any war, for its character was instead that of a holy crusade. This is how the tsar wanted to sell the war to his people, and at least at the outset he was successful. Even the Duma fell into line. On July 26 (August 8), at a special session of the parliament, deputies (including many radical liberals and socialists) vied with one another in testifying to their solidarity with the government and their unswerving commitment to the war effort. Within a matter of weeks Nicholas took other steps to reemphasize the sacerdotal character of the struggle. On August 22 he decreed that a total prohibition on the sale of alcoholic beverages would be in effect until the end of the war. And on August 31, he changed the name of his capital city ("Peter's town") from the Germanic St. Petersburg to the Slavic Petrograd. The empire's subjects were to be morally purified, just as the empire and even the Russian language itself were to be purged of insidious German influences.

Miasoedov in the Army

Hundreds of thousands of people were swept up in the mood of national unity and reconciliation that hung in the air during the first months of the war; Sergei Miasoedov was no exception. Moved by a patriotic article Boris Suvorin had recently published, Miasoedov impulsively dashed off a letter to the journalist, magnanimously forgiving him for the part he had played in Guchkov's plot back in April 1912. Suvorin answered that he had been very glad to receive Miasoedov's note, adding that "for my part I am delighted to extend my hand to you and consign the entire past to oblivion"—words that he would later find it difficult to explain away.[5]

In the same spirit, but with greater calculation, Sergei also sought to square accounts with his former patron, War Minister Sukhomlinov. In a letter of July 29 (August 11), Miasoedov implored the minister to excuse any conscious or unconscious

---

sufficient evidence to substantiate its claim that the war "had been unpopular from its inception." (See p. 289.)

4. Bernard Pares, *The Fall of the Russian Monarchy* (New York, 1961), p. 187.

5. Suvorin to Miasoedov, July 26, 1914, RGVIA, f. 962, op. 2, d. 68, l. 13.

120 transgressions he might have committed and concluded by begging Sukhomlinov's help in arranging a posting to the regular army. Miasoedov received the minister's laconic reply the very same day. "Personally," Vladimir Aleksandrovich wrote, "I have nothing against your entry into active military service."[6] Although this statement could not be construed as anything other than a decidedly cool *nihil obstat,* Miasoedov tried to use it as if it were some sort of glowing testimonial.

He had reason to, for as he had accurately foreseen, finding a suitable position with the regular military establishment was not going to be easy for him, despite the state of emergency occasioned by the war. After all, his last stint of field service had been twenty-three years before. Then, too, the fumes of the scandal of 1912 had not entirely dissipated. At that time the scabrous newspaper coverage of his duel with Guchkov had made him notorious throughout the empire. The ensuing years had doubtless clouded most people's recollection of the incident's details, but Miasoedov feared that the residual impression was that of an unsavory person who had never been fully exonerated of the grave accusations made against him. Miasoedov's particular worry was that his sullied reputation would prevent him from getting a job in the intelligence field, in which he believed he could best deploy his talents for the benefit of his country. He wrote P. G. Kurlov that his "excellent knowledge of East Prussia, of the local language, customs and population" eminently qualified him for work as a scout or as an interrogator of enemy prisoners of war.[7] In pursuit of this ambition, Sergei dutifully visited all the staffs and headquarters accessible to Petrograd, offering his services as an intelligence officer. Initially, there were no takers.

Desperate to get into the war, even in the most humble of capacities, Miasoedov finally approached an acquaintance of his on the staff of the Sixth Army, Staff-Captain V. V. Kryzhanovskii, and asked him for a posting to the *opolchenie,* or home guard. When Kryzhanovskii said he could not necessarily guarantee even this position in view of the negative publicity that still attached itself to Miasoedov's name, the retired colonel insisted that he had been completely cleared of all charges and produced Sukhomlinov's note as proof. After all, would the minister of war really write such a letter about a man tainted by the slightest suspicion of treason?[8] The upshot was that Miasoedov was offered and eventually accepted an inglorious billet with the workers' home guard based in Peterhof.

He was not content with this, however, and immediately began to lobby for a better appointment. Finally, in October 1914 one of his petitions hit its mark. Impressed by Miasoedov's familiarity with East Prussia and his fluency in German, the chief of staff of the Tenth Army, which fronted the Eydtkuhnen sector of East Prussia, invited the former gendarme to take up a post as an interpreter in the army's intelligence section. Wearing the uniform of a colonel in the regular infantry, Miasoedov was at the front and hard at work by early November.

6. Miasoedov to Sukhomlinov, July 29, 1914; Sukhomlinov to Miasoedov, July 29, 1914, RGVIA, f. 962, op. 2, d. 66, ll. 34, 35.

7. Miasoedov to P. G. Kurlov, August 13, 1914, RGVIA, f. 801, op. 28, d. 166, l. 153.

8. V. V. Kryzhanovskii interrogation, February 3, 1917, RGVIA, f. 962, op. 2, d. 55, l. 61.

The Tenth Army was part of the Russian Northwest Front, a group of armies commanded by General Ruzskii, which was deployed against East Prussia and German Silesia on an irregular line that extended from the Baltic Sea to central Poland. It was Miasoedov's duty as a staff intelligence officer to find out as much as he could about the dispositions of the enemy confronting the Russians in his particular sector. Such information was, of course, chiefly of tactical utility, but it was extremely important notwithstanding. In today's era of sophisticated electronic sensors, night-vision equipment, and satellite surveillance it is easy to forget the fact that armies in the early stages of World War I were for all intents and purposes quite blind. Military aviation was still in its infancy, which meant that information about the enemy had to be arduously collected by human beings on the ground. As local success either in the attack or on the defense could hinge on the precision with which the enemy's changing strength was known, the responsibilities of the staff intelligence section were of the utmost gravity. In the main, three methods were available to compile a portrait of the enemy: infiltration, interrogation, and armed reconnaissance. Miasoedov employed all three.

Infiltration was facilitated by the extreme attenuation of the front along which Russia squared off against Austria and Germany. In the west, static trench warfare had superseded mobile operations by December 1914; the trench networks dug by the belligerents extended slightly more than four hundred miles, from the Swiss frontier to the Belgian port of Nieuport on the English Channel. By contrast, the Eastern front stretched almost one thousand miles from the Baltic Sea to the Rumanian border. This of course meant that the lines in the west were manned and held with a density of troops impossible in the east. As a result, inserting an agent behind enemy lines in the west was a virtual impossibility: for instance, although the British made repeated efforts to do so, they never succeeded in infiltrating a single operative through the German positions during the entire war.[9] But precisely because the Eastern front was less continuous, and consequently more porous, than the Western front, infiltration was an option available to the intelligence services of every warring power. Despite the dangers involved (after all espionage was a capital offense), these services routinely dispatched scores of agents on missions behind enemy lines for periods ranging from a few hours to several weeks. The Austrians, for example, employed two thousand persons in this capacity from 1914 through 1918, six hundred of whom survived the war.[10]

Who were these people? A handful were officers or civilians with rare linguistic and thespian talents, motivated by patriotism to hazard their lives for their country. Miklos Soltesz, a boy barely out of high school, was recruited by Austrian intelligence in 1914 because of his fluent Russian and made several successful forays behind Russian lines over the next three years, sometimes tricked out in a tsarist uniform.[11]

---

9. Michael Occleshaw, *Armour Against Fate: British Military Intelligence in the First World War* (London, 1989), p. 217.

10. Maks Ronge, *Razvedka i kontrrazvedka*, 2d ed. (Moscow, 1939), p. 239.

11. Nicholas Snowden, *Memoirs of a Spy: Adventures Along the Eastern Front* (London, 1933), pp. 4, 11, 37, 45, 130.

122 However, the largest number (perhaps even the majority) of agents came from the ranks of the carters, peddlers, tanners, and lumber sellers native to the prewar border zones. Such people (of whom many were Jews) had long had business dealings and contacts in adjacent countries. Under the cover of their itinerant and ostensibly harmless occupations, they could pass from one zone of occupation into another, returning with valuable information for their officer-handlers. At least, this was the hope.[12]

The problem was that there were often serious doubts about the reliability and quality of the information purveyed by agents of this class. As most, although not all, of them spied for money, how likely were they to run the risks that were often necessary to collect truly accurate and timely intelligence? Then, too, how confident could an intelligence service be that such an agent was working exclusively on its behalf? There were entrepreneurs among them who were willing to sell information to more than one side. On the Eastern front it was also not uncommon for one's own agent to be captured and doubled. There were also episodes in which spies were tripled or even quadrupled.

Despite the problematical character of intelligence collected in this fashion, every frontline intelligence officer attempted to enlist agents of this sort. Here Miasoedov would seem to have had a natural advantage; owing to his many years in Verzhbolovo, he was acquainted with large numbers of people on both sides of the Russo-Prussian border, and Russia was at this point momentarily in possession of a band of Prussian territory. This advantage soon proved illusory, however, for his efforts at recruiting spies among the East Prussian population were rebuffed at every turn. He reported (January 1915) to the intelligence chief of the Tenth Army that there were, in his opinion, three reasons for this. Some local residents indignantly rejected his offers to spy for Russia because they were solidly loyal to their own government. Others feared the vengeance of the German army, should it manage to oust the Russian invaders and reassert control. But he was also constrained to observe that the outrages committed by Russian soldiers in East Prussia (the burning of villages in particular) had poisoned the minds of many against the Russian Empire and all it stood for.[13]

Miasoedov's attempts to sign up spies among Russian subjects in the immediate border zone were also unfruitful. He complained that his best prospects had been arrested and/or exiled into the interior on vague suspicions of unreliability by the Russian civil and military authorities themselves.[14] Miasoedov did, however, pursue other avenues of organizing espionage against Germany. The most important of these involved one of his business partners, David Freidberg. Freidberg, who was the manager of the Northwest Russian Steamship Company's Odessa office, had been in Hanover on business on the day the war had broken out. He had managed to avoid internment and had escaped Germany by using the U.S. passport of an American cousin of his. Upon his return to Russia, he had been approached by Miasoedov, who

12. Dennis E. Showalter, *Tannenberg: Clash of Empires* (Hamden, Conn., 1991), p. 101.
13. Miasoedov to chief of intelligence, Tenth Army staff, January 1915, RGVIA, f. 801, op. 28, d. 166, l. 159.
14. Ibid., l. 157.

persuaded him to agree to travel to Germany again, in the guise of an American commercial traveler. This time, however, he would be on assignment for Russian military intelligence. Miasoedov accompanied Freidberg to an interview at the Russian General Staff in Petrograd, where he was briefed on his mission and given a list of ten questions of great interest to the Russian secret service. The plan was for Freidberg to make his way to Copenhagen on the pretext of visiting his brother, Samuel, who had moved there at the beginning of the war. He was then to cross over from Denmark into Germany under the cover of his bogus passport. In the event, however, this mission had to be aborted; upon his arrival in Copenhagen Boris informed him that he had gotten word that the German police had learned of his earlier misuse of the American passport back in August 1914. David Freidberg was a wanted man in Germany and had no choice but to take the train back to Petrograd. But although his espionage mission had been canceled, Freidberg was still in a position to do a small covert service for his government. At the request of Russia's ambassador to Denmark, he smuggled two packages of secret diplomatic dispatches back into Russia, dispatches that were apparently needed so urgently by the central Ministry of Foreign Affairs that they could not wait for the usual couriers.[15]

During his brief months of service at the front, Miasoedov thus failed to arrange any significant infiltration operations against the Germans. He was, however, extremely successful in developing information about the enemy by means of interrogation and reconnaissance. Then, as now, prisoners of war were not supposed to answer any but the most trivial questions put to them by their captors. But with the correct mixture of threat and reassurance POWs—most of whom were frightened, tired, and hungry—could often be induced to say more than they intended. Miasoedov soon became known for his extraordinary effectiveness as a debriefer of enemy prisoners, an effectiveness to which his imposing physical presence, his fluent and idiomatic German, and his outward facade of bonhomie all contributed.

Armed reconnaissance complemented interrogation, for the purpose of nocturnal raids against enemy positions was frequently the acquisition of prisoners. On several occasions in December 1914, Miasoedov personally led patrols into the Johannisburg forest (at the southern extremity of the Masurian lakes) in order to probe the German lines and seize German scouts. On the nights of December 4, 7, and 12 Miasoedov and his party engaged in firefights with the enemy. His conduct on these occasions and his performance in general won him the enthusiastic commendation of his superiors. On January 20, 1915, Major General Arkhipov, commander of the Johannisburg detachment, reported to the chief of staff of the Tenth Army that Miasoedov had been of "substantive value" as an intelligence officer, and praised him for his uncanny ability to worm "valuable information" out of German POWs. When he had come under fire, his personal example of "fearlessness and courage" had inspirited his men, "who were in action against much stronger forces of the enemy."[16] The

15. RGVIA, f. 2003, op. 2, d. 1063, ll. 117–119.
16. Commander of Johannisburg detachment to chief of staff, Tenth Army, January 20, 1915, RGVIA, f. 962, op. 2, d. 113, l. 380.

124 Germans themselves developed a healthy respect for the intelligence operations of Miasoedov, whom they described as "an intelligence pro" and "a particularly good judge of the German military mind."[17]

But if Sergei Nikolaevich experienced a renewed sense of professional purpose and worth as a result of his work with the army, his personal life remained chaotic and unstable. The scandalous scene between Klara and Stolbina had not in fact resulted in the collapse of his marriage. His daughter, Musa, who remained devoted to her father, had once again served as a mediator and had somehow negotiated a temporary marital truce. Klara sent frequent letters to Sergei at the front. The endearments these missives contained, however, bespoke not so much sincere affection as Klara's desperate need for money. Sergei had sent her only 200 rubles since he had left to join the Tenth Army, a sum entirely inadequate to support the family. The bills were piling up. Klara was in arrears to the Petrograd Conservatory for Musa's piano lessons and owed the landlord so much back rent that she feared he would withhold the firewood she needed to heat the Kolokol'naia apartment that winter. "I don't understand," went a letter of December 18, "why you do not write us, although the children and I have written you many times."[18]

The chief reason for Klara's distress was the fact that Miasoedov was still devoting a significant proportion of his salary to the upkeep of his mistress. In January and February of 1915, he instructed the Russo-Asiatic Bank to make payments from his account of 210 and 250 rubles, respectively, to Stolbina's roommate, Nina Petrovna Magerovskaia, a crude subterfuge that was supposed to keep the transactions secret from his wife.[19] Indeed, despite the pressure of his military duties, Miasoedov nonetheless carved out the time for trysts with Evgeniia Stolbina, and rendezvoused with the twenty-four-year-old beauty in Warsaw at the end of December and again in Vilna in early February.[20]

Miasoedov's arrangement with Stolbina was not, however, an exclusive one. Together with Nina Magerovskaia, Evgeniia Stolbina continued to seek out the company of lonely and "generous" clients. At their flat in Rozhdestvennskaia Street they received male guests, including highly placed military officers, at all hours of the day and night. Among their frequent visitors were D. Ia. Dashkov, a major-general of the Imperial Suite, Lieutenant General P. A. Smorodskii, the head of the Alexander Committee on the Wounded, as well as one of the sons of the Grand Duke Konstantin Konstaninovich, who had become smitten with Stolbina ever since he had first clapped eyes on her in a Petrograd restaurant.[21]

17. Heinz Höhne, *Der Krieg im Dunkeln. Macht und Einfluss des deutschen und russischen Geheimdienstes* (Munich, 1985), p. 177.

18. Klara to Sergei, December 18, 1914, RGVIA, f. 801, op. 28, d. 166, ll. 11–12 (quotation on l. 12).

19. Miasoedov to Russo-Asiatic Bank, February 16, 1915, RGVIA, f. 801, op. 28, d. 164, l. 261; N. F. Magerovskaia testimony, April 16, 1915, RGVIA, f. 801, op. 28, l. 165, l. 123.

20. Hotel receipts, RGVIA, f. 801, op. 28, d. 169, l. 137.

21. Minister of justice to M. V. Alekseev, November 13, 1913, RGVIA, f. 2003, op. 2, d. 1073, l. 203; surveillance report, February 12, 1915, RGVIA, f. 801, op. 28, d. 163, ll. 53, 55. It was this latter liaison that gave rise to the persistent but false rumor that the real reason Miasoedov had been executed as a spy had been

Her promiscuity had nonetheless come to bore and disgust Evgeniia; in her let- 125
ters to Sergei she never failed to remind him of his promise to seal their relationship
with marriage. Sergei's answer to this appeal was the same as it had been prior to the
outbreak of the war: marriage was an impossibility at present both because of the difficulty of getting a divorce from Klara and because of his limited financial resources.
He did, however, write Evgeniia that he had concocted a plan, which he hoped would
turn him a quick profit of 100,000 rubles—an amount more than adequate for the
couple to start a new life together. Evgeniia later told government investigators that
she presumed that this anticipated windfall was somehow connected to the shipping
business with which Miasoedov had long been associated.[22]

What was the meaning of Miasoedov's remark about the 100,000 rubles? Regardless of what tsarist investigators subsequently came to believe (or pretended to believe), he was obviously not boasting to Evgeniia about the sizable payments that he
expected to receive from his German spymasters. But equally, he could not have been
thinking of extracting profits from the day-to-day operations of the Northwest Russian Steamship Company; the German High Seas Fleet had closed the egress from the
Baltic to Russian shipping, which meant that passenger traffic was suspended for the
duration of the war. We are left with only two possibilities: either Sergei was counting
on the Freidbergs to cut him into one of the large importing contracts they were
managing through Copenhagen, or, more probably, he believed, as he had prior to
the war, that he could persuade them to liquidate the entire assets of Northwest, including its two steamships, and give him a hefty share of the proceeds. Although in
either case Miasoedov was deluding himself, he nonetheless went out of his way to do
favors for his old partners even while at the front. In December 1914, for instance,
when David Freidberg asked him to find a place for his son in a Russian university to
complete the medical degree he had been working on in Leipzig, Miasoedov gamely
vowed to do what he could to help.[23] When later in the same month Boris Freidberg
asked him to intercede in the case of Robert Falk, another company associate, who
had been exiled to Dvinsk on suspicion of political unreliability, Sergei Nikolaevich
approached his old acquaintance P. G. Kurlov, then governor-general of the Baltic,
and also wrote letters of recommendation to Kurlov's adjutant on Freidberg's
behalf.[24] Miasoedov also met with Boris and David Freidberg in Belostok, Vilna, and
Riga to discuss company affairs on three occasions in early 1915.[25]

Miasoedov's conduct during the war thus displayed both the strengths and the
weaknesses of his complex character, for it was an admixture of bravery and greed, of

---

the desire of a "high ranking person" to eliminate a romantic rival. I will take this subject up in the next
chapter.

22. Assistant Warsaw procurator to Stavka, February 5, 1916, RGVIA, f. 2003, op. 2, d. 1073, l. 222.

23. RGVIA, f. 962, op. 2, d. 112, l. 148.

24. Freidberg to Miasoedov, December 24, 1914, RGVIA, f. 801, op. 28, d. 167, l. 47; Miasoedov interrogation, March 15, 1915, RGVIA, f. 962, op. 2, d. 160, ll. 94–95.

25. Matveev findings, April 30, 1915, RGVIA, f. 801, op. 28, d. 167, l. 33.

126 patriotism and concupiscence, of generosity and meanness. Yet virtually everything Miasoedov did after he joined the Tenth Army in November 1914 would eventually be viewed as sinister and suspect. For Miasoedov's fate would be inextricably entwined with Russia's disappointing performance on the battlefield and the collapse of any hope that Russia could achieve a swift victory.

Russia at War

The most curious feature of the war plan Russia attempted to implement against her enemies in August 1914 was the fact that it divided Russia's armies into three parts: a northwest group of armies, or front, designated for action against Germany; a screening force in central Poland; and a southwest front, concentrated against Austria-Hungary. The rationale for each of these deployments was different. Alliance considerations lay behind the plan for the invasion of Germany in the north. Aware in general outline that Germany intended to strike France with the bulk of its strength at the beginning of any general war, Russia had promised its French ally in 1912 that in that event it would attack Germany with eight hundred thousand men no later than the fifteenth day after the declaration of mobilization. It was hoped that this blow would disrupt Germany's western offensive, thus helping the French resist the German onslaught. The deployment in central Poland was, by contrast, explicable in terms of the hard facts of geography. Russian Poland was an enormous salient two hundred by two hundred and thirty miles projecting into central Europe, flanked by German territory to the north and Austrian to the south. The large number of troops Russia amassed to the west of Warsaw therefore represented not only an essential general reserve but also a force capable of repelling an incursion into Poland by either Germany or Austria or by both working in tandem. Finally, the southern offensive was at least in part the result of strategic opportunism: the Russian High Command was much more confident about its chances in a fight against the Austrians than it was about its prospects in a contest with the Germans. But Russia's nationality policy also figured into the decision for a southwestern offensive. The policy of "Russification"—involving as it did discrimination against Polish culture and restrictions against the use of the Polish language—was heatedly resented in the Transvistula provinces. There was an authentic fear in Petrograd that if an Austrian army succeeded in erupting into Poland, the sullen local population would immediately rebel in its support, thus confronting Russia with a nightmarish combination of foreign war and internal insurrection. It was believed that the best prophylaxis against this eventuality would be a rapid offensive thrust into Austrian Galicia so as to pin down Austria's armies before they could launch their own invasion. Thus it was that as opposed to adopting what might appear to be the most logical course—attacking against one enemy and merely defending against the other—Russia instead embarked on two simultaneous (and consequently diluted) offensives.[26]

---

26. In a superb article, Bruce Menning has definitively reconstructed the circumstances that led to the adoption of this plan in May 1912. See Bruce Menning, "Fragmenti odnoi zagadki. Iu. N. Danilov i M. V.

The Northwest front, consisting of the First Army and the Second Army under Generals Rennenkampf and Samsonov, respectively, invaded East Prussia on August 17. While Rennenkampf was to strike north of the Masurian lakes toward Königsberg, Samsonov was to sweep south and then west of the lakes, thus trapping the German defenders between both Russian forces and the Baltic coast. At least at first the campaign seemed to be unfolding perfectly. On August 20 Rennenkampf had forced the German Eighth Army to withdraw after a bitter fight at Gumbinnen, twenty miles to the west of Eydtkuhnen; by the twenty-fourth he had occupied Insterburg. Meanwhile, Samsonov had crossed the Narew and within a few days had occupied Niedenburg and was moving on Allenstein. Then, as is well known, disaster overtook him. Taking advantage of the large gap that had opened up between the First and Second Russian Armies, and well informed about Russia's plans owing to the interception of uncoded Russian radio messages, the Germans encircled Samsonov at the very end of August in the Komusinsk forest and utterly annihilated him.[27] This catastrophic battle of Tannenberg was succeeded by the first battle of the Masurian lakes, in which the Germans failed to entrap Rennenkampf but succeeded in inflicting heavy damage and expelling him from East Prussia. In its disastrous invasion of Germany, Russia had incurred casualties of two hundred fifty thousand men killed, wounded, or taken prisoner. And as if this were not bad enough, the Russians had lost or abandoned virtually all of the artillery they had committed to the campaign as well as four hundred thousand shells.[28] Neither the troops nor the ordnance could easily be replaced.

The news from the Southwest front was, however, much more encouraging and muffled the public impact of the East Prussian debacle. In a series of confusing engagements spread two hundred miles across Galicia, Austrian and Russian forces blundered into each other at the end of August. The ensuing Galician battles lasted until the end of September, by which point the Austrians had been driven back almost to the Carpathians. The Russians had seized Lemberg and had swept past the important fortress of Przemysl, whose Austrian garrison desperately held on though it was cut off miles behind the Russian lines. Austria's losses in this campaign were even worse than Russia's in East Prussia: one hundred thousand of the Dual Monarchy's soldiers were dead, another hundred thousand were POWs, and almost a quar-

---

Alekseev v russkom voennom planirovanii v period predshestvuiushchii Pervoi Mirovoi Voine," in *Posledniaia voina imperatorskoi Rossii,* ed. O. R. Airapetov (Moscow, 2002), pp. 65–87.

27. On the reasons for Samsonov's defeat see *Vostochno-Prusskaia Operatsiia. Sbornik dokumentov mirovoi imperialisticheskoi voiny na russkom fronte* (Moscow, 1939), pp. 559–560. The Russian army has of course received considerable criticism for its practice of broadcasting radio messages en clair. It is often overlooked, however, that the German Eighth Army during the Tannenberg campaign was guilty of exactly the same thing: Showalter, *Tannenberg,* p. 169. One reason that has been adduced for this practice in the Russian case was the extraordinary complexity of Russia's field ciphers. To encrypt and decrypt any message was apparently so time-consuming that army, corps, and divisional staffs evidently came to prefer speed to security in military communications. L. G. Beskrovnyi, *Armiia i flot Rossii v nachale xx veka Ocherki voenno-ekonomicheskogo potentsiala* (Moscow, 1986), p. 148.

28. Sir Alfred Knox, *With the Russian Army 1914–17: Being Chiefly Extracts from the Diary of a Military Attaché,* vol. 1 (London, 1921), pp. 91–92; Robert Wilton, *Russia's Agony* (London, 1918), p. 221.

128 ter of a million had been wounded. Thus the Austrian army's combat strength had been reduced by a third in less than a month.[29] The Russian Southwest front was, however, in no condition to press its advantage: its troops were exhausted by weeks of continuous movement and fighting; moreover, its logistical apparatus had broken down completely. By September 24, for example, the Russian Fourth, Fifth, and Sixth Armies were each almost seventy kilometers ahead of their supply depots.[30]

Grand Duke Nikolai Nikolaevich, the Russian commander in chief, consequently ordered offensive operations suspended, intending to use the breathing space to rest his weary men and bring up new equipment and reinforcements before attempting a drive due west into German Silesia. The enemy was not inclined to cooperate with Nikolai's plan. Realizing that he had to prop up the tottering ally, Germany's eastern commander, General Paul Hindenberg, formed a new Ninth Army that he rushed into position on the Austrian left. Aware of Nikolai's designs, Hindenberg ordered an offensive to preempt Russia's Silesian attack with a sudden outflanking maneuver against the Russian Second and Fifth Armies. The upshot was the battle of Lodz (mid-November to early December 1914), which concluded with the Russian forces withdrawing under heavy pressure in order to straighten their front. The new Russian position in the center and south was a virtual straight line running from the town of Plock on the Vistula to Gorlice in the Carpathian foothills.

By the end of 1914 Russia had taken a terrible bludgeoning but had nonetheless survived the first five months of the war. A levelheaded analysis of the situation, however, did not provide reason for optimism. Every European army had gone into the field with a plan for a short war, and none of these plans had succeeded. By December it was evident that the war was going to be protracted, and a protracted war would place unanticipated strains on the economies and societies of all the belligerents. Russia in particular was by this point already running low on resources crucial to her war effort; although there were shortages of all kinds, three areas were of the gravest concern: artillery shells, rifles, and military manpower.

Russia's military leaders, like its counterparts elsewhere in Europe, had presumed that a great continental war would be fought with the equipment and munitions stockpiled in peace. They had accordingly established procurement norms that, for example, mandated the acquisition of fifteen hundred rounds per artillery tube. The problem was that no one had foreseen the scale of the conflict, or the dizzying rate with which ammunition would be expended. More than any other weapon, artillery dominated the World War I battlefield and shaped its tactical environment. It was in fact responsible for the majority of casualties inflicted on all armies on all fronts. The possession by every power of accurate, quick-firing field guns had forced troops to dig in, thus giving birth to trench warfare. Without artillery preparation, an infantry attack against enemy positions was deemed equivalent to suicide. Equally, if one's own guns remained silent in the face of the concentrated fire of enemy batteries, the

---

29. Showalter, *Tannenberg*, p. 327; Holger H. Herwig, *The First World War: Germany and Austria-Hungary 1914–1918* (London, 1997), p. 94.

30. A. Beloi, *Galitsiiskaia bitva* (Moscow, 1929), p. 321.

result could be the demoralization of the troops through naked fear or shell shock. Ominously, Russia had nearly exhausted her prewar supply of artillery rounds by the end of 1914. Between August and December 1914, over 85 percent of Russia's total reserve of 5.6 million shells had *already* been delivered to the front.[31] To be sure, virtually every warring power ran through its stock of ammunition as quickly as did Russia in the first phase of the war. The difference was that Russia's industrial sector was less robust than those of Germany, Britain, and even France. It was possible for these countries to mobilize their factories for the war and achieve feats of production that Russia could not dream of equaling.

Rifles posed a similar problem. Russian General Headquarters, or Stavka, calculated in late 1914 that the Russian army required a hundred thousand new rifles every month, whereas the maximum output of domestic industry was only forty-two thousand. One reason for this high demand for rifles was the alarming propensity of Russian soldiers to cast their arms aside during retreat, flight, or medical evacuation. That the weapons of the dead and those of POWs were rarely recovered exacerbated the problem.[32]

Then there was the manpower crisis. Despite the chatter in the London newspapers about the irresistible power of the "Russian steamroller," Russia began to experience a severe shortage of trained troops by the end of 1914. Russia had had 1.4 million soldiers under arms when the war began. An additional 5.1 million men had been called up in the first five months of the conflict. But Russia's losses had been unprecedentedly enormous. At least one million of her soldiers had been taken prisoner. The Germans had virtually wiped out five Russian army corps during the East Prussian battles of August and September. Even when Russia had prevailed on the battlefield, it had done so at high cost: the average casualty rate of the units of the Southwestern front stood at 40 percent by year's end. Indeed, by that point possibly as many as four million sick or wounded soldiers had been withdrawn from the firing line and dispatched to hospitals and infirmaries in the rear. To make matters worse, the relentless pace of combat operations had substantively degraded the military effectiveness of those troops who remained at the front; by mid-November there were Russian soldiers who had been in battle for fifty days straight. At Stavka, General Iurii Danilov observed that to date the Russian army had managed to hold its own in the face of enemy attack by sheer weight of manpower; Russia had prevented a German breakthrough at Lodz by feeding in thousands of fresh troops. But the time for such profligacy with men, he gloomily observed, was now past; Russia's manpower reserves had begun to dry up. The army would really be fully capable of renewing offensive operations only in April 1915, when the recruits called up for that year had finished their preliminary training. Even then an attack would be based on the

---

31. A. L. Sidorov, *Ekonomicheskoe polozhenie Rossii v gody pervoi mirovoi voiny* (Moscow, 1973), p. 20.

32. See P. P. Petrov, *Rokovye gody 1914–1920* (California [*sic*], 1965), pp. 23–24. In early September Stavka tried to organize the general collection of rifles on the battlefield; two months later General Ruzskii, commander of the Northwest front, announced a program to pay bounties to civilians who brought in either Russian or enemy rifles. See Mikhail Lemke, *250 dnei v tsarskoi stavke (25 sent. 1915–2 iuliia 1916)* (Petrograd, 1920), p. 97.

130   assumption that Russia's allies had replenished its stocks of arms and ammunition.[33] If that hypothetical condition could be fulfilled, Russia might be able to stage an operation that would win the war: a general offensive with the chief axis of advance running from central Poland into Silesia and then extending to Berlin.

A sine qua non of this plan was the preliminary occupation of East Prussia. Were this not accomplished, the Germans could easily exploit their flanking position to get in the rear (and consequently cut off) Russia's advancing columns. On January 4 (17), 1915, a military council on the problem of East Prussia was held at Sedlets, the headquarters of the Northwest front. The conferees, who included front commander N. V. Ruzskii, front quartermaster general M. D. Bonch-Bruevich, and Danilov himself, agreed that in February the Russian Tenth Army should attempt to breach the German fortified lines north and south of the Masurian lakes and drive the Germans back to the Vistula. This decision was taken despite the obviously weakened condition of the Tenth Army, for it was believed that the German Eighth Army, its main antagonist, had been equally battered by wartime attrition. The Germans were, moreover, outnumbered, for the Russian Tenth Army contained nineteen divisions, while the German Eighth comprised a mere eight.

But the calculations made at Sedlets had been founded on erroneous information. The most important principle of war is interactivity; Stavka seemed slow to grasp the truth that a military operation whose plan presupposes total enemy passivity is usually a recipe for disaster. At the end of 1914 a heated debate had taken place within the German military leadership about whether the Eastern or the Western front should receive strategic priority in the coming year. After much wrangling, the German High Command authorized the transfer of four complete army corps from the Western front to the Eastern. Three of these corps were constituted as a new army, the German Tenth, which was deployed north of the Eighth with its left flank on the Nieman and its right on Insterburg. Hindenberg and his chief of staff, Erich Ludendorff, were intent on employing these reinforcements to preempt Russia's offensive by enveloping and pulverizing the Russian armies in East Prussia.

To keep the Russians off balance, the German Ninth Army launched a diversionary strike at Bolimov in Central Poland on January 31, 1915. The Germans began their attack with a preparatory barrage of eighteen thousand shells filled with poison gas—the first ever use of chemical weapons in the Great War. But the real German target was farther to the north. On February 7 both the Eighth and Tenth Armies were on the move: the Eighth in a direct line toward Margrabovov and Lyck, and the Tenth in a great turning maneuver, at first driving east along the banks of the Nieman and finally swinging south toward Suvalki. The weather conditions were far from auspicious. A blizzard, which had blown up on February 4, tormented attackers and defenders alike, obscuring visibility, freezing steam locomotives solid, choking the roads with drifting snow, and suspending deliveries of food, water, and ammunition.

33. I. I. Rostunov, *Russkii front pervoi mirovoi voiny* (Moscow, 1976), pp. 186–187; General-Lieutenant Khol'msen, *Mirovaia voina. Nashi operatsii na Vostochno-Prusskom fronte zimoiu 1915 g.* (Paris, 1935), p. 17; *Rossiia v mirovoi voine 1914–1918 goda (v tsifrakh)* (Moscow, 1925), pp. 17, 32.

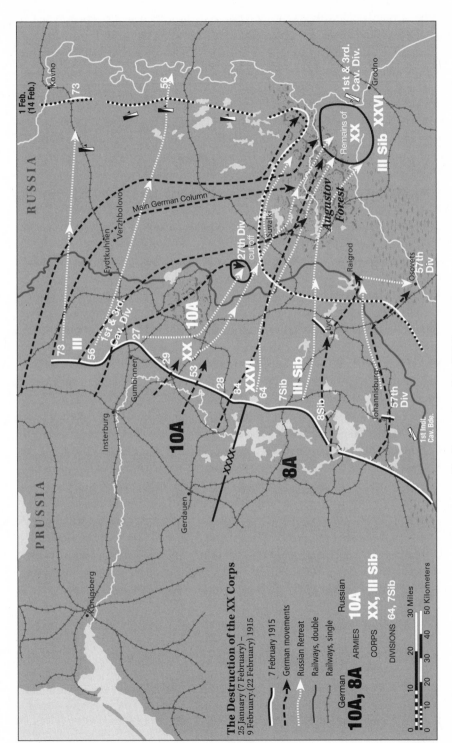

The Destruction of the XX Corps, 1915

The Russian Tenth Army was caught totally by surprise. Holding a line some 170 kilometers in length, with only one regiment in its reserve, the Tenth was completely incapable of dealing with the furious German onslaught. As communications among the various units of the army and general headquarters failed, the army disintegrated into its constituent formations, with decisions being made by officers on the spot. When German forces began to flank the Verzhbolovo group, the right wing of the Tenth army, its commander, N. A. Epanchin, ordered a retirement upon Kovno. The Germans immediately dashed into the gap that was thus created. The Russian XX Army Corps was completely surrounded in the Augustov forest. On February 18, after several attempts to break out had misfired, the corps—or what was left of it—surrendered. As a result of this operation the Germans bagged 110,000 Russian prisoners and over three hundred pieces of artillery. Another 100,000 soldiers were either dead, or were shortly to die, from battlefield wounds, disease, or freezing.[34]

For a moment it appeared that the entire Russian Northwest front was on the verge of collapse. It was the amalgamated effect of weather, geography, and quick thinking that retrieved the situation. When the blizzard lifted, there ensued freakishly high temperatures, which transformed the terrain into an impassable morass of water and mud, but not before the remaining units of the Tenth Army had retired on Grodno and Kovno. As they had burned the bridges within the Bobr swamps during their retreat, this avenue of pursuit was effectively pinched off. Finally, the Russian Twelfth Army, deployed on the Narew between Polotsk and Ostralenka, struck north toward Johannisburg—a threat to the right flank that halted the German advance in its tracks.

The so-called winter battle of Masuria had been dramatic, bloody, but oddly indecisive. Germany's spoiling attack had utterly ruined Russia's plan for the conquest of East Prussia. But Germany had not obtained very much in the way of strategic results either. It had chalked up an impressive tactical victory but had been incapable of exploiting it to shatter and penetrate the Russian front. Nonetheless, the psychological impact of the battle on the population of the Russian Empire cannot be overestimated. In a very real sense the news of this defeat elicited more anger, grief, and bitterness on the home front than even the defeat at Tannenberg had done. In February 1915 there were no Galician victories to distract public attention from the destruction of the XX Corps of the Tenth Army. It will be recalled, of course, that it was precisely to the staff of Siever's Tenth Army that Miasoedov had been attached.

Lieutenant Kolakovskii

It was Iakov Pavlovich Kolakovskii who provided the link between Russia's military disasters and Colonel S. N. Miasoedov. Kolakovskii, a second lieutenant in the

---

34. Khol'msen, *Mirovaia voina*, pp. 277–280; N. A. Epanchin, *Na sluzhbe trekh imperatorov. Vospominaniia* (Moscow, 1996), pp. 30–32; W. Bruce Lincoln, *Passage through Armageddon: The Russians in War and Revolution, 1914–1918* (New York, 1986), pp. 118–120; General Ludendorff, *My War Memories*, vol. 1 (London, n.d.), pp. 125–128.

Twenty-third Nizovsk Infantry Regiment, arrived by train in Petrograd on December 13(30) with an astonishing tale to tell. Between December 23 and December 25 (January 5–7) he was exhaustively debriefed at the general staff.

Kolakovksii explained that he had been attached to Samsonov's Second Army. By ill chance, while conducting reconnaissance his patrol had been overrun by a strong party of Germans on August 17(30), the first day of the Russian invasion of East Prussia. Taken prisoner, he had been rowed over to Denholm Island, off the Baltic coast, where he had been incarcerated in a camp with five hundred other Russian officers. Conditions in this *Lager* had been atrocious. The German guards had routinely beaten the inmates, had starved them on a meager diet of bread and water, and, against all usages of war, had demeaned them by making them dig ditches. Determined to get out any way he could, Kolakovskii devised an ingenious plan to effect his release: he would offer his services as a spy for Germany. But there was more to his scheme than escaping from the mistreatment and monotony of the camp, for if the Germans took him seriously, he might be able to trick them into divulging critical information about their espionage program against Russia.[35]

On November 28 (December 11) he approached the camp authorities with his proposition. In short order he was taken to the staff of the German XX Army Corps in Allenstein. On December 3 (16) a certain Captain Richard Skopnik, the corps' intelligence chief, had interviewed him. Skopnik told Kolakovskii that the German army had decided to take him on as its agent; he would be furnished with money and sent back to Russia. In the course of the conversation, Skopnik observed that the number one priority of the German secret service was arranging the assassination of Russia's supreme commander, the Grand Duke Nikolai Nikolaevich, a man who represented "all evil" for Germany. Kolakovskii recalled that Skopnik also added that "in the highest circles of Russia there is a strong influence in Germany's favor, but the Grand Duke and his staff stand for war with Germany and oppose the interests of the Germans."[36]

To prepare him for his new duties, the Germans then transferred Kolakovskii to the headquarters of the Eighth Army in Insterburg, where he was put into the hands of another intelligence officer, the fluent Russian speaker Lieutenant Alexander Bauermeister. Bauermeister proved to be just as loquacious and candid as Skopnik. On December 8(21) he pointed out that Germany was lucky that there were two groups of Russian subjects who were its natural sympathizers and allies: the ethnic Germans and the Jews. Every German serving in the Russian army "recognizes the pointlessness of this war for the Russians. . . . He knows that the Germans will improve Russia once they have conquered it and will save the people from ruin." The presence of such men in the Russian ranks was consequently "an enormous benefit." With regard to the Jews, "the more conscious and cultured element in the Russian

---

35. Kolakovskii statement, December 25, 1914, RGVIA, f. 801, op. 28, d. 163, l. 13.

36. Kolakovskii deposition, December 26, 1914, RGVIA, f. 962, op. 2, d. 160, l. 7. On Skopnik as a German intelligence officer see also Vladimir Orloff, *The Secret Dossier*, trans. Mona Heath (London, 1932), pp. 42–43.

134 population," the hatred and persecution they met with in the Russia had induced them "to render us an important service in espionage," for which "they will be richly rewarded by our government."[37] Of course, added Bauermeister, there were also pure-born Russians who were ready to collaborate with the Germans, including one particular colonel who had already worked on their behalf for five years.

The next day Bauermeister was even more forthcoming. His long residence in Petrograd, where his late father had owned a flourishing business, explained his excellent command of Russian. He had two brothers, both also German officers, one of whom had been killed on the Western front. All three brothers, as well as their mother, had belonged to a network of German spies in Russia prior to the war. He was now prepared to reveal that the colonel to whom he had referred the day before was Sergei Miasoedov, who had once been stationed in Verzhbolovo with the Separate Corps of Gendarmes. Bauermeister hinted that Miasoedov, whom he said his entire family knew very well, had been affiliated with his espionage ring.

The German lieutenant now got down to business. He provided Kolakovksii with a list of the German secret service's desiderata, along with a schedule specifying the fees Kolakovskii would earn for completing each assignment. Were he able to contrive the murder of Nikolai Nikolaevich, he would be paid one million rubles; if he persuaded the commandant of the Novogeorgievsk fortress to hand it over, he would receive another million; while if he managed to blow up the principal railway bridge in Warsaw, he would earn 200,000. The Germans also expected him to build up an independent espionage web of his own through the recruitment of subagents. For help in all these undertakings, Kolakovskii was advised to make contact with Lieutenant Colonel Miasoedov. Bauermeister knew that Miasoedov lived in Petrograd. Although he declined to supply the address, he insisted that it would be easy to ferret out the former gendarme there. Kolakovskii was to frequent the city's restaurants, where he would doubtless bump into Miasoedov sooner or later. Shortly before the lieutenant's release on December 11(24), Bauermeister introduced some refinements to the mission: Kolakovskii could forget about the Warsaw railway bridge, which other agents would sabotage. He was to proceed directly to Petrograd, where he was to rendezvous with Miasoedov, conspire against the life of Nikolai Nikolaevich, and penetrate the capital's highest official and social circles to determine the attitudes toward the war that obtained there. He was expected to return to Germany in four weeks. Bauermeister then equipped Kolakovskii with a German passport, a safe-conduct good for passing through the German lines, and 500 marks. The Russian lieutenant was driven to Stralsund and placed on a steamer for Sweden. Upon arriving in Stockholm, Kolakovskii had immediately proceeded to the Russian embassy, where he laid the entire matter before the military attaché.[38]

37. Kolakovskii deposition, December 23, 1914, RGVIA, f. 801, op. 28, d. 163, l. 16.

38. Kolakovskii deposition, December 26, 1914, RGVIA, f. 962, op. 2, d. 160, ll. 7–15, 20–21,30–35, 42–49.

As might be expected, these bizarre allegations elicited consternation through-out the war ministry and the general staff. How much of what Kolakovskii had said could be believed? On the face of it there were several details that tended to corrob-orate the lieutenant's testimony. For one thing, Russia's military attaché in Stock-holm had inspected Kolakovskii's passport and his German secret service pass and had pronounced them genuine; these documents were soon on their way to Petro-grad by diplomatic pouch.[39] For another, Russian military intelligence believed Skopnik and Bauermeister to be German spies, which in fact they actually were. Ac-cording to the staff of Warsaw Military District, Richard Skopnik, a Grenz-Kommissar or senior official in the border police in the town of Illov, had been the director of one of Germany's most important intelligence bureaus in East Prussia before the war. In 1913 the Russian police had apprehended a Prussian spy named Ernst Bem; documents found in his possession conclusively proved that he was act-ing at Skopnik's direction.[40] As for Alexander Bauermeister, he had indeed lived in Petrograd with his mother, Ada, and his two brothers, although all of them had de-parted the Russian Empire in the summer of 1914. Moreover, one of the brothers, Paul, had died while on active duty in France, just as Kolakovskii had reported.[41] It was also true that Alexander Bauermeister was attached to central German military intelligence in Berlin. Indeed, after the war Bauermeister published a memoir in which he admitted this and boasted of his undercover exploits, while categorically denying that Miasoedov had worked for Germany or that he, Bauermeister, had ever even spoken to him.[42] It is also worthy of notice that very early in the war Bauermeister is known to have advocated recruiting imprisoned Russian officers to be sent back to Russia to spy, and that the German army experimented with such a program in late 1914 and early 1915.[43]

However, the most chilling bit of evidence in Kolakovskii's favor came from the mouth of one Frantz Rutsinskii, who had been caught red-handed attempting to in-filtrate Russian lines near the Polish village of Kamion on the night of December 12, 1914. Rutsinskii, a Russian subject, confessed that he was a German spy; his instruc-tions on this mission had been to learn as much as possible about troop dispositions in the Warsaw region. He had also been ordered, however, to assassinate the Grand Duke Nikolai Nikolaevich if he got the opportunity; for this he, like Kolakovskii, had been promised a huge cash bonus.[44] It is, by the way, quite possible that Rutsinskii

39. Military attaché, Sweden, to general staff, December 12, 1914, RGVIA, f. 801, op. 28, d. 164, l. 35. I have also examined these documents, which are contained in a folder sewn into *papka* 164 after l. 36. Prussian passport no. 741 dated December 12, 1914, is made out in the name of the Danzig merchant "Anton Kulakowski."

40. Note of staff of Northwest front, March 8, 1915, RGVIA, f. 801, op. 28, d. 164, l. 161.

41. Counterintelligence memorandum, February 1915, RGVIA, f. 801, op. 28, d. 163, ll. 56–57.

42. Lieutenant A. Bauermeister, *Spies Break Through: Memoirs of a German Secret Service Agent*, trans. Hector A. Bywater (New York, 1934), p. 7.

43. Höhne, *Der Krieg im Dunkeln*, p. 170.

44. Matveev report on Rutsinskii, January 28, 1915, RGVIA, f. 801, op. 28, d. 169, l. 102.

136 was accurately repeating the orders he had been given; it is now evident that in December 1914 German Foreign Ministry official Curt Riezler seriously proposed that the German army arrange the grand duke's murder as a way of breaking Russia's will to fight.[45]

On the other hand, however, there were (to put it mildly) odd inconsistencies and logical flaws in Kolakovskii's statements. Many of these concerned the activities he ascribed to Miasoedov. If Miasoedov really was an important German intelligence asset, why would the Germans identify him as such to a newly recruited and untested agent? Then, too, the method Kolakovskii was told to use to locate Miasoedov—by sequentially dining in all the capital's most popular eateries—seemed unbelievably slipshod, particularly since the colonel was by November no longer in Petrograd but at the front. Kolakovskii's insistence that he had never heard of Miasoedov until Bauermeister mentioned him also struck the lieutenant's interrogators as odd. When gently reminded that the former gendarme was the notorious officer who had exchanged shots with Duma politician Guchkov, Kolakovskii suddenly "remembered" that he had of course read about the incident. He admitted he had even seen an artist's imaginary reconstruction of the duel in one of the newspapers.

Doubts about Kolakovskii's credibility aside, the war ministry could not overlook even the slightest possibility that the Germans really were plotting a campaign of sabotage and mayhem. At a bare minimum, Nikolai Nikolaevich, whose life might be in danger, had to be put on his guard at once. Sukhomlinov ordered Colonel Erandakov of counterintelligence to travel immediately to general headquarters in Baranovichi and provide Stavka with a complete briefing.

In the meantime Kolakovskii was given the freedom of Petrograd but was put under discreet surveillance all the same. Other than a few sexual contacts, nothing of any significance was observed; Kolakovskii did not appear to be engaging in any suspicious activities. Eventually it was decided to treat the lieutenant as a hero. He was awarded a decoration and was thoughtfully reassigned to the Caucasus, or Turkish front, to preclude his recapture and conceivable execution by the Germans.[46] He survived both the war and the revolution and died many decades later in Buenos Aires.

Arrest of Miasoedov

Kolakovskii's testimony had damned S. N. Miasoedov as a traitor: a charge that Russian counterintelligence definitely felt worth looking into. The central CI office at the general staff in Petrograd ordered a thorough investigation of the lieutenant colonel and the social milieu he inhabited. An army of secret agents immediately placed Miasoedov's apartment under observation, closely questioning his friends, neighbors, and acquaintances. Their summary report, dated February 12 (25), 1915, was replete with particulars about Miasoedov's wife, children, in-laws, and various of

---

45. Holger H. Herwig, *The First World War: Germany and Austria-Hungary 1914–1918* (London, 1997), p. 111.

46. Chief of staff, Northwest front, to Ianushkevich, March 9, 1915, RGVIA, f. 2003, op. 2, d. 1073, l. 50.

his associates, including Baron Grotgus, the exiled former newspaper correspondent Anna Aurikh, and the pharmaceutical importer Valentini.[47] Meanwhile, the CI office of the Northwest front had not been idle. In early January Colonel N. S. Batiushin, its head, instructed a civilian surveillance agent by the name of Distergof to attach himself to Miasoedov, pose as his new "assistant," and compile a daily record of everything he did. For over a month Distergof stuck to Miasoedov like a limpet, accompanied him everywhere, and shared meals, lodging, and transportation with him. Although Distergof did not personally see Miasoedov engage in any felonious activities, he wrote his boss that he had come to the conclusion that whereas the colonel was ostensibly collecting information about the Germans, he was actually collecting information *for* them.

On February 17 Lieutenant General A. A. Gulevich, chief of staff of the Northwest front, ordered Miasoedov's arrest. This was accomplished by means of a crude ruse. On February 18 (March 4), the head of the local gendarme administration in Kovno sent Sergei Nikolaevich a dinner invitation. Shortly after his arrival at his host's apartment, he was called to the telephone. Laying aside his sidearm, he advanced to the instrument and picked up the receiver. At that instant, three policemen who had been hiding in an adjacent room burst in and took him from behind.[48] So oblivious was Miasoedov to the identity of his enemies and the nature of the trap closing around him that later that evening in his Kovno jail cell he slipped Distergof a message intended for his mother. Distergof pocketed this note (in which Sergei begged his mother to appeal to Front Commander Ruzskii) and promptly turned it over to military-judicial authorities.[49]

The prosecution of Miasoedov was marred by egregious procedural irregularities from the very beginning. Despite the fact that the law demanded that accusations against serving officers be handled by military investigators exclusively, it was initially decided to assign the case to the office of the civil Warsaw District Court that specialized in political crime, on the excuse that significant numbers of civilians might be implicated. But this disposition of the matter was soon countermanded. On the advice of the quartermaster of the Northwest front, General M. D. Bonch-Bruevich, the Grand Duke Nikolai Nikolaevich commanded that Miasoedov instead be judged in a special military-field tribunal to be held in the citadel of Warsaw.[50] In theory such military-field courts were supposed to be convened only "when the commission of a criminal act is so obvious that there is no need to investigate it"—an article that certainly applied when a murderer was apprehended standing over his victim with a bloody knife in his hand but that scarcely fit the facts here.[51] The police

47. Surveillance report on Miasoedov and his associates, February 12, 1915, RGVIA, f. 801, op. 28, d. 163, ll. 52–55.

48. O. G. Freinat, *Pravda o dele Miasoedova i dr. Po offitsial'nym dokumentam i lichnym vospominaniiam* (Vilna, 1918), p. 50.

49. Note in pencil by Miasoedov, RGVIA, f. 801, op. 28, d. 166, l. 17.

50. Warsaw procurator to Matveev, March 16, 1915, RGVIA, f. 962, op. 2, d. 160, l. 36.

51. Freinat, *Pravda o dele Miasoedova*, p. 58.

138 immediately transferred the doomed man to the Alexander Citadel (Cytadela Aleksandrowska), the enormous, brooding edifice that towered over the Vistula in the northern part of the Polish capital. The citadel contained a chapel, a barracks, and an armory, as well as an infamous political prison, in which generations of Poles had expiated their desires for national independence.

Despite Distergof's treachery, Miasoedov was eventually able to send word of his arrest to several members of his family. His mother and sister soon arrived in Warsaw, where they were joined on March 2 (15) by Nikolai Nikolaevich Miasoedov, Sergei's older brother. All three of them wrote petitions and appeals asking for a speedy and favorable resolution of Sergei's case. Typical was Nikolai's letter to General Ruzskii of March 6 (19). "The horrible shame that has fallen on our family," Nikolai began, "has compelled me to disturb you at this busy time." If his brother had committed even a portion of the crimes he was apparently accused of, then Nikolai averred that he would ask Ruzskii's permission "to hang him with his own hands." But Nikolai's heart and head told him that Sergei was totally innocent and had been falsely arrested. If Ruzskii were personally to look into the case, he, too, would have to agree.[52] Ruzskii left this petition without issue, which was the fate of all the other letters the Miasoedov family addressed officialdom about the case.

Sergei Nikolaevich had in the meanwhile been interrogated by a Warsaw official of the Ministry of Justice named Matveev, who was in charge of prosecuting any civilians who might be shown to have abetted Miasoedov in his crimes. As a result of Matveev's questions, Sergei did at least get an inkling of what these "crimes" purportedly were. First, he was charged with having committed espionage for Germany prior to the outbreak of the war (although it was not specified whether he was supposed to have done so in Verzhbolovo, Petrograd, or both). Second, he was accused of having resumed his treasonous activities by giving aid and comfort to the enemy after he joined the staff of the Tenth Army. Matveev was particularly interested in a document Miasoedov had had in his possession at the time of his arrest. Entitled "Addresses 19 January 1915," this note listed the dispositions of the units of the Russian army in the Nieman region on that date. It was Bonch-Bruevich who first stressed the sinister implications of Miasoedov's possession of the "Addresses." In a letter to Matveev of March 11(24) he declared that "communication of information from this document to our enemies might have led to the failures of our forces in the battles that began after 19 January of this year, as they would have made it possible for the enemy to act without taking any chances, instead of having to resort to the unreliable means of using petty spies to penetrate the veil of secrecy about the moves we were likely to make, moves that were implicit in the preliminary grouping of our troops."[53]

In short, Bonch-Bruevich was giving first expression to the idea that Miasoedov had lost the winter battle of Masuria all by himself, and that the calamitous destruction of the XX Corps could be laid exclusively at his feet. In addition to asking Mia-

---

52. Nikolai Miasoedov to General Ruzskii, March 6, 1915, RGVIA, f. 801, op. 28, d. 164, l. 47.
53. Bonch-Bruevich to Matveev, March 11, 1915, RGVIA, f. 801, op. 28, d. 164, l. 19.

soedov to account for his relationships with the Freidbergs, Evgeniia Stolbina, War Minister Sukhomlinov, Boris Suvorin, Aleksandr Guchkov, and a host of other people, Matveev was curious about one final matter. He had been told that Miasoedov had stolen various items from houses abandoned by enemy civilians: was it true that he had committed this offense, a capital one in wartime?

Given the vagueness of these charges—after all, no specific acts of espionage or treason were spelled out—Sergei Nikolaevich had serious difficulty rebutting most of them. He categorically denied that he had ever committed treason and (a move that was doubtless a mistake) denied as well that he had ever had anything to do with espionage while working for the central Ministry of War. He insisted that he had never been a Germanophile: "While I always loved German culture and German orderliness, I always remained a Russian patriot." As for the "Addresses," this secret paper had been sent to him lawfully since it was essential to his job. One of his duties as a staff intelligence officer had been to travel the length of the Tenth Army's front, making liaison with headquarters of frontline formations in order to canvas them about their tactical intelligence requirements. If he was to visit these units, it was obvious he had to know where they were—hence his need for a copy of the "Addresses." Moreover, he had received the document only on January 26 (February 8)—one day *after* the Germans had launched their winter attack. With regard to enemy property, Miasoedov confessed that he had in fact taken certain articles from the house of a forester near Johannisburg. These included a set of wall-mounted antlers, some books, two oil paintings, one or two gravures, a table, and a plaque commemorating Alexander I's stay there in 1812. But he wanted to dispel the impression that this act had been looting in either the moral or legal sense. Competent Russian military authorities had ordered the cottage in question put to the torch along with many other structures in the Johannisburg Forest. Salvaging these objects could therefore hardly be construed as theft. Still further, he had taken some of items with the explicit permission of his commanding officer, among them the 1812 plaque, which he had intended to donate to a museum.[54]

As we have already seen, Miasoedov's trial took place on March 18 (31); and as we have also seen, his conviction was a foregone conclusion. (The death warrant was in fact signed without first being confirmed by higher military authority, as the law demanded). But there were, notwithstanding, some additional anomalies about the verdict that deserve special attention. In the first place, Miasoedov was convicted of having spied for Germany prior to August 1914, although no witnesses had testified to this and there was no material evidence to substantiate it. However, espionage in peacetime, unlike espionage in time of war, was punishable by imprisonment, not death. And Miasoedov was *completely exonerated* of committing any acts of treason after the war had begun, including sharing the "Addresses of January 19" with the

54. For Miasoedov's interrogation see RGVIA, f. 962, op. 2, d. 160, ll. 91–101 (quotation on l. 100). Miasoedov actually sent the plaque to Stolbina for safekeeping, along with a letter explaining that it was eventually to be donated to a museum. Miasoedov to Stolbina, January 21, 1915, RGVIA, f. 801, op. 28, d. 169, l. 138.

140   enemy. To be sure, Sergei Nikolaevich was found guilty of *maroderstvo*, or looting of the enemy, which was a hanging offense under the articles of war. However, as one eyewitness to the trial later observed, if the law against this behavior had really been strictly enforced, *every* Russian officer and soldier who had marched into Austrian or German territory since the war began would have been found in violation of it.[55] Regarding the fateful charges of espionage, however, there was no proof laid before the tribunal that positively incriminated Miasoedov either prior to or after 1914. The court was thus prepared to convict the ex-gendarme for treasonous conduct before the war began in the absence of any evidence one way or the other. Guchkov's charges of 1912, which were alluded to during the proceedings, confirmed precisely nothing. But even a court as flaccid and supine as this one would not convict in the presence of evidence that Miasoedov was innocent, and there was abundant proof on this score that covered the colonel's tenure with the staff of the Tenth Army. If Miasoedov had really given the Germans the intelligence that had enabled them to obliterate the XX Corps, he clearly had to have been in contact with them sometime in January. At the very least he would have had to signal them in some way. Yet Distergof had been in Miasoedov's company almost twenty-four hours a day during the entire month, and he had never detected Miasoedov in communication with the enemy. The precise details of what Miasoedov had been convicted of and what he had been acquitted of were, however, deliberately withheld from the public. On March 21 (April 3) Stavka issued an official communiqué about the affair. It stated that surveillance of Miasoedov had established his "indubitable guilt." Miasoedov had been found to be in contact with the agents "of one of the powers fighting against us." And it was on this basis he had been condemned by a military-field court and hanged.[56]

Reactions to Miasoedov's Execution

The news of Miasoedov's treason and execution shocked educated Russia to the core. In the Duma, there were those who, in the words of M. V. Rodzianko, "were inclined to assign Miasoedov responsibility" for all of Russia's military disasters. Many recalled Guchkov's denunciation of the colonel back in April of 1912, and lauded the foresight and acumen of the Octobrist politician.[57] For his part, Guchkov looked on Miasoedov's execution as a total vindication: letters of gratitude did in fact stream to Guchkov from all quarters, including one from an officer named D. M. Miasoedov, who belonged to a collateral branch of the family of the late "traitor." "When they discuss our lack of sufficient vigilance in Russia today they clearly don't remember

55. V. V-ago [B. Buchinskii], "Sud nad Miasoedovym," *Arkhiv russkoi revoliutsii*, vol. 14 (Berlin, 1924), p. 145.

56. "Voina. Ot Shtaba Verkhovnago Glavnokomanduiushchago," *Novoe vremia*, March 21 (April 3), 1915, p. 1.

57. M. V. Rodzianko, *Krushenie Imperii. Gosudarstvennaia duma i fev. 1917 goda revoliutsiia* (Valley College, N.Y., 1986), p. 115.

the matter you raised in 1912 . . . it is shameful to think that such a person has turned up in the 450 years of our valorous clan."[58]

There were also Duma deputies who saw political opportunities in the Miasoedov scandal to weaken and humiliate the government. One was A. F. Kerenskii, a radical lawyer and fire-breathing orator who would lead the Provisional Government after the February Revolution.[59]

It happened that, unlike other socialist parties, the Russian Social Democrats strongly opposed the war effort. The Bolshevik faction of the SDs was more extreme than the Mensheviks in this regard, maintaining with its leader Lenin that a German victory over tsarist Russia in the "imperialist war" was positively to be welcomed. The SDs, and the Bolsheviks in particular, consequently became special targets of the Russian police, which arrested and exiled all five Bolshevik deputies to the Duma at the end of 1914, excusing this illegal breach of their legislative immunity with a reference to their unpopular stance on the war.[60] On February 25, 1915, Kerenskii wrote a supposedly "private" letter to Duma president Rodzianko comparing this event and the recent arrest of Miasoedov. With characteristic intemperate exaggeration, Kerenskii began by noting that not long ago "several" bureaucrats and officers of the Department of Police had been apprehended on charges of high treason (after all, Kerenskii doubtless thought, Miasoedov had once been a gendarme, hadn't he?). This had happened shortly after the government had had the effrontery to broadcast the lie that there were deputies in the Duma who desired the defeat of the Russian army. But Russian society would not be distracted from recognizing the truth, for it was now apparent that "in the bowels of the Ministry of Internal Affairs a tight organization of real traitors has been calmly and confidently at work." The government could not be trusted to rid itself of the traitors in its midst; only the Duma could do this, and Kerenskii called on Rodzianko to summon that body into emergency session.[61] Of course, Kerenskii had intended from the beginning that his "private" letter have the widest possible public circulation. Using the local networks of the Socialists-Revolutionaries, another radical party, he saw to it that Russia was blanketed with thousands of hectographed copies of his alarmist screed. The scrupulously accurate press statement released by the commander of the corps of gendarmes in rebuttal— that no one currently enrolled in the corps or any members of their families had been arrested for espionage—utterly failed to tranquilize the public.[62]

The combination of Stavka's authoritative but sketchy pronouncement about Miasoedov's guilt and Kerenskii's inflammatory slurs soon gave rise to the most outlandish tales. Anxiety about secret treason within the state became so intense that encouraging tidings from the front, such as that of the fall of Przemysl on March 9 (22), were totally disregarded. One story had it that Miasoedov's safe had been found

58. Letter of April 10, 1915, GARF, f. 555 (A.I. Guchkov), op. 1, d. 1005, ll. 1–2.
59. Richard Abraham, *Alexander Kerensky: The First Love of the Revolution* (New York, 1987), p. 86.
60. See Leonard Shapiro, *The Communist Party of the Soviet Union* (New York, 1960), p. 142.
61. Kerenskii to Rodzianko, February 25, 1915, GARF, f. 110, op. 1, d. 923, l. 11.
62. Ibid., l. 3.

A. F. Kerenskii

stuffed with 600,000 rubles' worth of German gold; another, that he had made regular flights behind German lines in an airplane to provide intelligence to his handlers; yet another, that his wife ("a German Jewess") had been deeply involved in his nefarious plot.[63] Yet the most destructive gossip concerned the magnitude of the conspiracy. According to some, the damage that Miasoedov had inflicted was so great that the Russian High Command did not dare to acknowledge it. In a letter of March 20, a junior officer with the Fourth Turkestan Marching Company insisted to a friend that "Miasoedov not only gave up Russia's plans [to the enemy], he also handed over all of the general plans of the allies."[64] Yet according to others Miasoedov had been only a courier, a relatively low-level member of a vast cabal. The American ambassador to Russia, George Marye, was told, for example, that the real source of the secrets Miasoedov had betrayed to the enemy had been none other than Ekaterina Viktorovna, the wife of War Minister Sukhomlinov.[65] It was even said that Russian military authorities deserved no credit at all for catching Miasoedov; rather, *French* military counterintelligence had unmasked him. General Pau had recently arrived in Petrograd from Paris bearing with him documents taken from a German officer slain in France that conclusively established the ex-gendarme's guilt. It was this, and this alone, that had forced the Russian army to take action. The incontinent haste of Miasoedov's trial and execution resulted from the need to obliterate the evidence that would inculpate other, much higher-ranking traitors.[66] The top echelons of the army and the bureaucracy were filthy with traitors, or so it was whispered.[67]

Other Arrests

Although the rumor mills continued to spew out wild stories about the involvement of prominent tsarist officials in Miasoedov's crimes, the people who were actually picked up in the immediate aftermath of Sergei Nikolaevich's arrest were those with personal ties to him, no matter how indirect. On the night of February 19–20 the Okhrana staged coordinated raids on the apartments of Miasoedov's friends, relatives, and acquaintances in Petrograd, Vilna, Kovno, Libava, and Odessa. Hundreds of premises were searched and thousands of pounds of documents seized. Evgeniia Stolbina and Nina Magerovskaia were detained on the morning of February 20, when they staggered back to their apartment after an all-night party at Shishkin's gypsy encampment; both were still wearing evening dress.[68] No sooner had Klara Miasoedova been picked up on February 24 than she was remanded to the Warsaw Citadel by

63. See A Russian, *Russian Court Memoirs 1914–1916* (London, 1917), p. 144; Bernard Pares, *The Fall of the Russian Monarchy: A Study of the Evidence* (New York, 1961), p. 213.

64. GARF, f. 102, op. 265, d. 1042, l. 135.

65. George Thomas Marye, *Nearing the End in Imperial Russia* (Philadelphia, 1929), pp. 116–117.

66. A Russian, *Court Memoirs*, p. 144; S. P. Melgunov, *Vospominaniia i dnevniki*, vol. 1 (Paris, 1964), p. 192.

67. V. V. Karrik, "Voina i revoliutsiia," *Golos minuvshago*, nos. 1–3 (1918): 13.

68. List of persons arrested, February 19, 1915, RGVIA, f. 801, op. 28, d. 168, l. 61.

144 order of the commander of the Northwest front.[69] Baron O. O. Grotgus, connected to Miasoedov through the Northwest Russian Steamship Company, was arrested in Petrograd, as was O. G. Freinat, a retired official of the Ministry of Justice, who sat on several corporate boards, knew Miasoedov, and had written a report favorable to the Freidbergs' emigration bureau back in 1908. Frantz Rigert, husband of Klara's sister, was arrested on his estate, and Miasoedov's brother-in-law Pavel Gol'dshtein at his home in Vilna. G. Z. Berend, a German subject who was the proprietor of a large steam-powered grain mill in Libava, was arrested in Viatka, to which he had been ex-iled at the beginning of the war. He, too, knew Miasoedov and had solicited the lat-ter's help in drafting a legislative proposal to tax German grain imported into Fin-land. G. A. Urban was arrested because he had been a hunting companion of Sergei's in Verzhbolovo years before.

Virtually everyone else associated with the Northwest Steamship Company on whom the police could lay their hands was taken into custody. Boris Freidberg had been out of town on business when his house was searched on February 19. After he learned what had happened, he immediately traveled to Petrograd to consult with at-torney O. O. Gruzenberg, the very same man who had cross-examined Miasoedov in Vilna district court back in 1907. When he asked the lawyer whether he should go into hiding or give himself up, the latter answered, "As for myself I would not run away. I would seek justice in order to cut the throats of my accusers."[70] Swayed by Gruzen-berg's recommendation, Boris voluntarily surrendered to the Libava police on March 1. In view of what subsequently transpired, this was a piece of advice for which Gruzenberg would forever after reproach himself.

Like so many of his codefendants, Boris was packed off to Warsaw to be inter-viewed by special judicial investigator Matveev. When Boris's brother David and the family attorney, A. I. Lipshits, visited the administration of the Warsaw prison where Boris was being held and offered money to purchase the confined man better food (a common practice then), both of them were also placed under arrest. All in all, by April 24, thirty people were behind bars in connection with the Miasoedov affair.[71]

Nor was the end in sight. A Lithuanian prostitute named Antonina Kedys was dragged into the case, as were the innkeeper Mateush Mikulis, the artesian well-diggers Shlomo and Aaron Zal'tsman, and Staff-Captain P. A. Benson, who had for-merly been attached to the office of the Russian military attaché in Paris. I. K. Kar-pov, the operator of the Verzhbolovo railway buffet, was arrested because Miasoedov had eaten meat pies in his establishment and had, moreover, gone duck hunting with him. The Vilna wine merchant Kaplan was arrested for having sold Miasoedov rum and cognac, and a man named Prager because he had once shared a hotel room in Libava with A. I. Lipshits.[72] The trail of Miasoedov's associations (and the associa-

69. Order of Petrograd gradonachal'nik, February 24, 1915, ibid., l. 9.

70. O. O. Gruzenberg, *Yesterday: Memoirs of a Russian Jewish Lawyer,* trans. Don C. Rawson and Ta-tiana Tipton (Berkeley, 1981), p. 135.

71. List of persons arrested, April 24, 1915, RGVIA, f. 2003, op. 2, d. 1073, l. 87.

72. Letters of Warsaw assistant procurator to Stavka, April 1915, ibid., ll. 264, 291.

tions of his associates) was followed to a degree of mindless, stupefying absurdity. The piano teacher Izabella Kan and the widow Elena Borshneva were arrested, Kan because she had been Stolbina's roommate before Magerovskaia had moved in, and Boroshneva for having been Kan's student.[73] By the summer, the proprietor of the "Boyar" boarding house in Petrograd, Frederica-Luisa Ambrecht, would fall under suspicion because Baron Grotgus's brother had once lived there.[74]

Military authorities decided the fates of many of these people administratively. Stolbina, for example, was exiled to Tomsk in Western Siberia.[75] But even when cases were brought to trial, the evidence was often ludicrously flimsy. Take, for example, the accusations leveled against retired Real Privy Councilor Freinat. Freinat was on the boards of the Wal'dgof Cellulose Company and the Russian branch of Schering Chemical (the ancestor of today's Schering-Plough), two firms that had large numbers of German stockholders. Various employees of Wal'dgof were Germans, and some of them who had been recalled to Prussia on the eve of the war actually held reserve commissions in the German army. The fact that Wal'dgof made cellulose, an indispensable ingredient in the manufacture of smokeless powder, meant that the Germans with Freinat's help were certain to attempt to sabotage it.[76] Freinat was, moreover, personally acquainted with Prussian intelligence officer Richard Skopnik. Skopnik, who had a reputation as an authority on canines, had in 1913 served as a judge at an international dog show in Petersburg, which Freinat had also attended. Skopnik had been indifferent to the competition until the military working dogs were put through their paces; he came alive as he watched German shepherds drag machine guns into position and transport ammunition belts, and he questioned the animals' trainers, using Freinat as his interpreter.[77] The innocent explanation for all of this—that Freinat was an enthusiast for German shepherds and was in fact the president of the breed's Russian kennel club—somehow escaped the investigators' notice.

With regard to the Freidbergs, prosecutors seemed to assume that the Northwest Russian Steamship Company was a prima facie front for espionage, despite information that came to them from both the Kovno and Kurland gendarmes that the Freidbergs were respectable businessmen who had been repeatedly and groundlessly denounced by their competitors. Captain Dmitriev of the Kurland gendarmes even identified one of the people who had been most active in maligning the Freidbergs: a certain Burshtein, a former employee whom they had fired for dishonesty.[78]

In Copenhagen, the third Freidberg brother, Samuel, had in the meantime tried the only thing he could think of to influence the outcome of his brothers' cases.

---

73. Freinat, *Pravda o dele*, p. 49.

74. Counterintelligence memorandum, June 19, 1915, RGVIA, f. 801, op. 28, d. 172, l. 88.

75. Warsaw assistant procurator to Stavka, February 5, 1916, RGVIA, f. 2003, op. 2, d. 1073, l. 219.

76. Chief of counterintelligence of general staff to staff of Northwest front, March 16, 1915, RGVIA, f. 801, op. 28, d. 164, l. 306.

77. I. P. Vasil'ev deposition, RGVIA, f. 962, op. 2, d. 160, ll. 50–51.

78. Assistant chief, Kurland gendarmes, to assistant chief, Kovno gendarmes, February 20, 1915, RGVIA, f. 801, op. 28, d. 168, ll. 35,63.

146 Shortly after Boris's arrest in early March Samuel had telegraphed the offices of the Cunard Steamship Company in Liverpool, beseeching the management of the firm (whose agent in Libava he had been for years) to intervene with the British Foreign Office on his brothers' behalf. On March 6 (19), the chairman of Cunard, Sir Alfred Booth, called at Whitehall and did precisely that. The aide-memoire of the conversation prepared for British Foreign Secretary Sir Edward Grey pointed out that

> The Company [i.e., Cunard] have the highest opinion of their agent and vouch for his business character and faithfulness to British interests. His brother, under arrest, is also personally known to the head of the Company's Passenger Department, who gives him the same good character. The Company feel sure a mistake has been made, as both brothers, though Russian subjects, have always been most loyal in defense of British interests and anti-German in sentiment.[79]

Booth's opinion was sufficiently weighty to induce the Foreign Office to ask Britain's ambassador to Russia, Sir George Buchanon, to look into the affair. Buchanon's characteristically mean-spirited reply of March 27 is reproduced in full below:

> Freydberg [*sic*] was arrested because he was in business relations with a Colonel of Gendarmerie who with some forty other persons is charged with communicating secret military information which enabled the enemy to inflict serious losses on the Russian army during recent operations in East Prussia. It is always difficult for me to intervene in favour of a Russian subject even when he represents important British interests and all the more so when as in the present case the individual in question is said to have been connected within a very grave affair of espionage. If Freydberg's relations with the Colonel were of a purely business character (which I believe to be the case although I cannot vouch for it) he will no doubt be shortly released.
>
> I have in the past few months had to make such frequent representations on behalf of British subjects or British firms that I am afraid that my representations may not receive the same attention in the future if I take up a case like Freydberg.[80]

This message, which inter alia betrayed an astounding ignorance of what was going on in wartime Russia ("will no doubt shortly be released"), left no doubt that Buchanon had no intention of lifting a finger to help the Freidbergs no matter how concerned Cunard might be; his last paragraph was virtually a threat to the Foreign Office not to push him any further about this issue.

79. PRO. FO. Russian Correspondence 371. vol. 2444. no. 3396. p. 232.
80. Ibid., p. 236.

The Trials

Regardless of the fact that after several months of digging Matveev and his team had accumulated only paltry and circumstantial evidence with respect to most of the accused, higher military authorities seemed determined to make examples of them. In order to mete out truly condign punishment, there would of course have to be a trial. On June 11, General Gulevich telegraphed Warsaw that Nikolai Nikolaevich had ordered the cases of the Freidbergs and twelve other defendants to be heard in a military-field court.

The court held its first session on June 15 and handed down its verdict two days later. Boris Freidberg was declared guilty of conspiracy to commit espionage on behalf of Austria and Germany before 1914 and of the actual commission of that offense thereafter. Shlomo and Aaron Zal'tsman were found to have provided the Germans with secret material about the fortifications of Grodno and were consequently deemed guilty of spying. David Freidberg, Mateush Mikulis, and Frantz Rigert were convicted of conspiracy to commit espionage but were acquitted of actual spying, while Klara Miasoedova, Frid, Falk, Grotgus, Urban, Berend, Lipshits, and Freinat were declared innocent of both spying and conspiracy. David Freidberg, Mikulis, and Rigert were all sentenced to terms of hard labor. Boris Freidberg and the Zal'tsman brothers were condemned to hang.[81]

That very same day, June 17, Boris's wife Minna sent a tearful appeal to Stavka imploring Nikolai Nikolaevich for mercy: "A wife and mother of three young children falls to the feet of Your Imperial Highness with an ardent prayer to spare her and the children." Boris, she declared, was the victim of a "fatal error." He simply could not be a spy, for as the manager of the Northwest Steamship Company he had "conducted a ruthless struggle against German firms."[82] But Minna had been too late. By the time her telegram reached Stavka Boris was already dead. In the company of Shlomo and Aaron Zal'tsman he had been hanged early in the morning of June 18 (July 1). Minna's second message to the grand duke, in which she asked for husband's body, was, if anything, even more pathetic. As her husband had been a convert to Christianity, she declared that she wanted to bury him in the Lutheran cemetery so that she could "preserve the children's memory of their father by taking them to his grave."[83] But Stavka denied even this modest request and ordered the mail of the remaining prisoners intercepted, including a letter David Freidberg wrote to Samuel in which he asked the latter to look after his wife, adding that "I envy Boris. His sufferings are already over; mine have only begun."[84]

Stavka's gratuitous cruelty is explicable (if not excusable) in terms of the outrage that obtained there over the "leniency" of the sentences handed down in Warsaw that

81. Field court sentences, June 17, 1915, RGVIA, f. 2003, op. 2, d. 1073, ll. 154–156.
82. Telegram to Nikolai Nikolaevich, RGVIA, f. 2003, op. 2, d. 1073, l. 149.
83. Telegram of June 20, 1915, ibid., l. 146.
84. Letter of June 18, 1915, RGVIA, f. 962, op. 2, d. 112, l. 170.

148 June. General A. A. Gulevich, by now chief of staff of the Southwest front, nonetheless continued to play the part of the grand duke's hatchet man. At the latter's command, he fired off a stern letter of complaint to Lieutenant General Aleksandr Trubin, commandant of the Warsaw Citadel. Gulevich let Trubin know that Nikolai Nikolaevich was extremely dissatisfied. Why had there been so many acquittals? Wasn't the military-field court competent to do its job? Or had the members of the court and Trubin himself (who after all had confirmed the sentences) surrendered to a misguided compassion?

Trubin's response makes for interesting reading. He defended the performance of the field court that had tried the Freidbergs, stressing that it had made "the most intensive efforts to establish the culpability of every defendant even if only by indirect evidence." The problem was that the culpability of every defendant *could not* be established. Trubin had listened to the entire proceedings, and when the verdict had been read, he "could not in conscience find any reason not to confirm it." Neither the judges nor the commandant had been moved by pity for the accused. "Even if my own son had been among them my hand would not have trembled as I signed his death warrant as long as his guilt had been proven both to the court and to me." Could Gulevich please send a copy of this letter to the grand duke's chief of staff? "A reprimand, especially one from His Imperial Highness, our highly respected Commander in Chief, is a measurelessly heavy burden for me, as I do not feel myself to be at fault."[85]

But at Stavka neither the Grand Duke Nikolai nor his chief of staff, Ianushkevich, had any use for Trubin's apologia or, it appears, for the letter of the law itself. An order had already gone out forbidding the release of *any* of the acquitted parties. All of them, in addition to the three condemned to hard labor, were to be taken to the city of Vilna, where they were to be tried again, this time by the Dvinsk Military-District Court then sitting there. A letter from the Stavka's judicial department to General Tolubaev, the president of that court, explained that the grand duke had decided to consider as validly confirmed only the sentences passed on the men who had already been executed. Under no circumstances was Tolubaev to allow civilian defense attorneys to take part in the case.[86]

The Dvinsk court tried all eleven defendants behind closed doors from July 8 through 12 (21–25). The verdict, which was read on July 14 (27), was evidently more to Stavka's liking. The court declared that Klara Miasoedova, Falk, Freinat, David Freidberg, Grotgus, and Rigert were all guilty of participation in a conspiracy, prior to the war, "whose goal was to aid the governments of Germany and Austria in their hostile plans against Russia by means of collecting and distributing to these governments information about the composition and numbers of Russia's armed forces, their movements and armaments, and in general information of all kinds making it possible to evaluate the military preparedness of the Russian army." All of these defendants had,

85. Trubin to Gulevich, June 25, 1915, RGVIA, f. 2003, op. 2, d. 1073, l. 140.
86. Freinat, *Pravda o dele,* p. 100.

moreover, "wittingly and in combination" collected such information and passed it to Vienna and Berlin. In addition, Grotgus, Freidberg, Falk, and Rigert were convicted of having continued to conspire and spy on behalf of the enemy after the war had broken out, a charge on which Freinat, Miasoedova, and Mikulis were acquitted. Mikulis was, however, declared to have committed independent acts of espionage for Germany during the war. Given its studied indifference to proof and logic, it is remarkable that the court declared Frid, Urban, Berend, and Lipshits innocent.[87]

Grotgus, David Freidberg, Fal'k, Rigert, Mikulis, and Klara Miasoedova were all sentenced to die, while Freinat was assigned an eight-year term of hard labor. The commander of the Northwest front, then General M. V. Alekseev, confirmed the sentences with two modifications. Perhaps due to a chivalric belief that it would be unseemly to string up a woman, he commuted Klara's punishment to administrative exile. Baron Grotgus was also the beneficiary of an act of clemency: hard labor for life, rather than the halter, now awaited him.

Freinat and Grotgus were sent to the Orel and Iaroslavl hard labor prisons, respectively, where prison flunkies welded them into the heavy leg irons they were condemned to wear for the duration of their sentences. And Klara Miasoedova would shortly set out on her dreary journey to her place of exile—Tomsk—where, by some ironic quirk of fate, her husband's mistress, Evgeniia Stolbina, had preceded her.

But the hangman was not to be cheated of all his victims. On the night of July 26 (August 8) prison guards marched David Freidberg, Robert Falk, Mateush Mikulis, and Frantz Rigert down from their cells into the courtyard of the Vilna Penitentiary. Within minutes all four of them were kicking away their last breaths of life as they dangled from the gallows. Since at a minimum the first three of these wretched men were completely without guilt, virtually every figure in the top leadership of Russian General Headquarters now had hands sticky with innocent blood.

---

87. Ibid., pp. 113–115 (quote from page 113).

6

The Roots of Spy Mania

I t is time to step back from the narrative and try to place the events we have related in a broader context by considering three sets of questions. First, while it
is patently obvious that Miasoedov, his wife, the Freidberg brothers, Freinat,
Grotgus, Falk, and many others were totally innocent of the crimes imputed to
them, were *all* the people swept up in the case also guiltless? Second, why was Sergei
Nikolaevich cast in the role of Russia's archtraitor? Why him and no other? Was his
fate merely an accident? Was he the butt of some cosmic practical joke? Or were there
other forces at work? A variety of possibilities suggest themselves, each requiring
close inspection. Finally, what was it about the trial of Miasoedov that ignited the
spy-catching frenzy that gripped Russia in early 1915 and did not abate until the Bolsheviks took Russia out of the war (and perhaps not even then)? What cultural and
psychological phenomena made wartime Russia particularly vulnerable to epidemics
of "spy mania"? Let us begin with the question of real as opposed to imaginary spies.

Were Any Guilty?

The destruction of the bulk of the records of the Wilhelmine secret service by allied bombs in the Second World War has deprived us of the ability to make categori-
cal judgments about the quality of the German intelligence effort against Russia in
the World War I. From the fragmentary evidence that survives, however, it would appear that that effort in the prewar era produced spotty and uneven results. In 1909 the
intelligence section of the German General Staff—the *Nachrichten Abteilung*
(N.A.)—spent 22,000 marks on the twenty-four Russian agents in its employ but
confessed that it utterly failed to recruit any Russian officers as spies, or to acquire

mobilization and deployment schedules from military district or central staffs.[1] In the years that followed, the accelerating tempo of European crises caused the section to devote ever-greater attention to acquiring military information about the Russian Empire. A concerted effort was made to enlist Russian officers into Germany's service, and some success was achieved; in 1911, for instance, Captains Bortkevich and Grensach signed on with the N.A. German intelligence was also able to hire agents (and thus gain footholds) in some of the most important garrison towns of Poland, Lithuania, and the Baltic. Particularly valuable information came from those German nationals who were sent into Russia posing as traveling salesmen. By late 1913 the N.A. was celebrating its greatest coup to date, for it had apparently induced a colonel[2] in Russian military intelligence department of the Russian General Staff to work on its behalf.[3] On the very eve of the war, according to one account, German intelligence may have been suborning the treason of as many as seventy Russian officers.[4]

Yet this record of accomplishment was only superficially impressive. The Nachrichten Abteilung's four-year summary report for 1911–13 was a catalog of frustration and disappointment: Russian military secrets were proving unexpectedly difficult to acquire. One reason for this was the low productivity of many agents. But another was what we might describe as their perishability. The typical German agent in Russia did not have a long, useful career. Every year the ranks of the agents were thinned by sickness, death, defection, and arrest, and heroic exertions were necessary to make good the losses. Indeed, some of these losses could not be made good. "The best agent material," concluded the summary report in 1913, "has been eliminated."[5] It is perhaps therefore not surprising that the German intelligence service botched its most important prewar task concerning Russia: determining the speed with which Russia would mobilize and, consequently, the timing of Russia's initial attack. When the Russian First and Second Armies invaded East Prussia scarcely two weeks after the declaration of war, the German secret service was as startled as the German army was unprepared.[6]

As additional mistakes on this order could not be afforded, the resources devoted to military intelligence increased tenfold after the war began. In addition to using lo-

---

1. Generalmajor A. L. Fritz Gempp, "Geheimer Nachrichtendienst und Spionabwehr der Heeres" (unpublished manuscript, Berlin, 1927), National Archives, microfilm T-77, pp. 149, 156. Gempp, who served in German military intelligence, evidently composed this history, which cites many intelligence documents verbatim, in order to help the new German army build up its own intelligence apparatus. On the organizational structure of German military intelligence see also Gert Buchheit, *Der deutsche Geheimdienst. Geschichte der militärischen Abwehr* (Munich, 1967), pp. 17–24.

2. By no stretch of the imagination can this person, a colonel in the regular army, be identified with Miasoedov. Miasoedov had retired again in 1912 and had no access to military information between that time and November 1914.

3. Gempp, "Geheimer Nachrichtendienst," pp. 165, 174. On the colonel see Felix Gross, *I Knew Those Spies* (London, 1940), p. 211.

4. Gross, *I Knew Those Spies*, p. 10

5. Gempp, "Geheimer Nachrichtendienst," pp. 165–166, 173, 174, 175 (quote from p. 175).

6. K. von Kuhl, *Der Deutsche Generalstab in Vorbereitung und Durchführung des Weltkrieges* (Berlin, 1920), p. 82.

152 cally recruited spies to penetrate the enemy, Berlin and Vienna built up networks of what were described as "distance agents" in important Russian cities who communicated in code or invisible ink with their large espionage bureaus in Stockholm, Copenhagen, Christiania (i.e. Oslo), and Bern.[7] Both powers placed considerable emphasis on cultivating and bribing Russian officers at the front, and each claimed to have dozens of mostly low-ranking officers willing to act as agents (or at least willing to take its money.)[8] Then, too, the Germans organized a full-blown espionage center in Odessa, while the Austrians profited from the services of a military officer attached to the consulate of a neutral country in Moscow, who was said to supervise one hundred and fifty agents.[9]

One of the few sources to reveal some of the names of the Russian subjects who spied for the Central Powers during the war is the postbellum general staff study of Fritz Gempp, who played a key role in the Germans' most important espionage operations in the east from 1914 to 1917. According to Gempp, members of the "V-Mann" (i.e., anti-Russian) intelligence organization he founded included the Kovno merchant Max Koslowitz, the paper manufacturer Eynar Kull, the Lyck agricultural colonist Arnold, and the wealthy lumber magnate Pupkow. Gempp even claimed to have agents in Stavka itself. A certain Bogdanova infiltrated Russian General Headquarters in the guise of a Red Cross nurse. Gempp is also supposed to have had on his payroll a waiter who occasionally doubled as a telegraph operator at Stavka, and who could therefore supply the Germans with copies of Russian orders from time to time. Among the intelligence coups with which Gempp credited his agent network was the provision of information about railroad utilization and details about the number of Russia's casualties, as well as advance warning about Italy's entry into the war on the Allied side.[10]

It is, however, important not to exaggerate the value to Germany and Austria of the human intelligence sources they cultivated during the war. Take the officer-spies, for example. Neither the Germans nor the Austrians could be entirely confident that the soldiers in question were actually working for them, rather than stringing them along as part of a deception operation directed by Russian counterintelligence. One German intelligence professional subsequently recalled that of the eighty Russian agents Germany had signed up in 1914 and 1915, "over sixty . . . proved to have been set loose on us by the Russian secret service."[11] Colonel Walter Nicolai, the seasoned veteran who headed German intelligence during the war, complained in his memoirs

7. Lieutenant A. Bauermeister, *Spies Break Through: Memoirs of a German Secret Service Officer,* trans. Hector C. Bywater (New York, 1934), p. 89.

8. Colonel W[alter] Nicolai, *The German Secret Service,* trans. George Renwick (London, 1924), pp. 123–124.

9. On Odessa: P. P. Zavarzin, *Rabota tainoi politsii. Vospominaniia* (Paris, 1924), pp. 164–168; on the officer from the neutral country: Nicholas Snowden (Miklos Soltész), *Memoirs of a Spy: Adventures Along the Eastern Front* (London, 1933), p. 130.

10. Heinz Höhne, *Der Krieg im Dunkeln. Macht und Einfluss des deutschen und russischen Geheimdienstes* (Munich, 1985), pp. 168–169.

11. Gross, *I Knew Those Spies,* p. 18.

that "espionage in the Russian theater of war . . . could only provide material for very limited local tactical success. Not even one of the big regroupings of the Russian army was reported by it in time."[12] In fact, there is little doubt that the most reliable and profitable information about the Russian army that fell into enemy hands from the beginning to the end of the war came from signals intelligence—that is, from tapping into Russian field communications, intercepting radiotelegrams, decrypting messages, and the like. The Austrians alone broke sixteen separate Russian codes.[13] Major Busso von Bismarck, the German military attaché in Bern, was so successful in gaining secret collaborators in the Swiss government that he regularly forwarded to Berlin copies of every Russian military telegram going in or out of neutral Switzerland. Since the Russian General Staff routed its entire secret correspondence with its western European military attachés through the Bern telegraph office, Bismarck had struck pure gold. Indeed, it is highly probable that it was this source that alerted the Germans to Russia's planned offensive in January 1915 and consequently made possible the German counteroffensive that culminated in the destruction of the Russian XX Corps the following month.[14]

Yet Germany and Austria did endeavor to recruit Russian agents on a large scale, regardless of how cost-effective the process was. Given this fact, and given the hysterical tenacity with which the Russian police hunted for traitors (as well as the size of the net they cast to pull their suspects in) it is, of course, quite possible that some guilty parties as well as innocent ones were picked up in the course of the Miasoedov dragnet.

To delve into this matter more deeply, it is best to begin with Antonina Kedys. Her case is unique in that Kedys, unlike all the other people arrested in the Miasoedov affair, actually acknowledged her involvement in espionage. A prostitute who had a long history of trouble with the authorities despite her nineteen years, Kedys had been taken into custody in Minsk at the end of October 1914. Officially charged with vagrancy, she was administratively sentenced to exile in Tomsk province as an "undesirable." Yet prior to her dispatch to the east, the police learned that she also was wanted on an outstanding warrant for theft. She was accordingly sent to the Grodno women's prison, where she was placed in a cell with Emma Reinert, a twenty-nine-year-old peasant from the Lithuanian village of Shestakovo, who was being held on suspicion of espionage. The two women struck up a conversation. According to Reinert's testimony, when she told Kedys she had been falsely denounced by her landlord, Mateush Mikulis, Kedys blurted out that she herself really was a German spy.[15]

When Reinert told the prison warders what Kedys had said, there ensued an immediate investigation. At her very first interrogation (April 21), Kedys confirmed that she had told Reinert the truth: "I admit my guilt in giving German soldiers informa-

---

12. Nicolai, *German Secret Service*, p. 123.
13. Maks [Max] Ronge, *Ravedka i kontrravedka*, 2d ed. (Moscow, 1939), p. 239.
14. Höhne, *Der Krieg im Dunkeln*, pp. 174–176.
15. Reinert testimony, May 26, 1915, RGVIA, f. 801, op. 28, d. 165, l. 194.

154   tion about the movement and deployment of Russian troops."[16] She explained that after her father's death, her mother had remarried a German national in Tilsit. This man had introduced her to the German officers who had recruited her for espionage in the spring of 1914. Most of the time she had served as a low-level courier, carrying messages and documents for other German agents in the Russian borderlands. Prodded by her questioners, Kedys described some of the missions she performed and also gave them the names of her coconspirators. In particular, she claimed that Shlomo and Aaron Zal'tsman had supplied her with photographs and plans of the fortifications of Grodno for transmittal to the German secret service. She also stated that one of her handlers on the Russian side of the frontier had been Frantz Rigert, who had once sent her to Shestakovo with a packet of intelligence material that she turned over to Mateush Mikulis, who was to forward it to the Germans.

It was on this basis that the police locked up Mikulis and the Zal'tsmans. Rigert (who was, after all, Miasoedov's brother-in-law) was already in jail when Kedys confessed. It is worth noting that there were some scraps of evidence to back up Antonina's statements about the four men. Although Mikulis accused Kedys of lying, witnesses from Shestakovo swore that Kedys had indeed come to the village and passed the night at Mikulis's house in September 1914. When the enemy had temporarily occupied the village in March 1915, Mikulis had also been observed in close conversation with a German officer. Moreover, when apprehended, Mikulis had been found in possession of a safe-conduct allowing him to pass through the German lines.

The Zal'tsmans similarly denied everything: they had never committed any acts of espionage nor had they ever even met Kedys. But when the police pointed out that a photograph of the woman had been discovered among their belongings, the Zal'tsmans altered their story: Kedys had plied her trade for a time in 1914 in the same Grodno hotel in which they were staying; the photograph was a keepsake of the physical relationship they had had with her. However, Aaron and Shlomo persisted in maintaining their innocence of spying. To be sure, they had subcontracted to drill artesian wells for the II Army Corps in Grodno, but they had never collected or delivered any information of military utility to anyone.[17]

As for Frantz Rigert, when the police had shown Kedys his photograph during her examination, she had identified him immediately and without hesitation. Yet Rigert was as emphatic about his blamelessness as the Zal'tsmans had been. Why, then, had he evinced such curiosity about the number of troops accommodated at the Alekseev artillery camp in Vilna province? Rigert's answer was that his estate (the same for whose purchase Miasoedov had arranged a fraudulent loan) abutted the Alekseev camp. He had won a contract for pumping out the camp cesspools in 1913, a job for which he was paid by the man.[18]

16. Kedys interrogation, April 21, 1915, RGVIA, f. 801, op. 28, d. 171, l. 23.
17. For the foregoing see report on evidence, May 30, 1915, RGVIA, f. 2003, op. 2, d. 1073, ll. 99–108.
18. Ministry of Justice to Warsaw Circuit Court, May 5, 1915, RGVIA, f. 801, op. 28, d. 170, l. 82.

It is difficult to know what to make of all of this. On the one hand it is possible that Kedys was a remorseful spy and was telling the unalloyed truth. Yet on the other, even if Kedys was herself a traitor, the four men she incriminated did have cogent explanations for many of their purportedly suspicious acts. Rigert really was in the insalubrious business of cleaning the Alekseev camp cesspools on a per capita basis. Mikulis did have a German safe-conduct but insisted he had wrangled it from the occupation authorities to take his sick daughter to the doctor (and indeed could prove that he had used it for this purpose). As for the Zal'tsman brothers, were they really guilty of anything more than sleeping with a whore and lying about it to keep their wives in the dark? This would have been shabby conduct, surely, but scarcely a hanging offense.

In any event there was no conclusive evidence against any of these men—no irrefutable documentary proofs, no eyewitness testimony to criminal deeds. It all came down to Kedys's word against theirs. And how reliable was her word anyway? Was it not possible that in her fear and panic, Kedys was actually trying to mitigate her punishment by giving up nonexistent accomplices? Was it not equally conceivable that her denunciation of the Zal'tsmans was an act of revenge against two of her least favorite customers? It is incontrovertible that the young woman was profoundly disturbed. She had already made one attempt at suicide while imprisoned in Minsk in early November 1914; on May 25 (June 7), 1915, she hanged herself in her jail cell.[19] But even if Kedys had been the spy she proclaimed herself to be, there were no direct links between her and Miasoedov, ironically enough. Sergei Nikolaevich had been executed over a month before Kedys confessed.

A stronger, albeit still circumstantial, argument can be built for the guilt of Staff-Captain Pavel Vladimirovich Benson of the Fifth Aleksandriiskii Hussars. Tall, urbane, and conventionally handsome by fin de siécle standards (he sported an impressively huge waxed mustache), Benson had exploited his social connections to win a series of diplomatic and special appointments that permitted him to avoid the drudgery of field service. He had served a tour as adjutant to the Russian military agent in Paris, had been attached directly to General Rennenkampf, and along with General Count Andrei Shuvalov and General Ermolinskii, had been a member of a roving commission formed during the war to investigate the abuse of power by military commanders.[20] There was, however, another side to Benson than that of the soigné socialite, diplomat, and bon vivant, for he was also a notorious sexual predator who specialized in seducing and swindling women.

Benson had been under suspicion for some time even prior to the war, not least because of questions about how a man with no private means could lead so opulent a life. On April 26, 1915, he was arrested in the apartment of one of his mistresses, Mariia Aleksandrova Iaruzel'skaia; the police made an exhaustive search of these

19. For her death certificate see ibid., l. 152.
20. Orlov report, RGVIA, f. 2003, op. 2, d. 1063, l. 17.

156   premises, as well as the room that Benson maintained at Petrograd's exclusive European Hotel. From this physical inspection and from interrogation, it emerged that
        Benson had in the past few years somehow mysteriously accumulated large assets. A
        professor in Berlin named Stein had sold or transferred to him a villa in Switzerland
        worth over half a million francs. Benson was also found to be in possession of promissory notes from two different German subjects totaling 155,000 rubles and 321,000
        marks, respectively. In addition to this, cash payments of 170,000 German marks had
        been made to him prior to the war, at which time he had insured his life for 500,000
        marks with the German firm of Victoria zu Berlin, a company in which he held stock
        and with which he conducted a voluminous correspondence. Then there was the
        matter of the "salary" of 400 rubles, automatically deposited every month in Benson's Swiss bank account. Benson really could provide no adequate or convincing explanation for any of these emoluments.[21]

        The police regarded other odd facts about Benson and Iaruzel'skaia as potentially
        incriminating. Although the Swiss management of the European Hotel had tipped
        off Benson that he was under surveillance a full two months prior to his arrest (which
        should have given him ample time to destroy any compromising material), a significant number of documents bearing on operational issues turned up among the captain's papers notwithstanding, including an appreciation of the strategic situation
        authored by his uncle, Leonid, a general on the staff of the Third Army. Iaruzel'skaia's
        correspondence also raised some eyebrows: since the start of the war she had received
        many letters from one "Marie-Louise Berlin," each postmarked from a different European city. Iaruzel'skaia also had a note dated September 5, 1914, from "Geren," in
        which he or she talked about mailing off all of Iaruzel'skaia's letters, except those that
        were going to Germany.[22]

        Benson's relationships with Baroness Ida Zeidlitz and Dr. Adrian Polli-
        Pollachek—both German subjects—were disturbing too. Before the war, Zeidlitz
        had made frequent visits to Russia and when in Petersburg had always stayed in the
        European Hotel, where she had had frequent tête-à-têtes with Benson, ostensibly
        about business matters. If their association had been purely commercial, it was rather
        interesting that Benson had made a considerable effort to conceal Zeidlitz's true
        identity from his friends and acquaintances, to whom in 1913 he had falsely introduced her as a Russian relative of his.[23] Zeidlitz and Benson were, moreover, both
        tied to Polli-Pollachek, a Hungarian who had served as the Russian correspondent of
        several German newspapers since his arrival in Petersburg in 1904. For a hack journalist Pollachek seemed to enjoy unusual access to the Austro-Hungarian embassy.
        Described in one Stavka document as "a notorious German and Austro-Hungarian
        spy," Pollachek had been arrested in July 1914. Indeed, Benson *himself* had accused

---

21. Papers seized from Benson, RGVIA, f. 962, op. 2, d. 117, ll. 1, 230; Orlov report, RGVIA, f. 2003, op.
2, d. 1063, ll. 10–16.
22. Orlov report, RGVIA, f. 2003, op. 2, d. 1063, l. 15.
23. Ibid., l. 13.

Pollachek of espionage in 1910, an act for which Pollachek had challenged him to a duel.[24]

One final connection of Benson's provoked the keenest interest. Countess Magdalena (Lilly) Nostits was the wife of Count Grigorii Ivanovich Nostits, a major general of the Imperial Suite. Magdalena was an American adventuress with a very healthy libido, whose first husband had been a Prussian officer by the name of von Nympsh. Upon his death she had married Count Nostits, who was then serving as Russian military attaché in Berlin. In Petrograd, where she is said to have won over everyone "by her tact, her charming manners and her magnificent receptions" she was an acknowledged leader of wartime society.[25] However, matrimony apparently was inadequate to contain her amorous impulses; since wedding Nostits she had entertained a succession of lovers. One of them had been Benson, with whom she had had an affair when both he and her husband had been attached to the Russian embassy in Paris. According to a rumor widely circulated at the foreign ministry, Count Nostits had misplaced some important dispatches about this time, which had led to a showdown with Russia's ambassador, A. Nelidov, and the count's removal from his position.[26]

The pursuit of Benson had put Countess Nostits squarely in the sights of military counterintelligence. The ubiquitous V. A. Erandakov personally organized the investigation of the countess, shadowing her with *filery*, bribing her servants, and perlustrating her mail. The material he collected soon filled a thick dossier at Stavka, for Erandakov was ordered to make regular reports about Nostits to Ianushkevich, the grand duke's chief of staff. (Inter alia, that file contained nude photos of the countess, which a leering Ianushkevich once displayed to Foreign Minister Sazonov on one of his visits to Baranovichi, much to the latter's revulsion)[27]. Erandakov learned that Magdalena Nostits was currently sleeping with Lalong, a councilor at the Belgian embassy, and also discovered that she was conducting her entire foreign correspondence through the Belgian diplomatic pouch. However, whether she was doing this out of a concern for the defense of her own privacy or for some conspiratorial purpose, Erandakov could not say. His agents could not detect her in the commission of any specific crimes.[28]

The possibility that the countess was working on behalf of the Central Powers was nonetheless taken very seriously and resulted in steps to render her harmless. There could not, of course, be any thought of an arrest or trial. The countess was too

24. Ibid., ll.13–14; RGVIA, f. 962, op. 2, d. 49, ll. 186–189.

25. [A Russian], *Russian Court Memoirs 1914–16* (London, 1917), pp. 293–294. On Countess Nostits's struggle to overcome the negative impression left by her past during her debut in Russian society see A. Bogdanovich, *Tri poslednikh samoderzhtsa* (Moscow, 1990), p. 468.

26. For example, see A. A. Ignat'ev, *50 let v stroiu*, vol. 1 (Moscow, 1952), pp. 498–499.

27. *Dnevnik Velikogo Kniaza Andreia Vladimirovicha 1915 god*, ed. V. P. Semenikova (Leningrad/Moscow, 1925), p. 69.

28. Testimony of Ianushkevich, September 13, 1916, RGVIA, f. 962, op. 2, d. 134, ll. 154–156.

158 highly placed in society and was a particular favorite of the diplomatic corps.[29] As a major general of the suite, the count was, moreover, directly attached to the person of the emperor. Yet if the countess was peddling secrets to the enemy, her husband was most likely her unwitting source, and it was decided henceforth to deny him access to any sensitive information. A Stavka order of April therefore detached the count from his billet as guards chief of staff and excluded him from any active-duty assignments with the field army. The count protested this treatment through the ministry of the court: he had been told orally that neither he nor his wife was accused of anything and he wanted that statement put in writing, since "[my] retirement without a written denial of this heavy suspicion places a blot on the honor of my wife and myself."[30]

In his reply to the court commandant Ianushkevich showed himself at his most mealy-mouthed and disingenuous: he asserted that Stavka had no knowledge compromising the count and possessed no data whatsoever about the countess as she was not a soldier but a civilian. Any further inquiries about her, he continued, should be addressed to the Corps of Gendarmes and the Ministry of Justice.[31] As this letter makes clear, Stavka authorities had come to mistrust the imperial court enough to deceive it brazenly about what military counterintelligence was up to.[32] The rupture between the army high command and the autocracy, of which this episode was a symptom, is a topic we will revisit shortly, as it exerted a profound influence upon the way in which the Miasoedov case played out.

Among all those arrested or placed under observation in the first phase of the Miasoedov affair, then, only Kedys and the men she denounced—in addition to Benson, Zeidlitz, Pollachek, and Countess Nostits—even remotely warranted consideration as espionage agents of the Central Powers. But Kedys aside (and there is reason for skepticism concerning her disclosures in view of her evident mental instability), what unequivocal proof impeached any of them? Without catching a spy in a restricted area, finding incriminating documents on his person, or squeezing a confession out of him, espionage can be an extremely difficult crime to substantiate conclusively. For instance, it is beyond dispute that Benson was a scoundrel and morally depraved libertine; the pattern of his associations with Germans as well as his inexplicable, recently acquired wealth fully warranted the most intense scrutiny of the Russian police and counterintelligence. Given the fact that most of wartime Russia was under a martial law that granted the authorities vast powers to protect the state from potentially harmful individuals, it would have been quite legal either to have held Benson indefinitely or to have exiled him to eastern Siberia administratively. He was instead tried,

29. George Thomas Marye, *Nearing the End in Imperial Russia* (Philadelphia, 1929), p. 396.
30. Nostits letter of July 16, 1915, RGVIA, f. 2003, op. 2, d. 1063, l. 370.
31. Ianushkevich letter, August 18, 1915, ibid., l. 368.
32. Indeed, the Empress Alexandra was incensed that Nikolai Nikolaevich, Russia's supreme commander, had dared to relieve Nostits from duty without first asking her husband's permission. Evidently believing that the Nostits couple were the victims of a shabby and underhanded intrigue, in a letter of May 11, 1915, she advised Nicholas to order a complete inquiry and "restore justice." *Perepiski Nikolaia i Aleksandry Romanovykh 1914–1915 g.g.* (Moscow/Petrograd, 1923), p. 194.

convicted of espionage, and sentenced to hard labor. But even if Benson was a traitor (and I would be willing to bet that he was) he was never *shown* to be so beyond the shadow of a reasonable doubt. The case against Benson was entirely inferential—just as that against Miasoedov had been.

The chief difference, of course, was that the circumstantial evidence against Benson was quite compelling, whereas that against Miasoedov was so weak as to be nonexistent. Miasoedov, who was innocent, went to the gallows, whereas Benson, who may well have been guilty, received less harsh punishment. To be sure, Benson had numerous, highly placed friends and protectors, but perhaps the unequal treatment accorded the two men was explained by more than that.

Why Miasoedov?

As Miasoedov was not a German agent, there remain five hypotheses that might account for his victimization. The first of these is that Miasoedov was a casualty of circumstance and accident. The second points to an amorous intrigue to explain Sergei's Nikolaevich's demise, while the third portrays him as the scapegoat in a military or a military/political conspiracy. The fourth possibility is that although innocent he was believed to be guilty by a military counterintelligence establishment run amok. A final conjecture, of course, is that the Germans framed him. Each of these deserves a look; as will be seen, more than one of these theories may be true simultaneously.

The first hypothesis holds that Miasoedov was destroyed by a sequence of evil coincidences and sheer bad luck. It was, for example, Miasoedov's bad luck to have hunted with the kaiser, to have served in the frontier zone, and to have associated with Jews in a steamship venture—activities that were individually unremarkable but that acquired a sinister cast when taken together and viewed in wartime hindsight. Miasoedov's testimony in the 1907 Vilna court, which was given under compulsion, also proved to be a curse, for it saddled him for life with the enmity of the police and the Okhrana. Sergei's friendship with Sukhomlinov and his appointment to a war ministry post, which must have seemed to the gendarme a fabulous stroke of good fortune, was actually anything but, for it antagonized the minister's disgruntled adjutants. After all, it had been Botkin and Bulatsel' who first brought Miasoedov to the attention of Guchkov, which in turn made possible the Octobrist politician's libels against him in 1912. It was of course Guchkov's underhanded campaign to unseat the war minister in that year that gave the initial charges of treason against Miasoedov a national airing, which consequently explained why the selfaggrandizing Lieutenant Kolakovskii had ever even heard of the former gendarme. As a result, Kolakovskii, who clearly wanted to inflate his own status as a patriot in the eyes of his general staff interrogators, possessed a name around which he could build up a fairy tale about treason and subversion. It did not help that Miasoedov was serving on the Northwest front with the Tenth Army, near the very sector where the Germans surprised and wreaked havoc on the Russians during the winter battle of Masuria.

160   As for the other persons arrested in the affair, it was the accident of a relationship with Miasoedov that brought almost all of them to the prisoners' dock. As far as I can ascertain, anonymous denunciations were routinely leveled at anyone who owned a successful business or accumulated substantial property anywhere in the northwest borderlands of the empire in the last years of the ancien régime; just as routinely the police dismissed these fetid scribblings as the tripe they obviously were. But in the atmosphere created by the conviction of Miasoedov, the anonymous denunciation acquired a new authority, particularly if the police knew that the person it concerned had been linked to the hanged gendarme. For example, when a note sent to the Vilna Okhrana in late March 1915 branded the entire Gol'dshtein clan as German spies and traitors, Miasoedov's brother-in-law, the tannery owner Pavel Gol'dshtein, was jailed forthwith.[33] There were other random events that also worked to the disadvantage of the accused. On April 16, 1915, an explosion ripped apart one of the smelting furnaces at the Okhtinsk munitions factory near Petrograd, killing ten men. Although the appalling safety regime at the plant was most likely the cause of the blast, it was widely ascribed to sabotage.[34] High-profile incidents like this one fed the general obsession with spies and led to public clamor for their swift apprehension and severe punishment—phenomena that did not benefit those who would be tried for treason in Warsaw and Vilna that summer.

There is obviously something to the "bad luck" hypothesis, for Miasoedov's life was punctuated by one calamity after another. However, it does not pass muster as a solitary and comprehensive explanation for the colonel's judicial murder. Ill fortune may have placed Sergei Nikolaevich on the edge of a pit, but it did not push him in. It took other parties to do that, parties who either needed Miasoedov eliminated regardless of the evidence or who believed in his guilt with a strength that was impervious to proof.

This brings us neatly to the second hypothesis: that Miasoedov was brought down by a sinister plot launched by a powerful and jealous man. Walter Nicolai of the German Secret Service propagated this theory in the pages of his memoirs, where he insisted that "the charge against him [Miasoedov] was merely an excuse, very effective in wartime, to get him out of the way, as he was the rival in a lady's affections of another highly placed person."[35] Nicolai is evidently alluding to Evgeniia Stolbina here. It will be recalled that although Stolbina was Miasoedov's mistress, her fidelity to him was exclusively conditional on his presence. When they were apart, she entertained plenty of other men, of whom one was a son of the Grand Duke Konstantin Konstantinovich, according to police reports. Now Konstantin (a talented poet and translator of Shakespeare) did father six sons despite his lifelong preference for sexual relationships with men: Ioann (b. 1886), Gabriel (b. 1887), Konstantin (b. 1891), Oleg (b. 1892), Igor (b. 1894), and Georgii (b. 1903). Since Georgii was underage and

---

33. Anonymous denunciation of March 1915, RGVIA, f. 801, op. 28, d. 164, l. 284.
34. Correspondence and reports on the explosion, RGVIA, f. 2003, op. 2, d. 797, ll. 1, 5–6, 10.
35. Nicolai, *German Secret Service*, p. 28.

Oleg was mortally wounded in combat in October 1914, any one of the remaining four sons might plausibly have been involved with Stolbina in 1915. Unfortunately, the available evidence makes it impossible to determine which of them it was. In any event, the implication of Nicolai's remarks is clear: Stolbina's lover from the imperial family was envious of Miasoedov's hold over her and trumped up a case against the gendarme in order to remove him from the scene permanently. This story made a nice romantic coda to Nicolai's treatment of the Miasoedov affair, but there is not a word of discernible truth in any of it. No records connect any of Konstantin Konstantinovich's sons to the colonel's espionage trial. All four of our hypothetical candidates served in the army, but none held a position of any consequence, and it was the army elite, and Stavka in particular, that directed the arrest, prosecution, and execution of Miasoedov from first to last.

Was the death of Miasoedov therefore the result of some tenebrous Stavka plot? To examine this charge, our third hypothesis, it is necessary to return to the subject of the war and the rift between Stavka and court to which we have already referred.

Although the patriotic ardor that had erupted with the outbreak of hostilities in August 1914 had not completely cooled six months later, it had begun to manifest itself in a different form. As we have seen, there was significant reason by that point for dissatisfaction with the conduct of the war. To be sure, the army was doing its duty; Russia's troops continued to fight with their legendary courage and tenacity. Their commander in chief, the splenetic and emotionally volatile Grand Duke Nikolai Nikolaevich, remained implausibly popular throughout Russia as a sort of living symbol of devotion to the national cause. But how effective could any commander or any army be if it was starved of the resources and materiel necessary for combat? Shortages of munitions and equipment had reached such critical levels that raw recruits, in many cases after no more than ten weeks' training, were being marched to the front without rifles, ordered instead to arm themselves at the expense of the dead. Army losses were averaging three hundred thousand men a month. Then, too, there was the succession of calamitous defeats that the army had suffered at the hands of the Germans—Tannenberg, the Masurian lakes, and Soldau among them. Even the news from the Southwest front was bad, for Russia's offensive against Austria had literally been frozen into immobility in the gelid Carpathian passes. All these things together deflated public expectations for a rapid and successful conclusion to the war. The prospect of victory seemed farther off than ever.

What could explain Russia's baffling misfortunes on the battlefield? If the army was in the main sound, the problem had to lie in the rear-echelon areas, or perhaps even the capital itself. Among educated opponents of the regime it soon became an article of faith that the government was to blame for the army's agony. One school of thought held that the war had demonstrated the government's fundamental incompetence. As long as corrupt reactionaries like Sukhomlinov and Maklakov staffed it, the Russian Council of Ministers could not be trusted to organize military supply, let alone mobilize the economy for war. The "sacred union"—that pledge of abstinence from political struggle for the duration of the conflict to which the majority of polit-

162 ical parties had subscribed in the summer of 1914—began to crumble to pieces. Kerenskii's "private" letter about the Miasoedov affair, discussed in the last chapter, was indicative of the new trend. Politicians on the moderate right, center, and left started to call on the emperor to remove the otiose ministers and to enlist society's help in waging the economic war. With the Russian army in pell-mell retreat in the summer of 1915, there were demands for the creation of a "responsible ministry," that is, a ministry responsible to the Duma and largely drawn from its membership.[36]

Yet there were those who wondered whether something more than mere governmental ineptitude was at work. Rumor had it that the court was a hotbed of Germanophiles and defeatists. The court camarilla, which contained shady financiers, sclerotic generals, and the unspeakable Rasputin, was said to have the emperor and empress in thrall to its serpentine intrigues. Some saw it as particularly sinister that Alexandra was by origin a German and that she had blood relatives in Germany, including her brother Ernest, the reigning duke of Hesse-Darmstadt. A typical joke of the time turned on the extensive skepticism about Alexandra's true loyalties:

> The heir to the throne cries every day. When he is asked why he answers, "Why shouldn't I cry? The Russians are beaten, Papa cries and I cry with him. The Germans are beaten, Mama cries and I cry with her."[37]

Thus it was that the court came to be seen as the army's precise antithesis, and the empress as the antipode of Nikolai Nikolaevich. Whereas Nikolai and his Stavka stood for the manly and forthright prosecution of the war until victory was achieved, Alexandra's clique embodied all of the "dark forces" that furtively sought Russia's defeat and humiliation. It went without saying that "honest men of all classes over the country" sided with the grand duke.[38] In any event, the idea that hidden enemies at the court were deliberately obstructing the Russian war effort acquired wide currency. Indeed, as Ianushkevich's less than truthful statement about Countess Nostits cited above illustrates, there were those at Stavka who believed in this version of events themselves.[39]

It was obvious that talk like this could only aggravate relations between Nicholas II and his supreme commander. Well aware of the potential for friction, Nikolai Nikolaevich sought to reassure the emperor about his loyalty, by keeping the Duma politicians at arm's length, for example. But it is also clear that Nikolai found the bruit about the court/Stavka discord to be useful. In the first place, it flattered his outsized vanity by casting him in the role of national hero. But it also provided him

---

36. On these developments see V. I. Startsev, *Russkaia burzhuaziia i samoderzhavie v 1905–1917 gg.* (Leningrad, 1977), pp. 131–146; Paul Miliukov, *Political Memoirs 1905–1917*, trans. Carl Goldberg, ed. Arthur Mendel (Ann Arbor, 1967), pp. 305–316.

37. V. V. Karrik, "Voina i revoliutsiia," *Golos minuvshago*, nos. 1–3 (1918): 11.

38. Princess Catacuzene, Countess Speransky, née Grant, *Revolutionary Days* (Boston, 1919), p. 51.

39. Admiral Bubnov, also attached to Stavka, shared Ianushkevich's concerns about the court. See A. Bubnov, *V tsarskoi stavke* (New York, 1955), p. 13.

with a permanent, ironclad excuse that absolved him of responsibility regardless of the disasters that occurred at the front. Credulous faith in the existence of a malignant "court camarilla" exonerated him and his favored subordinates of any charges of command failure or military bungling. Under Nikolai's leadership there had, of course, been an abundance of both. But these phenomena would be overlooked if the majority of people were persuaded that defeat had been contrived by the court or by spies planted on the army by unknown parties there.

It is here that the conviction of Miasoedov could be most helpful, for it would focus public attention on treachery and deflect it away from the deficiencies of the Russian high command. The reputations and careers of persons other than Nikolai Nikolaevich were at stake. When considering those senior officers who directly took part in the case, one is immediately struck by the fact that each of them was connected to the Masuria catastrophe in some way. As a result, each would personally benefit from the colonel's defamation. General N. V. Ruzskii, who ordered Miasoedov's arrest, had been command of the Northwest front at the time of the battle. His chief of staff, General A. A. Gulevich, in effect ran the entire prosecution of Miasoedov from his office in Sedlets. General M. D. Bonch-Bruevich and Colonel N. S. Batiushin were the Northwest front's quartermaster general and intelligence chief, respectively. In these positions they bore technical responsibility for failure to supply the timely tactical intelligence about German troop movements that might have averted the destruction of the XX Corps. Yet they conducted the military investigation of Miasoedov, and Bonch-Bruevich himself selected the judges for the court-martial.[40]

From the fact that all these officers were complicit in the Russian army's failure at Augustov, and consequently stood to gain if the disaster could be chalked up to espionage, it does not necessarily follow that they knowingly conspired to sacrifice the life of an innocent man. But some of their other activities, particularly their blatant interference in the judicial process, tend to bolster that conclusion. As we have seen, Nikolai Nikolaevich removed the Miasoedov case from the regular military justice system and entrusted it instead to a field court, evidently in the interest of a speedy and predetermined outcome. Pains were taken to script the trial by sanitizing the information the judges would be permitted to hear. In his March 8, 1915, testimony, for example, Lieutenant Colonel Pavel Shirinov, who also served on the staff of the Tenth Army, praised Miasoedov's bravery and loyalty and maintained that the "Addresses of 19 January" was a document to which any intelligence officer would routinely have access. Not content with suppressing Shirinov's deposition, Stavka ordered up administrative punishment for him. At the command of Ianushkevich, Shirinov was immediately expelled from the ranks of the regular army and placed in the reserves.[41] Also revealing is a March 1915 letter from Ianushkevich to War Minister Sukhomlinov in which the former, while asserting that there was not the slightest doubt about Miasoedov's "vile treason," also explained that it was essential to "definitely liqui-

---

40. Bonch-Bruevich telegram, March 15, 1915, RGVIA, f. 962, op. 2, d. 104, l. 22.
41. RGVIA, f. 2003, op. 2, d. 1073, ll. 346–347, 352, 365.

164 date" the court case within the next day or two "in order to calm public opinion before the [Easter] holidays."[42] After the execution, Ianushkevich upbraided Gulevich because the field court had found Miasoedov innocent of espionage in wartime. Ianushkevich insisted that the preliminary military investigation had completely substantiated this charge (actually it hadn't), that this information had been included in the order for the colonel's trial, and that therefore the judges had had a *duty* to convict him on this count. But as they had shirked this duty, Ianushkevich declared that they were "unsuitable to participate in field courts-martial concerning especially important cases" and demanded that they be excluded from such courts in the future.[43]

Stavka was nonetheless aware of how weak its case against the former gendarme had been; in order to strengthen it (at least on paper) it kept Matveev and a team of detectives busy into 1916 vainly hunting for nonexistent evidence of Sergei Nikolaevich's crimes. In a real sense, Miasoedov was executed first and investigated later. Even after the colonel was dead and buried, Stavka continued to manipulate the courts in related treason cases. On the eve of the first trial of Miasoedov's "accomplices" the Stavka's judicial section prepared a note informing the field court in advance what verdicts it would reach. The judges were told that the Freidbergs, the Zal'tsmans, Falk, Mikulis, and Rigert were not to be acquitted of espionage "under any circumstances." By contrast, Israel Frid and Klara Miasoedova "may be acquitted (although it is not absolutely necessary to acquit them)."[44]

Penultimately there is a tantalizing but, alas, ultimately unverifiable anecdote that relates to the question of an army conspiracy against Miasoedov. In the beginning of the 1930s, A. A. Samoilo, a former tsarist intelligence officer who survived into the Soviet period, occupied a chair at Moscow's Hydrometeorological Institute. Learning that Sergei Miasoedov's brother Nikolai was to be appointed to a teaching post, he fired off a letter of protest to the institute's director: the brother of a notorious traitor (even a traitor to the tsarist regime) was obviously unfit as an instructor for Soviet youth. Nikolai thereupon paid a visit to Samoilo and begged him to withdraw his objections; his brother, he insisted, had been innocent. Indeed, Nikolai claimed once to have seen a report written by a military prosecutor in March 1915 that fully exonerated Sergei. He also swore that at the bottom of this document Grand Duke Nikolai Nikolaevich had scrawled the words "Hang him anyway."[45] If this document once existed, it does no longer, at least in the archives.

Finally, an appeal to common sense is in order. If the Stavka generals had really believed Miasoedov to be a master spy, why were they so eager to accelerate the proceedings against him? Why was he executed with such abrupt dispatch? If Nikolai Nikolaevich, Ianushkevich, and Gulevich had truly been convinced of the colonel's treason, none of this would have made any sense whatsoever. Rather than hustling

---

42. "Perepiska V. A. Sukhomlinova s N. N. Ianushkevichem," *Krasnyi arkhiv* 3 (1923): 44.
43. Ianushkevich to Gulevich, April 4, 1915, RGVIA, f. 2003, op. 2, d. 1073, l. 81.
44. Note concerning defendants, ibid., ll. 157–158.
45. A. S. Samoilo, *Dve zhizni* (Leningrad, 1963), p. 167.

Miasoedov to the scaffold, they would have kept him alive until they had extracted every scrap of relevant information—every date, every name, every detail—that bore on his espionage career and the Germans who had recruited and handled him. They might even have tempted the colonel to cooperate with an insincere promise of a commuted sentence. But what they most definitely would not have done is execute Miasoedov before they had squeezed him as dry as a desiccated lemon.

Although in my view the probability is high that several of the highest-placed officers at Stavka arranged the condemnation of Miasoedov despite knowing that nothing had been proved against him, the possibility cannot be ruled out that among the colonel's nemeses were those who had a blind and unshakable faith in the colonel's perfidy, evidence or no evidence.

Mikhail Bonch-Bruevich may have fallen into that category. Bruevich was another tsarist officer who successfully negotiated the transition to Soviet power, doubtless with the assistance of his brother Vladimir, who had been a member of the Bolshevik party since 1895 and would later serve as Lenin's personal assistant. Mikhail lived to the ripe old age of seventy-six and completed a memoir that appeared in print one year after his death. This self-serving and mendacious volume devoted considerable space to its author's World War I exploits, particularly his claim to have been Imperial Russia's spy-catcher extraordinaire. According to Bruevich, wartime Russia was plagued by a total infestation of enemy spies. There were spies in the Red Cross, spies in the universities, spies among the Baltic Germans, and spies among restaurant waiters, janitors, and doormen. Bruevich and his able assistant, Colonel N. S. Batiushin, engaged in a lonely and unequal battle with this verminous army of miscreants, constantly frustrated by their superiors' boneheaded indifference to the danger on the one hand and by the machinations of the court in defense of the guilty on the other. As a result far too many spies and traitors escaped justice, quite frequently the biggest fish among them. One agreeable exception to this pattern had been the arrest of Miasoedov, on which accomplishment Bonch-Bruevich fulsomely congratulated himself.[46]

How accurate was Bonch-Bruevich's depiction of his wartime vigilance? How closely did his memories of the period coincide with reality? It is undeniably true that during the war Bonch-Bruevich did claim that there were spies and enemy agents lurking under every rock. He was constantly agitating for the arrest and deportation of more "suspicious" individuals, regardless of the army or front to which he was attached. *Prior* to the arrest of Miasoedov (which, inter alia, did not occur as he described it in his book) he had already instigated treason cases against ninety-two people in the region of Mitau alone, much to the disgust of P. G. Kurlov, then the governor-general of the Baltic.[47] Kurlov, whom we have met before in these pages, was scarcely a paragon of honesty or rectitude, but it is hard not to sympathize with his keen resentment at the challenge to his authority represented by Bruevich's out-

46. M. D. Bonch-Bruevich, *Vsia vlast' sovetam* (Moscow, 1957), pp. 56–104, passim.
47. Aleksandr Tarsaidze, *Chetyre mifa* (New York, 1969), p. 98.

166 of-control counterintelligence establishment. Under the direction of Bruevich and Batiushin, counterintelligence was growing within the Russian state like a mestatisizing tumor, responsible to no one, trumping the power of the regular civil administration, and justifying its most outrageous actions by an appeal to "national security." Military CI was intruding in matters far removed from its charter, such as the struggle against speculation and price gouging, political propaganda, and labor unrest. One incident particularly stuck in Kurlov's throat, an occasion on which Bonch-Bruevich had presented him with a warrant for the administrative exile of eight prominent Baltic landlords and refused to provide any reasons, arguing that they were all classified. "Thus," wrote Kurlov, "data that was in the hands of subalterns of the reserve [i.e., low-level counterintelligence officers] was forbidden to the viceroy of the region, who according to a law confirmed by the Commander–in Chief had the prerogatives of an army commander with regard to the civil administration."[48]

Perhaps the most extreme example of Bruevich's inquisitorial zeal occurred in the summer of 1915 and concerned the Singer Sewing Machine Company. The American-owned firm, which had an 80 percent share of Russia's market for the machines, had a large network of stores throughout the empire staffed by a sizable sales force. It was exactly the scale of Singer's operation that Bonch-Bruevich regarded with a jaundiced eye, for it was in his opinion the most perfect cover that could ever be devised for the collection of grassroots intelligence by Germany. When Kel'pin, the director of Singer's Petrograd office, sent circulars out to all the company's Russian salesmen soliciting information about the operation of factories in their territories, Bruevich concluded that this "completely substantiates the firm's character as an espionage organization, since the particular interest the firm has evinced in the organization and work of Russian industry is doubtless connected to the growing intensiveness of the work of industry for the needs of the army at the present time."[49] Bonch-Bruevich then somehow managed to sell Ianushkevich on the need to take steps against Singer. In the second and third weeks of July, at Stavka's command, police agents fanned out throughout Russia, arresting Singer's branch managers and closing hundreds of its stores. Singer's Russian operations crashed to a halt; in Petrograd and its contiguous provinces alone five hundred Singer offices were shuttered and six thousand employees were thrown out of work.[50] Yet on this occasion Bonch-Bruevich had overreached himself. In September the Council of Ministers, which had taken up the Singer case, issued a ruling that found that the shutdown of the company had harmed the interests of Russian consumers while poisoning Russia's relations with the Americans. Although there might be some dubious persons in the firm's employ, the company was clearly not an espionage ring. Outside the direct theater of military activity, Singer's stores were to be reopened.[51]

48. P. G. Kurlov, *Gibel' imperatorskoi Rossii* (Moscow, 1992), pp. 181–182 (quote from p. 182).

49. Bonch-Bruevich to Stavka, July 5, 1915, RGVIA, f. 2003, op. 2, d. 1063, l. 375.

50. Ibid., l. 393. See also Eric Lohr, *Nationalizing the Russian Empire: The Campaign against Enemy Aliens During World War I* (Cambridge, 2003), pp. 79–82. N. V. Grekov, *Russkaia kontrrazvedka v 1905–1917 gg.: shpionomaniia i real'nye problemy* (Moscow, 2000), pp. 252–260.

51. Note on Council of Ministers' decision of September 18, 1915, RGVIA, f. 2003, op. 2, d. 1063, l. 469.

By this point it had been decided to reduce Bonch-Bruevich's public profile: he was ordered out of Stavka to Petrograd to become the chief of staff of the Sixth Army, an inactive force. However, before his departure for the capital he had had the time to revise and promulgate a new organizational statute for Russian military counterintelligence. Bruevich's new system established identical CI bureaus in every Russian army, which helped disseminate and institutionalize his own extremist views on treason throughout the theater of war. One feature of Bruevich's organizational statute deserves special mention, for it stipulated that the leading positions in counterintelligence were to be filled by general staff officers, not officers on loan from the gendarmes or Okhrana. This requirement, apparently based on the a priori assumption that the police were at best generally incompetent and at worst collectively disloyal, produced a general purge of high-level police agents from all the important organs of CI during the summer of 1915. For much of the rest of the war Russian counterintelligence largely operated as Bruevich had intended, and he deserves the lion's share of the blame for its grotesque excesses.[52]

What explains Bonch-Bruevich's obsession with treason and subversion? The possibility cannot be dismissed out of hand that the general's inexhaustible suspiciousness and paranoia disguised an underlying skepticism. Perhaps Bruevich's insistence that thousands of spies were at large in Russia was a convenient fiction propagated out of a desire to build a counterintelligence empire and consequently to maximize his personal power. However, the content and tone of the scores of reports by him that I have consulted indicate otherwise. Bonch-Bruevich's correspondence with his superiors, as well as his public pronouncements, stinks of authentic and fanatical belief.

Now it could be the case that social, psychological, and ideological conditions within the wartime empire helped to feed the general's espionage mania, as they did that of many other Russians. These are developments that I will take up shortly. Then, too, if one worked in counterintelligence, it was extremely easy to fall in with

52. The ups and downs of Batiushin's wartime career are also of interest. In April 1915, for reasons that are not entirely clear, he was removed from counterintelligence and assigned command of a cavalry regiment. In August of 1915, however, he was promoted to general and attached to the staff of the newly created Northern front as chief of intelligence and counterintelligence. In May 1916 he was placed at the head of a special commission to investigate "anti-state activity and espionage." Batiushin's Commission targeted several high-profile figures in finance and the sugar industry, including the banker Dmitrii Rubinshtein, whom it accused of speculation and profiteering. Rubinshtein was arrested in July 1916 and imprisoned in Pskov. In December 1916, however, at the empress's insistence, Rubinshtein was released to house arrest. (Rubinshtein had ties to Rasputin and had served as Alexandra's agent in transferring money to her German relatives—a matter that the imperial family, for obvious reasons, wished to keep secret.) After Rasputin's assassination, Rubinshtein was arrested again and was condemned to administrative exile in Siberia on the eve of the February Revolution, only to be freed by the Provisional Government. According to one of his victims, from May to December 1916 Batiushin used his commission to make himself "the dictator of Russia." See M. Iu. Tsekhanovskii, "General Batiushin i ego kommissiia," addendum to *Dvoinoi agent,* by Vladimir Orlov (Moscow, 1998), pp. 179–181; I. I. Vasil'ev and A. A. Zdanovich, "General N.S. Batiushin. Portret v inter'ere russkoi razvedki i kontrrazvedki," afterword to *Tainaia voennaia razvedka i bor'ba s nei,* by General'nogo Shtaba Gen.-Maoikr Batiushin, pp. 218–234 (Moscow, 2002); Alex Marshall, "Russian Military Intelligence 1905–1917: The Untold Story behind Tsarist Russia in the First World War," *War in History* 11, no. 4 (2004): 415–418.

168 the view that the threat from hidden spies was very grave. Such attitudes were manifested by intelligence professionals in other belligerent countries as well. According to Tristan Busch of Austrian military intelligence, Austria's wartime censors came to see "a collective spy in the public." So fanatically did those censors pursue their quest for spies that over one ten-week period in 1915 they treated a quarter of a million letters with iodine fumes looking for messages in invisible ink.[53] Yet it is worth emphasizing that there were at least two anxieties common to *Russian* counterintelligence officers, distinct from their institutional point of view, that may well have made them especially susceptible to infection by "spy mania." The first was a fear about the vulnerability of their own organization; the second was dismay about the stability of their country.

As we have already seen, one of prewar Russia's greatest intelligence coups had been the recruitment of Colonel Alfred Redl, once the Austro-Hungarian CI chief, whose traitorous revelations had considerably enhanced Russian confidence in victory if it ever came to a contest of arms with the Dual Monarchy. Now in May 1913 the Austrian authorities closed in on Redl: he had become careless and was eventually caught after picking up two money-stuffed envelopes at Vienna's central post office. It was apparently the Germans who had made the stakeout possible by alerting their allies to the general delivery alias Redl was using, information they had acquired from steaming open suspicious letters addressed to the same fictitious individual.[54] The precise circumstances of Redl's arrest were not, however, known in Russia. Within the Russian intelligence service feelings ran strong that Redl's discovery had to have been the result of betrayal, that a Russian mole had blown the identity of Russia's most valuable agent to the Central Powers. This of course meant that Russia's intelligence efforts were themselves compromised and would remain so until the dangerous traitor within had been unmasked.[55] The possibility that Russia's enemies had breached the inner sanctum of the country's security poisoned the working environment in Russia's intelligence bureaus, sowing mistrust and contributing to the distinctly paranoid intellectual style regnant there.

If rumors of a mole accentuated the unease within Russian CI, that service had another reason for concern more solidly grounded in fact. It did not take a mental giant to realize that one cause of Russia's defeat in her previous war with Japan had been the outbreak of revolution in 1905. Arguably, if the revolution had not come when it did, Russia might well have prevailed in the Far East. Although they had not "started" the revolution in any way—existing preconditions in the country being more than adequate for the purpose—the Japanese had been its beneficiaries, and

53. Tristan Busch, *Secret Service Unmasked,* trans. Arthur V. Ireland (London, n.d.), pp. 91–92. Despite all the trouble they took, the censors only detected two messages by real spies out of the whole 250,000 letters.

54. Ian D. Armour, "Colonel Redl: Fact and Fancy," *Intelligence and National Security* 2, no. 1 (1987): 179.

55. On the unease in Russian intelligence after 1913 see the comment by a contemporary Austrian intelligence operative in Busch, *Secret Service Unmasked,* p. 58.

they had made strenuous if sporadic efforts to assist it, by covertly funneling cash to revolutionary organizations, for instance.[56] What if the Germans tried to do the same thing? To be sure, the population of the empire seemed in the main to be firmly united behind the war effort, but would this attitude persist indefinitely? Perhaps the war had only temporarily papered over the deep strains and unresolved conflicts within Russian society. If so, would these not provide the Germans with excellent opportunities for fomenting sedition? There was evidence that the Germans were thinking along exactly these lines. The week before Miasoedov was hanged, the Russian military attaché to Holland telegraphed Petrograd that

> among German military people there are many discussions about the way in which the widely organized propaganda within Russia during the Russo-Japanese war led to disorders within the country. It is said that if the Japanese were able to do this then they, the Germans, will succeed at this all the more, by means of targeting Finland, revolutionary elements and the poorer classes. According to information in my possession, this question is currently being worked through in Germany.[57]

Reports like this one understandably made the Russian government apprehensive, but military counterintelligence was even more nervous, for it was the empire's first line of defense against covert enemy action. Firmly convinced that the Germans had unleashed a vast campaign of subversion and espionage against Russia, CI officers were all too prone to construe accidents, mishaps, and other random events as evidence of German conspiracy and all too inclined to see a German spy in every eccentric, dubious, or multilingual individual.

There is one final explanation, or partial explanation, for the origins of the Miasoedov affair: that the Germans were behind it and had deliberately sought to incriminate the colonel. To be sure, the information about Lieutenant Kolakovskii that is contained in surviving German sources suggests that he did indeed fool the Germans into thinking that he was eager to work for them, and that the Germans repatriated him in the expectation that he would become a useful spy. But perhaps this information conveys a false impression. After all, who was fooling whom?

Once Kolakovskii had been recruited, Lieutenant Bauermeister of the German General Staff briefed him on his mission. During this briefing Bauermeister either named Miasoedov as a German agent or did not. These are obviously the only two possibilities, and the logical inference to be drawn from *either* is that Miasoedov was innocent. If Bauermeister did not mention the former gendarme in connection with espionage, then clearly Kolakovskii made up a whole series of lies about him to im-

---

56. See D. B. Pavlov and S. A. Petrov, "Iaponskie den'gi i russkaia revoliutsiia," in *Tainy russko-iaponskoi voiny*, p.68 (Moscow, 1993).

57. Cable of March 13, 1915, Arkhiv Vneshnoi Politiki Rossiiskoi Imperii (hereafter AVPRI), f. 133 (chancellery), op. 470, d. 165 1915 g., l. 24.

170 press his Russian interrogators.[58] But if Bauermeister actually did describe Sergei Nikolaevich as a top German spy, this proves that he was in fact guiltless, for no sane intelligence professional would have been so cavalier about the identity of his operatives. In that event Bauermeister's real game would have been to dupe the gullible Kolakovskii into believing that Miasoedov really was a traitor, so as to ensure that this malignant falsehood reached the ears of the Russian authorities as soon as the lieutenant got back to his country.

If the Germans actually attempted to frame Miasoedov, what might their motivations have been? It does not tax the imagination to come up with several. In the first place, Germany did indeed consider the social and political fault lines within the Russian Empire as ripe for exploitation. There is every reason to believe that the report from Holland cited above genuinely reflects German intentions in this regard. The land hunger of the peasants, the volatility of the proletariat, and the grievances of the national minorities were all potential Russian weaknesses. But the Germans realized that Russia also suffered on account of the schisms and dissension both within and among her political and military elites. Falsely implicating Miasoedov in espionage might then be a crude act of psychological warfare, designed to exacerbate the factionalism and recrimination that obtained in Russia. With any luck, fingering Miasoedov might tar the gendarme's former patron, War Minister Sukhomlinov himself, with suspicions of treason, thereby eliciting confusion and panic at the highest levels of the Russian polity.

Second, to disinform the Russian government about Miasoedov might have been one of the best methods available to Germany to protect her real agents. By luring Russia's police and counterintelligence service into a futile investigation of Sergei Nikolaevich and his friends, Berlin could hope to siphon off the resources that might otherwise have been devoted to apprehending those who were authentically spying on its behalf.

Finally, in addition to the charges made against the colonel in 1912, another consideration might have militated in favor of framing Miasoedov, for German intelligence could very well have nurtured a long-standing grudge against him. We are obviously crawling out on a speculative limb here, but the record contains some scattered hints tending to support it. Like every other German memoirist who discussed the matter, German intelligence chief Nicolai subsequently denounced the tsarist government for its cruel execution of the innocent gendarme colonel. But why should Nicolai have shed any tears for Miasoedov? Elsewhere in his book he observes that the colonel was one of the best border reconnaissance officers prewar Russia had ever had, and when he describes Miasoedov's efficiency and effectiveness, his exasperation is very close to the surface.[59]

It could, of course, be objected that if the Germans' secret goal had been to mire Miasoedov in the quicksand of false accusations, merely to stuff Lieutenant Ko-

58. The German historian of intelligence Heinz Höhne believes that Kolakovskii's Russian interrogators coaxed him into denouncing Miasoedov during his interrogation. See *Der Krieg im Dunkeln,* p. 194. The exhaustive précis of the interrogation fails to support this, however.

59. Nicolai, *German Secret Service,* pp. 26–27.

Iakovskii's head with derogatory misinformation was a rather dilatory and casual way of going about it. Yet it is possible that this bid to lay a trap for the colonel, if it took place, may not have been the only effort of its kind. One person who had been quite active in denouncing the Freidberg brothers, both for corrupt business practices prior to the outbreak of the war and for treason thereafter, was a certain Fishka Braunshtein. As might be expected, Braunshtein was affiliated with Danish and German steamship concerns that had a vested interest in seeing the Freidbergs' rival company closed down. Drumming up business among potential emigrants was not Braunshtein's sole occupation, however, for he also moonlighted as an agent of Hauptmann Flek, chief of the German military intelligence bureau in Eydtkuhnen.[60] Did Braunshtein consign his lies about the Freidbergs to paper at the behest of his superiors in commerce or intelligence? Unfortunately there are no data available that conclusively resolve this question.

At the end of the day, however, the preponderance of the evidence suggests that it was more likely that Kolkakovskii was a fabulist pure and simple rather than the unwitting instrument of an audacious German disinformation campaign. The odds are better than not that his lies, rather than German ones, brought Miasoedov to grief. Nonetheless, even if the Germans did not conspire against the colonel, the utility to them of his destruction could not have been greater if they had.

One of Clausewitz's central theoretical principles concerns the interrelationship among the elements of what he calls the "paradoxical trinity of war." These three elements are reason and the logical assessment of ends and means, typically embodied by the government; inspiration and insight, usually represented by the military; and irrational passion and will, incarnated by the people, more often than not. To prevail in a war, particularly a total war like that of 1914–18, all three portions of a country's trinity had to coexist in harmonious balance. As Clausewitz held that the proper purpose of war was the attainment of political objectives, he believed that if military considerations came to predominate over political ones in the direction of a war, or if a war was unnecessarily protracted by an insensate tide of popular hate, catastrophe would inevitably ensure. But he was also of the opinion that no government, no matter how wise, could win a major war without the passion and support of the people, both in and out of uniform, or absent the skillful planning and leadership contributed by its generals. Yet there was an additional complication, for although a balanced trinity was a necessary condition for victory, it was not a sufficient one because war was an interactive process in which each side tried to inflict damage on the other. It therefore behooved a belligerent country to defend its own trinity with the utmost care while simultaneously launching attacks on that of the enemy.

This brief digression is germane to an understanding of the impact of the Miasoedov affair, for it delivered terrible wounds to the governmental and popular components of Russia's trinity. The Miasoedov case and the series of additional inquiries and prosecutions that grew out of it envenomed political discourse, debased the prestige of the house of Romanov, played an instrumental role in shattering wartime Rus-

60. RGVIA, f. 2003, op. 2, d. 1063, l. 237.

172 sia's fragile unity of purpose, and at the same time (to appropriate Nietzsche's term) facilitated a bizarre "transvaluation of values" whereby monarchism came to be equated with treason. In these respects the case furthered the German cause more than some of *OberOst*'s (i.e., Supreme Command East's) most celebrated victories on the Eastern front.

"Espionage" and Mass Psychology: The Anatomy of Spy Mania

It must be observed that the notorious espionage scandals that shook Russia from 1915 to 1916 did so much damage to the war effort because the charges of treason that emerged from them were regarded as plausible by hundreds of thousands, if not millions, of people. One reason for this plausibility is obvious: the Russian government had formally declared that Miasoedov, the Freidbergs, and all the others were in truth enemy agents. There were, however, many who had learned from experience that not every statement by the imperial regime should be taken at face value. But the accusations made in the Miasoedov/Sukhomlinov cases acquired a greater credibility than an official imprimatur alone could bestow because they coincided with and tapped into certain noxious, preexisting trends in public opinion that the war had amplified. It was popular attitudes that magnified the significance of the spy scandals in Russia to grotesque proportions, like hot air inflating a balloon. In a very real sense, the public was already primed to believe in the treason of Miasoedov before it was even known that he had been arrested.

The obverse of the popular patriotism and enthusiasm in every belligerent country in the war's initial stages was an intensification of chauvinistic and xenophobic sentiment. Everything connected to the hated foreign enemy was ostentatiously rejected and publicly scorned. In Britain the editors of the *Cambridge Medieval History* ostentatiously announced that they would henceforth publish no more chapters by Germans; Booth Chemists placed large advertisements in the newspapers explaining that the eau de cologne it sold was not actually from Cologne but was rather exclusively of English manufacture; and rumors abounded that itinerant bands of foreign agents were taking advantage of the cloak of night to poison wells and reservoirs.[61] After the onset of trench warfare in December 1914 had dashed hopes in Germany for a quick victory, an eyewitness observed that "anyone with black hair or a beard was arrested as a Russian while whoever appeared in an English-looking raincoat was brought by a cheering mob to the nearest police station."[62] Nor was the United States immune. An explosive outburst of anti-German feeling accompanied American entry into the war in 1917. The teaching of the German language was suspended in many high schools, sauerkraut was renamed liberty cabbage, and "Alsatian" became the term preferred for German shepherd dogs. "If you turn Hell upside down," thun-

61. Trevor Wilson, *The Myriad Faces of War: Britain and the Great War 1914–1918* (Cambridge, 1986), pp. 170–171, 402–403.
62. Gross, *I Knew Those Spies*, p. 12.

dered the famous American evangelist Billy Sunday, "you will find 'Made in Ger- 173
many' stamped on the bottom."[63]

Russia experienced the same upsurge in nationalist passion, hysteria, and intoler-
ance that was observable elsewhere in Europe and America during the world war. But
like Austria-Hungary and unlike France and Germany, Russia was a multinational
empire, not a relatively homogeneous nation state. What this meant was that the increasingly strong Russian nationalism of the war years defined itself in opposition
not only to the external enemy but also to the "internal" enemy—that is, some of the
other ethnic, religious, and national groups with which the Russians had cohabited,
in many cases for centuries. Two groups of tsarist subjects in particular became the
focus of nationalist prejudice and hostility: the Jews and the Germans. To Russian nationalists the fact that virtually all of Miasoedov's alleged accomplices and helpers
were either Jewish or ethnically German made emotional sense and helped "explain"
why the gendarme had become the traitorous ringleader of an espionage cabal.

It is beyond dispute that there were significant numbers of Russian Jews and ethnic Germans who spied against the Russian Empire during the First World War. It
was a Jewish merchant and Russian subject by the name of Pincus Urwicz who was
the first to bring the German Secret Service a Russian mobilization poster on the very
eve of the war.[64] After war broke out, as we have already seen, the Germans were heavily dependent on the Jewish agents they hired in Russian Poland and Lithuania for the
collection of tactical intelligence. For many of them, espionage was doubtless a purely
business arrangement, and they would work for whoever paid the most. Indeed, when
Miasoedov was with the staff of the Tenth Army, he tried to recruit informants from
among the same populations and communities as the Germans did. Other Jews, however, may have been driven to spy for Germany by the ill usage and abuse they suffered at Russian hands. The great Jewish historian Simon Dubnow observed in his
diary that although the Jewish masses had initially supported the war with the same
patriotic fervor as had the other inhabitants of the tsar's dominions, by November
1914 pro-German views had made large inroads among them. Nor was this surprising, given "the violence of the Russian army against the peaceable Jewish population
of Poland and Galicia, whose men are bleeding for the [Russian] Fatherland."[65]

Numbering roughly three million in 1914, the ethnic Germans had represented a
small but influential minority within the Russian Empire since the eighteenth century. Peter the Great's annexation of the Baltic territories had brought a sizable number of Germans under Russian control, a number that increased when his successors
set aside enclaves along the Volga for immigrants from the German states. Still more
Germans had headed for the east in the next century in search of greater economic or
commercial opportunities. Among the most recent arrivals there were those who
clearly retained a sense of affiliation to their original homeland; many retained Ger-

63. Robert H. Ferrell, *Woodrow Wilson and World War I* (New York, 1986), p. 205.
64. Dennis Showalter, *Tannenberg: Clash of Empires* (Hampton, Conn., 1991), p. 102.
65. Simon Dubnow, *Mein Leben* (Berlin, 1937), p. 193.

174   man citizenship and some, like the Bauermeisters, returned to Germany when called up for military service. Indeed, the Imperial German Government went out of its way to accommodate such people, as for example by passing a law in the 1870s that permitted German nationals to hold dual citizenship. It is evident that some ethnic Germans resident in Russia did undertake espionage assignments on behalf of German intelligence, although we have no details on exactly how many. At any rate, we do know that the German secret service had high hopes for them.[66]

There can be little doubt, however, that the majority of Nicholas II's Jewish and German subjects were loyal and had no involvement with treasonable activity of any kind. Yet innocence was not enough to preserve the groups to which they belonged from general stigmatization. For many years prior to the outbreak of war the Jews had been both feared and despised. Germans had been admired, envied, and feared all at the same time.

Of course, anti-Semitism in Russia had a long and ignoble pedigree. From the standpoint of the Russian anti-Semite the Jews were collectively presumed to be untrustworthy cosmopolitans and unpatriotic as a matter of course; many were supposed to be eager for the rule of an imperial Germany that would treat them less harshly than did the tsarist regime. Regardless of the abject poverty in which the greater part of them lived, they were also associated with capitalism, liberalism, and modernity—phenomena that Russian nationalists largely deplored.[67] The anti-Semitism of the wartime era may therefore be treated as a mere extension and amplification of preexisting sentiment.

Attitudes toward the Germans were considerably more complex. For generations, Russified families of German origin, especially those of the Baltic provinces, had produced illustrious men who had risen to the highest echelons of the military and the bureaucracy, making distinguished contributions to the defense and governance of the empire. Then, too, traditional Russian monarchists had in the past often found much to praise in the conduct and deportment of Russia's German subjects collectively, perceiving them as more industrious, law-abiding, and cultured than the Russians among whom they lived. But there were also Russian nationalists who resented the Germans for these very attributes, viewing them as vices rather than virtues. Such nationalists held that by dint of their superior culture, cunning, and disciplined plotting the Germans had finagled themselves into too many prominent positions in industry, commerce, and the civil service. Since many Russians were too direct and guileless to compete with their sly German rivals, the Germans had come to exert an excessive and baleful influence on Russian life. The German, wrote one Russian nationalist, therefore had to be recognized "as the foe who has usurped all that is best in the country."[68] As might have been expected, the war considerably intensified Germanophobic attitudes, and the popular image of the German as a

---

66. Gross, *I Knew Those Spies*, p. 9.

67. On prewar attitudes toward the Jews see Theodore R. Weeks, *Nation and State in Late Imperial Russia: Nationalism and Russification on the Western Frontier, 1863–1914* (DeKalb, Ill., 1996), pp. 34–36, 61–62.

68. *Russian Court Memoirs*, p. 113.

greedy, sinister exploiter supplanted that of the sober and upright burgher. Still worse, the concentration of so much economic and political power in German hands not only deprived honest Russians of their fair share, but it also made it possible for the evil-minded Germans to level heavy blows against the Russian war effort.

Yellow journalism and popular political pamphlets fed these negative stereotypes. Russian newspapers printed exposés of "German factories in Russia," and A. S. Rezanov, a military prosecutor, published a tract on German espionage that charged that "it took the war to show how many German officers were installed in Russia in the guise of employees of all kinds in the plants, factories and offices."[69] Nikolai Polivanov's *O nemetskoi zasilii* (*On German Exploitation*), a booklet that was in its sixth edition by 1916, taught that all Germans were moral degenerates and that the real danger to Russia was not to be found at the front but "in the marsh slime of the Germanophile chancelleries" in the rear.[70] In other words, Russia's Germans were as a class maliciously hostile to the Russian state and were engaged in a ruthless struggle against it from within.

These prejudices against the Germans and Jews, like a pair of optically distorted spectacles, shaped the "reality" that many Russians perceived. Because there was such widespread belief that neither the Jews nor the Germans were up to any good, evidence that tended to confirm this judgment was accorded an automatic credibility that counterevidence was not. Lieutenant Kolakovskii's testimony is a case in point. One reason that military interrogators may have been inclined to give him the benefit of the doubt despite his weird lapses and inconsistencies was the highly anti-Semitic and Germanophobic character of much of what he said. By telling his debriefers that the Jews of the borderlands were helping the German army with willing enthusiasm and that every ethnic German in the Russian army was a secret servant of the kaiser, he was parroting the standard bigoted line of the Russian nationalists. By strongly playing to the preconceptions of his interlocutors, he probably increased his chances of being regarded as honest and truthful.

In any event, at least up until the February Revolution of 1917, increasing anxiety about treason marched in tandem with increasing persecution of Jews and Germans. Anti-Semitism and Germanophobia were the catalysts of Russian spy mania.

Anti-Semitism

The war gave a renewed impetus to anti-Semitism almost from the very beginning, a tendency that was particularly strong in the Polish, Lithuanian, and Ukrainian borderlands. As early as August 14 (27), the gendarme administration of Warsaw province was reporting to Petrograd that hostility to the Jews on the part of the Poles was definitely on the rise, since the Jews were suspected of collaboration with the enemy.[71] Wild rumors about the Jews circulated: they were accused of poisoning wells, supplying the advancing Germans with horses and provisions, harboring

---

69. A. S. Rezanov, *Nemetskoe shpionstvo* (Petrograd, 1915), p. 203.
70. RGVIA, f. 2003, op. 2, d. 1083, l. 40 (pps. 6–8).
71. Report of August 14, 1914, RGVIA, f. 2003, op. 1, d. 494, l. 23.

176 enemy soldiers, and signaling the enemy about Russian troop movements.[72] The commander of the First Army wrote the commander of the Northwest front on September 26 that in some of the territory that the Germans had recently seized, a certain "exclusively Jewish" element in the local population had delivered both information and provisions to the German army and had demanded that the rules of military judicial procedure be relaxed in cases of espionage and treason.[73] Nikolai Nikolaevich's response to this was to promulgate a decree authorizing officers down to the level of regimental commander to set up field courts-martial "for condemning those guilty of espionage on the spot."[74] As one might expect, many of the victims of these new judicial institutions were Jews, who were often convicted on the flimsiest of evidence. One particularly notorious case involved Herschanovich, a Jewish resident of Mariopol, found guilty of collaboration on October 2, 1914, on the exclusive strength of a deposition by a Muslim cleric, one Imam Bairashevskii, a real collaborator who had denounced an innocent man to divert the attention of the authorities away from his crimes.[75] As a result of the labors of his attorney, Herschanovich was in the end exonerated and released in 1916. Many others were far less lucky. Toward the end of November 1914 Nikolai Nikolaevich issued a secret order that required military units to round up civilian hostages from Jewish towns and villages in their zones of occupation. Should anyone in the community be detected in acts of treason or espionage, the hostages would forfeit their lives.[76] It is unclear how many people were hanged or shot under the terms of this regulation; the account of the three Jewish hostages executed on December 24 in the village of Sokhachev was one of the few that made the national press.[77]

Matters deteriorated still further in 1915. In March of that year Jews were forbidden to reside in any territories abutting the Gulf of Finland (presumably to prevent them from engaging in treasonous communication with the German navy).[78] In the same month the army began to implement a general deportation of Jews from the western quarters of the empire; by the beginning of the summer the roads would be clogged by over six hundred thousand homeless refugees streaming east.[79] In May derogatory stories about the Jews once again dominated the national news. *Russkii invalid,* the daily newspaper of the Ministry of War, erroneously reported that in April Jews in the settlement of Kushi, Kurland province, had hidden and abetted

72. Abraham C. Duker, *The Jews in the World War* (New York, 1939), p. 5.

73. Commander of First Army to commander of Northwest front, September 26, 1914, RGVIA, f. 2003, op. 1, d. 494, l. 101.

74. Ianushkevich to Ivanov, September 30, 1914, ibid., l. 71.

75. O. O. Gruzenberg, *Yesterday: Memoirs of a Russian-Jewish Lawyer,* trans. Don C. Rawson and Tatiana Tipton (Berkeley, 1981), pp. 163–166.

76. "Dokumenty o presledovanii evreev," in *Arkhiv russkoi revoliutsii,* vol. 19, pp. 247–248 (repr., The Hague, 1970).

77. Jacob Frumkin, "Pages from the History of Russian Jewry," in *Russian Jewry (1860–1917),* ed. Jacob Frumkin, Gregor Aronson, and Alexis Goldenweiser, trans. Mira Ginsburg, p. 63 (New York, 1966).

78. Louis Greenberg, *The Jews in Russia: The Struggle for Emancipation,* vol. 2 (New Haven, 1951), p. 98.

79. Duker, *Jews in the World War,* p. 7.

German incendiaries who had put the town to the torch. Although once again the truth eventually came out (there were no Jews actually residing in Kushi at the time) the "Kushi incident" became the pretext for a new wave of Jewish expulsions, this time from the provinces of Kovno and Kurland.[80]

What made all these atrocities possible was the extraordinary power vested in Russia's commander in chief by the field ordinance that had come into effect with the declaration of war in 1914. The articles of this document gave Nikolai Nikolaevich dictatorial control over all administration both civil and military in the front zone. Since he was not responsible in any way to the central government back in Petrograd, he was, for all intents and purposes, a second tsar. Thus it was that the deportations ordered by him went forward, regardless of the crises in public health, transportation, and housing that attended them and regardless as well of the protests lodged against them by the Council of Ministers. The middle and higher echelons of Russia's military leadership at the front appear to have been in the grips of an anti-Semitic frenzy. Nikolai's right-hand man, Chief of Staff Ianushkevich, was notorious for his pathological hatred of the Jews.[81] Count Pavel Ignat'ev, who spent much of 1915 working in the counterintelligence bureau of the Southwest front, subsequently complained that his office was inundated with denunciations of the Jews, of which over 90 percent were absurd and utterly without merit. "Every Jew," he wrote in amazement, "was seen as a spy."[82]

But there was an explanation other than mass psychosis to account for what was going on. Prince N. B. Shcherbatov, minister of the interior and definitely no liberal, saw Ianushkevich's campaign against the Jews as being driven more by policy than bigotry. At the August 4, 1915, meeting of the Council of Ministers he expressed his mounting frustration at the government's impotence; the "all-powerful" Ianushkevich refused to ease up in his persecution of the Jews, despite the fact that it was creating unprecedented human suffering, destabilizing the empire domestically, and complicating relations with Russia's allies, to boot. Shcherbatov declared that it was Ianushkevich's plan "to maintain the army's prejudice against the Jews, and to represent them as responsible for the defeats at the front." It was Shcherbatov's strong suspicion that Ianushkevich was employing the Jews as "an alibi" for military catastrophe.[83]

In fact, concern about friction with allies as well as with neutrals due to Russia's treatment of the Jews had preoccupied the government at various points since the start of the war. A particular worry was Russian access to British and American capital markets, over which prominent Jewish financiers were presumed to have consid-

---

80. Frumkin, "Pages," p. 66; Greenberg, *Jews in Russia*, vol. 2, p. 99.

81. Simanovich, Rasputin's not always reliable secretary, ascribed Ianushkevich's enmity to his once having been refused financing for an estate by a Jewish banker. Aran Simanovich, *Rasputin i evrei* (Moscow, 1991), p. 49.

82. Colonel Comte Paul Ignatieff, *Ma mission en France* (Paris, n.d.), p. 20.

83. Michael Cherniavsky, *Prologue to Revolution: Notes of A.N. Iakhontov on the Secret Meetings of the Council of Ministers, 1915* (Englewood Cliffs, N.J., 1967), p. 57.

178 erable influence. As early as August 13 (26), 1914, Russia's ambassador to the Court of St. James, Count Benckendorff, was writing the emperor that perhaps some small concessions to Russia's Jews might now be in order to make a favorable impression on foreign public opinion, an idea which at that time Nicholas II would not entertain.[84] Some months later, in April of 1915, Minister of Finance Bark suggested to Foreign Minister Sazonov that Russia might smooth the way for future banking transactions in London if it could foster a positive view of itself among the leaders of all the political forces in Great Britain. The problem, of course, was the Labour Party, which still espoused vaguely Russophobic views chiefly owing to "Jewish agitation." In Bark's opinion, the Russian government needed to invite a prominent Labour Member of Parliament from the House of Commons on a junket to Petrograd, where he could associate "with the English colony in Russia, which is extremely well disposed towards Russia and holds decidedly anti-Semitic views." If this experiment succeeded in building support for Russia within the British left, it might be followed by a visit from an entire delegation from the Labour Party.[85] Such ham-fisted efforts at public relations could not, however, efface the negative impression left by the Russian army's reprisals and atrocities against the Jews of Poland and Galicia. A British relief worker, John Pollock, who spent three months in Poland in the spring of 1915, informed Whitehall that the persecution of the Jews was being deliberately promoted for political purposes; there was no substance to the indiscriminate charges of treason levied against them:

> The politicians have undoubtedly taken advantage of the War to prejudice the Russians against the Jews by representing the latter generally as traitors to the Russian cause. In this they were well seconded by reactionary Russian elements, such as surrounded the late Minister of the Interior, who is credited with saying that he did not accuse all Jews of being traitors, but only all traitors of being Jews (forgetting, it would seem, Colonel Myasiedov [*sic*]). From inquiries made in Poland there seems slender foundation for the general accusation of treachery made against the Jews. Undoubtedly some cases have been proven, and a substantial part of local information obtained by the Germans may have been given by Jews, although there are pro-Germans and may have been spies among the Poles also. This however was to be expected. In the first place it is only the Jews in Polish villages who have local information; in the second the Germans would naturally go to the Jews not only because of their livelier intelligence but also because the Yiddish jargon spoken by the Jews is a debased German, and with the aid of threats or a little torture they would probably get what they wanted. On the whole, taking these special conditions into account, it appears improbable that there has been more or-

84. AVPRI, f. 134, op. 473, d. 25:12, l. 2.
85. AVPRI, f. 134, op. 473, d. 71:60, ll. 20–21.

ganized spying amongst the Polish Jews than there would be among any
frontier population; it is understood that there has been quite enough on the
Belgian and French frontier.[86]

Despite its own anti-Semitism and its reluctance to interfere in the domestic affairs of
an allied state, the British government nonetheless was motivated enough by reports
like the foregoing to remonstrate with Count Benckendorff about his government's
Jewish policy. Indeed, the abolition of the Pale of Settlement in Russia (August 1915)
was promoted by the Russian Ministry of the Interior in part to stifle criticism in the
foreign press about the empire's abuse of the Jews. The other reason, of course, was
that the enormous flood of refugees expelled from the front zones had filled what remained of the Pale to the bursting point. At the August 6, 1915, sitting of the Council
of Ministers, State Comptroller P. A. Kharitonov pointed out that "the existence of
an irresistible force is clear—the transport by military authorities of hundreds of
thousands of Jews into the interior of Russia . . . and for whom there is no room in
the Pale of Settlement."[87]

The empire's Jewish population mobilized itself to care for its own and combat
the rising tide of anti-Semitism with all the means in its power. The Jewish Association for the Relief of War Victims (EKOPO) was founded in Petrograd in the spring
of 1915 to do something to alleviate the suffering of the scores of thousands of Jewish
refugees.[88] A group of prominent Jewish leaders, including several deputies to the
Duma, established an information bureau to collect information about the treatment
of the Jews and to fight the lies spread against them with the truth. The Jewish press,
particularly the newspaper *Novyi Voskhod* (*New Dawn*), made efforts to publicize the
heroism of Jewish soldiers at the front as an antidote to the pernicious slander about
"Jewish treason"; *Novyi Voskhod* was closed down by the authorities for its pains. The
most interesting defense against attacks on the loyalty of the Jews mounted by their
supporters was the assertion that they were being scapegoated so as to conceal the
identities of the *ethnic Russians* who were the real German and Austrian spies. This
line of argument was common on the political left. In a report to the Central Committee of the Kadet Party, the renowned lawyer M. M. Vinaver actually blamed Miasoedov himself for the spread of anti-Semitism since the beginning of the war; noting
that the most serious accusations leveled against the Jews had originated in the armies
of the Northwest front, Vinaver insisted that the traitorous colonel and his henchmen
had disseminated malicious tales of Jewish treason in order to deflect suspicion from
themselves. The chief Kadet newspaper, *Rech'*, featured Vinaver's interpretation of

---

86. PRO.FO. Russian Correspondence, 371. Vol. 2445. No. 121172, pp. 305–306.
87. Cherniavsky, *Prologue to Revolution*, p. 69.
88. Peter Gatrell, *A Whole Empire Walking: Refugees in Russia During World War I* (Bloomington, Ind.,
1999), pp. 148–150.

180 the persecution of the Jews in an article of July 28, 1915: "A screen is thereby put up for the Miasoedovs and other of our traitors behind which they may take shelter."[89]

Germanophobia

Whereas the army appears to have been the chief sponsor of the campaign against the Jews, it was the civil administration under the pressure of the center and right-wing press that implemented the anti-German agenda. Some of the restrictions placed on Germans in the empire stemmed from at least partially comprehensible issues of security. Given its interpretation of the war—that the struggle was against the German people, not just the regime of Wilhelm II—the interior ministry issued a circular on August 11, 1914, to all the governors of Russia's provinces that declared that as of that date all male German or Austro-Hungarian subjects from the ages of eighteen to forty-five capable of bearing arms were to be considered prisoners of war. All persons who fell into this category were to be subject to immediate arrest and were to be transported at their own expense to places of exile in eastern Russia, Siberia, and Turkestan.[90] Great numbers of Austrian and Germans who were long resident in Russia immediately appealed for Russian citizenship to evade the application of this cruel act, with many directly petitioning the emperor.[91]

There was, of course, a popular dimension to anti-Germanism that was a feature of Russia's wartime life, just as it was in all the other allied countries. Germanophobia was exceptionally pronounced among the members of the empire's educated classes, who should have known better. When the Moscow Literary and Artistic Society met on October 10 and voted to expel all persons with German names, the accomplished historian S. P. Melgunov resigned in protest and got to read about his "treasonable" deed in that evening's right-wing newspapers.[92] The most innocent expression of fondness for German writing, music, or art was enough to elicit torrents of abuse and occasionally worse. In April of 1915 the famous opera singer Dal'geim included a couple of arias in German at a private recital. He was denounced by a concertgoer to the police for this, and the latter actually opened an official inquiry into the incident.[93]

Eventually public rancor against "Germans" came to focus on two topics: first, the enormous damage that highly placed Germans were allegedly doing to the war economy; and second, the need to reduce the Germans' capacity for mischief by stripping them of land and property. M. V. Rodzianko, president of the Duma,

89. Greenberg, *Jews in Russia*, vol. 2, pp. 96, 101.

90. RGVIA, f. 2003, op. 2, d. 1066, l. 34.

91. V.I. Mamantov, *Na gosudarstvennoi sluzhbe. Vospominaniia* (Tallin, 1926), p. 227. Mamantov, the head of the Imperial Chancellery for Petitions, observed that one reason why foreigners were often reluctant to seek Russian citizenship prior to 1914 was the requirement that they simultaneously enroll themselves as either peasants or *meshchane* (members of an urban class of petty tradesmen and artisans).

92. S. P.Melgunov, *Vospominaniia i dnevniki*, vol. 1 (Paris, 1964), p. 187.

93. Ibid., p. 193.

charged that there were still German subjects employed in responsible positions at state factories five months into the war and condemned a congeries of grand duchesses, court cliques, and bureaucrats for protecting them. In his memoirs he subsequently wrote that "treason was sensed in this, for there was no other way to explain the unbelievable events that were taking place in front of everybody's eyes."[94]

As for the confiscation of the assets and wealth of individual Germans, newspapers and political pamphleteers declared that this was essential if Russia was to "break the German yoke" that had long held it in thrall. It was the two papers owned by the Suvorin family—*Novoe vremia* and *Vechernee vremia*—that took the lead in demanding that the government act decisively to liberate the country from German economic influence. In an article of January 6, 1915, *Novoe vremia* published a list of "German" factories currently operating in Russia and implied that their directors were deliberately sabotaging goods produced for military purposes. Shark, Hervager, Dich, and Bonmüller—all of them German subjects—were the directors, part owners, and managers of the Vargunin Paper Factory, the United Cable Factory, the Russian Book Association, and the "Culture" Partnership. Dozens of other examples were adduced.[95] *Vechernee vremia* started to run a weekly column by the firebreathing nationalist Osendovskii that subjected the government to a barrage of criticism for dragging its feet in the struggle against "German exploitation."[96]

There were other, calmer voices. V. N. Shakovskoi, minister of trade and industry, warned that the blanket closure of "German" business would harm, not help, the war economy, a position echoed by the trade journal of the Permanent Council on Trade and Commerce.[97] Yet such responsible views could not prevail against the geyser of nationalist hysteria and superpatriotism then spewing up in Russia. On January 11, 1915, Nicholas II approved a law drafted by the Council of Ministers that forbade the issuance of annual business licenses to nationals of countries at war with the empire, or to any of the commercial firms with which they might be associated. It was the first in a whole series of legislative acts that over the ensuing two years would sequester many factories owned by enemy aliens, liquidate others completely, and deprive them of the right to hold stock even in Russian concerns.[98]

In February 1915 it was the turn of agriculture. Three laws promulgated on the February 2 began the process of confiscating not only the lands of "enemy nationals" but also those of so-called enemy settlers—that is, persons whose families had resided in Russia for decades and, in some cases, centuries. By the early summer of 1916 it was estimated that over 7.9 million acres owned by people in the latter category were targeted for expropriation.[99] By the end of the second month of 1917 at

---

94. M. V. Rodzianko, *Krushenie Imperii* (Valley College, N.Y., 1986), p. 120.
95. A. S. Rezanov, *Nemetskoe shpionstvo* (Petrograd, 1915), pp. 203–208.
96. Vsevolod Nikolaevich Shakhovskoi, *"Sic Transit Gloria Mundi" 1893–1917 gg.* (Paris, 1952), p. 172.
97. Ibid., pp. 171–175; Baron Boris E. Nolde, *Russia in the Economic War* (New Haven, 1928), pp. 77–78.
98. Nolde, *Russia in the Economic War,* pp. 81–100 passim.
99. Ibid., pp. 107–115.

182 least 16 million "German" acres had been declared subject to seizure (although only a small proportion had actually been taken before the coming of the February Revolution caused the program to be suspended.)[100]

In the spring of 1915 anti-German passions boiled over in Moscow.[101] A. P. Martynov, head of the local gendarme administration, alerted the city commandant that the explosive mixture of high inflation, overcrowding, and anti-German agitation by the yellow press could very well lead to massive unrest, only to have his prescient counsel dismissed.[102] On May 29 angry crowds took to the streets and began to wreak destruction on German stores, or at least stores with German-sounding names. Encouraged by the apparent indifference of the police, the rioters graduated from throwing stones through shop windows to pillage, arson, and physical assault. When the dust settled after the two days of this vicious anti-German pogrom, 475 stores, offices, and factories had been plundered, 207 apartments had been looted, and almost 700 people had been beaten, in some cases fatally. A factory owner named Schrader had, for example, been dragged from his office by a howling mob, stripped naked, and thrown into a ditch to drown.[103] Because a couple of defense factories had been attacked, there were those, such as the overly credulous British ambassador George Buchanon, who believed that the "Germans" had actually instigated the riots themselves in order to cripple munitions production.[104] More insightful observers thought that something quite different had happened: noting the sluggish reaction of the police to the outbursts of violence, they suspected that local authorities had initially decided to wink at the pogrom in order to build up public morale and were caught off guard when it rapidly accelerated out of control.[105] Both the city commandant and the governor-general of the Moscow region were removed from office owing to this outrage.

The mise en scène for Russia's espionage cases of 1915 and 1916, then, was provided by the upsurge of jingoism, anti-Semitism, and Germanophobia in the country as well as the efforts of Stavka, the government, and elements in the press to encourage and exploit all three. Of course the goals each pursued were different. Stavka wished to insulate itself from criticism and provide the Russian public with an alternative explanation for military defeat. By cracking down on "Germans," the government sought to validate its commitment to the national cause in a vain bid for greater popularity. And in stoking the fire of xenophobia, the yellow press wanted both to sell newspapers and to score points against the government. Yet it is obvious that these crude attempts to play at mass politics came freighted with danger. The army's savage

100. Lohr, *Nationalizing the Russian Empire*, p. 108.
101. Lohr, ibid., provides an excellent and persuasive analysis of this entire episode. See pp. 31–54.
102. A. P. Martynov, *Moia sluzhba v otdel'nom korpuse zhandarmov. Vospominaniia*, ed. Richard Wraga (Palo Alto, Calif., 1972), pp. 267–271.
103. Nolde, *Russia in the Economic War*, p. 82; Melgunov, *Vospominaniia*, p. 195.
104. Buchanan to Grey, June 12 and June 14, 1915, PRO. FO. 371. Vol. 2452, pp. 345, 349.
105. Melgunov, *Vospominaniia*, pp. 194–195.

policy of hostage taking, execution, and deportation plunged the rear-echelon areas into chaos, helped wreck the country's transportation system, and furnished hundreds of thousands with more than sufficient reason to hate the empire and the system that oppressed them. The government's policies of sequestration and expropriation delivered a series of body blows to the wartime economy even as they failed to appease rabid nationalists, who regarded them as too little too late. And in lambasting the government for its timidity in dealing with the internal foe, the nationalist press accelerated the process of imperial decomposition that was already well under way prior to the 1917 revolutions, for the implicit logic of the right-wing position was that the state should defend national interests above all other considerations, including dynastic ones. All of these things—the severity against the Jews, the confiscation of "foreign" property, the tub-thumping in the press—tended to reinforce the perception that treason was stalking the land. Of course, politics informed the view one took of exactly what that treason was. If Jews, Germans, and Austrians were all traitors, then they clearly deserved harsh punishment. If the government had been slow to take the necessary punitive measures, or had obstructed the army's effort to clear the front zones of undesirables, perhaps it was harboring traitors itself. But what if the Jews and the "foreigners" were largely innocent? If they were, what was being done to them was not only monstrous but potentially subversive, for the architects of persecution within both army and government might well be using these groups as scapegoats to conceal their own treason. The paranoid environment in which political forces on the left, center, and right were accusing high figures in the state as well as one another of treasonable activities did not augur well for the stability of the regime or the success of its war effort.

Moreover, even if there was disagreement about the identities of Russia's real internal enemies, virtually everybody, regardless of politics, concurred that Miasoedov had truly been a German spy. Because by this stage mere propinquity was taken as tantamount to proof of guilt, the next stage of the tragedy could not be averted. Who had originally appointed Miasoedov to the war ministry? Whose testimonial had propelled him into a job with army intelligence at the front? In late April 1915 the Petrograd police forwarded to the staff of the Northwest front an anonymous letter denouncing Russia's minister of war. The author of this note, who had to have been either Andronnikov or Chervinskaia, asserted that "General Sukhomlinov is selling Russia out wholesale and retail" and demanded that both he and his wife be investigated for their connections to Colonel Miasoedov, the most infamous traitor in the country's history.[106]

---

106. RGVIA, f. 962, op. 2, d. 164, ll. 5–6.

7

The Great Retreat

In the spring and summer of 1915 Russian arms suffered a defeat so enormous that it dwarfed every previous catastrophe that had afflicted Russia in the war. It is a matter of some irony that the seedbed of this disaster was actually Russian military success. In March 1915 Austria's important Galician fortress of Przemysl, which had been under Russian siege for the previous six months, finally ran up the white flag; almost 120,000 Austro-Hungarian troops marched from the city into Russian captivity. The shock of this event could not but focus Germany's attention on the debility of her Hapsburg ally. Capitalizing on the momentum generated by the fall of Przemysl, the Russians appeared to be on the verge of erupting into Hungary while the Austrians seemed incapable of stopping their advance. Still worse, it was increasingly probable that Italy, which had sat out the early phase of the war, would soon join the Entente powers and open up a new front against Austria in the Trentino.

The Austrian High Command consequently made frantic appeals to Berlin for help: Austria's chief of staff, Conrad von Hötzendorff, insisted that without immediate German support the collapse of the Dual Monarchy was only a matter of time. It was on the basis of this argument that Conrad's German opposite number, Erich von Falkenhayn, reluctantly decided to reinforce the Eastern front. Reorganizing his forces in France and Belgium, Falkenhayn detached eight divisions for operations against Russia. Supplemented by three Austrian divisions, the German forces transferred from the Western front comprised a new German army, the Eleventh, which secretly concentrated near Krakow. The new formation was placed under the command of the talented General August von Mackensen, who was ordered to attack and annihilate the Russian Third Army along a thirty-five-kilometer length of front that extended from Gorlice to Tarnow.

Mackensen launched his assault on the morning of April 19 (2 May), 1915. At that point his local numerical superiority to his adversary was more than two to one. But still more significant was his advantage in artillery, for he had 144 pieces of medium or heavy ordnance to Russia's 4. Unleashing a devastating preliminary bombardment in which 700 guns dropped over half a million shells onto Russian positions, Mackensen in five hours utterly demolished the enemy network of shallow, waterlogged trenches that lay athwart the axis of his advance, killing over a third of their occupants in the process. The Russians were caught almost completely by surprise; within four days the embattled Third Army had ceased to exist as a recognizable military force. Unable to plug the gap with reinforcements because of a lack of reserves, the Russian army was impelled into headlong retreat. By the end of the summer the Gorlice-Tarnow breakthrough had produced a general German and Austrian advance along the entire extent of the Eastern front. By late May Przemysl was again in the hands of the Central Powers. By the end of June Austria and Germany had reconquered Galicia. By July Kurland, Lithuania, and Russian Poland were in danger. On July 14 General Danilov, quartermaster general of Russia's field armies, was telegraphing Petrograd to advise that public opinion had to be prepared for still further losses of territory: Russia would have to shorten her front "so as to place our glorious armies in a more advantageous position for defense."[1] In August the Russians evacuated Warsaw, Kovno, and Brest-Litovsk one after the other. At that stage Russia disposed of 1,800 battalions of troops to her enemies' 1,550, but many of Russia's "battalions" were merely notional, since they could muster no more than two to three hundred men, that is, 20–30 percent of the strength mandated by statute.[2]

By the end of September the impetus of the advance of the Central Powers had spent itself. One reason for this was a breakdown in their military logistics, which were placed under greater and greater strain the farther the troops marched away from the depots and railheads. The heavy rain that fell in September and October compounded the problem, for it transformed the roads into oceans of impassable mud. But the Russian High Command also deserves some credit: the cavalry army it hastily improvised that fall managed to thwart German efforts to achieve and exploit yet another breakthrough, this time in the northern theater of operations.[3] By the time it stabilized, the new frontline in the east ran from the outskirts of Riga along the Dvina to Dvinsk, then south to Baranovichi, Dubno, and Czernovitz. All of Russian Poland, as well as Kurland and large portions of Lithuania and Belorussia, were under enemy occupation—territories that amounted to a full quarter of the Russian Empire in Europe. As if this were not bad enough, the campaigns of the spring and summer resulted in a shocking casualty toll. From May to September 1915 Russia's armies were losing on average three hundred thousand men per month to combat deaths or wounds as well as an additional two hundred thousand to surrender or capture.[4] Still

---

1. AVPRI, f. 133, op. 470, d. 165 (1915 g.), l. 55.
2. Iu. N. Danilov, *Rossiia v mirovoi voine 1914–1915 gg.* (Berlin, 1924), p. 382.
3. I. I. Rostunov, *Russkii front pervoi mirovoi voiny* (Moscow, 1976), pp. 272–273.
4. P. P. Petrov, *Rokovye gody 1914–1920* (California [sic], 1965), p. 31.

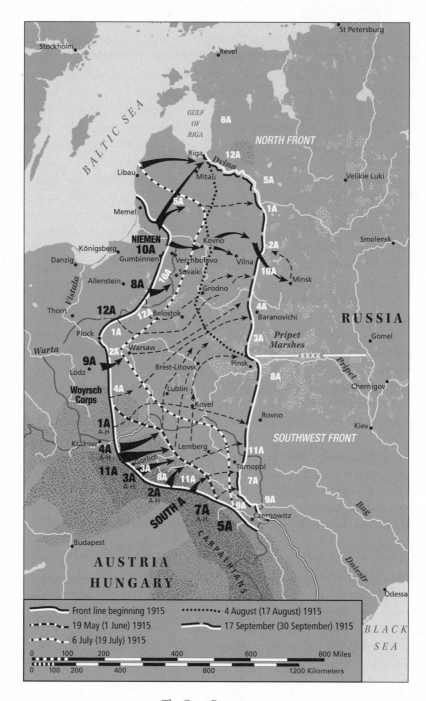

The Great Retreat, 1915

further, the Russian military's "Great Retreat" created a flood of civilian refugees in its wake, amounting to at least three million people, according to the most conservative estimate.

Russia's defeats in 1915 stemmed from several causes. Superior German generalship was certainly one, as was the mediocrity of the Russian generals who were fated to bear the responsibility for the defense of the most critical sectors. The uninspiring and inflexible General N. I. Ivanov, whose acquaintance we have already made, was then in charge of the Southwestern front. General Aleksei Brusilov, a truly brilliant commander who served under Ivanov at the time, later pointedly observed that the latter was a near defeatist without the foggiest conception of strategy.[5] General Anton Denikin, subsequently a noted White leader, who was also subordinate to Ivanov that spring, had nothing but contempt for his chief's "defective military qualifications."[6] As for R. D. Radko-Dmitriev, a Bulgarian in Russia's service who had given a good account of himself during the battle of the San in 1914, he proved to be fatally indecisive in the teeth of the German onslaught against his III Caucasus Corps. "We do not fear the Germans but rather our own generals," complained one disgruntled junior officer in April 1915.[7]

Then there was Russia's decentralized military command structure. This also deserves a share of the blame since it tolerated the procrastination of quasi-autonomous front commanders in coming to the assistance of their colleagues with reinforcements. The relative weakness of Russia's transportation infrastructure—of its network of railways and roads—also played its part in the debacle, because it hampered the redeployment of troops in response to enemy attacks, thus often placing a Russian commander in the unenviable position of accepting the risk of being outflanked or ordering yet another retreat. However, while the impact of all of the foregoing on the outcome of the battles in Galicia and Poland ought not to be minimized, the single most significant contribution to Russian defeat was made by an acute shortage of munitions.

There were several facets to this problem. First, there was the dearth of rifles for the infantry. As noted in chapter 5, Russia simply had too few rifles to arm all the men it called to the colors in the first months of the war. The Russian High Command was sensitive to the scarcity of rifles from the very beginning. As early as August 26, 1914, Stavka was ordering the collection of the rifles of the dead and wounded. Two months later the commander of the northwest front[8] began to pay bounties to civilians who brought in even Austrian or German rifles discarded on the battlefield.[9]

---

5. Brusilov wrote of Ivanov that "as for winning the war or even checking the enemy advance he did not think it could be done." General A. A. Brussilov, *A Soldier's Notebook 1914–1918* (London, 1930), p. 193.

6. Anton I. Denikin, *The Career of a Tsarist Officer,* trans. Margaret Patoski (Minneapolis, 1975), p. 266.

7. Letter of A. E. Orlov, April 22, 1915, GARF, f. 102, op. 265, d. 1042, l. 130.

8. Russia divided its forces into groups of armies known as fronts. There were initially two of these, the Northwest and the Southwest. In 1915 the West front was added, and in 1916 the Rumanian front.

9. Mikhail Lemke, *250 dnei v tsarskoi stavke (25 sent. 1915–2 iuliia 1916)* (Petersburg, 1920), p. 97.

188 Frantic attempts were made to replenish Russia's arsenals through foreign purchases, but contracting procedures were slow and deliveries both tardy and sporadic. In May 1915, 150,000 men of the Southwest front still had no rifles, and 286,000 soldiers of the West front were without them in January 1916.[10] In fact, taken together, Russia's armies in Europe were by then short by some 666,000 rifles—a full third of the number they needed.[11] As a result, wrote one high war ministry official, "our army is drowning in its own blood."[12]

Second, and even more dire, was the crisis in ordnance and shells. When the German attack occurred in the spring of 1915, Russia's reserve of artillery ammunition was so depleted that, as one officer recalled, shells were doled out "as in a pharmacy, by the teaspoon."[13] That this was not a mere exaggeration is proved by Stavka's desperate attempts to conserve ammunition during the ensuing campaign, which included an order subjecting battery commanders who shot off more than five shells per artillery tube per day to court-martial.[14] Moreover, the bulk of such artillery ammunition as Russia *did* have consisted of light, antipersonnel rounds; by contrast, the Germans seemed abundantly supplied with shells of all calibers. The psychological impact on Russian troops of cowering helplessly under the pulverizing bombardment of German high explosives while their own artillery was powerless to respond cannot be overestimated. Dispatch after dispatch from the front emphasized that the enemy's superiority in heavy artillery was responsible for the collapse of the Russian line that spring. As the commander of the Eighth Army reported, "The enemy is not frightening face to face but whole units are deranged almost to a man by his numerous heavy guns."[15] Given the terrible imbalance in ordnance, the Russian High Command tried to expend men to compensate for its lack of steel. In the absence of heavy artillery, noted one general in his diary, "we are fighting with human bodies."[16] Of course, a contest between steel and flesh was really no contest at all. Britain's military attaché explained to London on May 13 (26) that the Russian army had no choice but to retreat under the unendurable pressure of German artillery fire.[17]

What accounted for Russia's inferiority in artillery? One reason, of course, was that no one had conceived of the rate at which shells would be consumed in the inferno of World War I combat, a failure of imagination of which every army in Europe, not merely the Russian, was guilty. But the relative weakness of the industrial

10. "Perepiska V. A. Sukhomlinova s N. N.Ianushkevichem," *Krasnyi arkhiv* 3 (1923): 70; Lemke, *250 dnei*, p. 459.

11. Stavka report, RGVIA, f. 2003, op. 1, d. 1165, l. 105.

12. General M. A. Beliaev, quoted in W. Bruce Lincoln, *Passage Through Armageddon: The Russians in War and Revolution 1914–1918* (New York, 1986), p. 145.

13. Erast Giatsintov, *Zapiski belogo ofitsera* (St. Petersburg, 1992), p. 54.

14. A. Bubnov, *V tsarskoi stavke* (New York, 1955), p. 100.

15. RGVIA, f. 2003, op. 1., d. 120, l. 71.

16. F. F. Palitsyn, "V shtabe severno-zapadnogo fronta (s kontsa apreliia 1915 goda po 30 avgusta togo zhe goda)," in *Voennyi sbornik obshchestva revnitelei voennykh znanii*, vol. 3, p. 164 (Belgrade, 1922).

17. PRO.FO.371.2450, p. 213.

sector hobbled Russia's ability to respond effectively to the crisis through a crash program of munitions production. The issue was not so much one of shell casings, which Russia's factories were able to turn out in quantity. The weak links in the chain were rather fuses, chemicals, and the artillery tubes themselves, for these were commodities that Russian industry could not manufacture fast enough to satisfy the army's needs.[18] On the eve of the war, for example, there were only 126 factories in the entire empire that made machines or machine tools, which meant that even then a full 53 percent of Russia's domestic demand for these articles had to be made up with foreign purchases. Indeed, the plurality of metalworking lathes then in use in Russia had been imported from Germany, while only a third had been produced at home.[19] There were bottlenecks in the chemical industry, just as in the machine tool sector. Because Russia had an insufficient supply of the raw materials to make sulfuric acid, a key ingredient in high explosives, the production target for the latter—5.9 million pounds a month—could never be achieved in 1915.[20] Despite all the success Russia eventually enjoyed in increasing the output of military matériel during the war (a subject that will be discussed later), these structural problems meant that until the very end the imperial army was always deficient in large-caliber artillery, machine guns, high explosives, poison gases, air-burst fuses, and rifles.[21]

The Mood in the Country

It is scarcely surprising that the munitions crisis and the concomitant Great Retreat fanned the flames of what one scholar has described as the "war psychosis" that swept through Russia in 1915.[22] It became an article of faith for hundreds of thousands of people that the true explanation for the disasters had to be treason. To be sure, there were a couple of episodes that lent a thin veneer of credibility to this belief. General V. N. Grigor'ev, the commandant of the fortress of Kovno, had cravenly abandoned his position without putting up a fight, an act that many ascribed to treason rather than cowardice. When the Germans seized Kovno, twenty thousand prisoners as well as 1,300 guns fell into their hands.[23] Yet in the most important respects

18. Stavka to military attaché, Paris, December 26, 1914, AVPRI, f. 133, op. 470, d. 379 (1914), l. 53.

19. *Doklad soveta s"ezdov o merakh k razvitiiu proizvoditel'nikh sil Rossii* (Petrograd, 1915), pp. 172, 175–176.

20. L. G. Beskrovnyi et al., eds., *Zhurnaly osovogo soveshchaniia po oborone gosudarstva 1915 god* (Moscow, 1975), p. 164.

21. [A. S. Lukomskii], *Vospominaniia Generala A. S. Lukomskago*, vol. 1 (Berlin, 1922), p. 68. In May 1917, the Russian High Command was still appealing in vain to its French allies for deliveries of heavy artillery; Denikin stated that "we are so weak in heavy artillery that any pieces with calibers larger than 6" would be highly desirable for us." RGVIA, f. 2003, op. 1, d. 1767, l. 73.

22. Michael Smilg-Benario, *Der Zusammenbruch der Zarenmonarchie* (Zurich, 1928), p. 29.

23. The German secret service had actually approached Grigor'ev, and had promised him a fee of one million marks as well as political asylum in Germany in exchange for handing Kovno over to them. Grigor'ev apparently accepted this proposition but then had second thoughts and changed his mind. No money was ever paid to him. When he bolted from Kovno on August 15, 1915, he did so apparently in the fear that it was on the verge of being cut off by German troops. See Heinz Höhne, *Der Krieg im Dunkeln. Macht und Einfluss des deutschen und russischen Geheimdienstes* (Munich, 1985), pp. 187–188. See also V. V.

190 the government's handling of the Miasoedov case had been the essential foundation for the association of defeat and treachery in the popular mind. By scapegoating Miasoedov for the destruction of the XX Corps of the Tenth Army, the authorities had conditioned the empire's subjects to presume that one or more Judases were skulking behind each of Russia's military defeats. Given the fact that Miasoedov himself was dead and buried, it followed that there had to be other, as yet undiscovered, traitors, perhaps in the highest echelons of the army command. "Our cause in the war is completely lost," wrote a soldier of the Nikol'skii Infantry Regiment in despair that summer, adding "and what's more, it has been completely sold out."[24] Such attitudes spawned a variety of curious urban legends, of which the most bizarre was that of the "traitor generals." According to this widespread rumor of late 1915, a large band of generals whose treason had come to light were being paraded through the streets of Russian cities in chains, with a salver carried before them on which was heaped "the money with which they had been bought."[25] Of course, the frontline traitors, bad as they were, were obviously not the authors of the munitions crisis. This had to be the work of people in the rear, who had either incompetently bungled Russia's preparations for war or had intentionally sabotaged them. Since the war ministry bore the ultimate responsibility for the empire's military readiness, it became a natural target of popular suspicion. Suppose the highest officials of the ministry, or even War Minister Sukhomlinov himself, had conspired to weaken the Russian army, particularly its artillery arm. If so, would that not completely explain Russia's recent humiliations on the battlefield? As a letter from the Twenty-sixth Foot Artillery Brigade put it in July 1915: "That son of a bitch Sukhomlinov should have been quartered long ago in Moscow at the Lobnoe mesto."[26]

The Tribulations of Sukhomlinov

The military crisis at the front thus produced a political crisis at home. It was obvious that the empire's munitions production had to be reorganized and that steps had to be taken to muffle public outrage at the abysmal conduct of the war. Nicholas II attempted to achieve these objectives by approving the creation of an unprecedented special commission on artillery supply, which included industrialists and Duma politicians as well as bureaucrats among its members. By August this was su-

---

Karrik, "Voina i revoliutsiia," *Golos minuvshago*, nos. 1–3 (1918): 20, 24; Lemke, *250 dnei*, pp. 252–255. In September 1915 Grigor'ev was convicted of negligence in the defense of Kovno and was sentenced to fifteen years at hard labor. However, it must be noted that Kovno was so weakly fortified that its capture by the Germans was virtually preordained. It was because of this that even prior to the war Nikolai Nikolaevich had crudely joked that Kovno ought to be renamed Govno (shit). Major General Sir Alfred Knox, *With the Russian Army 1914–1917: Being Chiefly Extracts from the Diary of a Military Attaché*, vol. 1 (London, 1921), p. 326.

24. "Soldatskie pis'ma v gody mirovoi voiny (1915–1917 gg.)," *Krasnyi arkhiv* 4–5 (65–66) (1934): 128.

25. Karrik, "Voina i revoliutsiia," p. 37.

26. "Soldatskie pis'ma," p. 128. The Lobnoe mesto, which stands before St. Basil's Cathedral in Red Square, was the traditional place of execution in Muscovite Russia.

perseded by a system of four special conferences (*Osobye soveshchaniia*) devoted to transportation, food, fuel, and general questions of defense. These new organs had the same mixed composition as the artillery commission that had preceded them: private citizens and Duma deputies were to work side by side with ministerial officials in solving the most pressing of the country's problems. Other manifestations of the regime's opening to "society" were the formation under Aleksandr Guchkov of the war industry committees—labor/management boards designed to coordinate and increase the output of smaller factories for the war effort—and the authorization of a national union of rural and urban councils, known as the *Zemgor,* which was devoted to furnishing the troops with extra stocks of medicine, food, boots, field telephones, clothing, and the like. To further bolster public confidence in the government, Nicholas II reshuffled his cabinet and fired several of his least popular ministers. V. A. Sukhomlinov was among the first to go.

Sukhomlinov had of course known for some time that he was in trouble, for the political environment sculpted by the war did not bode well for his continuation in office. In the first place, at the very beginning of the war supreme command had gone to the Grand Duke Nikolai Nikolaevich, who, as we have seen, passionately hated Sukhomlinov. When Duma President Mikhail Rodzianko visited Stavka in November 1914, the grand duke had already begun to denounce the war minister as the chief culprit behind the army's supply shortages.[27]

Second, there was the Miasoedov case, which gave Sukhomlinov ample grounds to dread that his former close association with the hanged gendarme would soon receive loud and dangerous publicity. To be sure, he had broken off relations with Sergei Nikolaevich prior to the outbreak of the war, but sooner or later someone was going to recollect that it was he who had ordered the investigations that had officially cleared Miasoedov of allegations of espionage back in 1912. Attention would then inevitably focus on the entire history of his contacts with Miasoedov, and the minister feared that his enemies Polivanov, Guchkov, and Andronnikov ("the most evil weed in our Petrograd swamp") were intriguing to exploit that history to further damage his crumbling reputation and deprive him of his portfolio.[28]

Finally, Sukhomlinov had to worry about his colleagues. By early 1915 the majority of the other ministers had concluded that Sukhomlinov had become a major liability. The war effort demanded that the government win the trust and cooperation of responsible Duma politicians, an undertaking to which Sukhomlinov, in view of his notorious disdain for the parliament, was a clear impediment. Then, too, Vladimir Aleksandrovich's administrative inefficiency, an annoyance in times of peace, was utterly intolerable in times of war. Given the fact that the Russian people were already inclined to blame the war ministry for the army's munitions crisis, his removal might provide a welcome boost to the government's public standing.

27. M. V. Rodzianko, "Krushenie Imperii," in *Arkhiv russkoi revoliutsii,* vol. 17, p. 86 (Berlin, 1926) (repr., The Hague, 1970).
28. "Perepiska V. A. Sukhomlinova s N. N. Ianushkevichem," *Krasnyi arkhiv* 3 (1923): 45–46, 48.

For these reasons, in the third week of May 1915 Minister of Agriculture A.V. Krivoshein, then the dominant personality in the cabinet, convened a secret meeting with five of his colleagues to discuss how to convince the tsar to discharge Sukhomlinov, as well as Interior Minister Makarov, Justice Minister Shcheglovitov, and Holy Synod Procurator Sabler, who were all widely despised for their reactionary views and in Sabler's case for toleration of Rasputin to boot.[29] By threatening to resign en masse, Krivoshein and his group managed to force Nicholas II to fire Makarov on June 3 (16). Getting the emperor to part with Sukhomlinov was going to be far more difficult, however. For one thing, Sukhomlinov remained the tsar's favorite among his ministers. For another, Nicholas was convinced that all the talk against the minister of war was baseless calumny, in large measure because Sukhomlinov had assured him that this was so. Unrivaled master of autocratic politics that he was, in April Sukhomlinov had taken the precaution of delivering a personal brief to his sovereign on the Miasoedov affair, a report that unsurprisingly vindicated the war minister of any wrongdoing and explained that although it was true that Miasoeodov had been involved in counterintelligence when he had been attached to the war ministry, this assignment had been made at the insistence of Stolypin (!). Nicholas, who was completely taken in by these lies, subsequently told one of his relatives that Sukhomlinov ("an unquestionably honest and decent person") had been targeted for destruction by a sinister cabal "which wants to implicate him in the Miasoedov case but will not succeed."[30]

Under these circumstances, Krivoshein resolved to enlist the help of Grand Duke Nikolai Nikolaevich. Knowing that the emperor had scheduled a visit to Stavka on June 10 (23), Krivoshein contrived to arrive there one day earlier for a private consultation with Russia's commander–in chief on the fate of the war minister. Although it is not known what was said at the meeting between Nicholas and Nikolai the following day, on June 11 (24) Sukhomlinov received a copy of an imperial rescript "retiring" him from office and appointing him to the Council of State:

> Vladimir Aleksandrovich, after long reflection I have come to the conclusion that the interests of Russia and the army require your departure now. Having just spoken with Grand Duke Nikolai Nikolaevich, I have become firmly convinced of this. I am writing you so that you will first learn of this from me. . . . We have worked together for several years and never had any misunderstandings. I give you my heartfelt thanks for your work and for your efforts on behalf of the army of the fatherland. Impartial history will render a verdict more generous to you than the judgment of contemporaries. . . . God be with you. With the deepest respect
>
> Nicholas[31]

29. Vsevolod Nikoaevich Shakhovskoi, "*Sic transit gloria mundi*" *1893–1917 gg.* (Paris, 1952) p. 92.

30. V. P. Semenikova, ed., *Dnevnik b. Velikago Kniazia Andreia Vladimirovicha. 1915 god.* (Leningrad/Moscow, 1925), pp. 31–32.

31. V. A. Apushkin, *General ot porazhenii V.A. Sukhomlinov* (Leningrad, 1925), p. 104.

The gracious cordiality of this missive as well as its expressions of regret were no compensation to Sukhomlinov for the humiliation of his preemptory dismissal; when he learned that A. A. Polivanov had been named to succeed him at the insistence of Nikolai Nikolaevich, he grew even more indignant.[32]

If the tsar was ambivalent about firing Sukhomlinov, he had serious reservations about the Polivanov appointment. Polivanov's friendship with the detested Guchkov, which Nicholas had not forgotten, compromised the new minister in his master's eyes. The empress was even more prejudiced against him, if that were possible. While she recognized that Sukhomlinov had to go because of the "colossal" rage of the army against him, she wrote her husband on June 12 in her characteristically erratic English: "Forgive me, but I don't like the choice of the Minister of War. You remember how you were against him and rightly. . . . I dread N[ikolai Nikolaevich]'s nominations. N[ikolai Nikolaevich] is far from clever, obstinate and led by others. Can the man [Polivanov] have changed so much? Has he dropped Guchkov? Is he not our friend's [Rasputin's] enemy?"[33] Regardless of Alexandra's misgivings, the momentum in favor of concessions to public opinion was at this point too strong for Nicholas to resist. Every day brought news of fresh disasters at the front; the country appeared to be headed for a total military collapse.

It was soon the turn of Shcheglovitov and Sabler to fall from power. Krivoshein, who by then had openly emerged as a convert to the cause of cooperation between government and society, also induced the emperor to issue a degree calling the Duma (prorogued since January) back into session that July. Despite these concessions (or perhaps because of them) when the Duma convened on the nineteenth, the majority of its deputies were in no mood to support the existing government; speaker after speaker rose to demand the resignation of the ministers and their replacement by a "government of public confidence."[34] In a secret session on July 23 the Duma voted 245 to 30 in favor of criminal proceedings against Sukhomlinov and all the others who were responsible for the shell crisis.[35] The speeches delivered from the rostrum on this occasion were inflammatory in the extreme. Thundered deputy I. F. Polovtsov:

> Where is the criminal who deceived everyone with his lies about our readiness for the terrible struggle . . . ? Who wallowed in the filth of corruption and treason? Who stood between the traitor Miasoedov and the punitive sword of the law? Indeed it is he, the minister [i.e., Sukhomlinov] who pledged his head on behalf of Miasoedov. Miasoedov has been executed, but where is the head of his protector? Still resting on his star-studded shoulders.[36]

32. K. A. Krivoshein, *A. V. Krivoshein (1857–1921 g.) Ego znachenie v istorii Rossii nachala XX veka* (Paris, 1973), pp. 231–232; V. A. Sukhomlinov, *Vospominaniia Sukhomlinova* (Moscow/Leningrad, 1926), p. 260.

33. *The Letters of the Tsaritsa to the Tsar 1914–16* (London, 1923), p. 91.

34. Paul Miliukov, *Political Memoirs 1905–1917*, ed. Arthur P. Mendel, trans. Carl Goldberg (Ann Arbor, 1967), p. 328.

35. V. V. Shulgin, *Gody-Dni-1920* (Moscow, 1990), p. 283.

36. M. V. Rodzianko, *Krushenie imperii. Gosudarstvennaia duma i fevral'skaia 1917 goda revoliutsiia* (Valley College, N.Y., 1986), p. 157.

194   On July 24 the Council of Ministers agreed to respond to this vote by ordering a comprehensive inquest into the army's logistical problems. Krivoshein made a forceful case for indulging the Duma on this issue:

> We must respond to the Duma's formula. It reflects the feelings which are permeating broad circles of society. We will show that the government is not afraid of the light and that we are ready to consider the legitimate and reasonable demands of the Duma. Such a course of action is the best, also because it will force the Duma to take account of our legitimate and reasonable demands. Dissatisfaction with the former Minister of War is not revolution. . . . It is advantageous for the government to shed light on this whole affair which has undoubtedly been exaggerated. The insufficiency of supplies is, in large measure, the consequence not only of our, but everybody's, mistaken notion that the war could not last long. For this notion our Allies are also paying. In any event, it is too early to assign guilt.[37]

An imperial decree of July 25 (August 7) proclaimed the creation of an ad hoc bureau of inquiry, which was given the grandiloquent title "Special Supreme Commission for the Thorough Investigation of the Reasons for the Slow and Inadequate Replenishment of the Army's Stocks of Military Supplies."[38] N. P. Petrov, an eighty-year-old general of engineers, was tapped to head up the new commission. Three of Petrov's colleagues from the Council of State—I. I. Golubev, A. I. Panteleev, and A. N. Naumov—were named as commissioners, as were Senator Posnikov and Duma deputies V. A. Bobrinskii and S. Varun-Sekret.[39]

The Petrov Commission (as I shall henceforth style it) apparently did accomplish one of Krivoshein's objects, for it did materially appease public opinion that July and August.[40] But Krivoshein had been naive when he assumed that the commission would produce a dispassionate analysis disproving the rumor that the munitions crisis was the deliberate creation of miscreants in the war department. From the very beginning several of its members made no bones about the fact that they wanted Sukhomlinov's head. General Petrov, a somewhat drab but scrupled bureaucrat, initially resisted investigating any specific individual prior to the accumulation of evidence to warrant it, but he backed down when Bobrinskii screamed at him that "if we do not at once undertake to expose all Miasoedovism and Sukhomlinovism I will immediately resign from this commission and will inform the entire country about the reason for my departure!"[41] Sergei Varun-Sekret, a right Octobrist, vice president of the Duma, and friend of Guchkov, supported Bobrinskii unreservedly. Sukhomli-

---

37. Michael Cherniavsky, *Prologue to Revolution: Notes of A. N. Iakhontov on the Secret Meetings of the Council of Ministers, 1915* (Prentice Hall, N.J., 1967), p. 30.

38. RGVIA, f. 2003, op. 2, d. 1081, l. 1.

39. A. N. Naumov, *Iz utselevshikh vospominanii 1868–1917* (New York, 1955), p. 310.

40. Ibid., p. 335.

41. Ibid., p. 315.

nov had spurned society in his official career, and now society was going to have its revenge.

Other Cases

It did not augur well for the fallen minister that shortly after his loss of office several of his friends and acquaintances were taken into custody. Although he was a Russian subject, Oskar Altschüller, Alexander's son, had been picked up as a "suspicious person" at the very beginning of the war. Sukhomlinov had at once interceded with the Ministry of the Interior to secure Oskar's release. But as soon as the authorities in Kiev learned that Sukhomlinov was out of power, they rearrested and jailed the younger Altschüller.[42] On the evening of July 18, the police arrested Anna Goshkevich in her room at the Hotel Astoria in Petrograd. Her ex-husband, Nikolai Goshkevich, soon followed her to prison, as did his old contact at the artillery department Colonel V. G. Ivanov; Ivanov's wife; Anna's former lover, Maksim Veller; and Sukhomlinov's nominal biographer, V. D. Dumbadze.

Altschüller owed his incarceration to the fact that his father was Austrian and had moved back to Austria on the eve of the war. Anna Goskevich was taken in because it had come out that she had at one point shared a compartment with Miasoedov on a train trip from Warsaw to Petrograd; Nikolai Goskevich, because a copy of the secret "List of the Most Important Measures Carried Out by the War Ministry from 1909 to March 1914" had been found in a search of his apartment; and Ivanov, because of his association with Goshkevich. Dumbadze had, of course, used the "List" (or rather his ghostwriters had) in the preparation of his manuscript on the life of the war minister, while Veller was linked to the Ivanovs and Goshkeviches, as well as to Dumbadze.[43] For good measure, Dumbadze and Veller had also been the targets of an anonymous denunciation authored by Prince Andronnikov, which had named them as participants in the Miasoedov spy ring.[44]

The cases of the Goshkeviches, Ivanovs, Veller, and Dumbadze were consigned to the military judicial apparatus of the Southwestern front. All of them were accused of having spied for Germany and Austria-Hungary since 1909. On February 21, 1916, a field court-martial in Berdichev announced its findings: while the two female defendants, Anna Goshkevich and Nina Ivanova, were declared innocent, all four men were convicted on every charge. Ivanov, Veller, and Dumbadze were sentenced to death by hanging and Goshkevich to four years at hard labor.[45] These were exactly the penalties that the prosecution had demanded.

But the court attached a peculiar addendum to its decision that bespoke an extreme discomfort with the flimsy evidence that had been introduced during the trial, for it requested the commutation of all four sentences in view of "mitigating circum-

---

42. RGVIA, f. 962, op. 2, d. 48, l. 136.
43. Ibid., ll. 143–146.
44. Aron Simanovich, *Rasputin i evrei* (Moscow, 1991), p. 76.
45. Commander of Southwest front to Stavka, February 1916, RGVIA, f. 962, op. 2, d. 167, l. 104.

196 stances." The court declared that Veller, Dumbadze, and Ivanov had rendered valuable services to the Russian state and the army since the outbreak of the war, and that Goshkevich had committed his crimes under the influence of others, owing to the essential weakness of his character. The commander of the Southwestern front, whose duty it was to review military court sentences, noticed the obvious contradiction here: how could the court convict the accused of wartime espionage, one of the gravest offenses on the books, and yet simultaneously applaud the zeal and skill with which at least three of the very same accused had contributed to the Russian war effort? The only possible explanation was that the members of the court were not "firmly convinced" of the guilt of the defendants, which suggested that they had not thoroughly mastered the details of the case. (Presumably if they had they would have been surer of themselves.) As a result, the Southwestern front rejected the field court's appeal for reduced punishment and let the original sentences stand.[46]

The relatives of the convicted "spies" now mobilized themselves to beg clemency for their kin. Nikolai Goshkevich's father, a provincial doctor, asked the authorities in Berdichev to spare his son the rigors of *katorga* in recognition of his own forty years of spotless service, which included stints in the army medical corps in both the Russo-Turkish and Russo-Japanese wars.[47] When headquarters in Berdichev proved to be deaf to this and other, similar pleas, the relatives of Veller and Dumbadze tried to bring their case to the attention of the imperial family itself. According to Rasputin's private secretary, Aron Simanovich, they sent a delegation to meet with the self-styled holy man and importuned him to intercede with the tsar on behalf of the convicted prisoners. If Simanovich is to believed (and his testimony is not always credible), Rasputin agreed to help and succeeded in persuading Nicholas II to show mercy to the four.[48] Whether owing to Rasputin's intervention or for some other reason, in early March the emperor commuted all of the Berdichev sentences: in lieu of execution Dumbadze was to suffer ten years at forced labor; Ivanov and Veller were to be exiled to Siberia; while Nikolai Goshkevich was to get off with a mere sixteen-month prison term.[49]

Russia Reorganizes for War

In the meantime, both the government and the direction of the war effort had undergone some momentous changes. In early August 1915 Nicholas II decided to relieve Nikolai Nikolaevich from his post and assume supreme military command himself. Anguished by the defeats his army had sustained in the spring and summer, Nicholas had come to believe that duty required him to take his place with the troops in the field. The ministers of state were, however, appalled when they learned of the

46. Ibid.
47. Ibid., l. 157.
48. Simanovich, *Rasputin*, pp. 76–77.
49. Commander of Southwest front to V. V. Frederiks, March 8, 1916, RGVIA, f. 962, op. 2, d. 167, l. 163.

tsar's intentions. Although he had had the rudiments of a military education in his youth, unlike Nikolai Nikolaevich, the emperor was no career soldier. Moreover, in taking personal command Nicholas would make the prestige of the dynasty hostage to the fortunes of war. If further military reverses occurred (and who could be certain that they would not?), the image of the monarchy might sustain blows from which it could never recover. Then, too, with Nicholas away at general headquarters, supervision of the day-to-day operations of the government would devolve on the Empress Alexandra, and the empress had already evinced an alarming tendency to listen to and heed the counsel of Rasputin. Indeed, the Siberian *starets* understood full well how the departure of the emperor from Petrograd would augment his power and encouraged Nicholas to go to the front with that very object in view. Attempts by the cabinet, eight of whose members threatened resignation, as well as several Duma politicians to persuade the emperor to change his mind were all unavailing. On August 22, 1915, Nicholas entrained for general headquarters in Mogilev; Nikolai Nikolaevich would shortly decamp for the Caucasus region to take up his position as viceroy and general in chief of the Russian army arrayed against the Ottoman Turks. The only ray of hope amid the general gloom occasioned by this change in the supreme command was Nicholas's uncharacteristic common sense in recognizing his own unsuitability for the exercise of military leadership. He consequently appointed M. V. Alekseev, an extremely competent but somewhat narrow man, as his chief of staff. Henceforth it would be Alekseev who would actually run Russia's war, with Nicholas as a figurehead.[50]

While all of this was going on, back in Petrograd the Duma was preparing to unveil its most audacious demands yet for political reform. Moderate right, centrist, and moderate left deputies had created an alliance, known as the Progressive Bloc, which came to comprise over 70 percent of the entire membership of the Parliament. On August 25 the bloc released a comprehensive program that—in addition to calling for justice for national minorities, amnesty for political offenders, religious toleration, and a thorough overhaul of all organs of local and provincial administration—insisted on the formation of a "unified government, consisting of persons having the confidence of the country."[51] If it had been accepted, this program would of course have required Nicholas to renounce for all time his prerogative of naming his own ministers; the emperor consequently would have none of it. His response was to direct that the Duma be recessed on September 3. It would be five months before it was permitted to meet again.

Nicholas's choleric refusal to consider the program of the Progressive Bloc was, of course, a slap in the face to educated society. In some interpretations, the emperor's decisions that summer—to assume military command and to rebuff the Duma—are depicted as perhaps the worst he made in his entire, sorry political ca-

50. V. Alekseeva-Borel', *Sorok let v riadakh russkoi imperatorskoi armii. General M. V. Alekseev* (St. Petersburg, 2000), p. 411.

51. Sir Bernard Pares, *The Fall of the Russian Monarchy: A Study of the Evidence* (New York, 1961), pp. 272–273; Richard Pipes, *The Russian Revolution* (New York, 1990), pp. 226–227.

198 reer, for by so doing he set in motion processes that would utterly debase the prestige of the monarchy and deprive it of those allies and supporters who might have been able to check Russia's descent into revolution.[52] In any event, however, Nicholas's attitude was not shared by all his ministers. The personnel shake-up of the spring and summer of 1915 had produced a cabinet that contained persons who were both sympathetic to educated society and eager to collaborate with it. Of these, the most visible and influential was the new acting minister of war, A. A. Polivanov.

Unlike Sukhomlinov, Polivanov has generally been favorably regarded by historians, who have viewed him as a principled, responsible advocate of reform and a top-flight administrator. It is undoubtedly true that during Polivanov's tenure at the Ministry of War there was a substantive amelioration of the military manpower problem as well as a striking improvement in the delivery of munitions to Russia's field forces.

As we have already seen, the near rout of 1915 had nearly bled the Russian army white. The losses from death, wounds, capture, and desertion had been so great that when winter came, the frontline army's strength had dwindled to a mere 650,000 men.[53] If the approximately thousand-mile trench line was to hold, it was a matter of the highest urgency to mobilize additional conscripts and equip, train, and dispatch them to reinforce the front. Polivanov responded to the emergency by raising draft quotas and by calling up groups of reservists that had previously been exempt, such as sole breadwinners, *ratniki* (militia) of the second class, men over forty, and the like. As a result, in the space of slightly more than eight months he inducted an additional two million men into the Russian armed forces. These new recruits, who were known as *Polivanovtsy* ("Polivanovites"), flooded into the army so rapidly that by mid-1916 there were 1.75 million troops at the front and an additional three-quarters of a million in reserve.[54]

The situation with regard to munitions and other military supplies also brightened. As minister of war, Polivanov chaired the special conference on defense, which emerged as the key institution in expanding the contribution of Russian industry to the war effort. Between the time of its creation in 1915 and September 1917 it disbursed 15 billion rubles' worth of defense contracts—a sum that was about a third of all the monies the Russian government spent during this period.[55] This lavish influx of cash stimulated a large increase in output; in 1916 the total value (in prewar rubles) of the products of Russian industry exceeded that of 1914 by over 21 percent.[56] Moreover, as was true of the economies of other belligerents, the primary focus of industry

---

52. See the recent and elegant restatement of this interpretation in Pipes, *Russian Revolution*, p. 228. In the opinion of General Brusilov, the emperor's assumption of command caused the fall of the monarchy. Brussilov, *Soldier's Notebook*, p. 172.

53. Knox, *With the Russian Army*, vol. 1, p. 348.

54. Lincoln, *Passage Through Armageddon*, p. 242; David Jones, "Imperial Russia's Forces at War," in *The First World War*, vol. 1 of *Military Effectiveness*, ed. Allan R. Millet and Williamson Murray, pp. 279–280 (Boston, 1988).

55. Norman Stone, *The Eastern Front 1914–1917* (New York, 1975), p. 205.

56. A. L. Sidorov, *Ekonomicheskoe polozhenie Rossii v gody pervoi mirovoi voiny* (Moscow, 1973), p. 350.

(and virtually all heavy industry) was now the satisfaction of military demand. By the end of 1916 there were 1,800 factories and plants exclusively involved in war production; 604 of these were manufacturing munitions, and the value of their output measured in constant rubles tripled during the course of the year.[57] In 1916 domestic industry turned out 3,721 3-inch field guns, as compared with 1,349 in 1915. Equally impressive results were achieved with regard to shells, with slightly less than 10 million coming off the production lines in 1915, and almost 31 million the subsequent year.[58]

An important factor in the Russian army's apparent recovery was this: the Eastern front was relatively quiescent from the fall of 1915 into the spring of 1916, principally as a result of decisions that had been taken at German General Headquarters. Throughout the war, German strategists debated which of their two fronts should receive priority in any given campaigning season. The Schlieffen plan of 1914 had, of course, assigned the greatest weight to operations against France and Belgium in the west. In 1915, however, the "easterners" had been temporarily dominant, and Generals Hindenberg and Ludendorff had sought to decide the war by utterly destroying the Russian army. Yet despite all the defeats Russia had suffered and losses it had incurred since the spring, its powers of resistance had not been broken. In August, the chief of the German General Staff, Erich von Falkenhayn, had concluded that a decisive victory over Russia was at that point unattainable, since as he put it, "it is impossible to annihilate an enemy who is far superior in numbers, must be attacked frontally, and has excellent lines of communication, and any amount of time and space at his disposal."[59] So convinced was he of this that he forced a reallocation of Germany's military assets from east to west, making the centerpiece of his 1916 plan a massive offensive against the French fortifications at Verdun. Given the German orientation toward France in 1916, the choice to fight or not in the east was Russia's to make. And knowing how desperately the army was in need of recuperation, Russia's generals opted for inactivity over battle more often than not that winter and spring.

In addition to the salutary impact of the hiatus in operations, the regeneration of Russian military power has typically been ascribed to the wise statesmanship of Polivanov, the economic rationalization of the special conference system, and the public-spiritedness and selfless zeal of the civic organizations. Indeed, the economic and military upsurge of 1916 is often represented as conclusive proof that the tsarist government had been foolish not to enlist "society" in the war effort from the very first day, for the embrace of "society" and acquiescence in its agenda for reform offered Imperial Russia its only chance for victory and survival. However, while it is undeniably true that Polivanov, the special conferences, and such organizations as the Zem-

---

57. Ibid., p. 369.

58. L. G. Beskrovnyi, *Armiia i flot Rossii v nachale xx v. Ocherki voenno-ekomicheskogo potentsiala* (Moscow, 1986), pp. 91, 105.

59. General von Falkenhayn, *The German General Staff and Its Decisions 1914–1916* (New York, 1920), p. 142.

200 gor did much that was positive, their efforts do not deserve the unqualified praise they have often received.

Take, for example, the issue of reinforcing the army. Polivanov's manpower program did indeed dress large numbers of men in uniforms and get them to the front, but how prepared were these men for the rigors of modern warfare? Given the age of many of these recruits, it is obvious that few of them could have been in prime physical condition. Moreover, so quick was the progress from the induction station to the marching company to the frontline trench that the training these troops received was evidently rudimentary in the extreme. General A. A. Brusilov, the most operationally gifted of all Russia's field commanders, scathingly dismissed the martial qualities of the Polivanovtsy : "The men sent to replace casualties generally knew nothing except how to march; none of them knew anything of open order and many could not even load their rifles; as for their shooting, the less said about it the better."[60] The acute insufficiency of noncommissioned officers and officers at the front (the army was short almost sixteen thousand officers by the beginning of 1916) made matters still worse, for the dearth of competent instructors limited the opportunities the new recruits had to train after they had joined their units.[61]

What about the services provided by society generally, as exemplified by the creation of the Zemgor, the war industry committees, and the special conference system? Because signing up with the Zemgor excused a man from active military duty, there were those in the army who regarded its numerous functionaries (who were jocularly dubbed *zemgusary,* or rural council hussars) as little more than draft evaders.[62] To a large extent, however, this criticism was unfair, for agents of the Zemgor performed superbly in providing the army with medical services and supplying it with such articles as greatcoats, uniforms, and boots. As early as the summer of 1915, the Zemgor was operating over fifty hospital trains fully staffed with doctors and nurses and outfitted with operating rooms, wards, and pharmacies.[63] Within a year of its formation, the Zemgor was presiding over a vast frontline network of canteens, clinics, retail stores, and mobile bathhouses. The efforts of the Zemgor on behalf of the well-being and hygiene of the Russian soldier were in fact so vigorous that at least one general subsequently commented that the army was actually healthier during the war than it had been in peacetime.[64]

The war industry committees were another matter. By any standard they were far less efficient than the Zemgor, for they often failed to complete orders, engaged in subversive political activity, and openly competed with official state organizations for

60. Brussilov, *Soldier's Notebook,* p. 94.

61. Jones, "Imperial Russia's Forces," p. 283.

62. P. P. Petrov, *Rokovye gody 1914–1920* (California [*sic*], 1965), p. 35. Petrov says that the Zemgor eventually enrolled 150,000 young men.

63. Tikhon Polner, Vladimir Obolensky, and Sergius P. Turin, *Russian Local Government During the War* (New Haven, 1930), p. 195.

64. General Basil Gourko, *War and Revolution in Russia* (New York, 1919), p. 157.

technical personnel and scarce raw materials.[65] Moreover, the quality of their product was often shoddy if not completely worthless. For example, while it is true that the committees manufactured and delivered over 14 million hand grenades to the army in 1915 and 1916—almost half the total number supplied in those years—field trials held in 1916 indicated that up to 65 percent of the grenades the army was receiving were duds.[66]

As for the special conference system, although its original inspiration had been Britain's Ministry of Munitions, it eventually deviated considerably from that model. While optimal industrial performance in World War I would have required the imposition of an economic dictatorship, the special conference system compartmentalized rather than coordinated the output of food, fuel, transportation, and munitions and therefore fell far short of the mark.[67] As a result, the system neither rationalized nor centralized the economy; instead, it engendered anarchy, redundancy, corruption, and waste. The lack of intelligent central planning led to dangerous absurdities: at one point in 1915, the plurality of railroad repair shops in the country were dragooned into shell production, heedless of the consequences for the empire's transportation network.[68] The slow decay of Russia's railways would in the end prove more ruinous to the Russian war effort than the lack of munitions had been, for it constricted the army's access to supplies of all kinds, undermined morale, and stirred up civil unrest. The February Revolution of 1917 began in Petrograd with food riots, caused not by an absolute shortfall of comestibles in the empire but rather by a lack of the necessary locomotives and rolling stock needed to ship a sufficient quantity to the capital.

A final point needs to be made about the special conference system, specifically about the special conference for defense. As it had been established to solve the army's artillery problem while simultaneously appeasing educated opinion, it was from its inception both a political institution and an economic one. The majority of its twenty-seven members were, after all, representatives of "society" rather than the bureaucracy or the higher echelons of the government, for it contained eleven Duma deputies, three delegates from war industry committees, and two from the Zemgor. But if the conference's economic record was no better than poor, its political performance was worse still. As the months went by, its decisions came both to reflect and pander to an increasingly hysterical public mood. In tandem with the public outcry about "German domination" within the country, the conference moved to persecute

65. Sidorov, *Ekonomicheskoe polozhenie*, pp. 193–201; Louis Siegelbaum, *The Politics of Industrial Mobilization in Russia 1914–1917: A Study of the War-Industries Committees* (New York, 1983), pp. 104, 118, 156, 158, 192.

66. Siegelbaum, *The Politics*, p. 95; L. G. Beskrovnyi et al., eds., *Zhurnaly osobogo soveshchaniia po oborone gosudarstva 1916 god* (Moscow, 1977), p. 252.

67. Naumov, *Iz utselevshikh vospominanii*, p. 377.

68. Vladimir N. Ipatieff, *The Life of a Chemist: Memoirs of Vladimir N. Ipatieff*, ed. Xenia Joukoff Evdin, Helen Dwight Fisher, and Harold H. Fisher, trans. Vladimir Haensel and Mrs. Ralph H. Lusher (Palo Alto, Calif., 1946), p. 192.

202 ethnic Germans and other minorities by seizing their assets and sequestering their property. This extrajudicial punishment was often administered even if the property concerned was a factory involved in war work.

Among the conference's victims were the Til'mans family of industrialists, whom we have already encountered in this book. One of the plants in Kovno owned by Richard Til'mans was the empire's largest manufactory of wood screws. The authorities had closed this facility down in early 1915, despite the fact that its screws were essential for the assembly of rifle crates. In October the Ministry of Trade and Industry proposed to the special conference on defense that Richard Til'mans be allowed to relocate his factory to central Russia[69] and reopen it: the army desperately required the factory's output; Til'mans was the man most qualified to manage it; and, since Til'mans had been a Russian subject for over thirty years, there could be no doubt about his allegiance to the empire. Although the special conference initially seemed inclined to accede to the trade ministry's request, a voluble group of deputies, including Duma President Rodzianko, won the other conferees over to the view that, far from reopening the Til'mans plant, the conference should categorically sequester it and transfer its buildings, machines, and land to the treasury. The arguments made in favor of this course of action illustrate the quality of reasoning that often held sway at the special conference on defense. The German character of the ownership of the company was "completely confirmed," while the suspicion that the firm was engaged in unspecified "criminal activity" was "extremely well founded." Then, too, one could not discount the "psychological effect on the working masses" of sanctioning the establishment of a business in the Great Russian heartland by an individual with a dubious German surname. Finally (and this was the clincher), it had been "conclusively proved" that Richard Til'mans and various of his employees had known Miasoedov, and that Miasoedov had typed "conspiratorial documents" in one of the company's offices. (Miasoedov had indeed gone hunting with Richard Til'mans during the Verzhbolovo years, and had also once borrowed a typewriter belonging to the Til'mans firm to write a letter to his mistress.) The special conference's vote for sequestration was unanimous.[70]

V. N. Shakovskoi, who served as minister of trade and industry from early 1915 to early 1917 was driven to distraction by such idiocies.[71] Former War Minister A. F. Rediger, an unusually sensible witness, dismissed the special conferences as virtually useless, and the brilliant chemist V. N. Ipatev, who had better ideas about the wartime organization of industry than almost anyone else in Russia, believed that

---

69. One interesting Russian response to the debacle of 1915, beginning in August, had been to organize the dismantling of entire industrial plants in such threatened cities as Riga, Revel, and Minsk and the transfer of all the machinery and key personnel to such interior provinces as Saratov and Samara. See E. D. Rumiantsev, *Rabochii klass povolzh'ia v gody pervoi mirovoi voiny i fevral'skoi revoliutsii* (1914–1917 gg.) (Kazan, 1989), p. 51.

70. L. G. Beskrovnyi et al., eds., *Zhurnaly osobogo soveshchaniia po oborone gosudarstva 1915 god* (Moscow, 1975), pp. 328, 339–341, 391–394.

71. Shakhovskoi, *"Sic Transit,"* pp. 171–175.

their formation had been an "overreaction" to the shell crisis, that their existence precluded the adoption of a central economic plan, and that their policy of indiscriminate sequestration was a pernicious disgrace.[72]

The Noose Tightens

If national chauvinism, demagoguery, and ulterior motives could corrupt the special conference on defense, it is hardly surprising that the Petrov Commission was even more biased and reckless. After all, in addition to burnishing the government's image, the special conference had serious economic duties to perform, while Petrov's committee had been politicized from its inception. Since the most influential members of the panel had already made up their minds about who was responsible for Russia's military unpreparedness in 1914, the commission actually did its work in reverse: instead of collecting facts and drawing impartial conclusions from them, it started with its foregone conclusions and sought evidence to back them up. In retrospect it is clear that the majority of the commissioners were less interested in getting at the truth about Russia's military supply problems than they were in laying the groundwork for the criminal prosecution of Sukhomlinov. And the barely hidden agenda here was to hold the emperor's right to choose ministers up to obloquy, thereby furthering the Progressive Bloc's ambitions for a "united government."

The most important element in the commission's surreptitious political offensive on the bloc's behalf was its final report. That document, dated February 9, 1916, insisted that the dearth of modern ordnance and ammunition that had caused the Russian army so much suffering was not the result of either accident or innocent error. The shell crisis was instead the consequence "of the shameful activities of the organs of the ministry of war."[73] The commission faulted the ministry for its underestimation of the stockpiles of ammunition necessary to wage war, for its lack of attention to industrial mobilization, for its incoherent organization and its misuse of funds. While admitting that the speed with which campaigns devoured the artillery parks had something to do with the crisis, the report quickly zeroed in on Sukhomlinov personally. The former minister's inexplicably large bank balances drew comment, but the heaviest stress fell on Sukhomlinov's pattern of friendship and association, particularly his association with the executed spy Miasoedov. The commission rehearsed the entire story: how in Verzhbolovo Miasoedov had been involved in a shady partnership with the Freidbergs, who were themselves traitors; how in Petersburg Sukhomlinov had finagled Miasoedov's recall to the service as well as his assignment to a sensitive post in intelligence; and how the Sukhomlinov/Miasoedov circle had eventually grown to include Altschüller, the Goshkevichs, Veller, Ivanov, and Dumbadze—all of whom had been indicted for crimes against the state. In summation, the

---

72. For Rediger's opinion see his memoir, RGVIA, f. 280, op. 1, d. 8, l. 56; Ipatieff, *The Life of a Chemist*, pp. 191–195, 212.

73. Petrov Commission report, February 9, 1916, RGVIA, f. 962, op. 2, d. 43, l. 4.

204 report declared that at a bare minimum Sukhomlinov had been gravely derelict in his duty during the entire six years and three months he had spent in office.[74]

This, of course, was little more than guilt by association and character assassination by innuendo. By its juxtaposition of topics and distribution of emphasis the report strongly implied (without saying so directly) that conscious treason, not insouciant light-mindedness, lurked behind Sukhomlinov's misdeeds.

Commenting that he "was constrained to make this sacrifice," on March 1 1916 (O.S.), Nicholas II signed a decree empowering the First Department of the Imperial Senate to determine whether Sukhomlinov should be brought to trial.[75] Although he had finally become convinced of the need to throw his former favorite minister to the parliamentary wolves, the emperor was by no means capitulating to society, as indeed he demonstrated almost immediately. On March 13 Nicholas unceremoniously dismissed his popular war minister, A. A. Polivanov, informing him that "the work of the war industry committees does not inspire me with confidence, and your supervision of them I find to be insufficiently authoritative."[76] As this suggests, Polivanov's fulsome collaboration with Guchkov, which Alexandra constantly harped on in her letters from home, obviously continued to disturb the emperor.[77] Moreover, Nicholas had never gotten over his resentment of the way in which Polivanov's candidacy had in effect been imposed on him nine months earlier, nor had he not forgiven Polivanov for his animosity against his predecessor. After some hesitation, the tsar chose D. S. Shuvaev, a colorless military logistician, as Polivanov's replacement. There ensued a period of chronic governmental instability in which ministers were appointed and discharged with giddying rapidity. Many ascribed this chaotic shuffling and reshuffling of the Russian cabinet to the noxious influence that Rasputin held over the empress. In any event, so-called ministerial leapfrog became a permanent characteristic of the Russian monarchy until its demise a year later.

Sukhomlinov may have reacted with glee to the ouster of his implacable antagonist Polivanov, but he reaped no personal benefit whatsoever. The law had been set in motion and it would take its course. In the months since his own fall he had turned his back on politics in favor of the comforts of private life. After vacating their official quarters, the Sukhomlinovs had stayed for some time in a furnished apartment lent them by a friend. In September 1915 they finally moved into a small flat of their own at the corner of Officers' Street and English Prospect. Here Vladimir Aleksandrovich led a hermetic existence. Shunning meetings of the Council of State, he occupied his time by working on a new series of "Ostap Bondarenko" essays, as well as a history of the Russo-Turkish War of 1877–78, apparently oblivious to the dangers that loomed

---

74. Ibid., ll. 2–26, passim. The commission also accused a handful of other former war ministry officials of nonfeasance and malfeasance, including Ia. G. Zhilinskii, chief of the general staff from 1911 to 1914, and Kuzmin-Karavaev, who headed up the Main Artillery Administration from early 1909 until the spring of 1915.

75. Rodzianko, *Krushenie imperii i*, p. 159.

76. Quoted in Pares, *The Fall of the Russian Monarchy*, p. 327.

77. *Letters of the Tsaritsa*, pp. 224–260 passim.

over him.[78] Thus he was stupefied when the head of the city *okhrannoe delenie* came pounding at his door at 10:30 in the morning of April 20 with a warrant for his arrest. As a squad of police fanned out through his apartment rifling through his private papers, the former minister was led to the street and bundled off to the Fortress of Peter and Paul. Either by accident or deliberate cruelty, he was assigned to the same cell (No. 43) that had once housed General Stessel', who had been convicted of treason against the state for his premature surrender of the fortress of Port Arthur to the Japanese back in 1905.[79]

In the meantime the police had thoroughly ransacked the Sukhomlinovs' quarters and had amassed four stout boxes of documents, which they sealed as evidence and carted away. Ekaterina Viktorovna was left alone to contemplate the shambles of her ruined apartment. Less than twenty-four hours after her husband's arrest, Prince Andronnikov would, with characteristic spite, phone to taunt her about her misfortunes.[80] As had already been amply demonstrated, however, Ekaterina was no weakling. Shaking off her depression, she immediately bestirred herself to find out what she could about the case against her spouse and if possible to secure his release. The first thing she learned was that the head of the Sukhomlinov investigation would be Senator I. A. Kuz'min of the Senate's Civil Cassation Department; his had been the signature on the warrant for her husband's arrest. Kuz'min had issued that warrant on the direct order of A. A. Khvostov, who had succeeded Shcheglovitov at the Ministry of Justice.

As might be imagined, there was jubilation in "social" and Duma circles at the news of the former war minister's imprisonment. The reactions of officers at the front were, however, mixed. While a majority approved, thinking that this act would strengthen the government, a substantial minority believed that the very principle of monarchical authority had been compromised, and that only the Germans and the revolutionaries would gain thereby. Others whispered that the real meaning of the arrest was the government's knowledge that Russia was going to lose the war and its need to identify a scapegoat to deflect the rage of the people. Even greater cynics dismissed the entire thing as a cheap stunt designed to mollify public opinion.[81]

A Pyrrhic Victory

While Ekaterina mapped out her campaign for her husband, Sukhomlinov paced his cell, and Kuz'min collected his evidence, spring gave way to summer. June and July 1916 brought one of the most surprising turnarounds in military history: Russia's unleashing of the Brusilov offensive.

In March 1916 in Chantilly the Entente Allies convened their third conference on a common strategy for the war. With the Germans battering away at Verdun, all

---

78. Sukhomlinov, *Vospominaniia Sukhomlinova*, pp. 261–263.
79. *Russkoe chtenie*, April 20, 1916, pp. 2–3.
80. Ekaterina Sukhomlinova interrogation, November 21, 1916, RGVIA, f. 962, op. 2, d. 136, l. 53.
81. Lemke, *250 dnei*, p. 773.

206 agreed that the coordination of military operations on all fronts was long overdue. The conference resolved that simultaneous offensives should be launched in the summer of 1916, in both the west and the east.

Because the epicenter of the war had shifted back to France, Russia now enjoyed a clear numerical superiority over Germany and Austria-Hungary. Its Northern front and West front, consisting of four and three armies, respectively, together disposed of 1,200,000 soldiers and were opposed by no more than 620,000 Germans. The balance of forces was less favorable farther south, where the 512,000 troops of Southwest front (four armies) faced off against 441,000 Austro-Hungarian, German, and Turkish soldiers. Believing, therefore, that an attack against the German army had the highest probability of success, Russian General Headquarters proposed a simultaneous strike by the forces of the North and West fronts in the direction of Vilna. The role of the Southwest front was limited to diversionary action designed to pin down the enemy and prevent his reinforcement of the authentically threatened sectors in the north.

It happened that the commander of the Southwest front at this time was A. A. Brusilov, an extremely aggressive and highly imaginative general of cavalry. To him, the overall campaign plan's relegation of his front to a subordinate role was not only inglorious but also potentially fatal. Observing that a diversion had the desired results only if the enemy remained uncertain where the main blow would fall, Brusilov begged Stavka for permission to conduct at least one real attack on his front. Warning him that he would receive no additional stocks of artillery or shells, Alekseev eventually (and with some reluctance) acceded to Brusilov's request.

To Brusilov's way of thinking, one reason that the conflict's tactical offensives had heretofore proved so costly and so indecisive was the failure to achieve surprise. The concentration of tens of thousands of extra troops and the accumulation of tons of supplies that preceded any attack invariably alerted the enemy that an assault was imminent. Determined not to repeat this mistake, Brusilov took every step he could to obscure his true intentions. In seeking to surprise the enemy he constructed *places d'armes* in some twenty locations along his front, exploited aerial photography to map every inch of the enemy's defenses, limited his preliminary artillery barrage, and trained special "shock" units to bypass enemy strong points and thus widen the ruptures he hoped to open in the lines.

By mid-May (O.S.) Brusilov was ready. Although he had hoped to act in concert with Russia's two other fronts as well as with the French and British armies in the west, an emergency developed that forced him to initiate battle prematurely and alone. That event was Austria's defeat of Italy in the Trentino, which caused Rome to appeal to the Russians to do something to relieve the almost unendurable pressure on the Italian army. In response to Alekseev's command, Brusilov advanced the date of his attack to May 22 (June 4), 1916.

The military success that was immediately achieved completely validated Brusilov's extensive preparations as well as his novel tactics. The Austrian line was broken in four places, Russian troops poured through the breaches, and Austro-

Hungarian troops began to surrender by the thousands. Within a week, a full third of the men that Austria had initially deployed in the combat zone were prisoners of war. By the end of the month of June alone, Brusilov had captured almost a quarter of a million men. To prevent the total collapse of the Eastern front, Germany was forced to withdraw eleven divisions from France and Austria six divisions from Italy.[82] Before it finally sputtered to a standstill, Brusilov's offensive inflicted a million and a half enemy casualties, took over 450,000 prisoners, seized 581 guns, and conquered 575,000 square kilometers—a territory larger in size than Belgium.[83]

Yet, although an operational triumph, the Brusilov offensive was a strategic disaster. In August Rumania was emboldened to enter the war on the side of the Entente, and promptly collapsed, thus delivering vast quantities of oil and wheat into the hands of the Germans and forcing Russia to extend her front an additional five hundred miles to the Black Sea. At the same time Russian casualties had been enormous, amounting to over half a million troops. Moreover, although the Russians had once again overrun Galicia, and although they had crippled the Austro-Hungarian army, that army, stiffened as it was by allied troops, continued to hold. The prospect of a complete victory seemed as remote at the end of the Brusilov campaign as it had before it began. As a consequence, far from lifting the spirits of Russia's soldiers, it engendered demoralization and despair. The horrific costs and discouraging results of the operation left even many officers wondering whether Russia could ever win the war, regardless of how well supplied her army was.[84]

Sukhomlinov Is Released

An official bulletin of October 12, 1916, announced that in conformity with the wishes of the emperor, at 7:45 the previous evening General Sukhomlinov had been freed from the Fortress of Peter and Paul. Escorted to his apartment at no. 53 Officers' Street by a detachment of gendarmes, he had been placed under house arrest. The news stunned all of Petrograd. What had induced Nicholas II to take this hugely unpopular decision?

Conceivably it was a lingering affection for his former minister, who had already languished in prison for six months on charges that Nicholas felt were manifestly false. Certainly there were people in the tsar's inner circle who reproached him for what he had allowed to happen to Vladimir Aleksandrovich. One such was P. A. Badmaev, an elderly savant of "Tibetan medicine" who specialized in treating male impotence.[85] Badmaev, a confidant of Rasputin's, wrote the emperor shortly after Sukhomlinov's arrest, pointing out that whether any of the allegations against the

---

82. Brusilov, *Soldier's Notebook*, pp. 230–243; Stone, *Eastern Front*, p. 254; V. A. Emets, *Ocherki vneshnei politiki Rossii v period pervoi mirovoi voiny* (Moscow, 1977), pp. 275–277.

83. Brusilov, *Soldier's Notebook*, pp. 256, 266; Rostunov, *Russkii front*, p. 325.

84. *Vospominaniia Lukomskago*, vol. 2, p. 105.

85. Edward Radzinsky, *The Rasputin File*, trans. Judson Rosengrant (New York, 2000), p. 146.

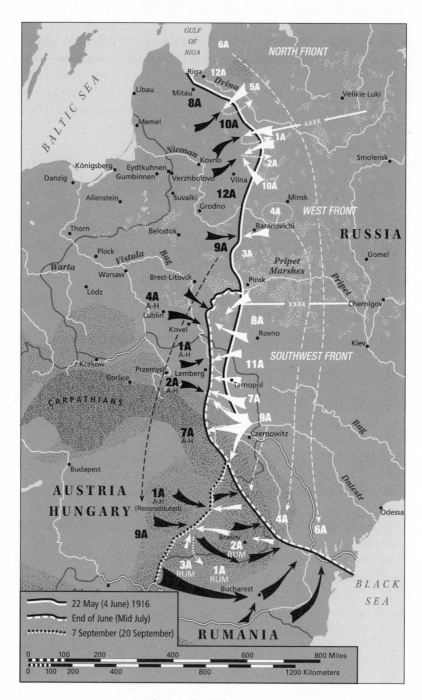

The Brusilov Offensive, 1916

general were true, "in any event he had been a loyal and useful servant to your majesty"—a person who ought not to suffer mistreatment.[86] A festering anger at the Duma, the civil politicians, and the public opinion on whose behalf Sukhomlinov had been sacrificed in the first place doubtless also swayed the tsar in the general's favor. However, it is apparent that Sukhomlinov regained his liberty chiefly because of the entreaties of two improbable suppliants—Rasputin and the Empress Alexandra.

The reason that their intercession for the ex-minister was so surprising was that neither of them had ever been known to be particularly fond of Sukhomlinov or the members of his household. Rasputin had not forgiven Vladimir Aleksandrovich for refusing to receive him and had openly spread derogatory gossip about the general in concert with Chervinskaia and Andronnikov. As for Alexandra, while she respected Sukhomlinov for his loyalty to her imperial husband, she simply could not abide Ekaterina Viktorovna, whom she described in a letter of November 1914 as "really the most *mauvais genre.*" Alexandra believed that Sukhomlinov's troubles were solely due to his amatory enslavement to this rude and aggressive social climber, and she wrote Nicholas in June 1915 that "it is [Sukhomlinov's] adventurer wife who has completely ruined his reputation . . . because of her bribes he suffers and so on."[87]

That the empress emerged as Sukhomlinov's champion was the result of the importuning of Rasputin. His transformation from enemy to friend of the ex-minister had in turn had been engineered by Ekaterina Viktorovna, who paid two visits to the apartment of the uncouth *starets* to plead her husband's case. There are several versions of what transpired between the Siberian peasant and the wife of the imprisoned general. According to one account, Rasputin was won over by the sheer eloquence of Ekaterina's forceful advocacy as well as the justice of her cause. In another, it was large monetary payments that actually lay behind Rasputin's change of heart. Finally, there is the unsavory, persistent rumor that Rasputin agreed to help Ekaterina but only in exchange for sex. After all, Rasputin's weakness for pretty women was legendary, and he was understood to have been strongly attracted to Ekaterina, perhaps even in love with her. As we have already seen, he once confided to one of his cronies that Ekaterina was "one of the only two women in the world to have stolen my heart."[88] As Court Commandant A. A. Mossolov subsequently remarked, "women know that there is only one way of paying a debt contracted towards Rasputin."[89] It is worthy of note in this regard that according to the police agents who had Rasputin under surveillance, the latter reciprocated Ekaterina's two trips to his home with sixty-nine visits to hers in the summer and fall of 1916.[90]

86. V. P. Semennikova, ed., *Za kulisami tsarizma. Arkhiv tibetskogo vracha Badmaeva* (Leningrad, 1925), p. 25.

87. *Letters of the Tsaritsa to the Tsar*, pp. 33–34, 89.

88. P. E. Shchegolev, ed., *Padenia tsarskogo rezhima. Stenograficheskie otchety doprosov i pokazanii dannykh v 1917 g. v Chrezvychainoi Sledstvennoi Komissii Vremennogo Pravitel'stva*, vol. 2 (Leningrad, 1924), pp. 13, 56.

89. A. A. Mosolov, *At the Court of the Last Tsar*, ed. A. A. Pilenco, trans. E. W. Dickes (London, 1935), p. 150.

90. O. A. Platonov, *Ternoyi venets Rossii. Zagovor tsareubiits* (Moscow, 1996), p. 190.

210

G. E. Rasputin

The *starets* was in a position to offer Ekaterina immediate and effective assistance. He arranged for her to meet Anna Vyrubova, the empress's favorite lady-in-waiting and trusted intimate (and inter alia, the second of the two women whom Rasputin claimed to have adored). Vyrubova eventually succeeded in persuading Alexandra to grant Ekaterina an audience. At this meeting, Ekaterina handed the empress a lengthy memorandum about her husband's travails that she had drafted herself. Her performance on this occasion was apparently impressive enough to overcome Alexandra's long-standing qualms about her personality and character.[91]

Thus it was that beginning in mid-July Alexandra's letters to Nicholas at general headquarters started to feature appeals for Sukhomlinov's discharge. Three letters composed in September were largely devoted to this topic. In one, the empress wrote, "Our Friend [i.e., Rasputin] has said that it is necessary to release General Sukhomlinov, lest he die in prison. . . . I have a petition that Madame Sukhomlinova addressed to me. Would you like me to send it to you? He has already been in prison for six months—which is long enough (*since he is no spy*). Despite all of his faults he is old, broken and won't live long. It would be horrible if he were to die in jail."[92] It was shortly after receiving this missive that the emperor ordered Sukhomlinov's transfer to the more comfortable circumstances of house arrest.

To understand the extraordinary intensity of the public outrage at Sukhomlinov's release it is essential to recognize that by this point relations between regime and parliament were not merely bad but hopeless. The ongoing process of ministerial leapfrog had stripped the imperial government of its last vestiges of dignity and credibility, as did the dreadful quality of the ministerial appointments, which many believed were the result of the malign influence of Rasputin. By way of illustration, take B. V. Stürmer, who served as Russia's premier from February to November 1916. A dyed-in-the-wool reactionary, Stürmer was suspected of being a closet Germanophile who was intriguing for a separate peace between Russia and the Central

91. *Padenie tsarskogo rezhima,* vol. 2, p. 13.
92. Quoted in Aleksandr Tarsaidze, *Chetyre mifa* (New York, 1969), p. 246.

Powers.[93] Then there was Minister of the Interior A. D. Protopopov, the former Duma deputy and toadying opportunist whose personal conduct was so odd that he was suspected by many (including the tsar himself) to be suffering from some form of mental illness.[94] Protopopov's visit to Sukhomlinov shortly after his homecoming fueled speculation that he had taken a personal hand in organizing the general's discharge from prison, and completed the destruction of his reputation.[95] At a meeting between Protopopov and the leaders of the Progressive Bloc in the apartment of Duma President Rodzianko on the evening of October 19th, the members of the Bloc spurned Protopopov's offer of a "comradely conversation." Paul Miliukov, distinguished historian and prominent figure in the Constitutional Democratic (Kadet) Party, spelled out why this would be impossible: "A person who serves with Stürmer, a person who freed Sukhomlinov, considered to be a traitor by the entire country, a person who persecutes the press and public organizations cannot be our comrade."[96]

The Duma's mistrust of the regime, exacerbated hugely by Sukhomlinov's release, reached a climax on November 1, when Miliukov took the floor to deliver an address that has ever since been known as the "treason or stupidity" speech. Waving an Austrian newspaper in the air, Miliukov punctuated his lengthy catalog of the government's misdeeds with the query, "Is this stupidity, or is it treason?" This diatribe had an electrifying effect on Miliukov's audience, which responded loudly and severally. While numbers of deputies shouted "stupidity" in response to Miliukov's rhetorical questions, others cried "treason," while still others chanted "Both! Both!" "It was as if," Miliukov later recalled, "a pus-filled sack had burst."[97]

The Miliukov speech soon circulated throughout the length and breadth of Russia. It is a sign of the total isolation of the regime that ultramonarchist V. M. Purishkevich, once the dynasty's most ferocious apologist, personally arranged for the distribution of tens of thousands of copies at the front by sanitary train.[98] The impact on the country was so electrifying that many contemporaries subsequently described the speech as the "storm signal" of the revolution, even the revolution's "first blow." This view is shared by at least some modern scholars, who argue that in the aftermath of Miliukov's address a violent revolution against the autocracy was only a matter of

93. See, for example, Princess Cantacuzene, Countess Speransky, neé Grant, *Revolutionary Days* (Boston, 1919), p. 87.

94. Pares, *Fall of the Russian Monarchy*, pp. 378–379, 394.

95. In his conversation with Sukhomlinov, Protopopov had informed him that while the tsar was still certain that he was innocent of treason, he was "grieved" by his financial dealings. See *Padenie tsarskogo rezhima*, vol. 4 (Leningrad, 1925), p. 29.

96. Shulgin, *Gody-dni-1920*, p. 314.

97. Miliukov, *Political Memoirs*, p. 377; see also the extremely unfavorable assessment of this speech by A. S. Rezanov, who wrote an entire book about it in emigration: *Shturmovoi signal P.N. Miliukova* (Paris, 1924). Rezanov, a trained military lawyer, observed that by the terms of Russia's arcane treason law of July 5, 1912, Miliukov's delivery of this speech was in itself an act of treason. The 1912 law stated that a person could be judged guilty of treason if he manifested "criminal indifference to the character of his actions, if their consequences might be harmful to the military defense of Russia." See p. 43.

98. A. I. Spiridovich, *Velikaia voina i Fevral'skaia Revoliutsiia*, vol. 2 (New York, 1960), p. 173.

212 time. Miliukov had strongly suggested that treason had insinuated itself so completely into the machinery of power that the regime had become utterly unfit to govern the country or prosecute the war. Moreover, he was understood to have implied that high figures at the court, perhaps including even the Empress Alexandra, were bound together in a traitorous league. What else could explain the unpardonable leniency recently shown to the odious Sukhomlinov? Rumor was rife that Miliukov knew much more than he had been able to say, and that the relatively innocuous Viennese newspaper article about the Russian "peace party" (from which he had quoted in the original) had actually been a document proving the empress's complicity in a seditious plot. Of course, Rasputin did indeed think that an exit from the war would be in Russia's best interest, but there was absolutely no meeting of minds between him and the empress on this subject. For although Alexandra had been born a princess of the House of Hesse-Darmstadt, and although she did secretly send money to relieve her poor relations back in Germany after the war had broken out (relying on the Petrograd banker Dmitrii Rubinshtein for this purpose), she was passionately devoted to the Russian cause and had nothing but hatred and contempt for the Prussianized Germany of Kaiser Wilhelm II.[99] Still, if it was true that she had intervened with the emperor on behalf of V. A. Sukhomlinov, for hundreds of thousands of Russians this act was in itself sufficient confirmation of her perfidy.

The Kuz'min Report

It was against this backdrop of social and political turbulence that Senator Kuz'min issued *his* findings about the Sukhomlinov affair. Dated November 7, 1916, the senator's report began by asserting that there could be no doubt that a dangerous Austro-German espionage ring had compromised Russia's most sensitive military secrets both prior to and after the outbreak of the European war: the military judicial system had exposed both the conspiracy and the conspirators, of whom the chief culprits had been Lieutentant Colonel Miasoedov, Colonel Ivanov, and Aleksandr Altschüller. Sukhomlinov had been in close contact with all three of these miscreants, as well as many of their accomplices. Indeed, Miasoedov had been the general's protégé, for he had openly socialized with the gendarme colonel despite the chasm of rank and status that lay between them, had employed him in the counterintelligence department in 1912 despite numerous official warnings of his untrustworthiness, and had given him the testimonial that had permitted him to reenter military service and join the active army in 1914. These irregularities were too numerous to be explained away as either coincidences or careless lapses in judgment. There was in fact a sinister pattern to the general's entire relationship with the executed spy, a pattern that led "to the unimpeachable conclusion that both Miasoedov and General Sukhomlinov

---

99. On the empress's anti-German sentiments see Mark D. Steinberg and Vladimir M. Khrustalëv, *The Fall of the Romanovs* (New Haven, 1995), pp. 27–28.

worked together to achieve the same criminal end—the betrayal of Russia in the interests of Germany."[100]

But there was more, for the disgraced war minister's associations with other key figures in the espionage plot were equally damning. He had had dealings with Colonel Ivanov behind the backs of the latter's superiors in the Main Artillery Administration and had attempted to secure the colonel's release upon his arrest. He had given Dumbadze a secret document about Russia's military reforms after the Japanese war on the ridiculous pretext of assisting in the preparation of his biography. Later, in April 1915, Sukhomlinov had helped Dumbadze make a trip to Germany, purportedly to spy on that country, but actually to deliver purloined documents and information to his German handlers. Then there was Altschüller, Sukhomlinov's "old friend" from Kiev, who posed as a businessman but who was actually one of Austria's most valued agents in the Russian Empire. When the police had ransacked Sukhomlinov's apartment, they had discovered no letters from Altschüller whatsoever, suggesting that the general who was otherwise so meticulous about saving every scrap of paper that passed over his desk had had the wit to burn the entire incriminating correspondence. Sukhomlinov's reliable helpmate in all his foul activities had been his shallow wife, Ekaterina Viktorovna, whose avarice and addiction to luxury had evidently led her husband both to accept bribes and to commit treason. Had not Butovich, her first spouse, testified that she was a stranger to any feelings of nationalism or patriotism, a woman whose motto had been "our fatherland is wherever we live well"? It was therefore not enough merely to indict Sukhomlinov, for Ekaterina Viktorovna was as guilty as he and equally deserving of punishment.[101]

Yet moving ahead with a criminal trial of either or both Sukhomlinovs required the consent of the tsar, who at least initially was determined to withhold it. Perhaps mindful of the opinion of Court Commandant A. A. Mossolov, who advised him that trying Sukhomlinov would inevitably do severe damage to the "monarchical principle," on November 10 Nicholas II telegrammed Justice Minister A. A. Makarov that he had inspected Kuzmin's report, had found nothing therein to justify a criminal prosecution, and commanded that the case against the general be closed.[102]

But as we have repeatedly seen, Nicholas was notoriously prone to vacillation and vulnerable to pressure. The tsar had fired Stürmer soon after Miliukov's speech, replacing him as premier with A. F. Trepov. On November 14 Trepov and Makarov together arrived at Stavka to implore the emperor to reconsider his decision. Trepov noted that when the Petrov Commission had wound up its labors in early 1916 it had confronted the government with the stark choice between going ahead with a legal case against the former minister of war or letting the matter drop. In the event, the

---

100. Findings of Senator I. A. Kuzmin, November 9, 1916, RGVIA, f. 962, op. 2, d. 52, ll. 2–3 (quotation from l. 3).

101. Ibid., ll. 4–14 (quotation from ll. 11–12).

102. Telegram of Nicholas II to minister of justice, November 10, 1916, RGVIA, f. 962, op. 2, d. 24, l. 2. On Mossolov, see Tarsaidze, *Chetyre mifa*, p. 218.

214 government had opted at that time to pursue the Sukhomlinov case; to close it down now would oxygenate the flames of malicious chatter and gossip like a bellows. Further, such a step would be deeply unpopular "with broad sectors of the population, who regard General Sukhomlinov as the chief culprit behind the military reverses experienced by our glorious army in the summer of last year." Trepov further hinted that unless judicial proceedings went forward, his new cabinet would not have a prayer of effective action. Albeit with misgivings, Nicholas reversed himself and scrawled a sullen "Agreed" on the memorandum authorizing Sukhomlinov's prosecution that Trepov had earlier prepared.[103] Expediency thus demanded that a trial take place and officials at the Ministry of Justice immediately set to work to prepare for one. Sukhomlinov's real ordeal had only begun.

103. Aide-mémoire, November 14, 1916, RGVIA, f. 962, op. 2, d. 124, l. 3.

8

Revolution and Final Act

The Case against V. A. Sukhomlinov

In mid-November 1916 Sukhomlinov was apprised that he had been formally indicted on felony charges and was told to prepare himself for trial. Thousands of pages of depositions and affidavits collected by Kuz'min and his fellow senators had served as the basis for the indictment. It is worthwhile at this point to take a look at the nature of the government's case and the quality of the evidence that buttressed it.

The general stood accused of three different categories of offenses: malfeasance with regard to the munitioning of the Russian army, peculation and other financial misconduct, and espionage for Germany and Austria-Hungary. All three were connected.

With regard to munitions and preparations for war in general, such controversial policies as Sukhomlinov's efforts to raze the fortresses in the western territories of the empire and disband the fortress artillery were cast in an entirely negative light, construed as purposeful attempts to degrade the empire's defenses. On the basis of testimony by the Grand Duke Sergei Mikhailovich, inspector in chief of the Artillery Department and an implacable foe of Vladimir Aleksandrovich, the general was also charged with obstructing the buildup of stocks of munitions both prior to and after the start of the war. He was blamed as well for his delay in applying to foreign sources for a solution to Russia's supply problem. In September 1914, for instance, he had banned the purchase of foreign-made rifles of calibers different from the Russian, although the army was by then chronically short of both rifles and cartridges. When the fact of the shell crisis was indisputable, he had not taken the decisive steps necessary to remedy it and had even had the temerity to deny that Russia was experiencing any real difficulties with military supply at all, as he asserted in a telegram to France's

215

216 Marshal Joffre on September 15, 1914. If he had instead promptly appealed to Russia's allies for help, this "might have had a substantive impact on the outcome of military operations in Galicia in the spring of 1915."[1]

Doubtless one explanation for the general's conduct was his desire to enrich himself by steering military contracts to firms that were paying him illegal kickbacks, a conclusion that was validated by an examination of his financial records. Clearly Sukhomlinov had been taking bribes. When he had become chief of the general staff in December 1908, his assets had been exceedingly modest: his bank balance had been a mere 2,908 rubles, while his holdings in stocks and bonds had amounted to another 54,000. He had owned no real estate. When he was elevated to the leadership of the war ministry, his annual salary and allowances had come to almost 63,000 rubles. Yet between December 1908 and September 1915 he had deposited 702,737 rubles in cash and securities in various Petersburg banks. His withdrawals had come to 279,311 rubles, which meant that his capital remaining should have stood at 423,426. However, try at they might, financial investigators could find no more than 80,000 rubles in the general's accounts.

These statistics raised at least three interesting questions. First, what had happened to the missing 340,000 rubles? Investigators noted that in July and September 1915 Sukhomlinov had emptied first one and then the other safe deposit box he rented at the Mutual Credit Company, which led them to assume that the general still possessed these assets but had secreted them somewhere unknown. Second, what had the ex-minister been spending his funds on? It was well established that Vladimir Aleksandrovich personally was not profligate with money. His housekeeper, Madame Kiun'e, recollected that he rarely gave her more than a hundred rubles for day-to-day expenses in any given month, and even then constantly urged her to economize. But Ekaterina Viktorovna's spending patterns were another matter entirely. Deposed in prison, Anna Goshkevich asserted that Ekaterina easily ran through 100,000 rubles or more every year on such items as medical bills, traveling expenses, and new clothes.[2] Chervinskaia, now allied with the vindictive Andronnikov, also weighed in on the subject of Ekaterina's extravagance, confirming Anna's portrait of her as an inveterate spendthrift. Finally, what accounted for Sukhomlinov's sudden and amazing acquisition of a fortune? Investigators discounted the general's own story—that his prosperity was entirely due to astute investing—by noting that his actual stock market profits from 1908 to 1915 could not have amounted to much more than 55,000 rubles. Since Sukhomlinov's legal income from state emoluments and investments could not explain his wealth, it followed that much of it had to have been illegally obtained. While greedy contractors and industrialists had obviously been among Sukhomlinov's clandestine benefactors, was not the probability high that foreign intelligence services had also been of their number? Would a man corrupt enough to accept bribes from companies and private parties refrain from accepting payments tendered by hostile foreign governments?

1. Indictment, November 1916, RGVIA, f. 962, op. 2, d. 48, ll. 128–132 (quotation from l. 132).
2. Anna Goshkevich deposition, October 18, 1916, RGVIA, f. 962, op. 2, d. 135, ll. 53–54.

The third and last battery of charges related to high treason, and here the government's case was largely circumstantial and inferential, based, as we have already seen, upon the general's suspicious relationships with convicted or indicted spies and traitors. But there was also the testimony of two witnesses who claimed to have solid proof that Sukhomlinov had spied against Russia. One of these men was Aleksandr Mashek, the other a certain "Franz Müller."

An ethnic Czech and Austro-Hungarian subject, Mashek had moved to Kiev in 1901 and had acquired Russian citizenship in 1911. He had spent much of his adult life drifting back and forth between the Austrian and Russian empires. For example, after teaching for a time at the Kuropatkin Forestry School in Ashkabad in Russian Turkmenia, he had gone to Bohemia, before returning in 1908 to Kiev, where he had been briefly employed by the intelligence department of Kiev Military District, presumably because of his facility with languages. When the war came, he served as a translator for the counterintelligence staff of the Ninth Army but soon applied for active military duty and was enrolled in the volunteer Czecho-Slovak rifle regiment that had been established under Russian auspices.

In February 1916, however, the counterintelligence staff of the Third Army, to which the Czecho-Slovak unit was attached, received information from soldiers in the regiment that Mashek was a long-standing Austrian agent and provocateur, who had spied on Czech nationalists in both Austria and Russia for years. In May military police arrested and questioned Mashek. Although there was insufficient hard evidence against him, Third Army staff concluded that he was a suspicious and potentially dangerous character and ordered him administratively exiled to Siberia that May.[3]

That might have been the last anyone ever heard of Mashek had it not been for the Sukhomlinov inquiry. In July 1916 Mashek had filed a report with Siberian military authorities, who dutifully passed it on to Senator Kuz'min, in which he alleged that the real reason for his exile had been to prevent him from testifying about the ex-war minister's treason, a subject about which he had firsthand information. The upshot was his transfer under guard from Siberia to Minsk, where he underwent an exhaustive series of interrogations in September.[4]

Mashek told his inquisitors that he had served as an operative for Kiev military intelligence from 1908 to 1913 under the direct command of its chief, Colonel A. A. Samoilo. According to Mashek, at some point 1908 he had become aware that General V. A. Sukhomlinov, then commander of Kiev Military District, was in actuality an Austrian spy. Unnamed comrades in Russian military intelligence who had penetrated the Austrian war ministry had found the documents that confirmed it and had so informed Mashek. But Mashek himself had had experiences that corroborated the general's treason. Mashek swore that he had twice personally witnessed Sukhomlinov paying surreptitious visits to the Austrian consulate disguised as a hackney cab driver. In mid-December 1908 he had also watched the general calling at the house of one Poliak, a wealthy sausage manufacturer and "renegade Czech." Mashek added

3. Report of May 7, 1916, RGVIA, f. 962, op. 2, d. 49, ll. 20–21.
4. Mashek report of July 7, 1916, RGVIA, f. 962, op. 2, d. 51, ll. 21–22.

218   that approximately one month prior to Austria's annexation of Bosnia-Herzegovina (September 23/October 6, 1908) Sukhomlinov had secretly conferred in Kiev with Austrian officials smuggled in from Przemysl.[5]

Of course, once Sukhomlinov had left Kiev for his new job as chief of the general staff in Petersburg, Mashek had had no further opportunities to observe the general's activities, but he insisted that he had other highly sensitive information about Austro-German espionage in Russia that had never been disclosed before. He knew, for instance, that prior to the war the Germans had set up a special "conspiratorial apartment" in the city of Warsaw, equipped with a private telegraph line that ran direct to the kaiser's office. He also stated that he was in a position to clear up the mystery surrounding the exposure of Russia's most valuable intelligence source in Austria, Colonel Alfred Redl. In 1913 the head of the Kiev Okhrana had sold Redl out to the Austrian police, and Mashek had unfortunately been unable to warn Redl in time. It was at that point that Mashek had resigned from the Russian secret service, frightened lest he himself become the next victim of the powerful traitors in Kiev. Mashek added that his wartime assignments had kept him abreast of many additional intelligence operations of the Central Powers; the staff of the Russian Third Army contained at least twenty-eight Austrian spies, or so he asserted.[6]

If Mashek claimed to be a dedicated Russian intelligence officer who had been unjustly exiled as part of a plot to suppress the truth, "Franz Müller" was a different sort of witness entirely and had a different tale to tell. In September 1915 two Austrian spies named Poket and Iakubets had been taken in the act of espionage behind Russian lines. The summary trial and hanging of Poket had not unnaturally made a considerable impression on Iakubets, who promised, in exchange for his life, to tell the Russians everything he knew about Austrian intelligence, including the identity of all Austrian agents known to him. One of the people whom he fingered was a certain Hungarian by the name of San-Kiraly, who had been posing as a barber in the town of Tarnopol. Counterintelligence immediately arrested San-Kiraly. When his apartment was searched, a considerable amount of incriminating material was found, including a photograph of San-Kiraly in Austro-Hungarian uniform. Confronted with this evidence, San-Kiraly confessed to espionage. He balked, however, at providing any additional information unless he received a firm assurance that first, he would not be executed and second, he would be given a passage to Brazil, where he claimed to have served as a military instructor prior to the outbreak of the European war. These conditions were soon granted, and San-Kiraly was assigned the cover name "Franz Müller," both to keep Austrian counterintelligence in the dark about who Russia's new source really was and also to shield him from possible Austrian vengeance later.[7]

The information initially provided by "Müller" proved to be quite reliable and allowed the Russians to roll up several local Austrian spy networks, such as the one

5. Mashek interrogation, September 19, 1916, ibid., ll. 22, 47, 56.

6. RGVIA, f. 962, op. 2, d. 51, ll. 45, 62, 208.

7. B. P. Poliakov interrogation, June 24, 1916, RGVIA, f. 962, op. 2, d. 49, ll. 174–176.

operating out of the Jesuit monastery in Tarnopol and the one headed by *prapor-shchik* ("subaltern") Pogoretskii of the staff of the Russian Ninth Army. Müller's helpful tips persuaded many people of his good faith, including Ninth Army head of intelligence Lieutenant Colonel B. P. Petrovich, who concluded that Müller/Kiraly "was actually an officer of the Austrian service, very experienced and clever in matters of espionage."[8]

But as time went by, Müller began to inflate his claims both about his importance and about his knowledge. He was, he insisted, no low-level Austrian operative but rather a first lieutenant of the Austrian General Staff who had been an initiate of the deepest secrets of Austrian intelligence and counterintelligence since 1908. His superiors' confidence in him was so great that he was one of the two officers personally ordered by Conrad von Hötzendorff, Chief of the Austrian General Staff, to arrest Colonel Redl. That confidence was also signaled by his selection as liaison to the German army's secret service. While serving in this capacity, he had attended a meeting in Berlin at which there was a discussion of Germany's top forty-eight agents in Russia. One of these men was General P. K. Rennenkampf, who would later play such an important part in Russia's failed invasion of East Prussia in 1914. Another of them was no less a personage than Minister of War Sukhomlinov himself. San-Kiraly explained that the prudent Germans did not deal with Sukhomlinov directly but rather employed a group of a dozen or so intermediaries to collect the documents he supplied and deliver the payments he demanded in return. San-Kiraly stated that he had been given access to many of these documents, as they were relevant to training he was undergoing for undercover operations in Galicia. In fact, his German hosts had on one occasion allowed him to handle their entire file on General Sukhomlinov, which Kiraly recalled as containing verbatim accounts of conversations between the war minister and Nicholas II.[9]

What is one to make of the evidence provided by Mashek and Müller/San-Kiraly? Senator Kuz'min, of course, took Mashek's allegations seriously enough to order that Sukhomlinov be closely interrogated about his relationship (if any) with Colonel Alfred Redl. With regard to San-Kiraly, the senator took the trouble to travel to Berdichev in the summer of 1916 to speak to him in person. Yet it is clear that Kuz'min both wanted and needed to believe that Mashek and San-Kiraly were telling the truth. A less partisan and more dispassionate evaluator, however, would have quickly recognized that neither of the two was particularly credible.

This was glaringly obvious in the case of Mashek, whose story was an amalgam of transparent lies and lunatic fantasies. The idea that the governor-general and military district commander could skulk around the nighttime streets of Kiev in the garb of a cabdriver without anyone's noticing it but Mashek simply boggles the mind, as does his weird canard about the Warsaw apartment with its direct line to Berlin. Moreover, there were many, more mundane details purveyed by Mashek that utterly failed to check out. For instance, Sukhomlinov could not have met with a recreant Czech

8. Ibid., l. 177.
9. Müller interrogations, February 2, June 11, June 16, 1916, ibid., ll. 89–94, 130–133, 136–137.

220   sausage maker in mid-December 1915, since he had already relocated to Petersburg at that time. Still further, the record decisively refuted Mashek's assertions about his service for Kiev Military District intelligence, for he had been fired after a couple of assignments in 1908, not kept on the payroll until 1913. Far from deeming him a faithful and useful employee, Colonel Samoilo of Kiev intelligence maintained instead that he was "undeserving of confidence," possibly even mentally abnormal.[10]

It is easy to see what was going on here. The Hapsburg Empire had long been sensitive about the loyalty of its ethnic minorities, particularly its large populations of Slavs, from whom it suspected that Russia would try to recruit spies. This anxiety was by no means groundless, for during the war Russia did make use of considerable numbers of Vienna's Slavic subjects for espionage purposes, including Professor Tomas Masaryk, the future president of independent Czechoslovakia.[11] It was only natural that the Austrians would seek to take countermeasures by dispatching their own agents to penetrate Czech nationalist circles abroad and keep an eye on Czech émigré communities generally. Mashek evidently belonged to their number, just as his comrades in the Czecho-Slovak Regiment had said. In making his preposterously false denunciations, Mashek was trying to wheedle his way out of his Siberian exile, while simultaneously revenging himself on the staff of the Third Army, which had ordered his banishment in the first place.

While superficially more plausible that the allegations of Mashek, San-Kiraly's statements were also replete with flagrant lies. For one thing, San-Kiraly could not possibly have been involved in the apprehension of Alfred Redl, for no one resembling him in either name or description belonged to the party of five men whose confrontation with Redl at the Hotel Klomser in May 1913 had precipitated the colonel's suicide.[12] For another, the transcripts of San-Kiraly's various interrogations contained repeated mistakes in dates, facts, and names, such as his erroneous references to Alexander Bauermeister as Baumeister or Burmeister.[13] Still further, although he may have convinced Colonel Poliakov that he was who he said he was, Staff-Captain Reek, his first interrogator, observed that his written German was only semiliterate, a fact that wholly deflated San-Kiraly's pretense of being an officer in the Austrian army, let alone an officer of the general staff.[14] This, of course, meant that he could never have served as a liaison to German intelligence, could never have attended the Berlin meeting on the subject of Russian espionage, and could never have handled a "Sukhomlinov dossier." The motive for all these prevarications was readily comprehensible: San-Kiraly feared that the Russians would hang him, as they usually did

---

10. Letter from intelligence division, West front, October 20, 1916, RGVIA, f. 962, op. 2, d. 51, l. 206.

11. On Masaryk see secret telegram from envoy in Bern, March 21 (April 4), 1915, AVPR, f. 134, op. 473, d. 57:49, l. 7.

12. These men were Major General Höfer, Colonel Urbanski, Colonel Ronge, Lieutenant Colonel Kunz, and Dr. Vorlicek. See Georg Markus, *Der Fall Redl. Mit Unveröffichten Geheimedokumenten zur Folgenschwersten Spionage-Affair des Jahrhunderts* (Vienna, 1984), p. 227.

13. Müller interrogations, February 2, June 15, 1916, RGVIA, f. 962, op. 2, d. 49, ll. 89, 131.

14. N. A. Reek testimony, August 28, 1916, RGVIA, f. 962, op. 2, d. 134, l. 137.

with the spies they arrested behind their lines. In his very first interview with Captain Reek, he made no secret of his belief that he would remain alive only as long as his captors found his information of interest.[15] He consequently had every incentive to represent himself as an intelligence mastermind, rather than the petty infiltrator he undoubtedly was. He also had to talk to his questioners and keep talking to them, telling them everything he actually knew, and diverting them with fables after his knowledge was exhausted. It was the only thing that stood between him and the gallows, or so he thought.

The testimony of Mashek and San Kiraly, purportedly impregnable substantiation of Sukhomlinov's espionage and treason, was consequently nothing of the kind. Internal inconsistencies and egregious lies besmirched their testimony and impeached virtually all that they had said. The government's case against the general for treason actually rested on a foundation not of rock but air. Yet this did not really matter, for as Miliukov had observed approvingly in his November 1, 1916, speech, Sukhomlinov had already been convicted by "the instinctive voice of the entire country and its subjective confidence."[16]

Sukhomlinov Defends Himself

Even though the prospects for a fair trial may have been quite dim, Sukhomlinov was determined to rebut the charges that had been leveled against him to the best of his ability. A whole series of depositions he made, first from his jail cell and then from his home in the spring and summer of 1916 and the winter of 1916–17, provide a comprehensive picture of the shape his defense would take.

With regard to his performance in preparing the Russian army for war and responding to the munitions crisis once the war had begun, the general noted that while it was quite true that he had not foreseen that the European war would be protracted, neither had anyone else in the Russian military hierarchy.[17] He might have added that almost no one in any of the belligerent armies had correctly anticipated the actual character of the conflict. Moreover, if the coming of the war had caught Russia with insufficient stocks of artillery and shells, it was necessary to emphasize that he, Sukhomlinov, did not bear the exclusive responsibility for this situation. The structure of Russia's military system conferred great power over the artillery department on its chief inspector, Grand Duke Sergei Mikhailovich, who frequently exercised that power to block the reforming initiatives of the regular organs of the war ministry. Sukhomlinov had for years complained of his frustration with the grand duke, but the latter was a member of the imperial family and in reality the war minis-

15. Ibid., l. 136.

16. Quoted in M. V. Rodzianko, *Krushenie imperii. Gosudarstvennaia duma i fevral'skaia 1917 goda revoliutsiia* (Valley College, N.Y., 1986), p. 357.

17. Sukhomlinov interrogation, March 28, 1917, RGVIA, f. 962, op. 2, d. 55, l. 358.

ter had little authority over him.[18] As for the wartime shortages of armaments, Sukhomlinov argued that his efforts to respond promptly to them had been undercut at Stavka, which, under the command of his personal enemy Nikolai Nikolaevich, had kept him in the dark about the authentic conditions at the front. When Sukhomlinov accompanied the emperor on visits to Stavka, for example, Nikolai Nikolaevich had refused him the right to be present for oral reports. The outcome was that after a few such episodes, Nicholas II discouraged his war minister from traveling to general headquarters at all.[19]

While Sukhomlinov's criticism of Stavka for withholding information did not hold water (after all, Nikolai Nikolaevich's chief of staff, Ianushkevich, corresponded with the war minister almost daily), his other arguments had considerable merit. First, it was obvious to any fair-minded observer that Sukhomlinov could not be faulted for not predicting a long war. The problem was that by this point there were few fair-minded observers left. When Sukhomlinov's predecessor as war minister, A. F. Rediger (inter alia no friend of his), protested the injustice of condemning Sukhomlinov for not acting to avert the shell crisis before he knew there was going to be one, this eminently sensible opinion evoked howls of derision from the members of the Petrov Commission.[20] Second, Sukhomlinov's criticisms of Sergei Mikhailovich and the Main Artillery Administration (GAU) were essentially justified. There had been something akin to a cold war between the war ministry and GAU prior to 1914, a fact that Sergei Mikhailovich admitted himself. But the record does not support his additional comment—that it had been Sukhomlinov who had impeded his constructive efforts rather than the opposite. Reasoning by analogy to the Russo-Japanese war, GAU had concluded that it was implausible that the typical Russian artillery piece would be fired more than five hundred times during the next conflict. For this reason a stockpile of 1,000 shells per artillery tube would be more than ample. This complacent forecast had been challenged by Sukhomlinov and his general staff, which had eventually succeeded in raising the ceiling to 1,500 shells per tube. The reason that the actual figure stood at only 850 rounds per gun in August 1914 is that the money to buy the additional munitions had only been appropriated the previous year, which meant that many of the necessary contracts had not even yet been awarded, let alone fulfilled.[21] To be sure, if Sukhomlinov had been doing his job properly, he *would* have been more energetic in dealing with the problems of guns,

18. Sukhomlinov had accurately represented the character of his references to Sergei Mikhailovich in his letters. See, for example, "Perepiska V. A. Sukhomlinova s N. N. Ianushkevichem," *Krasnyi arkhiv* 3(1923): 34. In his published memoirs he expanded on his criticisms of Sergei Mikhailovich. See V. A. Sukhomlinov, *Vospominaniia Sukhomlinova* (Moscow/Leningrad, 1926), p. 213.

19. *Vospominaniia Sukhomlinova*, pp. 242, 250.

20. Rediger memoir, RGVIA, f. 280, op. 1, d. 8, ll. 54–55, 57.

21. [A. S. Lukomskii], *Vospominaniia generala A. S. Lukomskago*, vol. 1 (Berlin, 1922), pp. 35–37. Lukomskii's views on this subject are uncommonly reliable. A brilliant military administrator, he served from 1910 to 1914 in the mobilization section of the general staff, before becoming head of the Chancellery of the War Ministry, a position he held from 1914 to the summer of 1915. From the summer of 1915 until April of 1916 he served as A. A. Polivanov's assistant minister.

shells, and rifles that arose by the end of 1914. But it is worth noting that GAU itself 223
was still maintaining, several months into the war, that reports of shell shortages were
gross exaggerations. General A. A. Brusilov, a near genius at tactics and operations
(although not strategy), made the technical insufficiency of the Russian army the central theme in the book he published about his wartime experiences. Yet he was much
harsher on Sergei Mikhailovich and GAU in his account of the origins of the shell crisis than he was on Sukhomlinov, of whose administration he largely approved.[22]

Of course, the charges of corrupt financial dealing were another matter entirely,
and with reference to them Sukhomlinov did not mount a sound defense. It would in
any case have been difficult for him to have done so, since he was guilty on these
counts. To be sure, he insisted that he had never accepted any presents or payments
from any firms or individuals in connection with war department business, but his
disavowal of wrongdoing and his statement that he had made all his money in the
stock market ring as false today as they did at the time. Similarly, his assertion that if
he had been distributing military orders in exchange for bribes his assets would have
run to "several million rubles," not the piddling 400,000 or so that investigators
could prove he still had on hand, also lacked persuasive force.[23] The fact that the au-
ditors who worked for Petrov and Kuz'min could turn up no more than 400,000
rubles did not prove that he possessed no larger sum than this, for he had had many
opportunities to conceal his assets both before and after he fell under suspicion.

Yet the gravest of the charges against Sukhomlinov concerned espionage and high
treason; were he to be convicted of these, he would very likely be sentenced to death.
The former war minister's exculpatory strategy here was three-pronged: first, he
loudly and repeatedly called attention to the essential improbability of many of the
accusations; second, he offered innocent explanations for the words and deeds that
were at the heart of his inquisitors' circumstantial case against him; and finally, he
advanced some strong reasons to explain why he was the target of a frame-up. The
first and third part of his strategy were eminently successful, the second somewhat
less so.

By way of illustration, take Sukhomlinov's response to the charge that he was the
head of a sizable network of spies. If he actually had been a traitor to Russia, why
would he have acted in concert with others? Would it not have been more logical
(and considerably more secure) for him to have operated alone? He noted that if he
had really been selling secrets, he would have approached the embassies of hostile
powers himself and would "never have turned for help to such persons as Lieutenant
Colonel Miasoedov, Colonel Ivanov, and the others named."[24] Moreover, what possible motivation did he have for betraying his fatherland? He was a patriotic Russian
and officer, loyal to his country and his sovereign. Why would he want to see Germany grind Russia into powder? He asserted that the investigators had come up with

22. General A. A. Brussilov, *A Soldier's Note-Book 1914–1918* (London, 1930), pp. 10–12.
23. RGVIA, f. 962, op. 2, d. 55, l. 46.
24. Sukhomlinov interrogation, November 9, 1916, RGVIA, f. 962, op. 2, d. 52, ll. 18–19.

224 no compelling motive for his treason other than money, and that if he had been giving up Russia's most sensitive secrets for money, he would clearly have enjoyed a higher standard of living than he actually did. To be sure, Ekaterina Viktorovna had many expenses (although the reports about them had been blown completely out of proportion), but he himself had been on a strict budget. How did the depiction of him as reaping enormous pecuniary awards from his treason square with the testimony provided by many that he was chronically short of cash?[25]

Sukhomlinov was equally contemptuous of the other numerous implausibilities imbedded in the government's reconstruction of the espionage conspiracy. A case in point concerned Alexander Altschüller. Altschüller had of course returned to his native Austria on the eve of the world war for reasons of health, but he had been indicted in absentia as an Austrian intelligence operative. In fact it was central to the prosecutorial argument that Altschüller was the Austrian archspy, the ringleader of all Austria's agents in the Russian Empire, and Sukhomlinov's trusted accomplice in crime. Anna Goshkevich had testified that Sukhomlinov's home office had abutted one of the rooms he used to entertain guests. On one occasion, she claimed to have observed Altschüller enter the office and devote several minutes to the scrutiny of secret documents that were carelessly scattered on top of the minister's desk.[26] As far as Sukhomlinov was concerned, this story made no sense at all. What kind of secret agent would Altschüller have been if he had been in the habit of peeking at war ministry documents in plain view of witnesses? Still further, if he, Sukhomlinov, had been in cahoots with Altschüller, why would the latter have had to rifle through his papers in the first place? While Vladimir Aleksandrovich's counterargument did not, of course, prove that Altschüller was not working for Austrian intelligence, it did effectively demolish Anna's statement: either she had not seen what she asserted she had seen, or if she had, Altschüller was in all probability no spy, which meant that he could not have been collaborating in espionage with Sukhomlinov.[27]

Vladimir Aleksandrovich also was effective in dealing with Mashek's and San-Kiraly's insinuations that he had been somehow involved in the exposure to the Austro-Hungarian authorities of Russia's spy Alfred Redl. Agreeing that Redl had indeed been "an enormous asset in espionage," Sukhomlinov told investigators that Redl had been recruited during the time that he, Sukhomlinov, had been Dragomirov's chief of staff in Kiev Military District (1899–1902). Through him, the Russian military had acquired access to priceless Austro-Hungarian General Staff reports and mobilization schedules. It was also thanks to him that several authentic Austrian spies within Russia had been caught, such as Grimm, the senior staff adjutant in Warsaw Military District. Yet Sukhomlinov asserted that he had had nothing to do with the unmasking of Redl and noted that the testimony of Mashek and

25. Nikolai Goshkevich interrogation, July 25, 1915, RGVIA, f. 962, op. 2, d. 134, l. 34.
26. Anna Goshkevich interrogation, October 18, 1916, RGVIA, f. 962, op. 2, d. 135, l. 56.
27. *Vospominaniia Sukhomlinova*, p. 315. In his memoirs, Sukhomlinov repeats the arguments he made both in depositions and in his subsequent trial with surprising fidelity.

"Müller" (whatever else one thought of it) bore him out on this point. Both Mashek and Müller had sworn that the man who had tipped off the Austrians in 1913 had been living in Kiev at the time. But whether this man was the head of the Kiev Okhrana, as Mashek had sworn, or the anonymous "Russian general" of Müller's version, Sukhomlinov obviously could be neither of those people.[28]

Yet when it came time to chip away at the wall of circumstantial evidence prosecutors had built up around him, Sukhomlinov found the going harder. The general was adamantly determined to present a facade of perfect innocence to his accusers. The problem was that although he was no spy, he was not entirely blameless. It would have been better for him if he had, for example, confessed to acts of common corruption, or if he had explained what his real purposes had been when he had attached Miasoedov to the Ministry of War back in 1911. But because he would not, he inevitably found himself distorting the truth and answering questions either evasively or cryptically.

For example, Senator Kuz'min and his team made much of the fact that in the correspondence among Colonel Ivanov, Nikolai Goshkevich, and Alexander Altschüller, Sukhomlinov had been referred to as "*tysiachnii*" ("thousander"), an appellation Kuz'min's people took to be a conspiratorial code name. When asked about this, Sukhomlinov replied that "tysiachnii" was instead a harmless, affectionate nickname derived from the number of his account (1,000) at the Guards' Economic Society. Unfortunately, this odd assertion was discredited the instant it became known that the general's account actually bore the number 1,007.[29] "Tysiachnii" clearly was a conspiratorial code name, but the goal of the conspiracy had been defrauding the treasury, not betraying the country to Germany.

Similarly, Sukhomlinov's statement that he had barely known Colonel Ivanov was conclusively refuted by the evidence of General Ianushkevich, who testified that after the colonel's arrest Sukhomlinov had defended him and agitated for his release.[30] Ianushkevich's deposition also exploded Sukhomlinov's pretense that he had always taken Altschüller for a Lutheran from birth and had not known that he was a Jew. Everybody around Sukhomlinov knew that Altschüller was Jewish and knew that Sukhomlinov was aware of this, for he often spoke of it.[31] By contrast, Sukhomlinov's explanation of the circumstances under which he had allowed Dumbadze to consult the secret "List of the Most Important Measures Carried Out by the War Ministry from 1909 to March 1914"—that he had handed over that document

---

28. Müller interrogation, June 11, 1916, RGVIA, f. 962, op. 2, d. 49, l. 137; Mashek interrogation, September 12, 1916, ibid., d. 51, l. 45; Reek deposition, August 28, 1916, ibid., d. 134, ll. 137–138. It is unclear to this day whether Redl was exposed as a result of treachery, his own carelessness, or the keen wits of an Austrian postal clerk who is said to have noticed an envelope with a general delivery address that was apparently stuffed with foreign cash and alerted the counterintelligence service.

29. Sukhomlinov interrogation, November 9, 1916, RGVIA, f. 962, op. 2, d. 52, l. 22.

30. Ibid., l. 19; Ianushkevich testimony, September 13, 1916, RGVIA, f. 962, op. 2, d. 134, l. 150.

31. Sukhomlinov interrogation, November 9, 1916, RGVIA, f. 962, op. 2, d. 52, l. 27.

226 only after the outbreak of war had deprived it of any utility to the enemy—was probably technically accurate but nonetheless bespoke a mind-boggling nonchalance about the handling of classified material.

Sukhomlinov's greatest difficulty, however, came in accounting for his association with Lieutenant Colonel Sergei Miasoedov. This was so because the very name "Miasoedov" had by this point become a symbol of depravity and treason for the overwhelming majority of the people of Russia. As Sukhomlinov knew nothing concrete about the circumstances of Miasoedov's arrest or the evidence introduced at his trial, he could not be certain himself that the gendarme had not actually been guilty. In speaking with his interrogators in 1916, then, Sukhomlinov had to proceed on the assumption that Miasoedov had actually been the agent of a hostile power and frame his statements accordingly. Even if Miasoedov had not been a traitor, virtually everybody strongly believed him to have been. Here is where the problem arose, for how would the history of the relationship between Miasoedov and the minister of war read in the newspapers? What inferences was the public liable to draw from Sukhomlinov's fraternization with Russia's most abominated spy?

Vladimir Aleksandrovich's approach to excusing his contacts with Miasoedov in the first instance involved transferring the responsibility for his assistance to the gendarme to others. It was true, of course, that he had hired Miasoedov, but he insisted that he had done so only upon the recommendations of such people as General P. P. Maslov, General S. S. Savich, and Baron Taube—all men with impeccable reputations in the military or police.[32] But Sukhomlinov also took pains to correct the misapprehension that Miasoedov had held an important position at the war ministry. Although the gendarme had keenly desired an intelligence post, Sukhomlinov had not given him one, and Miasoedov had never been entrusted with any secrets. According to Sukhomlinov, the colonel had been nothing more than a low-level general factotum, albeit one with delusions of grandeur.[33] (Unfortunately for the accused minister, Colonels Erandakov and Vasil'ev were still around to contradict him.)

But if Sukhomlinov had hired Miasoedov, he had also fired him. Queried about this, Vladimir Aleksandrovich replied that he had dismissed the gendarme in 1912 not because of the letter about him from the ministry of the interior or the newspaper attacks on him, nor because of any, even inchoate suspicion of him, but rather owing to "the public scandal that Miasoedov had made at the races." Subsequently, Sukhomlinov had ordered Miasoedov investigated (which he acknowledged he had done to quiet the press), but the surveillance had turned up no proof of wrongdoing. Sukhomlinov consequently had no reason to suspect the colonel of espionage. In fact, Miasoedov's most relentless tormentor, A. I. Guchkov, obviously had not thought at the time that the colonel was a traitor either. After all, he had accepted the colonel's challenge to a duel, hadn't he?[34]

32. Sukhomlinov interrogation, July 28, 1916, RGVIA, f. 962, op. 2, d. 134, l. 69; also *Vospominaniia Sukhomlinova*, p. 311.

33. Sukhomlinov testimony, July 29, 1916, RGVIA, f. 962, op. 2, d. 134, l. 83.

34. Sukhomlinov testimony, July 28, July 29, August 3, 1916, ibid., ll. 70, 81, 92.

Of course, the events of the spring of 1912 had caused a rupture between Sukhomlinov and Miasoedov. After that time, the two men had scarcely ever seen each other. The general's interrogators seemed to be puzzled by this. If that was the case, why then had the general written the letter of July 29, 1914—the document that Miasoedov had used to worm his way into the intelligence department of the Tenth Army? Sukhomlinov's response to this was to emphasize that the letter had also been misinterpreted. In the first place the letter had not been official. But second, it had not been an enthusiastic recommendation of the gendarme, merely a statement that he, Sukhomlinov, had no objection to the colonel's return to active duty, adding disingenuously that this was the sort of innocuous favor that one acquaintance might be expected to do for another.[35]

The weakness of the general's reconstruction of his ties to Miasoedov was not so much that it played fast and loose with the facts (although it certainly did) but that it amounted to a confession of incompetence if not insanity on Sukhomlinov's part. To swallow Sukhomlinov's story one had to believe that despite many warnings from many quarters, the minister had decided to bring Miasoedov to the war ministry anyway and that he had thereafter failed to notice the espionage that went on for months under his very nose. At best this meant that he had to have been either criminally negligent in the stewardship of his ministry or non compos mentis at the time. There was, of course, a third possibility, for why would a man admit to professional ineptitude or imbecility on this scale if he did not have something to hide?

After Sukhomlinov had read some of the materials pertaining to the Miasoedov case, including a transcript of the court's verdict (to which he was granted access after the February 1917 Revolution) he changed tack. He began to maintain that although Miasoedov had been justifiably executed, his crime had been the theft he had confessed to, not espionage. He noted that, due to insufficient evidence, the court had acquitted the colonel of providing the Germans with information prior to the winter battle of Masuria. But he also noted that although the court *had* convicted Miasoedov of committing espionage in 1907 and from 1911 to 1912, the evidence for these offenses was not only insufficient but also nonexistent. The conclusion he arrived at was that the treason charges had been a smoke screen sent up to conceal the mistakes of army high command. "It is a psychological feature of this war," he told Senator Kuz'min "that all failures are before anything else ascribed to treason. . . . If a dubious operation miscarries, it is due to treason, because the enemy was informed." He illustrated this proposition by referring to the letters Ianushkevich had sent him from Stavka, such as the one in which the latter had written that the collapse of the Carpathian offensive in 1915 had caused him to worry that the Southwest front had "its own Miasoedov."[36] In view of the army's propensity to hide behind scapegoats, Sukhomlinov came around to the belief that not only Miasoedov but most probably *all* of the members of the so-called espionage ring—the Goshkevichs, Altschüller, Ivanov, Dumb-

35. Kuz'min finding, February 7, 1916, ibid, l. 93; RGVIA, f. 962, op. 2, d. 52, l. 2.

36. Sukhomlinov testimony, March 28, 1917, RGVIA, f. 962, op. 2, d. 55, ll. 358–360.

228 adze, Veller, Freinat, and the others—had been innocent of spying. Vladimir Aleksandrovich had discovered that the most logical and honorable way he could defend himself from the accusation of treason was to defend the integrity of everyone that had been named or charged as members of Miasoedov's "conspiracy." And he would courageously attempt to do exactly this when he was placed on trial himself.

"Treason" and the February Revolution

In February 1917 (O.S.) a few days of revolution sufficed to sweep away the Russian autocracy, as well as the dynasty that had ruled Russia for over three hundred years. Yet although the revolution itself can be compared to a brief and violent explosion, it was an explosion that had been primed by an entire series of dangerous economic and social developments, themselves the spawn of the war.

In the first place there was the question of the money supply. When the war began, the Russian Empire had in short order been deprived of two of its principal sources of revenue. The closure of the Black Sea and Baltic to commercial shipping had meant an end to duties on imports and exports, while the emperor's imposition of prohibition had shut down the lucrative state alcohol monopoly, which prior to the war produced approximately a quarter of the state's income.[37] At the same time the war naturally resulted in a substantial rise in state outlays. At the beginning of 1917 Finance Minister Bark reported to Nicholas II that state expenses directly related to the war amounted to over 25 billion rubles.[38] How was the Russian State to cope with this financial crisis? It could, of course, have recourse to foreign loans, but the slightly less than 6 billion rubles that Petrograd was able to raise abroad during the war was a mere palliative rather than a cure for Russia's fiscal woes.[39] Domestic loans and treasury bills supplied an additional 10.4 billion, but there was still a significant shortfall, which could not be covered from regular tax receipts.[40] The upshot was the government's decision to defray part of the cost of the war by printing money: whereas in July 1914 there had been 1.6 billion paper rubles in circulation, by January 1916 that figure had risen to 5.5 billion and by January 1917 to over 9 billion.[41] The inevitable consequence of this was a staggering increase in inflation. It has been estimated that if the urban consumer price index for 1913 is taken as 100, on the eve of the February Revolution it stood at 259.[42] Owing to the increased demand for workers, as well as labor militancy, industrial wages did rise but always lagged behind the ascent of prices, which led to a pronounced decay in living standards within Russia's cities.

37. Alexander M. Michelson, Paul N. Apostol, and Michael W. Bernatzky, *Russian Public Finance During the War* (New Haven, 1928), pp. 39–40. The average payout of the alcohol monopoly from 1909 to 1914 had been 500 million rubles a year, while the average size of the state budget had been 2 billion rubles.

38. M. Frenkin, *Russkaia armiia i revoliutsiia 1917–1918* (Munich, 1978), p. 12.

39. T. M. Kitanina, *Voina, khleb i revoliutsiia (prodovol'stvennyi vopros v Rossii 1914–oktiabr' 1917 g.)* (Leningrad, 1985), p. 18.

40. Calculated on the basis of Michelson, *Russian Public Finance*, pp. 323–326.

41. Ibid., p. 379

42. Ibid., p. 259.

Compounding the problem was the upsurge in the urban population, which grew from 22 to 28 million people during the war as peasants streamed from country to town to take advantage of job opportunities in the empire's expanding war industries. Most of these new arrivals were packed into unsanitary dormitories in already overcrowded slums, placing an ever-increasing strain on dwindling stocks of food, fuel, and medicine.

Conditions were better in the countryside, where peasants could grow food for themselves. In fact, the war brought a measure of prosperity to many of Russia's villages. The amount of money peasants held in Russia's rural savings banks—480 million rubles in 1913—had jumped to 638 million in 1915.[43] There were a variety of reasons for this, including the pensions the state paid out to the relatives of soldiers on active duty, as well as prohibition, which reduced the typical peasant's alcohol consumption, thus leaving him with more money in his pocket. But perversely, another result of the war was a decline in rural Russia's output of foodstuffs. The amount of land sown with edible crops decreased over 16 percent from 1914 to 1916. A number of factors were also at work here. The army's massive conscription of men and horses from the villages obviously bore fruit in a fall in labor power, which consequently made it harder to till the land. But shortages in consumer goods also played a part in the food problem. Since much of Russian industry had converted to war-related work, there were fewer plants producing the articles that rural folk wanted. The output of scythes, for example, was 8,200 in 1916—only 17 percent of what it had been before the war. Finding that they had little or nothing to buy, many peasants grew disinclined to work hard to keep up their grain yields, and some evidently withdrew from the market entirely. The gross grain harvest of 1916–17 came to slightly more than 71 million tons, almost a quarter lower than the prewar figure.[44]

What transformed the food supply problem into a crisis was the collapse of Russia's transportation network, particularly its railways. The railroads literally deteriorated under the stress of war, since Russia lacked enough plants or workshops capable of manufacturing or producing rails, signaling equipment, and rolling stock. The number of locomotive engines in service in January 1917 was half that of July 1914. This meant that it was harder and harder to convey supplies of food and fuel to the hungry and cold. Not even the army was immune. By the end of 1916 the frontline army had no more than a ten-day supply of food on hand, and General Brusilov was telegraphing the Ministry of Agriculture that "in the very near future the literal starvation of the army will begin."[45] On the very eve of the revolution, Alekseev would be reporting to the emperor that the unreliability of rail transport meant that the only long-term solution to the army's provisioning difficulties would be for Russia's soldiers to establish farms in the immediate rear areas and grow their own victuals (an expedient that the Red Army actually turned to during the Civil War).[46]

43. John L. H. Keep, *The Russian Revolution: A Study in Mass Mobilization* (New York, 1976), p. 31.
44. Ibid., pp. 29–34.
45. Kitanina, *Voina, khleb i revoliutsiia*, pp. 217–218.
46. Alekseev to Nicholas II, February 25, 1917, GARF, f. 601, op. 1, d. 674, l. 1.

230　　But it was in Russia's swollen cities, particularly Petrograd, that the food crisis bit the sharpest. It did not help at all that the winter of 1916–17 was unspeakably frigid. There was one snowstorm after another in January 1917. Temperatures plunged to −35°C (−21°F) and stayed there. Under these circumstances, many locomotives could not build up a head of steam adequate for moving any but the most insignificant of loads.[47]

If the immiseration of urban Russia largely accounts for the outbreak of revolution in February 1917, it does not explain that revolution's easy triumph. Tsarism died a rapid death because almost no one was prepared to come to its defense. That, in turn, was the product of the political environment created by thirty months of total war. Nicholas II's pigheaded refusal to countenance reform, the whirligig of incompetent ministerial appointments, and the growing perception that the fate of the empire lay in the unwashed hands of the licentious and dissolute Rasputin had combined to strip the monarchy of mystery, as well as dignity and respect. Indeed, by the end of 1916 it was an article of faith among members of the extreme right that only the physical removal of the Siberian *starets* could arrest the empire's precipitous descent into revolution. It was with this goal in mind that a small group of conspirators, including the wealthy degenerate Prince Feliks Iusupov, archreactionary V. M. Purishkevich, and Grand Duke Dmitrii Pavlovich, the tsar's own cousin, came together to plot against Rasputin's life. Iusupov cultivated the friendship of the *starets* and induced him to pay a visit to his palace, where, after Herculean efforts on the part of the assassins, he was finally killed in the early morning of December 17, 1916.[48] Although loudly applauded throughout Russia, the murder of Rasputin was no anodyne to the political decomposition, which ironically enough it may have helped to accelerate. Nicholas II ordered the arrest of all of those involved in the murder, including his cousin Dmitrii. The effect of this was to suggest to the country at large that the influence of Rasputin had been more extensive and more pernicious than hitherto suspected; why else would a member of the imperial family sully himself with the blood of a peasant?[49]

Thus it was that the circumstances of Rasputin's death reinforced the idea that the court was awash in filth and treason. The scarlet thread of treason spooled out from Lieutenant Colonel Miasoedov to his protector General Sukhomlinov to Rasputin, who had in turn secured the general's release from jail, into the very bosom of the tsar's family. For if the emperor himself was not a traitor, the empress probably was, and this amounted to the same thing. As the noted liberal V. D. Nabokov (the novelist's father) observed in a memoir he wrote of the revolution: "Advanced Rus-

47. See General Basil Gourko, *War and Revolution in Russia 1914–1917* (New York, 1919), p. 256.

48. At Iusupov's Rasputin was served sweet cakes and Madeira, both poisoned with potassium cyanide. He was also shot three times and beaten about the temples for approximately ten minutes with a two-pound rubber dumbbell. His body was then cast from a bridge into the Neva River. Apparently, the actual cause of death was drowning: the lungs of the corpse were discovered to be full of water.

49. Andrei Maylunas and Sergei Mironenko, *A Lifelong Passion: Nicholas and Alexandra: Their Own Story* (New York, 1997), pp. 510–511.

sian public opinion, which had long ago lost confidence in Nicholas II gradually came to realize . . . that it was impossible simultaneously to be for the tsar and for Russia, since to be for the tsar meant to be against Russia."[50]

This attitude was not confined to the political elite that Nabokov was describing. Fragmentary evidence exists that the idea that the monarchy was utterly compromised by treason had penetrated the consciousness of the lower classes. Toward the end of 1916, a Kadet working for the zemstvo union in the countryside near Riga wrote a friend with his impressions of local conditions. This letter, which was promptly intercepted by the police, observed that "in the village they no longer believe in the success of the war." Yet the author added that he did meet peasants who were somewhat more optimistic, ones who told him that "we've got to hang Sukhomlinov" and "if we string up 10–15 generals, then we will begin to win."[51] The concept that the army and the entire war effort had been sold out by high-ranking traitors resonated with at least some industrial workers, too, if we are to credit contemporary reports. On February 23, there was a large-scale walkout from the Arsenal munitions factory in Petrograd. When factory managers sought to shame the departing workers into returning to their lathes by yelling, "What are you doing? You are aiding our enemy, the Germans! Traitors to the fatherland!" they were shouted down by cries of "What about Miasoedov? Sukhomlinov? The Empress herself is a German spy!"[52] Now it is possible that this exchange was not so much spontaneous as a reflection of the headway that left-wing political parties had made in disseminating their propaganda, for we know that socialist organizations in Petrograd, including the Bolshevik apparatus, had placed emphasis on espionage at court in the leaflets with which they were blanketing the city at that time.[53] But it really did not make much difference. Once Russians by the hundreds of thousands had come to believe that tsarism incarnated espionage and treason, the monarchy in Russia was no longer defensible.

While the tinder for the revolution in the capital was the dearth of bread, the spark was a sudden uptick in the temperature. Loaves were in short supply not only because stocks of flour were low but also because the fuel was so scarce that many bakeries could not even fire up their ovens. Empty shelves in the bread stores generated both hunger and anger, particularly in the working-class districts of the Vyborg side and Vasilevskii Island. When on February 23 the cold wave broke and the temperature shot up to 8°C (47°F), crowds of people began to swarm into the streets to protest.[54] By the late afternoon possibly as many as a hundred thousand workers had

50. Vladimir Nabokov, *Vremmenoe pravitel'stvo i bol'shevistskii perevorot* (London, 1988), pp. 95–96.

51. "Politicheskoe polozhenie Rossii nakanune Fevral'skoi revoliutsii v zhandarmskom osveshchenii," *Krasnyi arkhiv* 17 (1926): 18.

52. Quoted in Tsuyoshi Hasegawa, *The February Revolution: Petrograd 1917* (Seattle, 1981), p. 220.

53. S. P. Mel'gunov, *Na putiakh k dvortsovomu perevorotu (zagovori pered revoliutsiei 1917 goda)* (Paris, 1931), p. 29.

54. Richard Pipes, *The Russian Revolution* (New York, 1990), p. 274.

232 gone on strike, demanding an immediate increase in the supply of provisions. This strike movement gathered momentum the next day and by the twenty-fifth had engulfed the entire city. Nicholas II's order from Stavka that the disorders be suppressed by armed force if necessary proved to be counterproductive, since the soldiers quartered in Petrograd almost immediately began to defy orders to fire on demonstrators. Indeed, it was the eventual mutiny of virtually all the city garrison's 180,000 troops that caused the revolution to burn to incandescence and ensured its ultimate victory. The reasons behind this military rebellion were numerous and complex, but it is clear that one of the most important was the loss on the part of the soldiers of any reverence for the authority of the tsar—gossip about Rasputin, the "German" empress, and espionage had put paid to that.[55] At the same time the neutrality or defection of the garrison did not mean that the consummation of the revolution was bloodless. Gunshots reverberated everywhere in the ensuing five days of anarchy, as Petrograd witnessed confused battles between mobs and rooftop police snipers, beatings and lynchings of police informants and petty officials, as well as pandemic looting and orgies of vandalism, rape, and drunkenness. At least fifteen hundred people were killed or wounded as a result of the violence, and some estimates range as high as seventy-five hundred.[56] On February 27, a substantial proportion of Duma deputies constituted themselves as a provisional committee for the restoration of order, which in turn announced that a Provisional Government had been selected from its ranks. On the very same day a self-appointed band of representatives from all the active socialist parties of the capital proclaimed the establishment of a worker's soviet, or revolutionary council, and called upon the workers of the city to elect delegates to it.

In the meantime the emperor had finally awoken to the seriousness of the situation, and on the twenty-eighth entrained at the front for Tsarskoe selo, the suburban palace outside Petrograd where his wife and children were residing. When it was discovered that the railway to that destination had been blocked by mutinous troops, the imperial train was diverted to Pskov, the headquarters of the Northwest front, where it arrived on March 1. The front commander, General Ruzskii, quickly broached the issue of political concessions with his sovereign, insisting that these had to be granted if Russia were to have a prayer of continuing to wage war. On the morning of March 2, Chief of Staff Alekseev conducted a telegraph poll from Stavka of Russia's leading generals in the field on the question of abdication and discovered that they were unanimously in its favor. On March 2, the emperor agreed to sign an act of abdication. As is well known, concern for the health of his son Aleksei, a hemophiliac, induced the emperor to edit the document that had been prepared so as to abdicate for both himself and his heir. The crown was to pass to his brother, Mikhail Aleksandrovich. Although motivated by the best of intentions, Nicholas's decision was bla-

55. Alan K. Wildman, *The End of the Russian Imperial Army: The Old Army and the Soldiers' Revolt (March–April 1917)* (Princeton, 1980), p. 156.

56. Orlando Figes, *A People's Tragedy: The Russian Revolution 1891–1924* (New York, 1998), p. 321.

tantly illegal, as he did not have the constitutional power to renounce his son's right to rule. But this decision was also fatal to the survival of the monarchy, for Mikhail refused to assume the throne unless it was granted him by a Constituent Assembly that had yet to be elected. As this was tantamount to abdication on Mikhail's part, tsarism as a political system was now defunct. At 1:00 a.m. on the morning of March 3, 1917, the train of the former emperor pulled out of Pskov station en route for general headquarters at Mogilev. "Everywhere," wrote Nicholas in his diary, "there is treason and cowardice and betrayal."[57]

Sukhomlinov Returns to Prison

The February Revolution had immediate and drastic consequences for Sukhomlinov. On the afternoon of February 27 large crowds of rebellious soldiers and workers had converged on the Tauride Palace, where both the Duma's Provisional Government and the Petrograd Soviet were in session. There they were addressed by Aleksandr Kerenskii, the socialist, radical attorney and Duma deputy, who announced that he had accepted the portfolio of minister of justice in the new government. "Comrades!" shouted Kerenskii, "all the former chairmen of the council of ministers and all the ministers of the old regime are under my authority. They will answer, comrades, for all their crimes against the people in accordance with the law!"[58] The real purpose of Kerenskii's fire-breathing oratory, of course, had been to appease the masses and thus avert the indiscriminate lynching of prominent servants of the tsarist state. The Provisional Government as a whole had already ordered the arrest of such of these men as could be rounded up. While some of them, such as former minister of justice Shcheglovitov, were hunted down by irregular posses of armed men, others, such as Protopopov, voluntarily surrendered to the Duma politicians in the hope of saving their lives. Over the next several days scores of former tsarist notables were escorted to the Tauride Palace, where they were detained in one of its wings, which had been converted into a temporary prison.

On the evening of March 1 a small party of sailors apprehended Sukhomlinov at his apartment on Officers' Street. He was driven away to the Tauride Palace in a truck, with a Browning automatic pistol pressed to his temple. The news that Sukhomlinov was coming had a galvanic effect on the hundreds of troops milling about the palace. When he arrived, he had to walk through a gauntlet of infuriated soldiers, all screaming that he should be turned over to them for execution on the spot. That he was spared this fate was due to the intervention of several members of the Provisional Government, particularly Kerenskii, who declared that the general was under the government's protection, warning the more ardent vigilantes that "if you permit yourselves, out of legitimate hatred for him, to inflict on him the punishment to which he is subject by trial, or exert violence, you will thereby help him avoid

234 the punishment to which he is subject by trial." Nonetheless, aware that the crowd had to be given something, Kerenskii did permit the epaulettes to be cut from the former minister's uniform and service overcoat, the operation on the latter garment being performed by the general himself, with his own penknife.[59]

Half an hour after this act of public humiliation, Sukhomlinov's guards loaded him again onto the truck and took him to the Fortress of Peter and Paul. In short order he found himself confined in the same cell he had occupied prior to his release five months earlier. The prison regime devised by Kerenskii's Ministry of Justice was, however, considerably harsher than anything he had experienced the last time. He was dressed in torn underwear and a threadbare smock—discards from a military hospital. He was permitted only a few brief minutes of solitary outside exercise each day, and he was fed on the coarsest of soldiers' fare: black bread, buckwheat groats, and cabbage soup. As if all of this were not bad enough, the window in the general's cell alternately froze and thawed the entire winter, and the resultant water puddled on the floor and caused mold to creep across the walls. It is scarcely surprising that his health deteriorated.[60] A journalist allowed to tour the facility and peer in at the prisoners held in the Trubetskoi bastion described Sukhomlinov as an emaciated man with a disheveled beard staring vacuously at the judas-hole in the door to his cell, and added that his appearance of overall dejection produced "a painful impression."[61]

Sukhomlinov was not, of course, the only person to endure these torments. On the same night that he had been remanded to prison, the process of transferring other particularly important tsarist officials to the Fortress of Peter and Paul had begun. Every cell in the Fortress was soon occupied and not exclusively by the general's former ministerial colleagues, for unbeknownst to him his wife Ekaterina Viktorovna had also been swept up in the wave of arrests and incarcerated in the Trubetskoi bastion. Anna Vyrubova, the empress's confidante and courier to Rasputin, slept in the adjacent cell. A sympathetic guard alerted Sukhomlinov to the presence of the two women in the prison several days after they had arrived.

Whatever one may think of Ekaterina, she was a person of undeniable bravery and force of character, qualities that particularly manifested themselves during times of adversity. She refused to be defeated by anything, prison included. Realizing how dangerous idleness could be, she developed a comprehensive plan to fill her every waking hour. Whenever books or paper were available, she read and wrote. When they were not, she fashioned sprays of artificial flowers out of sun-dried prison bread, which she colored with dyes made of wallpaper and tea wrappers. She learned how to communicate with other prisoners by tapping on the walls of her cell and taught Vyrubova to do the same. She smuggled messages of encouragement and support to her husband. She petitioned officials for better food, clothing, and medicine for the prison population as a whole, and to some extent succeeded in wearing them down

59. Robert Paul Browder and Alexander F. Kerensky, eds., *The Russian Provisional Government 1917. Documents,* vol. 1 (Stanford, 1961), pp. 48–49.

60. *Vospominaniia Sukhomlinova,* p. 295.

61. Spirin, *Rossiia 1917 god,* p. 83.

through raw persistence. Professor G. E. Rein, also a prisoner at that time, later lauded Ekaterina as "an angel" for these efforts.[62] She also exerted a strange, intimidating moral force that was recognized and respected by the prison's turnkeys and troops alike. As Vyrubova put it, Ekaterina "became universally respected by the soldiers and I am confident that this alone saved us both from far worse indignities than those which we were called upon to bear."[63]

Ironically enough, it was the realization that his wife shared his imprisonment that roused Sukhomlinov from his melancholic stupor. Her energy and indomitable spirit seem to have inspired him to get busy too. He devised a crude drainage system to keep the walls of his cell dry. He laboriously made two miniature packs of cards from scraps of paper, sent one as a gift to Ekaterina, and retained the other for games of patience. He also started to devote some serious thought to the defense he would offer when he was publicly tried for treason. He demanded that judicial authorities allow him to examine the records of the military field court proceedings against Colonels Miasoedov and Ivanov. These were eventually brought to a special room in the Fortress for his use. Although the temperature in this room was less than 32 degrees F., he diligently worked his way through all the documents, taking copious notes.[64]

The Provisional Government and Its Discontents

The dominant figures in the new provisional government were Kerenskii, who, as we have seen, took the post of minister of justice; Miliukov, who became minister of foreign affairs; Guchkov, who fulfilled his lifelong ambition by taking over the war ministry; and Prince G. L'vov, a liberal noblemen from the zemstvo movement who served as premier. These men and their colleagues faced a host of well-nigh insurmountable obstacles in their efforts to wield effective power. Some of these were outside their control; others they themselves made worse.

In part because of its lack of a mandate, the Provisional Government found itself in essence sharing power with the Petrograd Soviet, which from the beginning had made its support for the government conditional upon the satisfaction of its demands. By agreement with the Soviet the Provisional Government pledged itself to grant amnesty to all tsarist political prisoners and to uphold freedom of speech and assembly as well as the workers' freedom to strike. But the Provisional Government also bound itself to abolish the old provincial administration, disband the tsarist police, and guarantee that all military units that had rebelled against the autocracy in February would be kept in Petrograd permanently and spared any transfer to the front. The consequences of these latter measures were disastrous. As the zemstvos and volost' committees proved to be incapable of taking the place of the old system of provinces, the countryside degenerated into anarchy. The dissolution of the police

---

62. V. Shulgin, *Gody-dni-1920* (Moscow, 1991), p. 289.

63. Anna Viroubova [Vyrubova], *Memoirs of the Russian Court* (New York, 1923), p. 191.

64. *Vospominaniia Sukhomlinova*, p. 296.

236 deprived the government of any reliable instrument of state coercion, since the popular militia that replaced it was incompetent, insubordinate, and of fickle loyalty. Moreover, the presence of tens of thousands of riotous soldiers in the capital was a latent threat to stability and order.

There was more. The Soviet did not hesitate to issue proclamations and decrees on its own, regardless of whether they complemented or contradicted the government's programs. One of the most famous examples of this was "order number 1," which the Soviet drafted on the first of March. Addressed to the troops of the Petrograd garrison, but subsequently interpreted as applying to the entire army, the order instructed every military unit to elect soldiers' committees on the soviet model, required the disarming of all officers, and insisted that the government's orders should be obeyed *only* if they were not in conflict with the decisions of the Soviet.[65] It required no imagination to foresee that the result of the order would be the disorganization of the army, the destruction of discipline, and the wasting away of morale. A telling index of military disintegration was the fact that by September of 1917 there were at least one million military deserters wandering throughout Russia, clogging the railroad stations, swelling the urban mobs, and engaging in mendicancy, vagrancy, and crime.[66]

In addition to bearing the burden of uneasy cooperation with the Petrograd Soviet (which by late March had transformed itself into the All-Russian Soviet of Workers' and Soldiers' Deputies and purported to represent the entire country) the Provisional Government had to cope with the social and political forces unleashed by the revolution. For hundreds of years, the peasants of Great Russia had dreamed of the "black repartition"—their appropriation of all the lands belonging to the gentry. Many peasants took the fall of the monarchy as the signal that the time of repartition had arrived. Beginning in the spring and intensifying that summer, peasants throughout the country physically seized gentry, church, and crown lands and incorporated them into their communal holdings. Although the Provisional Government was itself committed to land reform, it argued that the future Constituent Assembly ought to determine its scale and shape, and only after a lengthy process of surveys and censuses at that. The postponement of decisions about land policy stripped the Provisional Government of both backing and credibility in the village, as the government learned when an All-Russian Peasant Congress convened in Petrograd that May. Nor was the government any more successful in stemming the growing militancy of labor. The Soviet granted the factory workers of the empire the eight-hour day, but this measure was not enough to pacify them. Battered by the rampant inflation, workers demanded ever-higher wages. Some spoke of the need for government or perhaps even the workers themselves to take over the factories and industrial plants. The workers' dissatisfaction with the order of things was expressed in strikes,

65. For the text of the order see Browder and Kerensky, *The Russian Provisional Government,* vol. 2, pp. 848–849.
66. Frenkin, *Russkaia armiia,* p. 197.

of which there were over a thousand involving 2.4 million persons during the eight months of the Provisional Government's existence.[67]

Then there was the entire battery of problems that the Provisional Government had inherited from its tsarist predecessor: the revolution did not abate the food, fuel, and transportation crises from which the country was suffering; indeed, in some respects it exacerbated them. The government was not at all successful in solving these problems, and some of the expedients it adopted were utterly counterproductive. The imposition of a total grain monopoly in May, which in theory nationalized the entire harvest, was unenforceable, further alienated the peasantry, and effected no increase in the food supply in urban areas. By August 1917 the bread ration in Moscow had fallen to 220 grams a day.[68]

Finally, the Provisional Government had the war to contend with. In the immediate aftermath of the February Revolution virtually all the political forces in Russia except the Bolsheviks favored the prosecution of the war to a victorious conclusion. Not only did the government think it important for the newly born Russian democracy to continue the struggle against German militarism, but it also was desperately reliant on Allied subventions and loans, in return for which the Allies insisted that Russia undertake an offensive on the Eastern front as early as possible. The Russian military elite also advocated an offensive, mistakenly reasoning that it would be the best medicine for Russia's ailing field forces. Messages from Russia's intelligence bureaus in Scandinavia tended to validate the wisdom of an offensive, too. Russia's intelligence chief in Christiana (Oslo) reported in May that he was convinced that Germany could not survive another winter of war. "Only the total passivity of the Russian front can make it possible for the Germans to conduct defensive war on the Anglo-French and Italian fronts."[69] Of course, given the condition of the Russian army, a general offensive was the last thing it needed. In hindsight it is clear that a strategic defense, which might have bought time for the reinforcement and recuperation of the troops, would have been much the wiser decision. Failing that, Stavka should probably have considered a limited, peripheral operation, such as the plan for an amphibious attack on the upper reaches of the Bosporus.[70] Under the circum-

67. Daniel T. Orlovsky, "Russia in War and Revolution," in *Russia: A History,* ed. Gregory Freeze, p. 244 (Oxford, 1997).

68. Keep, *Russian Revolution,* p. 178.

69. Report of May 12, 1917, AVPRI, f. 134, op. 473, d. 188:182 (1917), l. 145.

70. Captain Bubnov's plan of March 1917 was for an economy-of-force operation in which three highly trained Russian divisions would make a surprise landing within the Bosporus fortified region, supported by the entire Black Sea fleet. Bubnov's concept was by no means outlandish, as often supposed. By the spring of 1916, Turkey had withdrawn many units based in Constantinople to reinforce her armies operating in the Caucasus and Middle East. At the same time an aggressive construction program had by that point significantly altered the naval balance in the Black Sea in Russia's favor. In addition, Russia's Black Sea fleet had built enough transport vessels to move an entire army corps at once and had acquired experience in successful amphibious warfare during its operations against the Turkish port of Trebizond. By the spring of 1917 Turkey was by then so hard-pressed in the other theaters of war that it had but two divisions available for service in the entire Bosporus region. Moreover, Russia had three divisions available near Odessa that had done nothing but prepare for this operation for months. See RGVIA, f. 2003, op. 1, d. 1133,

238   stances, to proceed with a massive land offensive in the summer of 1917 was the greatest command error committed by Russia in the war.

After four postponements, General Brusilov, who had replaced Alekseev as commander in chief, launched the attack on June 18. The main blow was to be delivered
by the four armies of the Southwestern front, which were supposed to break the
enemy's hold on the right bank of the Zlota Lipa and then wheel north to take L'vov.
Despite the fact that the Russian army enjoyed a clear advantage in artillery at the
point of the attack, as well as a three-to-one superiority in manpower over the German, Austrian, and Turkish troops it opposed, the entire operation catastrophically
misfired.[71] Two days after its inception, the Germans counterattacked and broke
through the Russian lines on the right flank of the front. There ensued a disorderly
rout as thousands of Russian soldiers fled the battlefield in panic. Within two weeks
the front had stabilized, but the Russian army had again been expelled from Galicia.
The army took two hundred thousand casualties in this botched offensive, which predictably led to a further degradation of morale.[72] Such were the fruits of order number 1, which had poisoned Russia's hierarchically organized military forces with a
toxic dose of democracy. The Russian High Command itself estimated in August of
1917 that it would require months to restore the army to combat readiness, and even
then only through the restoration of draconian military discipline.[73] This, however,
was not a course for which the provisional government in Petrograd had any stomach. The failure of the offensive resulted in a massive disaffection with the war both at
the front and in the rear, of which Lenin and the Bolsheviks would eventually be the
prime beneficiaries.

The Provisional Government and the Concept of Treason

Lenin once famously observed that the Provisional Government had in short
order transformed Russia from a decrepit despotism into the "freest country in the
world," and implied that it was this that gave him and his party the necessary maneuver room to make Russia's second revolution of 1917.[74] There is a great deal of
truth in this judgment, for the Provisional Government was simultaneously so weak
and so scrupulous (on the whole) about civil rights that it proved both unable and
unwilling to take the steps necessary to defend itself. (The government made an exception for V. A. Sukhomlinov, whose civil rights, as we shall see, it trampled upon.)
After the defeat of the abortive Bolshevik uprising in July 1917, for example, the gov-

---

ll. 358–360; A. Bubnov, *V tsarskoi stavke* (New York, 1955), pp. 215, 279; Stavka to Ministry of Foreign Affairs, February 16, 1915, AVPRI, f. 138, op. 467, d. 472/492, l. 13; Paul Halpern, *A Naval History of World War
I* (Annapolis, 1994), pp. 238–245.

71. Major General Sir Alfred Knox, *With the Russian Army 1914–1917: Being Chiefly Extracts from the
Diary of a Military Attaché*, vol. 2 (London, 1921), p. 641.

72. N. M. Iakupov, *Revoliutsiia i mir (soldatskie massy protiv imperialisticheskoi voiny 1917–mart 1918
gg.)* (Moscow, 1980), p. 91.

73. RGVIA, f. 2003, op. 1, d. 1242, l. 24.

74. Robert V. Daniels, *Red October: The Bolshevik Revolution of 1917* (New York, 1967), p. 4.

ernment did not move immediately to arrest the entire Bolshevik leadership, in large measure because, as a historian has noted, it feared "offending the non-Bolshevik socialists, whose notion of civil liberty included the right to preach armed insurrection, mutiny and desertion in time of war."[75] Of course, toleration of such phenomena was scarcely a cogent strategy for political survival, let alone military victory.

In addition to the standard freedoms of speech, assembly, conscience, and association, the Provisional Government thus guaranteed the population a right to sedition. The Russian people also enjoyed other freedoms de facto, for they were free to loot, free to confiscate real property, free to take part in pogroms, and free to lynch. In addition, it seems as if everyone in the Russia of 1917 had what might be described as a right to paranoia. Liberals and conservatives worried about Russian civil society—perhaps even Russian civilization itself—disintegrating in the acid bath of revolutionary excess. Workers and socialists believed that counterrevolutionaries were squatting in every corner, conspiring to overthrow democracy and restore the monarchy or establish a military dictatorship. And the government and its military intelligence services agonized about the deeds of enemy spies and the cunning homegrown fifth columnists who willingly assisted them. That all these preoccupations and anxieties were *to some extent* anchored in reality, however, ought not to obscure the fact that they were also carried to fantastic, irrational extremes. This was particularly so with regard to the fear of counterrevolution and the fear of espionage.

In part because of their fascination with models and parallels derived from French history, the Russian socialist intellectuals in 1917 were conditioned to anticipate that the most serious threats against the gains of the revolution would come from the right. After all, Bonaparte had destroyed the first French republic, just as his nephew, Napoleon III, had destroyed the second. Seduced by these analogies, Russia's socialists expected that a charismatic figure, most likely a military man, would emerge and unite all the reactionary forces in the country to overthrow the revolution. Now it is true that at the front many generals were in despair about the havoc that the revolution had wreaked upon the armed forces. At a conference held at Stavka on July 16, Russia's most prominent frontline commanders told Kerenskii that unless political agitation among the troops was banned, soldiers' committees abolished, and the military death penalty reinstated in the rear, the army would never regain cohesion.[76] Then, too, there was the notorious Kornilov affair. This was the bid in late August by Brusilov's replacement as commander in chief, General Lazr Kornilov, to march on Petrograd and establish martial law in the inaccurate belief that the Provisional Government was in imminent jeopardy of falling to the Bolsheviks. In an effort to shore up public support, Kerenskii deliberately misrepresented this event as an attempt at a counterrevolutionary coup d'état. Nonetheless, the radical left consistently overestimated the strength of the right in 1917. The right was poorly

75. David Shub, *Lenin: A Biography* (Baltimore, 1966), p. 242.

76. Alan K. Wildman, *The End of the Russian Imperial Army: The Road to Soviet Power and Peace*, vol. 2 (Princeton, 1987), pp. 153–156.

240 organized, had no synoptic political program, and, most important, had little in the way of a mass base. Kornilov's troops had moved on Petrograd to defend the Provisional Government and ceased moving when they learned that that government was not in peril. But the non-Bolshevik socialists, including Kerenskii himself, remained in thrall to the false belief that counterrevolution was growing every stronger and more menacing. They would have done well to have taken the threats that loomed from other quarters more seriously.

If the danger of counterrevolution was exaggerated, so, too, was the danger posed by espionage. We have seen how as early as 1915 Russian military intelligence had fallen into the insidious mental habit of seeing espionage conspiracies everywhere. The February Revolution did not break but rather reinforced this cast of thought. Prominent counterintelligence officers, such as Bonch-Bruevich, had long maintained that a great deal of Russia's suffering was attributable to spies who in turn owed their success to the protection afforded by powerful figures in the tsarist regime. With the demise of tsarism, it followed that now was the perfect moment for CI to root them out to the last man. But this would not be an easy job, for the Germans would surely try to exploit the environment that the revolution had created.

It was indeed the case that Germany saw potential opportunities in the post-February Russian political landscape. In 1917 the stresses of war weighed heavily on every belligerent nation, not least because governments by then understood and acted on the understanding that the war was not merely the clash of armies but a struggle among entire societies. The British naval blockade of Germany was contributing to the Allied war effort not only by interdicting shipments of foreign arms and explosives but also by depriving Germans of foodstuffs and fertilizers, in the hope of shattering their collective will to fight. Similarly, Germany's reintroduction of unrestricted submarine warfare (February 1, 1917) was supposed to starve the British people into submission within six months. The rules of war had changed, and under the new rules it made excellent sense for the Germans to look for weapons to use against Russian, no less than British, society.

Such weapons were at hand because there existed within Russia political factions that advocated a withdrawal from the war. Of these, the most important was the Bolshevik Party. When Lenin returned to Petrograd from Swiss exile in April 1917, he promulgated his notorious "April Theses," which denounced the Provisional Government, demanded the dissolution of the regular army, and called for an immediate end to the war. It was because they were familiar with Lenin's views on the war that the Germans had permitted him to cross German territory on his trip back to Russia in the first place. It was also because they expected the Bolshevik Party to agitate for peace that they additionally supported it with financial subventions. The Provisional Government had very good information about this arrangement, including details from sources inside the German Social Democratic Party. Moreover, the Russian Foreign Ministry expressed a grudging admiration for Germany's cleverness in utilizing the Bolshevik Party to distribute antiwar propaganda and advocated reciprocating the favor by smuggling money to pacifist and defeatist groups within the German

Reich itself.[77] It was on the basis on the Bolshevik Party's collusion with Imperial Germany that the Provisional Government eventually ordered the arrest of some of its leaders as well as restrictions on its activities in the aftermath of the July uprising.[78] However, during the "emergency" of the Kornilov affair, the government rescinded these orders, freed several prominent Bolsheviks, including Trotskii, and distributed more than forty thousand rifles and revolvers to party members and sympathizers. As these weapons were not relinquished after the emergency was over, the Provisional Government had made the mistake of topping up the arsenal of the sole political body in Russia that had sworn to overthrow it by force.

If the Provisional Government made a total hash of dealing with the connection between the Bolsheviks and the Germans, the most serious and unambiguous instance of German subversion that occurred on its watch, it also utterly misman-aged military counterintelligence. One consequence of the revolution had been a massive disruption of the CI apparatus. In Petrograd, for example, rioting mobs put the offices of district counterintelligence (along with their archives) to the torch. Si-multaneously, a general amnesty resulted in the release of a good number of people who had been imprisoned or exiled on the orders of imperial CI. In April the Provi-sional Government reorganized army counterintelligence and expelled from its ranks all officers with any prior service in the gendarmes or Okhrana. In the same month, several of the most prominent figures in the old regime's counterintelligence service, including General Batiushin and several members of his commission, were them-selves arrested on charges of corruption and abuse of authority.[79] In short order the government established a special commission to investigate malfeasance in military CI.[80] Yet if these developments disorganized counterintelligence and deprived it of its most experienced officers and agents, they made no change at all in its institutional culture. In the months after February, the counterintelligence service grew more and more prone to ascribe any untoward incident, even the most minor, to enemy ac-tion.[81] German and Austrian spies were assumed to be behind everything from a

---

77. AVPRI, f. 134, op. 473, d. 188:182 (1917), ll. 161, 189, 193–194, 197.

78. The fact that the Bolsheviks accepted some financing from Berlin did not, however, make them "German agents," as some of their enemies charged. Rather, at this point they had one goal in common with the Germans: Russia's withdrawal from the war. Yet the Bolsheviks were extraordinarily sensitive about accusations that they had received German support and consistently denied them. Interesting in this regard is the memoir of the important Petrograd Bolshevik A. Shliapnikov, *Kanun semnadtsatogo goda*, pt. 2 (Moscow, 1920). Here (pp. 77–78) Shliapnikov asserts that although German and Austrian agents sought to infiltrate and "help" the Bolsheviks from the very beginning of the war, these offers were always re-buffed.

79. Vasil'ev and Zdanovich, "General N. S. Batiushin," biographical appendix in *Tainaia voennia razvedka i bor'ba s nei*, by General'nogo Shtaba Gen.-Maior Batiushin, p. 254 (Moscow, 2002). Batiushin, who remained imprisoned until the October Revolution, clearly had been guilty of abuse of power, al-though not of financial misdealings. However, there was conclusive evidence of extortion against certain members of his commission, particularly A. S. Manasevich-Manuilov.

80. A. A. Zdanovich, "Kak 'rekonstruirovali' kontrrazvedky v 1917 god," *Voenno-istoricheskii zhurnal*, no. 3 (1998): 54–55.

81. Ibid., pp. 53–54; Mikhail Alekseev, *Voennaia razvedka Rossii. Pervaia mirovaia voina*, bk. 3, pt. 2 (Moscow, 2001), pp. 198–200.

242 stockyard fire to a missing railway spike to a shoddily manufactured pair of boots. Russia's CI agents in the field were encouraged to think in these terms, with the result that the reports they submitted routinely blamed the enemy for what were obviously simple accidents.[82] In August the counterintelligence section of the general staff would cable the military districts that it was impermissible for their CI organs to limit themselves to the protection of military secrecy. This was because Russia's foes "persistently work not only in the area of military espionage in its purest form, but also are trying by all means possible to destroy Russia's military power, for example by spying on trade and commerce, by smuggling in contraband as well as pacifist, nationalist, political and all other forms of propaganda, by arson, and by bombing factories and other structures." It was consequently the duty of counterintelligence to detect and foil enemy initiatives in every one of these areas.[83] This was a breathtakingly ambitious agenda that reflected CI's underlying hallucination that the enemy espionage and subversive activity had attained such monstrous proportions that CI had the obligation to insinuate itself into every nook and cranny of the country's national life in order to stamp them out. In the last months of the tenure of the Provisional Government, military counterintelligence appears to have wanted to become something approximating the Soviet NKVD (the Stalinist secret police) and lamented its inability to effect the metamorphosis.

It did not do the Provisional Government any good that the urban newspapers were chock-full of squibs and stories about espionage. In part, this was due to the total press freedom introduced by the revolution, which meant that anything, regardless of how improbable or false, could find its way into print. But it also resulted from a decision, which seems to have been taken by War Minister Guchkov himself, to give greater publicity to the government's triumphs in the war against enemy spies.[84] Presumably his motivation was to impress the reading public with the vigilance and energy the new government was bringing to the task of spy catching, but if so his initiative seriously backfired. So much sensational material appeared in the press that the public could be excused for concluding that espionage and treason were flourishing under the Provisional Government to an even greater degree than under the tsar. This perception eroded one of the last remaining validations of the Provisional Government's right to rule.[85]

The Provisional Government and the Sukhomlinov Trial

As 1917 progressed, the debility of central authority, the raging inflation, food crisis, strike movement, land confiscations, and a sense of the futility of the war all

---

82. For examples, see Orlov report, April 3, 1917, RGVIA, f. 2003, op. 2, d. 797, ll. 137 ff.

83. War ministry circular to military districts, August 12, 1917, RGVIA, f. 2000, op. 1, d. 8319, l. 79.

84. For just one example of the sort of material Guchkov began to release see "Arest germanskago shpiona," *Novoe vremiia*, March 9 (13), 1917, p. 3.

85. In August, General Kornilov himself had apparently come to believe that enemy agents had bored their way into the Provisional Government. See Pipes, *Russian Revolution*, p. 464.

tended to further radicalize the population of Russia in village and town alike. This seemingly irreversible shift to the left in political attitude found belated reflection in changes in the composition of the Provisional Government. By early May both Guchkov and Miliukov had been forced from power, in large measure because of their support for "annexationist" war objectives (including Russia's acquisition of Constantinople and the Bosporus and Dardanelles). Such a traditionally tsarist foreign policy agenda had by that point become unpalatable to the urban masses. A coalition government was established by negotiation with the Soviet, and Kerenskii, the sole socialist in the original cabinet, acquired the portfolio of minister of war as well as five ministerial colleagues drawn from the Menshevik and Socialist Revolutionary Parties. In early July the Bolshevik insurrection provoked another shakeup as the Kadets withdrew their support from the government, leaving the majority of the ministries in the hands of socialists of one stripe or another. While retaining his post at the war ministry, Kerenskii simultaneously assumed the premiership. This arrangement endured for less than twenty days: on July 22, Kerenskii announced the formation of a yet another coalition government entirely selected by him, which as an effort at political reconciliation brought some Kadets back into office. Kerenskii also declared that his new government would take a new tack in dealing with Russia's manifold problems, stating, "The national work of the salvation of the country ... must proceed under conditions and in forms dictated by the severe necessity of continuing the war, supporting the fighting capacity of the army and restoring the economic power of the nation."[86] This bloated rhetoric, which was typical of Kerenskii's oratory throughout 1917, did, however, have a subtext of real meaning, for the premier was promising that the government would henceforth do everything in its power to crack down on anarchy and indiscipline. As it transpired, that power proved to be small.

Nonetheless, it was this fourth cabinet of the Provisional Government that resolved in August 1917 to proceed with the public trial of Vladimir Aleksandrovich Sukhomlinov and his wife, Ekaterina Viktorovna. These judicial proceedings were for all intents and purposes the first important show trial held in twentieth-century Russia. Several considerations apparently shaped Kerenskii's decision to stage it at that time and with the maximum possible publicity. First, Sukhomlinov was such an unpopular figure that his conviction would be almost a foregone conclusion. He would therefore serve as a convenient stand-in for the tsarist system: when Sukhomlinov was found guilty, tsarism would be also. This would demonstrate to the country that the revolution's triumph was complete and that there was no possibility of a return to the monarchical past. Second, the trial would also substantiate the notion that the Provisional Government was a government of laws that respected the rights of the accused and afforded them due process, in bold contrast to the administrative arbitrariness (*proizvol*) and secrecy that had so often characterized the handling of polit-

---

86. Quoted in Richard Abraham, *Alexander Kerensky: The First Love of the Revolution* (New York, 1987), p. 239.

244 ical offenses under the ancien régime. Third, and finally, Kerenskii clearly anticipated that this piece of judicial theater would raise his standing as well as that of his government with the people of Russia. Unlike the traitorous monarchists and equally traitorous Bolsheviks, the Provisional Government and its supporters were true patriots devoted to the regeneration of the nation. In particular, the gray-coated soldiers at the front would be impressed with the government's fearless exposure of evildoing in the war department, as well as the government's sincere commitment to the welfare of the army and to victory in the war. This at least was what Kerenskii hoped.

Convinced that the trial would attract a throng of spectators too large for an ordinary courtroom, the government elected to hold the proceedings in the enormous concert hall of the Petrograd Army and Navy Club, an impressive late-nineteenth-century edifice on the corner of Liteinyi Prospect and the Kirochnaia. On the morning of August 10 (23), 1917, the trial convened for its first session.

At 11:45 the Sukhomlinovs were led into the hall and seated in armchairs that had been placed behind the long table provided for their defense attorneys. Vladimir Aleksandrovich was dressed in a general's tunic to which he had proudly pinned his St. George's Cross, the decoration he had won for valor against the Turks almost forty years previously, while his wife wore a simple black dress and hat. The pair seemed subdued but composed and were observed talking to each other from time to time. Five minutes later the judges trooped in and the proceedings began.

The form of the trial was somewhat peculiar, even awkward, for the case was to be tried by a jury in front of appellate judges. All the judges—Iurshevskii, Liadov, Chebyshev, Menshutkin, with N. N. Tagantsev presiding—were senators and jurists from the senate's criminal cassation department. But they were most familiar hearing cases in camera, for the criminal cassation department was exclusively a court of procedural appeals in which juries never took part. Prosecutors V. N. Nosovich, M. E. Feodos'ev, and later D. D. Danchich represented the state, while Sukhomlinov was defended by two lawyers named Zakhar'in and Tarkhovskii, and Ekaterina Viktorovna by M. G. Kazarinov. The government's witness list consisted of 130 persons, of whom only 69 were present. The Sukhomlinovs were even less fortunate. Less than half of the 67 witnesses their attorneys had subpoenaed had turned up in court.[87]

It was this circumstance that occasioned the first challenge to the legitimacy of the trial by the defense. Arguing that the absent witnesses had testimony of extraordinary importance to their clients, the Sukhomlinovs' lawyers filed a motion for the dismissal of charges, a motion on which the court declined to rule. Kazarinov then immediately issued his second challenge, for he insisted that the court as constituted was an improvised body that, under a law that the Provisional Government had enacted itself, had no right to try the accused. He reminded the court that this law had mandated that former ministers and other prominent persons from the tsarist regime were to be tried by a court drawn from the first department of the senate, as well as from the department of cassation. Kazarinov observed that he was not merely

---

87. "Sud nad Sukhomlinovym," *Novoe vremia*, August 11 (24), 1917, p. 3

raising a technical quibble here, for the material collected in the investigation of the Sukhomlinov case had been turned over to the Provisional Government—a political, rather than a juridical body—and it had been the government, not the courts, that had ordered the trial. Implying that the motivation for the trial was thus more political than legal, Kazarinov once again moved to dismiss. Nosovich rose to object. The Provisional Government, which possessed "absolute state power," enjoyed "even more privileges than the former monarch had." It therefore could choose to assign the case of Sukhomlinov to any court it wished, even to a court especially constituted for that purpose. Obviously displeased by this attack on his competence as a judge, Tagantsev sided with Nosovich. Kazarinov's motion was overruled. The rest of the day was spent in the task of jury selection. Once that had been accomplished, the court adjourned until the next day. The empaneled jurors were all assigned rooms in the Army and Navy Club, where they would be sequestered for the duration of the trial.[88]

The second day of the trial was almost totally consumed by the public reading of the bill of indictment against the Sukhomlinovs, a document of 116 pages of minuscule print. Sukhomlinov was charged with ten felony counts and his wife with two. At 7:30 in the evening, when the hoarse and exhausted clerk finally completed his marathon recitation, the court announced that it would hear the pleas of the accused. Trembling with the effort to control himself, Sukhomlinov stated that he was not guilty of any of the charges. Ekaterina seemed to bear up better under stress than her husband. When her turn to reply came, she calmly yet forcefully said, "I consider myself unconditionally innocent. Only the consciousness of my absolute innocence permitted me to endure all of the horrors of the last two years."[89] There were loud exclamations throughout the spectators' gallery.

When the tumult had subsided, the foreman of the jury begged leave to make a request of the bench. The jury had listened to the indictment with the greatest possible attention, but owing to the intricacy of the charges and the large amount of factual information it contained, it was clearly impossible for them to remember everything. Would it be possible to have two copies of the indictment made available for the jury's perusal? While granting that to do so would be a technical breach of Russian law, Nosovich responded that in view of the special circumstances surrounding this case, he saw no reason why the court could not permit the jury to examine one copy of the indictment, under a strict time limit, of course. At this Kazarinov bolted from his chair. Doing this would be "an unheard of violation of the law," he said hotly. In Russia, a bill of indictment was the prosecution's interpretation of the evidence in the case. For the jury to consult it during the trial even for a brief interval would be to blatantly disregard the principle of impartiality. After all, it was the state's job to *prove* that its version of what had happened was true in a fair court of law. The only way in which such an act would be even barely tolerable would be if he

88. Ibid.
89. Ibid., August 12(25), 1917, p. 4.

246 and his colleagues were given the right to prepare a counterindictment for the jury that refuted the arguments in the indictment and pointed out its egregious errors of fact. After Kazarinov's forceful outburst even a court as biased as this one had to reject the jury's request, for under Russia's version of adversary criminal procedure his was the correct interpretation of what the law required.[90]

The presentation of evidence began on August 12, the third day of the trial, and concluded on September 5. In this twenty-five-day period over one hundred witnesses were called to the stand. The court heard testimony from such high-ranking military men as Ianushkevich, Polivanov, Ivanov, Danilov, and Alekseev. The Grand Duke Sergei Mikhailovich spoke about the origins of the artillery crisis, as did Generals Vernander, Kuz'min-Karavaev, and Smyslovskii. Sukhomlinov's old nemesis from the Ministry of Finance, V. N. Kokovtsov, testified along with Admiral Grigorovich, the former minister of the navy; S. I. Timashev, former minister of trade and industry; and A. A. Makarov, who as minister of the interior in 1912 had sent Sukhomlinov the official letter denouncing Miasoedov. Savich, Rodzianko, Miliukov, and Guchkov, who answered questions for several straight hours, represented the Duma. Prince Andronnikov, Madame Chervinskaia, Klara Miasoedova, Sukhomlinov's former adjutants, Nikolai and Anna Goskevich, and Oscar Altschüller all appeared in court, as did police officials, ex-military attachés, and criminal investigators. In addition, large quantities of written material were read aloud to the jury—among them the transcript of Miasoedov's interrogations, extracts from Sukhomlinov's diaries, Sukhomlinov's correspondence with Ianushkevich in the first months of the war, affidavits from witnesses who could not be in Petrograd because of service at the front or illness, and Andronnikov's letters to Ekaterina Viktorovna and the former Empress Alexandra.

On September 6 the closing arguments began. Nosovich was the first to speak. With whom had the war minister surrounded himself? What did it mean that Sukhomlinov had consorted with such scoundrels and undoubted spies as Miasoedov, Dumbadze, Altschüller, Andronnikov, and all the rest? To drive his point home, Nosovich had recourse to a visual aid, unveiling a huge "Cartogram of Espionage" in front of the jury. This was a chart, consisting of forty-two circles with a name neatly inscribed in each. Sukhomlinov's and Miasoedov's names were at the very center, and straight lines radiated out from them directly or indirectly connecting every other name—a sort of grotesque sunburst of treason. The circles were also color-coded: light red meant a person was suspected of espionage, dark red that he or she had been indicted for espionage, while dark red with a small black dot indicated a conviction for the same offense. Six of the circles featured a large black dot, which connoted an execution.[91] If these sinister patterns were not enough to implicate Sukhomlinov in treason, added Nosovich, there was also the testimony of Franz Müller, the Austrian

90. Ibid.
91. This chart is preserved in the archives. See RGVIA, f. 962, op. 2, d. 120.

spy who had sworn that he had seen documents in Vienna that proved that Sukhomlinov was an agent of Austria-Hungary.

Turning to the question of the country's preparation for the war, Nosovich drew an elaborate verbal picture of the suffering and defeat the army had endured owing to the shortages of munitions. Sukhomlinov had been responsible for these, and it was simply untrue that "everyone" had counted on a general European war being short. His indifference to the authentic needs of national defense had been tellingly expressed in his contempt for the Duma prior to the war. "Two paths stood before the Russian minister of war," Nosovich thundered. "One path involved working hand in hand with the State Duma to strengthen the combat power of the army, although at the risk of falling from office. The other path was clinging to power at any cost. And General Sukhomlinov went down that second path, and openly proclaimed himself an enemy of the Duma."[92] The choices that Sukhomlinov had made continued to bear evil fruit even after he had been removed from power, and in large measure explained the dire military straits in which Russia now found herself.

Nosovich concluded with this peroration to the jury:

> Before you stands a man accused of treason. Consider. Has it been proven? If it has been proven, gentlemen, than let the voice of the court of Russia's public conscience pronounce its terrible word against treason. Let it crush the serpent of the past, groveling before the throne and the serpent of the present, raising its head and preparing to strangle in its embrace our bleeding fatherland, our maligned mother Russia![93]

The speech of the second prosecutor, D. D. Danchich, was considerably more subdued, in welcome contrast to Nosovich's histrionics. Danchich noted that the dramatic events of the summer and fall (presumably he had the July days, German advance, and Kornilov "plot" in mind) had tended to deflect public attention away from the Sukhomlinov trial. But these proceedings were of vital importance notwithstanding. The recovery of the honor and dignity of the army and the people depended on the verdict in this case. The jury should understand, he averred, that "when you bring in a verdict in the case of Sukhomlinov . . . you will also be bringing in a verdict in the case of the old regime."[94]

It was now the turn of the defense to wrap up its arguments. On the ninth of September Sukhomlinov's lead attorney, Zakharin, made his statement. It was not a particularly effective performance, as it rather quickly degenerated into a feeble attack on A. I. Guchkov. Zakharin charged that it was exclusively owing to the machinations of the Octobrist that his client had been indicted on criminal offenses. A great

---

92. "Sud nad Sukhomlinovym," *Novoe vremia*, September 9 (22), 1917, p. 4.
93. Ibid.
94. Ibid.

248   deal of the government's "evidence" related to Sukhomlinov's acquaintance with Miasoedov. But it was Guchkov who had "created" the Miasoedov espionage case, it was Guchkov who had poisoned the relations between the Duma and Sukhomlinov, and it was Guchkov who had instigated vicious newspaper attacks on the war minister. Why had he done all these things? The answer was simple: out of an incontinent ambition to become minister of war himself. The only result of this speech, described by a journalist as "chaotic in form and perplexing in content," was to make a negative impression on the members of the jury.[95] Tarkhovskii, the junior attorney on the Sukhomlinov defense team, did little to repair the damage. He spent most of his time trying to impugn the competence of the Warsaw court-martial that had convicted Miasoedov of espionage, as if to suggest that if the gendarme had been innocent, the former minister was innocent too.[96]

    Yet M. G. Kazarinov's speech on behalf of Ekaterina Viktorovna was accorded an entirely different reception. His summation, delivered on September 10, was interrupted so often by open applause from the public gallery that the alarmed presiding judge, Tagantsev, finally gave the order to clear the spectators from the courtroom. The powerful reaction that Kazarinov elicited was the result not only of his sharp wits and logic but also of his formidable rhetorical skill and his nearly flawless emotional communion with his audience.

    What, asked Kazarinov, was this trial actually about? Since no evidence of specific treasonable acts had been introduced, it followed that the heart of the prosecution's case concerned the inadequate preparation of the Russian army for the great European war. If this was so, what part could Ekaterina Viktorovna possibly have played in the matter? She made no military decisions, she did not preside over the Military Council, and she did not draw up military budgets or award government arms contracts. Still further, she could not have exerted a malign influence over her husband even if she had wanted to, since reasons of health obliged her to spend large portions of every year abroad. The inference to be drawn was that the "evidence" that the government had put into the record about her divorce, spending habits, and so forth was not only scurrilous, unsubstantiated, and false but was also entirely *irrelevant,* since even it were true it would not convict her of any crime whatsoever. "They say that the wife of the war minister ordered ten hats a season and wore a diamond necklace? What of it? If the minister of war himself wore the necklace and the diamonds and went around dressed like that then I would understand." What Kazarinov was driving at was the point that although the government had implied that Ekaterina's extravagance had driven Sukhomlinov to peculation and treason, this had not been proved.

    Kazarinov then turned to Ekaterina's character, which he argued had been maliciously slandered in the preceding weeks of testimony. The claim made by her churlish ex-husband Butovich that she had no patriotic feelings for Russia was utterly re-

95. Ibid., September 10 (23), 1917, p. 4.
96. Ibid.

futed by her record of work during the war. Kazarinov pointed to Ekaterina's impressive accomplishments: she had organized hospital and bath trains, she had distributed presents at the front to the soldiers, and she had personally raised over 2.5 million rubles to purchase small comforts for the troops. These were hardly the deeds of a flighty sybarite, let alone a traitor. Moreover, her conduct since her husband's troubles had begun had also been exemplary. She had stood by him and had provided him with complete moral and spiritual support. If she had truly been guilty of something, she would have fled the country. But she did not, for "her conscience was clean, and she calmly awaited the future."

What, then, of the circle of dubious individuals who surrounded her husband? The prosecution had itself conceded that Ekaterina could be condemned only if were shown that she was consciously aware that there were spies among her friends and acquaintances. But the sole evidence that she had been so aware came from the meretricious lips of Prince Andronnikov, and if this trial had shown anything, it had shown that Andronnikov's statements were not to be trusted.

Kazarinov concluded with an eloquent appeal for the rule of law in Russia. "The prosecutor has told you you must pronounce a guilty verdict in order to calm outraged public opinion, and he demands a guilty verdict from you in the name of this public opinion. . . . But a court must render a verdict on the basis of facts, not under the pressure of some sort of public opinion. In this case there is no evidence, there are no manifest facts, and it is terrible for the future of the new Russia when demands are heard to convict someone of anything at all on the basis of such unfounded data as the prosecution has introduced in these proceedings."[97]

On September 11, Sukhomlinov and his wife were each permitted to make a last statement to the court. In a series of terse, cogent remarks the former minister defended his stewardship of the Russian army during his years in power. He described the weakness of the army in the aftermath of the Japanese war and detailed the most important steps he had taken to build it back up. He laid particular stress on his introduction of a reserve system, which had increased the size of the army in both peace and war, and on the substantive improvements made in Russia's mobilization system, accurately pointing out that the speed of Russia's mobilization and concentration had astonished the Germans in 1914. His voice trembling with emotion, he closed by saying, "I may have made mistakes. I may even have made miscalculations, but I committed no crimes. If the Lord God has helped me endure all of the horror of the past two years, all of the burden of slander, if I have borne everything up until now, it is only because before God, before the fatherland and before the former supreme commander, my conscience is clear."[98] It must be noted that Sukhomlinov's judicious and dignified assertion of his innocence contrasted sharply with the curiously inept defense his lawyers had offered during the trial. When it came time for Ekaterina Viktorovna to speak, the self-possession and serenity that she had dis-

97. Ibid., September 12 (25), 1917, p. 4.
98. Ibid.

250 played throughout the proceedings finally deserted her. "Neither I nor my husband are criminals," she declared, "I have nothing left in my life. It is all the same to me." A fit of sobbing then overcame her and she could say no more.[99]

The court reconvened on September 12 at three in the afternoon. For the ensuing four and a half hours, presiding judge Tagantsev read his instructions to the jury. At 7:30 the jury was sent away to begin its deliberations. At 8:00 the following morning the jury returned to the court with its verdicts. General Sukhomlinov had been found guilty on nine of the ten charges against him, including treason. Ekaterina had been acquitted. The judges immediately sentenced Sukhomlinov. As the death penalty was in force only at the front, they imposed the harshest penalty available to them: complete loss of rights and hard labor for life. Sukhomlinov, who is said to have listened "calmly" to both the verdict and the sentence, was then taken back to the Fortress of Peter and Paul, where he was to be temporarily held until a permanent place of confinement had been designated. Ekaterina, accompanied by some of her relatives, left the Army and Navy Club at once.[100] The trial had lasted thirty-three days. The overthrow of the Provisional Government by the Bolsheviks was less than one month away.

Anatomy of a Fiasco

Although Kerenskii and his associates were doubtless elated at the news of Sukhomlinov's conviction, if not Ekaterina's acquittal, the judicial proceedings taken as a whole had utterly failed to accomplish any of their intended purposes. In fact, in several respects the trial backfired, producing results that were exactly the opposite of those anticipated.

In the first place, Danchich had been correct when he complained in his summation that the public was not all that interested in the Sukhomlinov case. By this point in 1917 there was simply too much else to worry about: the possibility that the Germans might seize the capital, the threats to democracy from both left and right, and the exhausting quotidian struggle for food and fuel. Although the court was crowded on the penultimate day of the trial when Tagantsev gave his charges to the jury, this was the only occasion during the entire trial when the members of the public had to be turned away for want of space. Published reports inform us that the rest of the time there were always plenty of vacant seats in the spectators' gallery. The citizens of Petrograd stayed away in droves, and by so doing they caused what was supposed to have been a dazzling public relations coup to sputter like a defective firecracker. This had to be a grave disappointment to a government that had, in the words of one newspaper correspondent, "attached an enormous social significance to the Sukhomlinov case."[101]

99. Ibid.
100. "Konets dela Sukhomlinovykh," *Novoe vremia*, September 14 (27), 1917, p. 3.
101. "Sud nad Sukhomlinovym," *Novoe vremia*, August 13 (26), 1917, p. 3.

Second, although the government had proclaimed that the proceedings would present the Russian people with the entire, unvarnished truth about treason in high places and the country's unreadiness for war, it was evident that simultaneously too much and too little of that truth had emerged. The very first witness had been Ianushkevich, who had been chief of the general staff at the time of the July crisis of 1914. During his cross-examination on August 12 he divulged the circumstances of the empire's mobilization during the crisis, explaining that the tsar had wanted to mobilize only against Austria-Hungary, not Germany, in the hope of averting a general war, only to be talked back into a general mobilization when Sukhomlinov and Sazonov objected that a partial mobilization would guarantee Russia's prompt defeat should Vienna not back down.[102] As the Reuters agency was covering the trial, Ianushkevich's story soon became known around the world. In Berlin, the German Press Bureau seized upon it with particular relish, arguing that it completely absolved the German Reich of any guilt for starting the war. Since it had been the Russian general mobilization that had *forced* an unwilling Germany to fight, the Russians were uniquely responsible for the outbreak of the Great War. The German interpretation of these revelations was embarrassing for both Russia and her allies. The *Times* of London, for example, printed articles to refute these German claims, and the German-Swiss journalist Richard Grelling rushed an entire little book into print with the same object in view.[103] Despite these efforts, the idea that the Russian mobilization somehow "caused" World War I took root, and it can occasionally be found in the historical literature even today.[104]

But if record of testimony such as Ianushkevich's inconvenienced the Provisional Government and strained its relations with its allies, other testimony was damaging by its absence. Consider the court appearance of Colonel V. A. Erandakov. Erandakov had been called to the stand by the prosecution on August 24 to establish that, despite his denials, Sukhomlinov had indeed entrusted Miasoedov with sensitive intelligence materials. The colonel was also supposed to offer expert commentary on the treason of Miasoedov and the espionage of various of his closest associates. But when it came time for the cross-examination, Kazarinov asked Erandakov to answer questions about other persons whom military counterintelligence had suspected of

---

102. Ibid.

103. See, for example, "The Mobilized Chancellor: A Futile Campaign," *The Times,* September 6, 1917, p. 5f.; Richard Grelling, *Die "Enthüllungen" des Prozesses Suchomlinow* (Bern, 1917). Grelling, who despised the Wilhelmine regime, denied that mobilization was the equivalent of an act of war and concluded on p. 63 that "Germany and Austria are and remain solely and exclusively guilty of the fact that the European war occurred."

104. See, for example, L. C. F. Turner, "The Russian Mobilization of 1914," in *The War Plans of the Great Powers 1880–1914,* ed. Paul M. Kennedy, pp. 252–268 (Boston, 1979). The international coverage of the trial made enough of an impression even to find its way into fiction. In *Mr. Standfast* (1919), one of John Buchan's novels devoted to the exploits of the intrepid Richard Hannay, Hannay is ordered to infiltrate a nest of German sympathizers, whose leader maintains that "the revelations of the Sukhomlinov trial in Russia . . . showed that Germany had not been responsible for the war." *Mr. Standfast* (Ware, U.K., 1994), p. 23.

252 spying both before and after 1914. What, for example, could Erandakov state about the American wife of a certain general of the Imperial Suite? Had she not been regarded as a potential enemy agent? If so, why had no one apprehended her? A frightened Erandakov blurted out that he had no information on the subject, and the presiding judge immediately shut down this line of questioning.[105] Kazarinov was, of course, referring to Countess Magdalena Nostits, the fortune hunter from Boston who had most likely been working for the Germans since her second marriage. He knew that the court wanted no mention of her since she was wildly popular with the American community in Petrograd, and the Provisional Government had no desire to antagonize Washington, which had entered the war on the Allied side only four months before. This tactic produced the exact effect he had planned: it was obvious that someone had ordered Erandakov to keep mum about the countess. This in turn implied that the supposedly impartial court had engaged in witness tampering and that these proceedings were not a transparent, honest quest for truth, as the Provisional Government had maintained. What was the government hiding? If the Provisional Government was itself protecting spies and traitors, as it claimed its imperial predecessor had, what ethical authority did it have to try the accused? Throughout the long weeks of the trial Kazarinov never passed up any opportunity to deflate the government's pretensions to the moral high ground.

A third reason that the trial misfired was the vertiginous incoherence of the case mounted by the prosecution. As is demonstrated by the published reportage and even more strikingly displayed in the stenographic record, there was no rhyme or reason to the prosecution's presentation and sequencing of the evidence.[106] One witness would testify about the shell shortages of 1915, only to be followed by another speaking about Miasoedov's activities in Verzhbolovo in 1906, and then by someone making allegations about the war minister's social contacts in 1911. The state's use of documentary evidence was if anything even worse, for the principles governing its selection were opaque and the timing of its introduction random. As the correspondent of *Novoe vremia* observed on August 24, "The trial moves slowly. A very great deal of time is absorbed in the reading of all manner of letters and documents. Frequently there is mystification about why all of this has to be made known."[107] As this comment suggests, the prosecutors did not adequately put all of this seemingly unrelated written and oral testimony into perspective or explain how it all fit together. There was therefore no logical progression to the prosecution's case, which was a particularly lethal failing in a case that was simultaneously so circumstantial and so complex. All of this, of course, stemmed from the negligent, slovenly manner in which the prosecution had prepared itself before going to trial.

Fourth, even if the prosecutors had been perfectly prepared, they still would have been incapable of getting around the ugly truth that the evidence they had to offer

---

105. Erandakov testimony, August 24, 1917, RGVIA, f. 962, op. 2, d. 145, l. 72.
106. The stenographic record is preserved in RGVIA, f. 962, op. 2, d. 139–155.
107. "Sud nad Sukhomlinovym," *Novoe vremia*, August 24 (September 6), 1917, p. 3.

did not substantiate the charges in their bill of indictment. For a show trial to be effective, it must instill at least some belief in the guilt of the accused. For that to happen, the evidence, even if doctored or perjurious, must at least on the surface appear
to be ironclad. But the evidence in the Sukhomlinov case did not fall into this category. In the first place, a great deal of it was contradictory. To be sure, the prosecution did call witnesses, such as General Velichko, who swore that Sukhomlinov was
completely responsible for the country's military unpreparedness in 1914 and that he
consequently was the father "of all of the failures of the current war." But there were
other credible witnesses, such former Quartermaster General Danilov, who denied
this, stating that in his opinion the shortages of guns and rifles were the result "of an
entire series of unfortunate conditions that did not depend upon the will of General
Sukhomlinov."[108] Second, the testimony of a large number of the witnesses was
tainted by partisanship, self-interest, or defensiveness in ways impossible to miss.
Velichko, for example, had been the chairman of the army's fortress committee and
had never forgiven Sukhomlinov for dissolving that body and putting him out of his
job. For witnesses from GAU to denounce Sukhomlinov for the munitions crisis was
essential to absolve their own organization of any blame. In a similar vein, the various
representatives of military counterintelligence and the police who condemned
Sukhomlinov for harboring nests of spies were always quick to add that of course it
had not been their fault that the traitorous scum had not been unmasked long ago.
This brings us to the question of espionage and treason. As already noted, there was
no evidence presented at the trial about any discrete acts of either. Instead the prosecution continuously described this or that individual as a spy apparently in the for-
lorn hope that mere repetition would alchemize an intimation into a fact. The problem with this expedient was that it did not work. Take the prosecution's treatment of
the "spying" of Altschüller. One of the experts it summoned to shed light on this
matter was M. V. Alekseev, former chief of staff of Russia's field army. In 1907 and
1908, however, Alekseev had been chief of staff of Kiev Military District, which placed
all intelligence and counterintelligence operations there under his supervision. Alekseev pointed out that at one stage Altschüller had been placed under surveillance as a
possibly suspicious person, but when the prosecutors eagerly asked Alekseev what the
results of that surveillance had been, the general snapped back that "if there had been
any results he [i.e., Altschüller] would have been placed under arrest." But Altschüller
had not been arrested because "nothing tangible was ever observed."[109] The prosecution fared still worse on the seventeenth day of the trial, which was entirely devoted
to trivial testimony about Altschüller. As a newspaper reported, this testimony "provided absolutely no data to suspect Altschüller of espionage for Austria, or even to establish that there was anything criminal in Altschüller's relations with Sukhomlinov
at all."[110] In fact, at the end of the day the core of the prosecution's case for Sukhom-

108. Ibid., August 15 (28), 1917, p. 3.
109. RGVIA, f. 962, op. 2, d. 145, ll. 12–13.
110. "Sud nad Sukhomlinovym," *Novoe vremia*, August 27 (September 9), p. 3.

254 linov's own commission of espionage and treason was its Cartogram of Espionage, which had no more evidentiary weight than a toddler's finger painting for all of its circles, lines, and arrows.

There is a fifth and final point worth making about the Sukhomlinov trial. So badly was it organized, so poorly scripted, so incompetently conducted, that it succeeded in accomplishing what most people as late as July 1917 would have found totally incredible: evoking sympathy for the disgraced ex-minister who heretofore had been the most pilloried and reviled man in Russia. Kazarinov's closing argument had brilliantly ridiculed the state's feeble case against Ekaterina, and in so doing had implicitly poked holes in the case against Sukhomlinov as well. That his speech was wildly applauded and cheered was therefore an ominous signal to the Provisional Government that the public trial had been a serious mistake. Sukhomlinov was convicted, of course, as was probably unavoidable given the fact that the majority of jurors had been government employees. But the blow that the government had aimed at Sukhomlinov had come back upon itself, like the spinning of a quintain. On September 15 N. P. Okunev, a middle-aged Moscow businessman, wrote the following lines in his diary: "That poor devil Sukhomlinov has been sentenced to life at hard labor. . . . Exceeding authority and nonfeasance certainly took place, but whether there was high treason, that is a question which history will eventually resolve, not those jurors . . . who pronounced their 'Yes, Guilty!' not without pangs of conscience."[111]

Coda

The Bolshevik Revolution of October found Sukhomlinov still in the Fortress of Peter and Paul. Under Lenin's government there were initially small improvements in the conditions of his imprisonment. He was, for example, permitted to walk outside more frequently and to attend divine services at the Cathedral of Peter and Paul. Despite these extra privileges, prison life undermined the general's health. After several months of petitioning, Ekaterina Viktorovna succeeded in having her husband transferred to "The Crosses," a special penitentiary for political offenders located in the Vyborg district of Petrograd. The Crosses included a hospital, and the cells there were considerably lighter, drier, and airier than those in the Fortress. Baths and showers were available on request, and, improbably enough, the prisoners were even provided the services of a skilled masseur.[112]

As part of its May 1, 1918, celebration the Bolshevik government issued a decree that granted amnesty to certain categories of prisoners; since he was over seventy years old, Sukhomlinov fell within its scope, and he was released on the very same day. He did not go to the small apartment Ekaterina had in the meantime found in the city but rather sought accommodation with friends. For the next several weeks, he

111. N. P. Okunev, *Dnevnik moskvicha (1917–1924)* (Paris, 1990), p. 84.
112. *Vospominaniia Sukhomlinova*, p. 322.

led a peripatetic existence, staying overnight with whoever would have him and changing his lodgings frequently. In the late summer of 1918, however, rumors began to circulate that the Communists were planning the wholesale roundup and execution of all former tsarist ministers. Sukhomlinov took these rumors seriously enough to begin to plan an escape from Russia. On the evening of September 22(October 5) he went to the Finland railway station, where he caught a train for Beloostrov Station. Upon his arrival, he walked northeast parallel to the shore of Lake Ladoga until he was so deep into the wilderness that he judged himself safe. Luckily, he found an abandoned hut, where he spent the night and rested throughout the next day. On September 24 he continued his trek until he reached the Sestra River, which marked the border between Finland and Bolshevik Russia. Here a fisherman was waiting in a small boat to ferry him over the river and out of the country. Finnish authorities immediately granted his request for asylum.

Ekaterina did not accompany him because she had by then initiated divorce proceedings. The physical and mental agony of the investigation, imprisonment, and trial all doubtless played a role in her decision, but she had also found a new romantic interest as well as a new political protector in the person of a Georgian engineer by the name of Gabaev, who at least temporarily was on good terms with the new regime. By 1919 Gabaev and Ekaterina had married, and the former was running a cooperative saccharin factory in Petrograd. He was also turning a substantial profit as an importer, traveling abroad to acquire various goods and articles that were in short supply in Russia. According to a visitor to their home, the Gabaevs had managed to construct a comfortable, even luxurious life for themselves. While the majority of Russians were struggling with the hunger that was the direct result of the regime's idiotic economic policies, the Gabaevs were dining on abundant, well-prepared food and drinking the finest of wines. The reversal in their fortune was, however, quick and dramatic. At some point in 1920, Gabaev was arrested and executed on the charge of spying for the government of Finland. Ekaterina was also arrested and sent to Moscow, where she was apparently shot by Lenin's political police—the Cheka—in 1921.[113]

What of the other figures in this tragedy?

The Bolsheviks shot Prince Andronnikov in 1919.

Aleksandr Guchkov got out of Russia and emigrated first to Berlin and then to Paris. He died of cancer of the throat in the south of France in 1936.

Nicholas II, his wife Alexandra, and all their children were murdered by the Bolsheviks in Ekaterinburg in July 1918.

The Grand Duke Nikolai Nikolaevich quit Russia for Italy in March 1919, and moved to France in 1921. He served as the head of the Romanov dynasty in exile until his death at the winter resort of Antibes in January 1929.

---

113. *The Life of a Chemist: Memoirs of Vladimir N. Ipatieff,* ed. Xenia Joukoff Edin, Helen Dwight Fisher, and Harold H. Fisher, trans. Vladimir Haensel and Mrs. Ralph H. Lusher (Stanford, 1946), pp. 291–293.

256   Vasilii Dumbadze emigrated to the United States and died in New York City in 1950.

The October Revolution precipitated Klara Miasoedova's release from exile. She apparently made her way back to Vilna, where she settled in what became the independent state of Lithuania. According to the Polish novelist Josef Mackiewicz, she lived long enough to see Lithuania overrun first by Stalin's Red Army and then by the Nazis.[114]

Sukhomlinov moved to Berlin. There he led a life of coarse poverty, of bickering with his fellow émigrés, and of work on his memoirs. His memoirs were published in German in 1924, and shortly thereafter the Soviets printed a Russian-language edition, doubtless because they found the general's diatribes against the liberals, the bourgeoisie, and the Provisional Government to their taste. Early in the morning one day in February 1926, two Berlin policemen attempted to roust an elderly man from a park bench in the Tiergarten. It was Sukhomlinov, who had frozen to death overnight. According to one story, the retired German general Count Rediger von der Jolts approached General Kurt von Schleicher with a request that Sukhomlinov be given a funeral with all military honors, in respect for the high military offices he had held in Imperial Russia. The request was denied.

---

114. Jozef Mackiewicz, *Sprawa Pulkownika Miasojedowa. Powiesc* (London, 1992). Mackiewicz claimed that his novel was based on fact, including evidence provided by informants in Vilnius. See p. 9.

Conclusion

Patriots and Traitors

For much of the history of Imperial Russia, the definition of political loyalty was uncomplicated. A loyal subject was one who was loyal to the ruling Romanov dynasty. Legal status, social class, ethnicity, and nationality were not important, for fealty to the crown was supposed to trump any other allegiances or affiliations. It followed that any ideology or system of beliefs that promoted a different principle of allegiance was ipso facto dangerous for the traditional monarchy. One such ideology was agrarian socialism of the kind espoused by Russian socialists-revolutionaries, who dreamed of overthrowing the monarchy and establishing a state devoted to the welfare of the peasants. Another was Marxism, in view of claims it made for the international solidarity and brotherhood of the working class. However, there was an ideology that antedated both of these and was just as much a challenge to the existing order, and that was nationalism.

Nationalism threatened the Russian monarchy just as it threatened the other conservative continental monarchies in Europe. This was so because the nationalist insisted on the creation of a Europe of nation states, in which ethnicity, language, and culture—not the divine rights of dynasties and kings—determined the just boundaries of political communities. Up until 1860, however, Europe was not on the whole politically organized in this fashion. Italy was disunited, German speakers resided in over forty discrete states, and Austria and Russia were vast multinational empires. Nationalism challenged all these arrangements.

In the early nineteenth century, conservatives and monarchists regarded nationalism as a profoundly destabilizing, highly combustible, and destructive force. It was believed that Napoleon had drawn a great deal of his power from the exploitation and channeling of French nationalism. After his defeat in 1815, a common objective of the

258   continental powers had been to defend the established order and ensure the general peace by suppressing nationalism and the liberalism that went hand in glove with it. It took Prussia's Otto von Bismarck to perform the alchemy whereby nationalism was converted from a force on the left to a force on the right. He did so by appropriating the nationalist project and unifying Germany, but unifying it in his own peculiar way under the sovereignty of the conservative Hohenzollern monarch of Prussia. The new Hohenzollern emperor of Germany retained all his rights, including his right to rule over his non-German subjects. In doing this, Bismarck reinvented nationalism and decoupled it from German liberalism entirely.

Given the history of the Russian Empire and the large number of national groups it had absorbed as it expanded, the development of national consciousness among any of the non-Russian peoples was an obvious matter for worry. The Poles, for example, had risen in violent rebellion against the Russian government in both 1830 and 1863. During the 1905–7 revolution serious nationalist insurrections in such regions as Transcaucasia and the Baltic provinces had imperiled the regime's efforts to restore its authority. It is therefore easy to understand why Petersburg looked upon non-Russian nationalism with abhorrence. However, for a great deal of the nineteenth century the tsarist government had also eyed *Russian* nationalism with distaste.[1] This was so because certain Russian nationalists, no less than other nationalists, were revisionists who sought to alter the status quo. For example, there were Russian nationalists who were attracted to the concept of Pan-Slavism—that is, the idea that St. Petersburg should mount crusades to liberate the Slavic peoples of eastern and central Europe from Turkish and Austrian domination, bringing them under Russia's political sway. The pernicious element in this grandiose imperialist delusion was its insistence that Russia conduct an aggressive foreign policy other than the one the regime preferred—an aggressive foreign policy that, moreover, came freighted with the risk of war.

In the last quarter of the nineteenth century, however, Russian nationalism became more respectable to Russian conservatives. The state itself contributed to this trend through its Russification programs within the borderlands of the empire and its increasing restrictions on the cultural life and opportunities permitted to such groups as the Poles, Latvians, and Jews. Nicholas II, who came to the throne in 1894, was himself attracted, rather than repelled, by nationalist ideas. His was a nationalism that was oriented simultaneously toward an imaginary future and an imaginary past. On the one hand he believed that it was Russia's irresistible destiny to increase in power and influence, while on the other he helped popularize the fatuous nostalgia for the Russian middle ages that was so conspicuous a feature of fin de siécle culture.

---

1. To be sure, "orthodoxy, autocracy and nationality" constituted the official ideology of the regime of Nicholas I (1825–55). But "nationality" as understood in conservative court circles of the time meant extolling the submissiveness and piety of the Russian people, not the adoption of a messianic program for the realization of the greatness of the nation. See Nicholas Riasanovsky, *Nicholas I and Official Nationality in Russia, 1825–1855* (Berkeley, 1969), pp. 137–140.

As we have already seen, the outbreak of the First World War had evoked a great upsurge in Russian national feeling and patriotism. For many Russians, the war was a just struggle that had united and energized the Russian people: victory in the war would vindicate the superiority of Russian civilization. At the same time, for millions of illiterate peasants nationalism in the modern sense was thoroughly incomprehensible. There were also those on the political right who were appalled by the war and believed that Russia's decision to engage in hostilities with the Central Powers was a fatal error. Such people included former Interior Minister P. N. Durnovo, the author of a prescient February 1914 memorandum predicting that the consequences of a European war for Russia would be social collapse, chaos, and revolution.[2] Others who felt this way were Count Witte, the former minister of finance; Baron Rosen, the empire's former ambassador to Japan; and G. E. Rasputin, who, upon learning of the declaration of mobilization had telegraphed the empress's confidante Vyrubova to warn that "war must not be declared; it will be the end of all things."[3] Then, too, there were those on the extreme left who repudiated the war and refused to support it, arguing that it was the bastard child of selfish imperialism. There were socialists of this stripe in every belligerent country, and they were collectively known as the Zimmerwaldists, after a town in Switzerland where in 1915 an antiwar European socialist conference had met. Lenin and the Bolsheviks, among others, exemplified this strain in Russian politics.

In general, however, most politically conscious people in Russia, whether right, center, or left, embraced the war and the new militant forms of patriotism that accompanied it. The patriotism of wartime was more than mere love of country, for various styles of patriotism from 1914 to 1917 offered competing interpretations of the purpose of the war. According to one version of patriotism, the war was being waged in the interests of the Russian people; according to another, in defense of the Russian state; and for yet another, to bring Russia at long last into the comity of progressive and democratic nations. But all forms of patriotism provided similar answers to the question about winning the war. There was, of course, common agreement that for Russia to prevail she had to defeat her external enemies: the German, Austro-Hungarian, and Ottoman empires. Yet, interestingly, there was also an agreement that Russia would not be able to achieve victory until it had obliterated or neutralized its internal adversaries. During World War I Russian patriots of every tendency became obsessed with unmasking and destroying the inner foe.

The reason for this was the general belief that Russia's reverses and calamities in the war were all or almost all attributable to treason. Treason was the supreme and comprehensive excuse for everything. From the time of the battle of Masuria in early 1915 the news from the front had been almost entirely bad. One report of military

2. For the text of this document see Frank Alfred Golder, *Documents of Russian History 1914–1917* (Gloucester, Mass.: 1964) pp. 3–23.

3. Ibid., p. 28; Edward Radzinsky, *The Rasputin File,* trans. Judson Rosengrant (New York, 2000), pp. 261–262.

260 failure succeeded another. There was word of shortages of vital munitions and supplies, of ignominious withdrawals, and of scarcely credible losses. Even Russian victories, such as the Brusilov offensive, had been achieved at an appalling cost in
human lives. What, other than clandestine treason, could possibly explain these disasters? Everyone knew that Russia possessed the might and capabilities to win the
war, but it was painfully evident that Russia was paying an excessive price, and that
even so, the eventual outcome might be defeat. It was self-evident to many that treason had to be at work.

The information provided by traitors was so voluminous that Russia's entire war
effort had become transparent to the enemy, who had prior knowledge of its best-laid
military plans, and each of its concentrations and movements of troops. There were
newspapers, like Moscow's *Russkoe slovo* [*The Russian Word*], which speculated that
at least 50 percent of Germany's victories on the Eastern front derived from the activities of traitors and spies.[4] Nor was that all. It was believed that traitors were also sabotaging war production, ruining the economy of the home front, and undermining
the transport of fuel, food, and supplies. Some were even hatching furtive plots to
surrender the entire country to the enemy. Popular culture fed these fantasies of treason. The ubiquity of foreign espionage was a theme central to many Russian films,
plays, novels, and even cabaret performances of 1914–17.[5]

The instinctive faith that at bottom treason was responsible for Russia's wartime
woes conferred profound emotional and psychological satisfactions on its patriotic
adherents. It was the uncomplicated key to understanding the great trauma that Russia was then suffering. It cast Russia as a victim, treacherously defrauded of the victory that rightfully should have been hers. It was also consonant with the Russian fascination with conspiracy, a fascination that was the outgrowth of centuries of
autocratic rule. As we have already seen, conspiracy was a political style that flourished under the tsarist regime. But it was a short leap from the insight that conspiracy
was one species of politics to the belief that all politics was conspiracy. To the Russian
of 1915 it was axiomatic that political effects were not the result of their ostensible political causes. Rather, hidden forces operating silently in the dark manufactured political effects. Only that which was secret could possibly be true. "Conspiracy theories
of history," in Walter Laquer's apposite judgment, "have been for a long time part of
Russian political psychology."[6] The belief that "treason is everywhere" consequently
became one of the most distinctive characteristics of wartime patriotism in Russia.
But this belief was also a call to action. It was the duty of the patriot to expose traitors,
punish them, and deprive them of the ability to do additional harm.

Not all of those who accepted this proposition agreed about who Russia's arch-
traitors were. To patriots on the nationalist right it was clear that Russia's most dangerous traitors were to be found among the disloyal nationalities: that is, those ethnic

4. Letter to the editor of *Russkoe slovo*, May 5, 1915, GARF, f. 102, op. 265, d. 1020, l. 867.
5. Hubertus F. Jahn, *Patriotic Culture in Russian during World War I* (Ithaca, 1995), pp. 112–113, 162–
163.
6. Walter Laquer, *Black Hundred: The Rise of the Extreme Right in Russia* (New York, 1993), p. 43.

and religious groups that were seditiously insubordinate to the Russian crown. Although Muslims, Armenians, Georgians, and Ukrainians were to be found in this category, its preeminent representatives were the Jews and the Germans. It was an article of faith on the nationalist right that the Jews of Poland, Ukraine, and Belorussia had been spying on the Russian army and selling their discoveries to the enemy since the very first day of the war. In the Russian heartland, it was those wealthy Jews involved in banking and industry who were first in the ranks of the war profiteers and speculators who were driving up the price of food and all other necessities.

As for Russia's German subjects, regardless of the length of time they or their families had resided in the country and despite any protestations they might make to the contrary, it was presumed that they gave their genuine fealty to Berlin, not Petrograd. They had succeeded in dominating a great deal of Russia's economy and consequently exerted an unwholesome influence on the country's development. But their motivation for doing this had been more sinister than mere greed. Who could doubt that in many cases they had chosen to involve themselves in certain critical industries in anticipation of the war, perhaps even at the direction of the German General Staff? Was it not a fact that they had thereby acquired the ability to wreak maximum havoc on the Russian war effort? Russian newspapers printed exposés of "German factories in Russia," and a popular tract on German espionage that charged that "it took the war to show how many German officers were installed in Russia in the guise of employees of all kinds in the plants, factories and offices."[7] Undercover German saboteurs were bad enough, but what about the imperial court? Was it not infested with people who bore German names? What of the empress's own German heritage?

By contrast, to the patriot on the nationalist left there were no unequivocal ethnic markers for treason. Traitors and spies came garbed in a variety of ethnic and religious identities. Certainly there were treacherous Jews and Germans, but there were also treacherous Poles, Lithuanians, Uzbeks, and even Russians. However, as time went on there was a general coalescing of opinion that the monarchy itself was a suspect, or even traitorous, institution. After all, it was the prime duty of any political regime to defend its subjects from enemies both foreign and domestic. The Russian monarchy, however, had signally failed on both counts. It had demonstrated that it was incompetent to wage war against the Central Powers, not least because of its reluctance to accept the political and economic collaboration of progressive society, but it had also become an impediment to the destruction of the internal enemy. Time after time it had been shown that the most dangerous traitors had congregated in the protective shadow of the throne. Take Sukhomlinov, for instance. Nicholas II had been personally responsible for choosing this traitor to head up the Ministry of War, and it was Nicholas who had stymied the judicial investigation of Sukhomlinov's evil deeds and who had later rescued the malefactor from his well-deserved incarceration in the Fortress of Peter and Paul. Monarchism was consequently the exact antipode of patriotism. Even right-wing patriots, who supported the monarchical principle in

---

7. A. S. Rezanov, *Nemetskoe shpionstvo* (Petrograd, 1915), p. 203.

262   the abstract, had to concede that this particular monarch and his court were threats to the national security. This is what V. D. Nabokov meant when he wrote that "to be for the tsar meant to be against Russia."

It is, of course, true that the appeal to "struggle with the internal enemy," regardless of who made it, could be construed as a functional political tactic. With the world war, the era of mass politics had finally arrived in Russia, and the army, the government, and the factions in the Duma all evidenced keen interest in mobilizing and motivating the population. One technique for doing this was to extol the valor and sacrifice of military paragons. Early in the war the Cossack Kozma Kriuchkov had become nationally famous for having fought eleven German uhlans single-handed and having killed them all despite the sixteen grievous wounds he had received. Kriuchkov's feat was publicized in the columns of the newspapers and in the crude woodcuts (*liubki*) distributed by the thousands to the soldiers and the peasants. But the reverse of encouraging hero worship was the incitement of hate, for it, too, could be a powerful tool for mobilizing the people. Stigmatizing Jews or Russian Germans or the traditional monarchists with charges of treason could generate an outrage that could be translated into a sense of resolve and common purpose. Such blanket accusations also served hidden political agendas. To condemn the Jews of the western borderlands of the empire for the Russian army's military debacles did indeed insulate the Russian military leadership from criticism. To revile the Germans and demand the expropriation of their lands and businesses advanced the cause of ethnic Russian nationalism: German economic domination would at last be broken and German wealth would flow into Russian hands. Many on the political left wanted to overthrow the Russian monarchy in any case. How convenient, then, was the equation of traditional monarchism and treason!

It would be inaccurate to suggest that all those who orchestrated these campaigns against internal enemies were pure cynics—cold-blooded manipulators fully conscious of the innocence of the majority of their chosen targets. Guchkov did in fact know when he denounced Miasoedov as a spy that his allegation had no evidence behind it. But Ianushkevich was so in thrall to a particularly imbecilic anti-Semitism that he may very well have believed in the collective depravity of Russia's Jews. Even if there were individual Jews who as of yet had committed no acts of treason, there were none who would not betray Russia if given the opportunity. To banish hundreds of thousands of them from the frontier zones was consequently a just and necessary precaution. In other words, many of those who spun the wartime fantasies of treason also truly subscribed to them. In the end, however, it is difficult to exaggerate the trauma and harm that resulted from this fixation on the internal enemy. Multitudes suffered directly, but there was also a sense in which everyone in Russia was victimized by the espionage hysteria. The belief that the Russian Empire was worm-eaten with traitors and spies undermined the legitimacy of a government that was apparently incapable of ferreting them all out. Still further, belief in pandemic treachery also robbed people of hope in victory, spread defeatism, and made a mockery of personal sacrifice for the Russian cause. To what purpose should Russians spill torrents of blood on the battlefield if their sanguinary offerings were canceled out by acts of betrayal behind the front lines?

Without the Miasoedov/Sukhomlinov affair it is highly improbable that these pernicious fantasies of treason could ever have put down such deep roots. Indeed, one of the most striking features of the case is the degree to which Miasoedov and Sukhomlinov fit the profiles of treason devised by both the right and the left. To be sure, both Miasoedov and Sukhomlinov were unquestionably Russian by birth. But with whom had they associated? Germans and Jews. The breadth and depth of Miasoedov's and Sukhomlinov's acquaintance and contact with members of these groups were taken as confirming that there was something wrong with them both. These were not the sort of companions that honorable, patriotic Russian officers were supposed to seek out. Miasoedov was married to a woman who came from a Jewish family, he worked with Jewish businessmen, and he accepted salaries from them. In a letter to his mistress he had described Boris Freidberg as "his boss."[8] In every official report devoted to the Miasoedov case, the same formulaic language was used to describe Miasoedov's activities after his first retirement from the gendarmes: "He completely immersed himself in German-Jewish business, and grew close to many suspicious individuals, particularly to the family of the Jew Freidberg."[9]

Then there was Miasoedov's strange attraction to Germans. The list of his German friends was a long one. There was Eduard Valentini, the Petrograd pharmaceutical importer. There was the Til'mans family of industrialists. There was the Baltic German Baron Grotgus, who served with Miasoedov on the board of the Northwest Russian Steamship Company. And there was Otton Freinat, who, while employed by the Russian Ministry of the Interior, had defended the Northwest Russian Steamship Company against charges of misconduct and who had later provided legal services to the German-controlled Wald'hof Cellulose Company and Schering Chemical Companies. Miasoedov had even been an intimate of Kaiser Wilhelm II, with whom he had lunched, hunted, and attended church.

As for Sukhomlinov, his disreputable taste for the company of Jews had been much remarked on ever since he had served as military district commander in Kiev. Consider his unsavory relationship with Alexander Altschüller. Altschüller was both a Jew and an Austrian subject, and yet he, a person of such untrustworthy background, was the single closest friend and confidant of the minister of war.

Of course, for patriots on the nationalist left, it was precisely the fact that Miasoedov and Sukhomlinov were *Russians* that was most significant. These two men were the most nefarious traitors who had been exposed to that time, and the lesson to be drawn from their perfidy was that treason was not exclusively confined to the empire's non-Russian minorities. But there was more. Sukhomlinov had initiated Miasoedov into the deepest secrets of Russian intelligence prior to the war. In the opinion of the nationalist left, Sukhomlinov's endorsement had made it possible for Miasoe-

8. Matveev finding, April 30, 1915, RGVIA, f. 801, op. 28, d. 167, l. 47.
9. Petrov Commission report, 1916, RGVIA, f. 962, op. 1, d. 43, l. 169.

264   dov to join the active field army after the war had begun and to win the winter battle of Masuria for the Germans. Sukhomlinov therefore bore responsibility for Miasoedov's crimes in addition to his own. In his turn, Sukhomlinov owed everything to his imperial patron, the tsar, who had prized him as one of the most faithful and devoted of his ministers. But the general's pose as the consummate monarchist camouflaged a very different reality. There were dung beetles swarming beneath the thin integument of dynastic loyalty.

Yet *why* had both Miasoedov and Sukhomlinov elected to sell out their country? What had motivated them? The answer was their gross moral corruption, for both men had been driven to treason by lechery. Neither of them had been able to control their sexual urges. The entire espionage case was permeated by the rancid aroma of sex. To many in wartime Russia this made emotional sense, for they believed that the unrestrained pursuit of selfish physical gratification was an impulse that directly contravened the desire to serve the nation and the common good.[10] In a sense, a complete surrender to lust was the first step toward treason. Miasoedov was a confirmed voluptuary who had doubtless turned to espionage to acquire the money to support his mistress, Stolbina, a woman of such low character that she was scarcely one rung above a common harlot. Sukhomlinov had also doubtless taken money from foreign paymasters to satisfy his much younger wife's love of extravagance and luxury. The general had been a slave to his ignoble passion for the calculating and grasping Ekaterina Viktorovna, whose own vices also included a total absence of anything approximating decent national feeling. Had not her ex-husband Butovich called attention to her tellingly flippant observation that "our fatherland is wherever we live well"?[11] The Miasoedov/Sukhomlinov case thus afforded Russians a glimpse into an antisociety, whose values and practices were inverted parodies of the accepted norms: this was a world in which Jews bossed Russian noblemen and in which foreigners bought and sold the ministers of state. Miasoedov's and Sukhomlinov's treachery proved that traitors could lurk anywhere. "There is not one layer of society that can be guaranteed free of spies and traitors," wrote military prosecutor Rezanov in 1915.[12]

If there was treason everywhere, it followed that anyone could be a traitor. Yet perhaps neither Miasoedov nor Sukhomlinov had been uniquely susceptible to corruption. Perhaps all people, or at least all Russians, were potentially as weak and fallible as they. This eventually became the working theory of Russian counterintelligence, which seemed to assume that everyone was a traitor until proved otherwise. In the outlook of the Russian counterintelligence officer of the First World War was the embryo of the future Stalinist mind, in which the left- and right-wing conceptions of treason fused, and which was intoxicated by visions of both disloyal nationalities and omnipresent treason.

10. See Joshua A. Sanborn, *Drafting the Russian Nation: Military Conscription, Total War, and Mass Politics 1905–1925* (DeKalb, Ill., 2003), pp. 162–163, for some interesting remarks about Russian anxieties about "undisciplined sex" undermining "civic virtue."

11. Kuz'min finding, November 7, 1916, RGVIA, f. 962, op. 1, d. 52, l. 8.

12. Rezanov, *Nemetskoe shpionstvo*, p. 115.

Sources

I. ARCHIVES

Arkhiv Vneshnoi Politiki Rossiiskoi Imperii (AVPRI) (Archive of the Foreign Policy of the Russia Empire, Moscow)

f. 133: Chancellery of the Ministry of Foreign Affairs (contains a great deal of correspondence with Stavka)
f. 134: "War" archive

Gosudarstvennii Arkhiv Rossiiskoi Federatsii (GARF) (State Archive of the Russian Federation, Moscow)

f. DP OO: Special Section, Department of Police
f. 102: Department of Police
f. 110: Staff of Separate Corps of Gendarmes
f. 555: A. I. Guchkov
f. 601: Nicholas II

Great Britain. Public Records Office, London

FO: Foreign Office papers, Russian correspondence

National Archives, Washington D. C.

Generalmajor A. L. Fritz Gempp, *Geheimer Nachrichtendienst und Spionabwehr der Heeres.* Unpublished ms. Berlin, 1927, NARS microfilm T-77.

Rossiiskii Gosudarstvennyi Voenno-Istoricheskii Archiv (RGVIA) (Russian State Archive of Military History, Moscow)

f. 280: A. F. Rediger

266   f. 801: Main Administration of Military Justice (op. 28, misfiled with documents from 1917; contains virtually all of the raw material turned up in the investigation of the Miasoedov affair)

f. 962: Special Supreme Commission for the Thorough Investigation of the Reasons for the Slow and Inadequate Replenishment of the Army's Stocks of Military Supplies (Petrov Commission) (contains investigation reports, interrogations, statistical studies, correspondence among figures identified in the case, depositions, stenographic reports of court proceedings, physical evidence)

f. 970: Imperial Military-Field Chancellery

f. 2000: Main Administration of the General Staff

f. 2003: Stavka (General Headquarters), World War I

II. PUBLISHED PRIMARY SOURCES

Baedeker, Karl. *Russia with Teheran, Port Arthur and Peking. A Handbook for Travellers.* Leipzig, 1914. Reprint, New York, 1970.

Batiushin, General'nogo Shtaba Gen.-Maior. *Tainaia voennia razvedka i bor'ba s nei.* Moscow, 2002.

Bauermeister, Lieutenant A. *Spies Break Through: Memoirs of a German Secret Service Officer.* Translated by Hector Bywater. New York, 1934.

Beskrovnyi, L. G., et al., eds. *Zhurnaly osovogo soveshchaniia po oborone gosudarstva 1915 god.* Moscow, 1975.

Bogdanovich, A. *Tri poslednikh samoderzhtsa.* Moscow, 1990.

Bonch-Bruevich, M. D. *Vsia vlast' sovetam.* Moscow, 1957.

British Foreign Office. *Russian Poland, Lithuania and White Russia: Foreign Office Publication no. 44.* London, 1920.

Brussilov, [Brusilov], A. A. *A Soldier's Notebook 1914–1918.* London, 1930.

Bubnov, A. *V tsarskoi stavke.* New York, 1955.

Buchinskii, B. "Sud nad Miasoedovym." In *Arkhiv russkoi revoliutsii.* Vol. 14, pp. 132–147. Berlin, 1924.

Busch, Tristan. *Secret Service Unmasked.* Translated by Arthur V. Ireland. London, n.d.

Catacuzene, Countess Speransky, née Grant. *Revolutionary Days.* Boston, 1919.

Denikin, A. I. *Ocherki russkoi smuti. Krushenie vlasti i armii. Fevral'-sentiabr' 1917 g.* Paris, n.d. Reprint, Moscow, 1991.

Denikin, Anton. *The Career of a Tsarist Officer: Memoirs, 1872–1916.* Translated by Margaret Patoski. Minneapolis, 1975.

Dnevnik Velikogo Kniaza Andreia Vladimirovicha. 1915 god. Edited by V. P. Semenikova. Leningrad/Moscow, 1925.

Doklad soveta s''ezdov o merakh k razvitiiu proizvoditel'nikh sil Rossii. Petrograd, 1915.

"Dokumenty o presledovanii evreev." In *Arkhiv russkoi revoliutsii.* Vol. 19, pp. 245–284. Reprint, The Hague, 1970.

Doumbadze [Dumbadze], V. D. *Russia's War Minister: The Life and Work of Adjutant-General Vladimir Alexandrovitsh Soukhomlinov.* London, 1915.

Dubnow, Simon. *Mein Leben.* Berlin, 1937.

Epanchin, N. A. *Na sluzhbe trekh imperatorov. Vospominaniia.* Moscow, 1996.

Freinat, O. G. *Pravda o dele Miasoedova i dr. Po offitsial'nym dokumentam i lichnym vospominaniiam.* Vilna, 1918.

Giatsintov, Erast. *Zapiski belogo ofitsera.* St. Petersburg, 1992.

Got'e, Iurii Vladimirovich. *Time of Troubles: The Diary of Iurii Vladimirovich Got'e.* Translated by Terence Emmons. Princeton, 1988.

Gourko, General Basil. *War and Revolution in Russia 1914–1917.* New York, 1919.

Grelling, Richard. *Die "Enthüllungen" des Prozesses Suchomlinow.* Bern, 1917.

Gross, Felix. *I Knew Those Spies.* London, 1940.

Gruzenberg, O. O. *Yesterday: Memoirs of a Russian Jewish Lawyer.* Translated by Don C. Rawson and Tatiana Tipton. Berkeley, 1981.

Guchkov, A. I., and N. A. Bazili. *Aleksandr Ivanovich Guchkov rasskazyvaet.* Moscow, 1994.

Gurko, V. I. *Features and Figures of the Past: Government and Opinion in the Reign of Nicholas II.* Translated by Laura Matveev. Palo Alto, 1939.

Hoare, Sir Samuel. *The Fourth Seal: The End of a Russian Chapter.* London, 1930.

Ignat'ev, A. A. *50 let v stroiu.* Vol. 1. Moscow, 1952.

Ignatieff, Colonel Comte Paul. *Ma mission en France.* Paris, n.d.

Ipatieff, Vladimir N. *The Life of a Chemist: Memoirs of Vladimir N. Ipatieff.* Edited by Xenia Joufkoff Evdin, Helen Dwight Fisher, and Harold H. Fisher. Translated by Vladimir Haensel and Mrs. Ralph H. Lusher. Palo Alto, 1946.

Isheev, P. P. *Oskokli proshlogo. Vospominaniia 1889–1959.* New York, n.d.

Kalmykow, Andrew W. *Memoirs of a Russian Diplomat: Outposts of the Empire, 1893–1917.* Edited by Alexandra Kalmykow. New Haven, 1971.

Karrik, V. V. "Voina i revoliutsiia." *Golos minuvshago,* nos. 1–3 (1918): 5–75.

Khol'msen, General-Leitenant. *Mirovaia voina. Nashi operatsii na Vostochno-Prusskoi fronte zimoiu 1915 g.* Paris, 1935.

Knox, Sir Alfred. *With the Russian Army 1914–17: Being Chiefly Extracts from the Diary of a Military Attaché.* 2 vols. London, 1921.

Kokovtsov, Count V. N. *Iz moego proshlogo. Vospominaniia, 1903–1919.* 2 vols. Paris, 1933.

Korostovets, Vladimir. *Seed and Harvest.* Translated by Dorothy Lumby. London, 1931.

Kurlov, P. G. *Gibel' imperatorskoi Rossii.* Reprint, Moscow, 1992.

Lemke, *250 dnei v tsarskoi stavke (25 sent. 1915–2 iuliia 1916).* Petersburg, 1920.

Ludendorff, General [Erich]. *My War Memories.* Vol. 1. London, n.d.

[Lukomskii, A. S.] *Vospominaniia Generala A. S. Lukomskago.* Vol. 1. Berlin, 1922.

Mamantov, V. I. *Na gosudarstvennoi sluzhbe. Vospominaniia.* Tallin, 1926.

Martynov, A. P. *Moia sluzhba v otdel'nom korpuse zhandarmov.* Edited by Richard Wraga. Palo Alto, 1972.

Marye, George Thomas. *Nearing the End in Imperial Russia.* Philadelphia, 1929.

Maylunas, Andrei, and Sergei Mironenko. *A Lifelong Passion: Nicholas and Alexandra: Their Own Story.* New York, 1997.

Melgunov, S. P. *Vospominaniia i dnevniki.* Vol. 1. Paris, 1964.

Miliukov, Paul. *Political Memoirs, 1905–1917.* Edited by Arthur P. Mendel. Translated by Carl Goldberg. Ann Arbor, 1967.

Mossolov, A. A. *At the Court of the Last Tsar.* Edited by A. A. Pilenco. Translated by E. W. Dickes. London, 1935.

Naumov, A. N. *Iz utselevshikh vospominanii, 1868–1917.* New York, 1955.

Nicolai, W. *The German Secret Service.* Translated by George Renwick. London, 1924.

Okunev, N. P. *Dnevnik moskvicha (1917–1924).* Paris, 1990.

Orloff, Vladimir. *The Secret Dossier: My Memoirs of Russia's Political Underworld.* Translated by Mona Heath. London, 1932.

268   *Padenie tsarskago rezhima.* Vols. 1–4. Leningrad, 1924–25.

Padenie tsarskago rezhima. Vol. 6. Moscow/Leningrad, 1926.

Paléologue, Maurice. *La Russie des Tsars pendant La Grande Guerre. 20 Juillet 1914–2 Juin 1915.* Paris, 1921.

Palitsyn, F. F. "V shtabe severno-zapadnogo fronta (s kontsa apreliia 1915 goda po 30 avgusta togo zhe goda." In *Voennyi sbornik obshchestva revnitelei voennykh znanii.* Vol. 3, pp. 158–185. Belgrade, 1922.

Pares, Bernard. *My Russian Memoirs.* London, 1931.

Perepiska Nikolaia i Aleksandry Romanovykh 1914–1915 g.g. Vol. 3. Moscow/Petrograd, 1923.

"Perepiska V.A. Sukhomlinova s N. N. Ianushkevichem." *Krasnyi arkhiv* 3 (1923): 209–262.

Petrov, P. P. *Rokovye gody 1914–1920.* California [*sic*], 1965.

"Politicheskoe polozhenie Rossii nakanune Fevral'skoi revoliutsii v zhandarmskom osveshchenii." *Krasnyi arkhiv* 17 (1926): 3–35.

Polivanov, A. A. *Iz dnevnikov i vospominanii po dolzhnosti voennogo ministra i ego pomoshchika 1907–1916 gg.* Vol. 1. Moscow, 1924.

Rezanov, A. S. *Nemetskoe shpionstvo.* Petrograd, 1915.

———. *Shturmovoi signal P.N. Miliukova.* Paris, 1924.

Rodzianko, M. V. *Krushenie imperii. Gosudarstvennaia duma i fevral'skaia 1917 revoliutsiia.* Valley College, N.Y., 1986.

Ronge, Max. *Razvedka i kontrrazvedka.* 2d ed. Moscow, 1939.

"A Russian." *Russian Court Memoirs 1914–1916.* London, 1917.

Samoilo, A. S. *Dve zhizni.* Leningrad, 1963.

Shakhovskoi, Vsevolod Nikolaevich. *"Sic Transit Gloria Mundi" 1893–1917 gg.* Paris, 1952.

Shavel'skii, Georgii. *Vospominaniia poslednego protopresvitera russkoi armii i flota.* Vol.1. New York, 1954. Reprint, Moscow, 1996.

Shliapnikov, A. *Kanun semnadtsatogo goda.* Pt. 2. Moscow, 1920.

Shulgin, V. *Gody-Dni-1920.* Moscow, 1991.

Sidorov, A. A. "V Kieve." *Golos minuvshago*, nos. 1–3 (1918): 221–229.

Simanovich, Aran. *Rasputin i evrei.* Moscow, 1991.

Smilg-Benario, Michael. *Der Zusammenbruch der Zarenmonarchie.* Zurich, 1928.

Snowden, Nicholas. *Memoirs of a Spy: Adventures along the Eastern Front.* London, 1933.

"Soldatskie pis'ma v gody mirovoi voiny (1915–1917 gg.)." *Krasnyi arkhiv* 4–5 (65–66) (1934): 118–165.

Spiridovich, General A. I. *Velikaia voina i fevral'skaia revoliutsiia.* 2 vols. New York, 1960.

Sukhomlinov, V. A. *Vospominaniia Sukhomlinova.* Moscow/Leningrad, 1926.

Teliakovskii, V. A. *Vospominaniia.* Moscow/Leningrad, 1965.

Topham, Anne. *Memories of the Kaiser's Court.* London, 1914.

Vsia Vil'na. Vilna, 1915.

Wilton, Robert. *Russia's Agony.* London, 1918.

Vitte, S. Iu. *Vospominaniia.* Vol. 3 Moscow, 1960.

Von Falkenhayn, General. *The German General Staff and Its Decisions 1914–1916.* New York, 1920.

Vostochno-Prusskaia Operatsiia. Sbornik dokumentov mirovoi imperialisticheskoi voiny na russkom fronte. Moscow, 1939.

Wood, Ruth Kenzie. *The Tourist's Russia.* New York, 1912.

Za kulisami tsarizma. Arkhiv tibetskogo vracha Badmaeva. Edited by V. P. Semennikova. Leningrad, 1925.

Zavarzin, P. P. *Rabota tainoi politsii. Vospominaniia.* Paris, 1924.

III. SECONDARY LITERATURE 269

Abraham, Richard. *Alexander Kerensky: The First Love of the Revolution.* New York, 1987.

Alekseev, Mikhail. *Voennaia razvedka Rossii ot Riurika do Nikolaia II.* Vols. 1 and 2. Moscow, 1998.

——. *Voennaia razvedka Rossii. Pervaia mirovaia voina.* Vol. 3, pt. 2. Moscow, 2001.

Alekseeva-Borel', V. *Sorok let v riadakh russkoi imperatorskoi armii. General M. V. Alekseev.* St. Petersburg, 2000.

Allfrey, Anthony. *Man of Arms: The Life and Legend of Sir Basil Zaharoff.* London, 1989.

Anfimov, A. M., and A P. Korelin, eds. *Rossiia. 1913 god. Statistiko-dokumental'nyi spravochnik.* St. Petersburg, 1995.

Apushkin, V. A. *General ot porazhenii V.A. Sukhomlinova.* Leningrad, 1925.

Armour, Ian D. "Colonel Redl: Fact and Fancy." *Intelligence and National Security* 2, no. 1 (1987).

Beloi, A. *Galitsiiskaia bitva.* Moscow, 1929.

Beskrovnyi, L. G. *Armiia i flot Rossii v nachale xix veka. Ocherki voenno-ekonomicheskogo potentsiala.* Moscow, 1986.

Bobrinskii, Aleksandr. *Dvorianskie rody vnesennye v obshchii gerbovnik Vserossiiskoi Imperii.* Pt. 1. St. Petersburg, 1890.

Bonsor, N. R. P. *North Atlantic Seaway.* Vol. 3. Jersey, Channel Islands, 1979.

Browder, Robert Paul, and Alexander F. Kerensky, eds. *The Russian Provisional Government 1917: Documents.* Vol. 1. Stanford, 1961.

Buchheit, Gert. *Der deutsche Geheimdienst. Geschichte der militärischen Abwehr.* Munich, 1967.

Cecil, Lamarr. *Albert Ballin: Business and Politics in Imperial Germany 1888–1918.* Princeton, 1967.

Chankowski, Stanislaw. "The Attitude of the Jewish Population of Augustow Province Toward the January (1863) Insurrection." *Landsmen* 2, nos. 2 and 3 (1991–92): 35–42.

Cherniavsky, Michael. *Prologue to Revolution: Notes of A. N. Iakhontov on the Secret Meetings of the Council of Ministers, 1915.* Englewood Cliffs, N.J., 1967.

Cion-Pinchuk, Ben. *The Octobrists in the Third Duma 1907–1912.* Seattle, 1974.

Daniels, Robert V. *Red October: The Bolshevik Revolution of 1917.* New York, 1967.

Danilov, Iu. N. *Rossiia v mirovoi voine 1914–1915 gg.* Berlin, 1924.

Diakin, V. S. *Samoderzhavia, burzhuaziia i dvorianstvo v 1917–1911 gg.* Leningrad, 1978.

Dubnow, S. N. *History of the Jews in Russia and Poland from the Earliest Times until the Present Day.* Translated by I. Friedlander. 3 vols. Philadelphia, 1920. Reprint, New York, 1975.

Duker, Abraham C. *The Jews in the World War.* New York, 1939.

Edelman, Robert. *Proletarian Peasants: The Revolution of 1905 in Russia's Southwest.* Ithaca, 1987.

Emets, V. A. *Ocherki vneshnei politiki Rossii v period pervoi mirovoi voiny.* Moscow, 1977.

Emmons, Terrence. *The Formation of Political Parties and the First National Elections in Russia.* Cambridge, Mass., 1983.

Fabre, René. *Les Grandes Lignes de Paquebots Nord-Atlantique.* Paris, 1928.

Falls, Cyril. *The Great War, 1914–1918.* New York, 1959.

Ferguson, Niall. *The Pity of War.* New York, 1999.

Ferrell, Robert H. *Woodrow Wilson and World War I.* New York, 1986.

Figes, Orlando. *A People's Tragedy: The Russian Revolution 1891–1924.* New York, 1998.

Freeze, Gregory L. "Krylov vs. Krylova: 'Sexual Incapacity' and Divorce in Tsarist Russia." In

The Human Tradition in Modern Russia, edited by William B. Husband, pp. 5–17. Wilmington, Del., 2000.

——. "The Orthodox Church and Emperor Nicholas II: A Confrontation over Divorce in Late Tsarist Russia." In *Stranitsy rossiiskoi istorii. Problemy, sobytiia, liudi. Sbornik statei v chest' Borisa Vasil'evicha Anan'icha,* edited by V. M. Paneiakh et al., pp. 195–203. St. Petersburg, 2003.

Frenkin, M. *Russkaia armiia i revoliutsiia 1917–1918.* Munich, 1978.

Frumkin, Jacob, Gregor Aronson, and Alexis Goldenweiser, eds. *Russian Jewry (1860–1917).* Translated by Mira Ginsburg. New York, 1966.

Fuller, William C., Jr. *Civil-Military Conflict in Imperial Russia 1881–1914.* Princeton, 1985.

——. "The Russian Empire" In *Knowing One's Enemies: Intelligence Assessment before the Two World Wars,* edited by Ernest R. May, pp. 98–126. Princeton, 1984.

——. *Strategy and Power in Russia, 1600–1914.* New York, 1992.

Gatrell, Peter. *Government, Industry and Rearmament in Russia, 1900–1914: The Last Argument of Tsarism.* Cambridge, 1994.

——. *A Whole Empire Walking: Refugees in Russia During World War I.* Bloomington, Ind., 1999.

Geifman, Anna. *Thou Shalt Kill: Revolutionary Terrorism in Russia, 1894–1917.* Princeton, 1993.

Gilensen, V. M. "Germanskaia voennaia razvedka protiv Rossii (1871–1917 gg.)." *Novaia i noveishaia istoriia,* no. 2 (1991): 133–177.

Gleason, William. "Alexander Guchkov and the End of the Russian Empire." In *Transactions of the American Philosophical Society.* Vol. 73, pt. 2. Philadelphia, 1983.

Golder, Frank Alfred. *Documents of Russian History 1914–1917.* Gloucester, Mass., 1964.

Grekov, N. V. *Russkaia kontrrazvedka v 1905–1917 gg.: shpionomaniia i real'nye problemy.* Moscow, 2000.

Greenberg, Louis. *The Jews in Russia: The Struggle for Emancipation.* Vol. 2. New Haven, 1951.

Halpern, Paul. *A Naval History of World War I.* Annapolis, 1994.

Hamm, Michael F. *Kiev: A Portrait, 1800–1917.* Rev. ed. Princeton, 1995.

Haskegawa, Tsuyoshi. *The February Revolution. Petrograd 1917.* Seattle, 1981.

Herrmann, David G. *The Arming of Europe and the Making of the First World War.* Princeton, 1996.

Herwig, Holger H. *The First World War: Germany and Austria-Hungary 1914–1918.* London, 1997.

Höhne, Heine. *Der Krieg im Dunkeln. Macht und Einfluss des deutschen und russischen Geheimdienstes.* Munich, 1985.

Holm-Petersen, F., and A. Rosendahl, A. *Fra Sejl til Diesel. Dansk Skibsfart, Søhandel og Skibsbygning.* N.p., n. d.

Hosking, Geoffrey. *The Russian Constitutional Experiment: Government and Duma, 1907–1914.* Cambridge, 1973.

Huldermann, Bernhard. *Albert Ballin.* Translated by W. J. Eggers. London, 1922.

Hyde, Frances E. *Cunard and the North Atlantic 1840–1973: A History of Shipping and Financial Management.* Atlantic Highlands, N.J., 1975.

Iakupov, N. M. *Revoliutsiia i mir (soldatskie massy protiv imperialisticheskoi voiny 1917–mart 1918 gg.)* Moscow, 1980.

Jahn, Hubertus. *Patriotic Culture in Russian during World War I.* Ithaca, 1995.

Jones, David. "Imperial Russia's Forces at War." In *Military Effectiveness,* edited by Allan R. Millet and Williamson Murray. Vol. 1, *The First World War,* pp. 249–328. Boston, 1988.

Joseph, Samuel. *Jewish Immigration to the United States from 1881 to 1910.* New York, 1914.

Kaledin, Viktor K. *F.L.A.S.H. D 13.* New York, 1930.

——. *14–O.M. 66. K: Adventures of a Double Spy.* New York, 1932.

Katkov, George. *Russia 1917: The February Revolution.* London, 1967.

Keep, John L. H. *The Russian Revolution: A Study in Mass Mobilization.* New York, 1976.

Kitanina, T. M. *Voina, khleb i revoliutsiia (prodovol'stvennyi vopros v Rossii 1914–oktiabr' 1917 g.)* Leningrad, 1985.

Kobylin, V. *Imperator Nikolai II I General-Ad''iutant M. V. Alekseev.* New York, 1970.

Kennard, Howard P., ed. *The Russian Year-Book for 1912.* London, 1912.

Kohut, Thomas August. *Wilhelm II and the Germans.* New York, 1991.

Krivoshein, K. A. *A. V. Krivoshein (1857–1921 g.) Ego znachenie v istorii Rossii nachala XX veka.* Paris, 1973.

Król, Stefan. *Cytadela Warszawska.* Warsaw, 1978.

Lange, Ole. *Den Hvide Elefant. H. N. Andersens Eventyr og ØK 1852–1914.* Viborg, 1986.

Laquer, Walter. *Black Hundred: The Rise of the Extreme Right in Russia.* New York, 1993.

The Letters of the Tsaritsa to the Tsar 1914–16. London, 1923.

Lewinsohn, Richard. *The Mystery Man of Europe: Sir Basil Zaharoff.* Philadelphia, 1929.

Lieven, Dominic. *Nicholas II: Twilight of the Empire.* New York, 1993.

Lincoln, W. Bruce. *Passage through Armageddon: The Russians in War and Revolution, 1914–1918.* New York, 1986.

Lloyd's Register of Shipping: From 1 July 1914 to 30 July 1915. Vol. 1. London, 1914.

Lohr, Eric. *Nationalizing the Russian Empire: The Campaign against Enemy Aliens During World War I.* Cambridge, Mass., 2003.

Los', F. E., ed. *Revoliutsiia 1905–1907 gg. na Ukraine. Sbornik dokumentov i materialov v dvukh tomakh.* Vol. 2, pt. 1. Kiev, 1955.

McDonald, *United Government and Foreign Policy in Russia 1900–1914.* Cambridge, Mass., 1992.

Mackiewicz, Jozef. *Sprawa Pulkownika Miasojedowa. Powiesc.* London, 1992.

Markus, Georg. *Der Fall Redl. Mit Unveröffichten Geheimedokumenten zur Folgenschwersten Spionage-Affair des Jahrhunderts.* Vienna, 1984.

Marshall, Alex. "Russian Military Intelligence, 1905–1917: The Untold Story behind Tsarist Russia in the First World War." *War in History* 11, no. 4 (2004): 393–423.

Mel'gunov, S. P. *Na putiakh k dvortsovomu perevorotu (zagovori pered revoliutsiei 1917 goda)* Paris, 1931.

Menning, Bruce W. *Bayonets before Bullets: The Imperial Russian Army, 1861–1914.* Bloomington, Ind., 1992.

——. "Fragmenti odnoi zagadki. Iu. N. Danilov i M. V. Alekseev v russkoi voennoi planirovanii v period predshestvuiushchii Pervoi Mirovoi Voine." In *Posledniaia voina imperatorskoi Rossii,* edited by O. R. Airapetov, pp. 65–87. Moscow, 2002.

Michelson, Alexander M., Paul N. Apostol, and Michael W. Bernatzky. *Russian Public Finance During the War.* New Haven, 1928.

Miliukov, Paul, et al. *History of Russia: Reforms, Reaction, Revolutions.* Translated by Charles Lam Markmann. Vol. 3. New York, 1969.

Nabokov, Vladimir. *Vremmenoe pravitel'stvo i bol'shevistskii perevorot.* London, 1988.

Noel-Baker, Philip. *The Private Manufacture of Armaments.* Vol. 1. London, 1936.

Nolde, Baron Boris E. *Russia in the Economic War.* New Haven, 1928.

Occleshaw, Michael. *Armour against Fate: British Military Intelligence in the First World War.* London, 1989.

272   Oldenburg, S. S. *Last Tsar: Nicholas II, His Reign and His Russia.* Vol. 3, *The Duma Monarchy, 1907–1914,* translated by Leonid I. Mihalap and Patrick J. Rollins, edited by Patrick J. Rollins. Gulf Breeze, Fla., 1977.

Orlovsky, Daniel T. "Russia in War and Revolution." In *Russia: A History,* edited by Gregory Freeze, pp. 231–262. Oxford, 1997.

Pares, Bernard. *The Fall of the Russian Monarchy.* New York, 1939.

Pintner, Walter McKenzie. *Russian Economic Policy under Nicholas I.* Ithaca, 1967.

Pipes, Richard. *The Russian Revolution.* New York, 1990.

Pisarev, Iu. A. *Tainy pervoi mirovoi voiny. Rossiia i Serbiia v 1914–1915 gg.* Moscow, 1990.

Platonov, O. A. *Ternoyi venets Rossii. Zagovor tsareubiits.* Moscow, 1996.

Polner, Tikhon, Vladimir Obolensky, and Sergius P. Turin. *Russian Local Government during the War.* New Haven, 1930.

Radzinsky, Edward. *The Rasputin File.* Translated by Judson Rosengrant. New York, 2000.

Riasanovsky, Nicholas. *Nicholas I and Official Nationality in Russia, 1825–1855.* Berkeley, 1969.

Rogger, Hans. *Jewish Policies and Right-Wing Politics in Imperial Russia.* Berkeley, 1986.

Rossiia v mirovoi voine 1914–1918 goda (v tsifrakh) Moscow, 1925.

Rostunov, I. I. *Russkii front pervoi mirovoi voiny.* Moscow, 1976.

Rowan, Richard Wilmer. *Spy and Counterspy: The Development of Modern Espionage.* New York, 1929.

Rubinow, Isaac M. *Economic Conditions of the Jews in Russia.* Washington, 1907. Reprint, New York, 1975.

Rumiantsev, E. D. *Rabochii klass povolzh'ia v gody pervoi mirovoi voiny i fevral'skoi revoliutsii (1914–1917 gg.).* Kazan, 1989.

Rutherford, Ward *The Tsar's War 1914–1917.* Cambridge, 1992.

Ruud, Charles, and Sergei Stepanov. *Fontanka, 16. Politicheskii sysk pri tsariakh.* Moscow, 1993.

Sanborn, Josh. *Drafting the Russian Nation: Military Conscription, Total War, and Mass Politics 1905–1925.* DeKalb, Ill., 2003.

——. "The Mobilization of 1914 and the Question of the Russian Nation: A Reexamination." *Slavic Review* 59, no. 2 (2000): 267–289.

Sarbei, V. G., et al., eds. *Istoriia Ukrainskoi SSR.* Vol. 5. Kiev, 1983.

Schindler, John. "Redl—Spy of the Century?" *International Journal of Intelligence and Counter-intelligence* (forthcoming).

Shub, David. *Lenin: A Biography.* Baltimore, 1966.

Siegelbaum, Louis. *The Politics of Industrial Mobilization in Russia 1914–1917: A Study of the War-Industries Committees.* New York, 1983.

Seton-Watson, Hugh. *The Russian Empire, 1801–1917.* London, 1967.

Shapiro, Leonard. *The Communist Party of the Soviet Union.* New York, 1960.

Shatsillo, K. F. "'Delo' Polkovnika Miasoedova." *Voprosy istorii* 42, no. 4 (1967): 103–116.

——. *Ot portsmutskogo mira k pervoi mirovoi voine. Generaly i politika.* Moscow: 2000.

Showalter, Dennis E. *Tannenberg: Clash of Empires.* Hamden, Conn. 1991.

Sidorov, A. L. *Ekonomicheskoe polozhenie Rossii v gody pervoi mirovoi voiny.* Moscow, 1973.

Sorin, Gerald. *A Time for Building: The Third Migration, 1880–1920.* Volume 3 of *The Jewish People in America,* edited by Henry L. Feingold. Baltimore, 1992.

Spiridovich, A. I. *Velikaia voina i Fevral'skaia Revoliutsiia.* Vol. 2. New York, 1960.

Spirin, L. M. *Rossiia 1917 god. Iz istorii bor'by politicheskikh partii.* Moscow, 1987.

Startsev, V. I. *Russkaia burzhuaziia i samoderzhavie v 1905–1917.* Leningrad, 1977.

Steinberg, Mark, and Vladimir M. Khrustalëv, *The Fall of the Romanovs.* New Haven, 1995.

Stone, Norman. *The Eastern Front, 1914–1917*. New York, 1975.

Sukhova, E. K. "Pogranichnaia strazha i kontrabanda v Rossii nachala XX veka." *Voprosy istorii,* nos. 7–8 (1991): 234–237.

Szajkowski, Zosa. "Sufferings of Jewish Emigrants to America in Transit Through Germany." *Jewish Social Studies,* 39, nos. 1–2 (1977): 105–116.

Tarsaidze, Aleksandr. *Chetyre mifa*. New York, 1969.

Tsekhanovskii, M. Iu. "General Batiushin i ego kommissiia." Appendix to *Dvoinoi agent,* by Vladimir Orlov. Moscow, 1998.

Turner, L. C. F. "The Russian Mobilization of 1914." In *The War Plans of the Great Powers 1880–1914,* edited by Paul M. Kennedy, pp. 252–268. Boston, 1979.

Wandycz, Piotr S. *The Lands of Partitioned Poland, 1795–1918*. Seattle, 1974.

Weeks, Theodore. *Nation and State in Late Imperial Russia: Nationalism and Russification on the Western Frontier, 1863–1914*. DeKalb, Ill., 1996.

Wildman, Allan. *The End of the Russian Imperial Army: The Old Army and the Soldiers' Revolt (March-April 1917)*. Princeton, 1980.

———. *The End of the Russian Imperial Army: The Road to Soviet Power and Peace*. Vol. 2. Princeton, 1987.

Wilson, Trevor. *The Myriad Faces of War: Britain and the Great War 1914–1918*. Cambridge, 1986.

Zdanovich, A. A. "General N. S. Batiushin. Portret v inter'ere russkoi razvedki i kontr-razvedki." In *Tainaia voennaia razvedka i bor'ba s nei,* by General'nogo Shtaba Gen.-Maior Batiushin, pp. 190–257. Moscow, 2002.

———. "Kak 'rekonstruirovali' kontrrazvedky v 1917 god." *Voenno-istoricheskii zhurnal,* no. 3 (1998): 50–58.

Index

Note: Page numbers in *italics* refer to illustrations.